S0-BRI-005

CATHOLICISM AND CRISIS IN MODERN FRANCE

French Catholic Groups at the Threshold of the Fifth Republic

Catholicism and Crisis in Modern France

FRENCH CATHOLIC GROUPS AT THE THRESHOLD OF THE FIFTH REPUBLIC

BY WILLIAM BOSWORTH

PRINCETON UNIVERSITY PRESS
PRINCETON, NEW JERSEY, 1962

L.C. Card: 61-7414

Publication of this book has been aided by the Ford Foundation Program to support publication, through university presses, of works in the humanities and social sciences.

William Bosworth has spent several years travelling and studying in France. A grant from the Social Science Research Council enabled him to spend 1958 and 1959 in Paris, where he personally contacted key Catholic groups at the very time when the French political crisis was reaching its height. He returned for further research and updating of his material during the summer of 1960. Dr. Bosworth, an alumnus of Stanford University, received his doctorate from Princeton University. He currently teaches in the Department of Political Science, Hunter College.

Printed in the United States of America
by Princeton University Press, Princeton, N.J.

To my family

Acknowledgments

I COULD not have written this book without the understanding and cooperation of all those who were interviewed. Special thanks are due to the officials of Catholic groups, who never allowed a crowded schedule to interfere with a cordial and educational chat. Whether professors or prelates, officials of laymen's groups or simple priests, all were interested in this project and willing to contribute their knowledge to it. It was a pleasure to meet these French men and women and to learn from them.

I am indebted to many students of French affairs for suggestions and corrections as this study was being prepared. Professor René Rémond of the *Institut d'Etudes Politiques*, Paris, was particularly helpful throughout the research. Professors Gabriel Almond, Henry Ehrmann, Edgar Furniss, Jr., Roy Macridis, Charles Micaud, and Philip Williams also helped hammer out some of the key ideas in this book. Maps and diagrams were prepared by the talented hands of Mrs. Marion Manfredi, Jerry Motyka, and the late Elmer Loemker. Jack Putnam's editing of the manuscript is also gratefully acknowledged. Of course, any errors or omissions are solely my fault.

The Social Science Research Council, through a Research Training Fellowship, made it possible for me to spend the fateful year from June 1958 to June 1959 in Paris. A grant from Hunter College allowed me to return to Paris in the summer of 1960, to study the effects of the new school aid law on Church-state relations. Finally, this book is being published with the help of a grant from the Ford Foundation. I am grateful to all these institutions for their indispensable aid.

Contents

Tables

Charts and Diagrams

Maps

Abbreviations

		CHAPTER
ACA	Assemblée des Cardinaux et Archevêques	THREE
ACGF	Action Catholique Générale des Femmes	FOUR
ACGH	Action Catholique Générale des Hommes	FOUR
ACI	Action Catholique Indépendente	FOUR
ACJF	Association Catholique de la Jeunesse Française	FOUR
ACO	Action Catholique Ouvrière	FOUR
AFC	Associations Familiales Catholiques	FIVE
APEL	Associations de Parents d'Elèves de l'Enseignement Libre	EIGHT
CCIF	Centre Catholique des Intellectuels Français	FIVE
CFPC	Centre Français du Patronat Chrétien	FIVE
CFTC	Confédération Française des Travailleurs Chrétiens	SEVEN
CTIC	Centrale Technique d'Information Catholique	SIX
FFEC	Fédération Française des Etudiants Catholiques	FOUR
ICI	Informations Catholiques Internationales	SIX
JAC	Jeunesse Agricole Chrétienne	FOUR
JEC	Jeunesse Etudiante Chrétienne	FOUR
JIC	Jeunesse Indépendente Chrétienne	FOUR
JOC	Jeunesse Ouvrière Chrétienne	FOUR
MFR	Mouvement Familial Rural	FOUR
MRP	Mouvement Républicain Populaire	SEVEN
RFD	Rassemblement des Forces Démocratiques	SEVEN
SIPEC	Service d'Information Politique et d'Education Civique	FIVE
TC	Témoignage Chrétien	SIX
UFCS	Union Féminine Civique et Sociale	FIVE

CATHOLICISM AND CRISIS IN MODERN FRANCE

To have a clear picture of our Nation, it is not enough to consider its apparent, momentary homogeneity. As in a laboratory, we must take apart its constituent elements and study them separately. We must see how they are tied together, test their comparative strength, find out if each element is correctly situated and functions quite normally, make sure that none is in danger of growing excessively or being abnormally stunted. In short, we must give the whole social structure a thorough check-up, and if this examination shows a pathological state, look for the cause and the remedy.

ETIENNE MARTIN-SAINT-LÉON, 1930

Catholicism and French Society: An Introductory Note

> Anyone who has written many pages about the Church must feel impelled to preface them with an apology. To have explored the plan of so vast an organization, tracing some of its devious ins and outs and peering into its dusty nooks and crannies, is to realize how much more is still unseen, unspoken of, and unguessed at. Whole wings remain unentered for lack of the knowledge of how to enter; whole stories remain unsurveyed for lack of the ability to climb them.[1]

I. The Nation and its Subgroups

"The Nation," says Jacques Maritain, "is one of the most important, perhaps the most complex and complete community engendered by civilized life."[2] For certain purposes a modern nation, this lofty example of human development, can usefully be considered as one single entity. But often national activities can best be understood if some of the constituent elements of the nation are examined first. This is particularly true in the case of France, where the fabric of historical evolution is rich with the multicolored threads of divergent groups and ideologies.

As a "complex and complete community," the nation resembles lower level communities—a town or village, for example. The constituent elements of a nation can be compared to the households which form the village. A household consists of a number of individuals, each with a fixed relationship to the others, and each identifying himself with a permanent location, or house. In the same way, subgroups, which are the basic con-

[1] Philip Spencer, *The Politics of Belief in Nineteenth-Century France* (London: Faber and Faber, 1954), p. 13.

[2] Jacques Maritain, *Man and the State* (Chicago: Phoenix Books, 1951), pp. 4-5.

stituents of a nation, have a fixed position in the nation similar to the house in the community. Groups, like households, are made up of individuals with certain interrelations. Groups and households can be influential or powerless, stable or ephemeral, well-integrated or socially isolated.

Students have long been concerned with the various subgroups into which French society can be divided.[3] However, too often the concern has been with the formal ideological position of the subgroup rather than its practical activities. Instead of observing what groups do, Frenchmen have listened to what they say they believe. The result has been too little information about such important French groupings as the business elite, the higher civil service, and even French Catholicism and French Communism.[4]

Despite their incomplete treatment of social groupings, French scholars have reached interesting and provocative conclusions about their importance. Many have warned that strongly organized groupings can endanger national unity and homogeneity.[5] André Siegfried reflects this line of reasoning in the following quotation: "It is not unusual since 1875 that a strong governmental regime was not established. The only two power centers capable of unleashing the masses are the Catholic Church and the trade union movement, but these two forces

[3] Montesquieu and de Tocqueville are among the many Frenchmen who emphasize pluralism in the nation. For years the political and sociological vocabulary of France has contained a number of words to express group phenomena: *groupement, tendance, famille idéologique, famille spirituelle*, and *corps intermédiaire*. See Claude Bernardin et al., *Libéralisme Traditionalisme, Décentralisation* (Paris: Armand Colin, 1952).

[4] One of the most significant books on French politics in recent years has helped to expand our knowledge of the French business elite. See Henry Ehrmann, *Organized Business in France* (Princeton: Princeton University Press, 1957).

[5] Only a few years after Madison and Hamilton wrote *The Federalist*, with its condemnation of "factions," the Le Chapelier law of 1791 in France legally abolished many of the established entities existing between the individual and the state. The separation of Church and state in 1905 culminated a half-century of bitter dispute over the place of French Catholicism in the nation. For more comment on this point, see G. E. Lavau, *Partis Politiques et Réalités Sociales* (Paris: Armand Colin, 1953), pp. 157-162.

are anticonstitutional or at least extraconstitutional, so that no secular authority can be established without relying on one or the other: outside of these two forces there is no ideological dynamism capable of galvanising the voting masses."[6]

The idea that Catholicism is one of the important social and political forces in France has long had currency among French political analysts. Siegfried's attitude has already been indicated. Other modern or near-modern analysts such as Albert Thibaudet, Jacques Fauvet, and François Goguel have also recognized the political importance of French Catholicism. For Albert Thibaudet, social Catholicism formed one of the six "ideological families" into which the France of the 1930's was divided.[7] For Jacques Fauvet, the MRP, as a political instrument of the Church, forms one of France's key political forces.[8]

Unfortunately, the awareness of the group phenomenon in France has not always produced a very healthy reaction toward groups in practical politics. Americans take for granted pressure

[6] André Siegfried, *De la Troisième à la Quatrième République* (Paris: Grasset, 1956), p. 47. See also p. 191. This quotation was originally in French. Like all the other French sources in this book, it was translated by the present writer.

[7] Albert Thibaudet, *Les Idées Politiques de la France* (Paris: Stock, 1932), pp. 81-118.

[8] Fauvet calls the force "Christian Democracy" but limits his study practically to the MRP. See Jacques Fauvet, *Les Forces Politiques en France* (2nd ed.; Paris: Editions Le Monde, 1951), chap. v, pp. 163-198. Fauvet believes that "the two churches" form one of the fundamental divisions in French life, with the Catholic Church facing the rabid anticlericals. See Fauvet, *La France Déchirée* (Paris: Arthème Fayard, 1957), pp. 52-70.

Anglo-American studies of the French political scene also have useful analyses of Catholicism as a social group. See David Thomson, *Democracy in France* (3rd ed.; London: Oxford, 1958) and Philip Williams, *Politics in Postwar France* (2nd ed.; London: Longmans Green, 1958), *passim.*

Most responsible analysts recognize competing groups within French Catholicism itself. See Joseph Folliet, "Catholiques de Droite? Catholiques de Gauche?" *Chronique Sociale*, LXIV, Nos. 7-8 (December 30, 1956). See also René Rémond, "Droite et Gauche dans le Catholicisme Français," *Revue Française de Science Politique*, VIII, Nos. 3 and 4 (September and December 1958), pp. 529-544 and 803-820. Note also Michel Darbon, *Le Conflit entre la Droite et la Gauche dans le Catholicisme Français: 1930-1953* (Toulouse: Privat, 1953).

groups and other social forces; they tolerate them but try to control their abuses. The French have usually stressed the threat which many important social groupings could pose to the nation. But often they have ignored or misunderstood the practical political impact of these groups. The result has too often been that groups, from the home distillers to the Catholic Hierarchy, have abused the powers accruing to them.

II. The Architecture of French Catholicism

Like other groupings within the French nation, French Catholicism is in many respects similar to a large household in a local community. Catholic groups have a political location much as a house has its own address. Members of Catholic groups are aware of being in a "family" and of having certain fixed relationships with one another. Just as each house has its own building plan, so Catholicism has a basic structural scheme which must be understood.

To be Catholic a group must have a publicly-affirmed link to the ecclesiastical nucleus of French Catholicism. This link can be established in several ways; the simplest is for a group to call itself officially "Catholic." By this act it is telling the world that it is prepared to accept completely the discipline which the Church requires of it. Or a group can show its Catholicism simply by designating officially an ecclesiastical advisor for questions on which the Church reserves a right to speak. Some groups without any of these formal ties to the Church must also be included here because of their universally recognized "Catholic inspiration." Among these the most important are the MRP, the CFTC, and the review *Esprit*.

At first glance the structure of French Catholicism seems impossibly complicated. It includes multitudes of individuals, each one with unique motivations and attachments, but it also includes the apparently monolithic Jesuit order. Room must be found somewhere under the roof of French Catholicism for religious orders and priests, close to the directives of the Hierarchy, and also for groups with only the most tenuous connections to Catholicism, such as *Esprit.* Some groups, notably the MRP, are primarily designed for political action, while others, such as Catholic Action or the religious orders, claim to stay aloof from partisan battles. And among the groups with a political orientation there are extreme rightists such as *Cité Catholique*, moderate if not extreme leftists, and a whole gamut in between. Can such differences be reconciled under the banner of Catholicism or any other single principle? It is hoped that the present study will help to give the answer.

III. Aims of the Study

As we have just noted, one of the major aims of the study is to see whether all French Catholic groups belong to one household, or whether they really live at different addresses. To find this out it will be necessary to examine several facets of French Catholicism, starting with the organization and activities of the most politically-significant Catholic groups and moving down to the level of the individual, analyzing his motives for joining Catholic groups and the consequences of his attachment to them.

First, however, the material presented in this study is designed to achieve a more immediate aim: it will catalogue the constituent elements of French Catholicism with political significance. An accounting of such groups has up to now been unavailable, and this has meant an initial stumbling block to anyone seriously desiring to study Catholicism as a social force in France. The study will then use the analysis of Catholic activities to provide a tentative judgment on the "efficiency" of French Catholicism in the political realm.

It must be noted at the outset, however, that most of the Catholic groups to be studied have a higher goal than political activity. This is the case for all but groups of "Catholic inspiration," furthest from the Church Hierarchy. The most fundamental goal of Catholic groups is spiritual, and this is not the kind of goal that can be properly evaluated here. Thus, any desire to judge Catholic groups harshly because they lack political efficiency should be abandoned. Generally it is not political efficiency that these groups seek.

Given the aims of this study, a number of questions arise. Which are the "leading" Catholic groups and which are the "followers"? Are there ways of better coordinating the efforts of Catholic groups in the civic and social domains? What is the actual and potential control of the Hierarchy? These and other questions will be considered in the chapters to follow.

One problem surely must baffle those—like the author—not expert in the discipline of psychology. Much of the effectiveness of French Catholicism comes not from its constituent groups as such but from the depths of attachment to French Catholicism shown by individuals. The reasons for individuals becoming attached to such groupings as French Catholicism are often complex.[9] Apparently the main reason for joining Catholic groups is to fulfill a religious need: a need to join with other Catholics to express religious dogma and moral sentiments in a secular context. This need is not a function of one's political views or his social position: notorious "leftists" and reactionary *intégristes* share the same religious need.

Attachment to Catholic groups can fulfill other needs as well. Catholic vocational organizations provide their members with the means of achieving their vocational interests. Identification with any Catholic organization can be vicariously pleasing through its connection with the Church nucleus. An individual quite closely bound to Catholicism, such as a priest, will make the goals of the Church his own goals, and will be prepared to sacrifice everything to attain them. Some people join Catholic groups because of the social prestige (these are not the most active members). For example, in many areas of Western France, membership in rural Catholic Action or the APEL is the "thing to do." One of the tasks of this study will be to at-

[9] See a general treatment of the nature of attachment, loyalty, and patriotism in Harold Guetzkow, *Multiple Loyalties: Theoretical Approach to a Problem in International Organization* (Pub. 4; Center for Research on World Political Institutions; Princeton: Princeton University Press, 1955).

tempt an analysis (albeit rudimentary) of these varied motivations.

It might be suggested that loyalty to the state would be adversely affected by attachment to social groupings like French Catholicism. André Siegfried seemed to have such fears. If this were true to any great degree, it would have the gravest possible consequences to the French political system. Already the Communist "household" has seceded from the rest of the community. If the Catholic "household" on the other side of the street were equally committed against the community, the prospects for long continuation of the village—or of France—would be dim indeed.

Loyalty to the French nation might be affected if the members of Catholic groups were told by the Church that they had to take political stands which were dogmatic and uncompromising. The Catholic schools, press, vocational groups, and so on could serve such a crusade, which could receive the highest moral sanction from the Hierarchy. Thus, a strong and coordinated stand by all French Catholicism on a controversial political issue might paralyze the French regime.

Catholics might endanger loyalty to the nation-state in other ways as well. If all Catholics were driven by basically nonreligious social and political motives, they might try to use their Catholic organizations to impose their ideas on the rest of society. Certain Catholic groups already exist for social and political action, and nonreligiously-motivated Catholics might want to multiply them and extend their range. Soon there could be Catholic political parties of all ideological tendencies, Catholic cells in the civil service and perhaps even in Parliament. The end result might be a "withering away of the state" because Catholic groups existed to perform all its functions. On the other hand, none of this would be possible if the only strong motivations to enter Catholic groups were religious. It would be impossible to agree on any common Catholic political position and coordinated Catholic activities could not be extended into the political sphere. This study will try to put into proper perspective the religious and the nonreligious motives for attachment to Catholic groups.

Catholics might modify their loyalty to the regime if there were a recurrence of the discrimination (even persecution) imposed on the Church at various times in French history. But for this to happen the state would have to emulate the Communist religious program. Any more tolerant position probably could not muster all Catholic opinion to effective opposition.

Because of the means which the nation-state possesses to exact loyalty from its citizens, including the monopoly of legal sanctions, it seems unrealistic to expect that Catholic groups could directly challenge one's attachment to the political society. However, there might be an indirect challenge of a more serious nature. In some areas of French society three groups exist side by side, each performing the same functions: a democratic Catholic group, a democratic "neutral" group, and a Communist group. Often, of course, there are more than three. Whether the attachment of Catholics to their group is motivated only by religious factors or also by egoistical, political, or other reasons, the existence of a separate Catholic group is desired by its members. But the existence of this group splits the democratic forces and thereby increases the possibility of stagnation, or even Communist domination, of a social area. This situation, it is suggested, is chronic throughout French society and breeds discontent with the effectiveness of the regime and the health of the society. Thus, attachment to Catholic groups would indirectly lessen attachment to the political society.[10]

This last proposition, like the others mentioned earlier, will be tested in the chapters to follow.

IV. Techniques

For greater clarity, Catholic groups have been divided into four categories, according to their relation to the central core of the Church. After a brief historical sketch, the first of these categories is analyzed: the ecclesiastical nucleus itself. The

[10] Suggested by Prof. Gabriel Almond, in several discussions.

Hierarchy, religious orders, and chaplains for laymen's groups all figure in this first category. The other three are made up of Catholic laymen. Closest to the Hierarchy are the Catholic Action groups. Farthest away are those of "Catholic inspiration." Between the two are Catholic "social action" groups.[11] The basis for distinguishing among these categories is the distance from the ecclesiastical nucleus, the heart of French Catholicism.

Separate consideration is needed for the Catholic press. Catholic publications, while all performing similar functions, have widely-varying relationships to the Church.

The study has been limited to Catholic groups of national scope, and many groups of a certain regional significance have been ignored. However, the regional bastions of key national organizations will be compared at the end of the study, and this should furnish useful information on the most "clerical" and the most "dechristianized" areas in France.

To understand fully the activities of Catholic groups, it is necessary to go beyond ideological abstractions, as has already been made clear. For the purposes of this study a more useful approach has been chosen. The opinions and activities of Catholic groups will be compared with respect to significant present-day political events. Two events have been emphasized here, because they seem of overriding importance. One is the question of state aid to Catholic schools—one of the most burning issues in France for a century or more—which has taken a dramatic turn since the laws of 1951 and 1959. The other event is the political crisis through which France passed in 1958. This crisis, which almost caused the death of French democracy itself, was a test for all forces in French society. For those which favored the parliamentary regime, immediate action was

[11] The term "social action" in this context may not be very accurate, but it is used by many French authors, among them V. L. Chaigneau, in *Les Ouvriers dans la Moisson* (Paris: Editions Spes, 1955). See Chapter VIII, pp. 105-115. Note also the important book by Henri Rollet, *Sur le Chantier Social: L'Action Sociale des Catholiques en France, 1870-1940* (Lyon: Editions de la Chronique Sociale, 1955).

necessary; for those wanting an authoritanian government or the personal rule of General de Gaulle, action was even more urgent. Only groups which had no political designs whatsoever, whose only City was the City of God, could afford to remain inactive. Thus, the crisis period offers a limit case for seeing which Catholic groups have political significance and what sort of action they take. The reader may be surprised that Catholic groups are being judged by their reactions to French domestic events rather than international issues. These latter issues have not been emphasized for two reasons. First, the position of Catholic groups in French political life can be judged far more accurately in referring to internal questions. Second, the force of events during the Fourth Republic's decline centered French interest on domestic and colonial questions.

Since 1958, crises in and near metropolitan France have made it more urgent than ever to dissect the nation in the manner proposed by Martin-Saint-Léon. France's curse of colonial wars seemed at one time to threaten moral and physical exhaustion, but at present perhaps the seeds of governmental stability have been sown. It is possible (though not certain) that the old bugaboo of the school question is at last near a settlement. It is more certain that France is in the throes of the most extensive social and economic renovation in her history. At such a time, there is a pressing need to add to the store of knowledge about a country which so many love but which so few really understand.

Historical Sketch: Catholic Institutions and the Laic Republic

I. Introduction

In France, at least among a certain educated elite, the legacy of the past largely determines present actions. For example, today's quarrels between *laïques* and *cléricaux* over the school question cannot be fully understood without referring to the events of the early 1900's.[1] Thus, without pretending to give a complete panorama of Catholicism in French history, this historical sketch will provide some of the background necessary for unlocking the mysteries of present-day Catholic behavior.

During two periods of recent French history the relations between Church and state were profoundly changed. Just after the turn of the century the Republic officially became "laic," for Church and state were separated by law. A generation later, after much of the old animosity between *cléricaux* and *laïques* had been forgotten in the holocaust of World War I, Catholic groups began developing radically new means of political and social action. Nothing could be more instructive than examining the differences among Catholic groups wrought by this generation of change.

It is usual in French historical studies of Catholicism to stress ideological factors. Without minimizing the value of this approach, the present chapter emphasizes the structure and activities of major Catholic groups, with the aim of clarifying the real political impact of French Catholicism. Since there has been very little systematic work in this field, no definitive conclusions should be expected.

[1] Throughout the book the noun *laïque*, used in the French sense, indicates one who opposes any Church interference in the political order.

In each period under consideration, it seems most meaningful to study Catholic institutions on three different levels: the Vatican, the French clergy, and lay Catholic groups, including the Catholic press. The behavior patterns of each of these groups, studied in turn, will serve as reference points for understanding how Catholic groups have changed as the laic Republic became a permanent fixture of French politics.

In both of the periods under consideration, the existence of a laic Republic, in which Church and state are separate, is by all odds the major question for Catholic groups. In the earlier period Catholics were fighting a losing battle to protect the century-old vested interests of the Church in the state. Between the world wars, Catholics were seeking ways of accepting the laic Republic without losing too much face. Again today, as Chapter Eight will show, the nature of the laic Republic is a key question for French Catholics.

A. THE POLITICAL CLIMATE AT THE TURN OF THE CENTURY

An intense antigovernmental campaign was waged by most Catholic groups at the turn of the century. It could not have developed without a long period of struggle between those favoring the vested privileges of the Church in the state and those favoring a complete separation of the two. The rabid *laïques* feared, with some justification, that the state-subsidized Church was a conspiracy designed to prevent at all costs the "true freedom" of the French government. When the government became *laïque*-oriented in the late nineteenth century, the Church feared persecution. For a generation before the separation of Church and state in 1905, the conflict between the two sides had increased in vehemence; a cause-effect spiral, for which both sides were responsible, culminated in vicious attacks on the foundations of both Church and state.[2]

[2] For the attacks on religious orders by the state, see R. P. Lecanuet, *Les Signes Avant-Coureurs de la Séparation (1894-1910)*, Vol. III of *L'Eglise de France sous la Troisième République* (Paris: Alcan, 1930), *passim.* See also Emmanuel Barbier, *Histoire du Catholicisme Libéral et du Catholicisme Social en France, 1870-1914* (Bordeaux: Imprimerie

A comment on the 1905 separation of Church and state from the Masonic paper *Lanterne* will indicate the views of a rather extreme section of *laïque* opinion: "Whoever believes that the clerical tribe would willingly accept the laws of the laic state is poorly acquainted with the clericals. And Republicans would be wrong to think that the struggle is finished. Tomorrow as yesterday we must defend ourselves against invading clericalism; and if the weapons that the new law gives us are not sufficient, we must forge others. . . . So here is the Church, mortally wounded. Soon it will fall into indifference and contempt. The Republic will finally triumph over the Church. Down with the Church, and long live the Republic!"[3] Clericals were equally intransigent against the Republic after the separation, and more particularly against the Jews and Freemasons who, they thought, threatened the existence of the Church. *La Croix*, now so respectable, was violently against Freemasonry, if not antisemitic. Professional bigots like Drumont ("The danger hanging over the heads of Frenchmen will never be lifted until the Jewish-Masonic regime which dishonors us and delivers us to the enemy is overthrown . . .") had a large following among Catholics.[4] Of course, the Dreyfus affair had served to make the battle-lines even more rigid, though it did not itself cause the opposition of most Catholics to the regime.

If most Catholic groups lent a sympathetic ear to the Royalist and Bonapartist causes, they were not primarily opposing the idea of the Republic itself. Pope Leo XIII had urged Catholics to make their peace with the Republic more than a decade before the separation, and more and more Catholics realized the wisdom of his words. They were not against the conservative

Cadoret, 1923), Vol. IV, pp. 19-20. See also J. Brugerette, *Le Prêtre Français dans la Société Contemporaine* (Paris: P. Lethielleux, 1935), Vol. II, pp. 524-528.

[3] *Lanterne*, December 8, 1905. Cf. the famous statement by Viviani in *Humanité*, October 4, 1904: "Neutrality was always a necessary lie." See *Cahiers d'Action Religieuse et Sociale*, Vol. 262, September 15, 1958, p. 497.

[4] Quotation from Drumont's newspaper *Libre Parole*, December, 1905, in *Archives Nationales*, F^{19} 1970.

Republic of Monsieur Thiers; but, they were unalterably opposed to the laic Republic of Monsieur Combes, the Republic which was taking away the vested interests of the Church.[5] The political system which the French people approved, with larger and larger majorities, down to the First World War was not disposed to compromise on the issue of the Church-state relations, so the bulk of Catholic sentiment turned toward the other dissenting elements—royalists, Bonapartists, authoritarian opportunists—to form what many thought was an opposition bloc. However, most Catholics were no more confirmed Royalists than they were confirmed anti-Republicans. Their activity was dictated by expediency.[6] Still, this alliance with the right-wing extremists set the tone for Catholic political activity at the time of separation.

II. Catholic Institutions and the Separation of Church and State

A. THE VATICAN

Paradoxically, at the very time when Catholicism was a national political issue, the French clergy had no organisms that could speak on behalf of the whole French Church. Succeeding French regimes during the life of the Concordat and succeeding Popes in Rome had both feared a resurgence of Gallicanism, so had worked together to restrict any institutions of the Hierarchy above the diocese level. Thus, at the time of the separation con-

[5] As early as 1890, Pierre Veuillot, a former Legitimist, stated the minimum aims of Catholics: "It would be very good to reestablish the Monarchy, of course, if we could! But since we cannot! Soon we shall have been working on this for twenty years, and still the Republic continues. In fact, we must admit that it draws new strength from each assault on it." And, according to Eugène Veuillot, "We shall continue our fight by constitutional means, in order to drive you from power, to demolish these criminal laws, and thus to make the Republic livable." (Quoted in Barbier, *op.cit.*, Vol. II, pp. 271-272.)

[6] The conservative Emmanuel Barbier confirms that many Catholics were Royalists only out of expediency: "The priests were not Republicans, and everyone knew it. Were they to any greater degree Monarchists or Royalists? It was thought so, but time was to dispel this illusion." (Barbier, *op.cit.*, p. 273.)

troversy, the real spokesman for the French Church was the Pope himself.

The next chapter will show how the personality of the Pope is an important factor in the political impact of the Church today. This was even more true at the turn of the century, and the repercussions were even greater for France because there were no institutions outside the Vatican to speak for the French Church. Pope Pius IX had laid the groundwork for Papal power as we know it today by promulgating the doctrine of Papal Infallibility. His *Syllabus* would become in later years the main inspiration for extreme-right Catholic groups in France. His authoritarianism and his uncompromising emphasis on Catholic dogma made the separation of Church and state in France virtually inevitable.[7]

Pope Leo XIII had very different personality traits from those of his predecessor: his willingness to compromise and his enlightened social views probably staved off the separation for a certain time. Leo's *Rerum Novarum* started a new era in Catholic relations with the working class throughout the world. But of more specific interest to France was his desire to compromise with the Republican regime. On February 16, 1892, Leo published a letter, *Au Milieu des Sollicitudes*, urging Catholics to adopt a conciliatory attitude toward the Republic. A letter like this would have been unthinkable from the pen of Pius IX, and illustrates the great differences in their personalities. However, not even the Pope could erase the memories of the *Ancien Régime* and of 1789. Leo could do nothing more than urge Catholics to rally to the Republic; he could not force them, and his urgings largely fell on deaf ears. At his death, over a decade after his call for rallying, Catholics were more than ever hostile to the Republic.[8] Moreover, the call to rally was seen by many diehard *laïques* as a subtle move by the "diplomat-Pope" to change the character of the regime from within: Catholics

[7] See the description in Brugerette, *op.cit.*, pp. 524-526.
[8] *ibid.*, p. 348.

could purge the Republic of its anticlerical elements and restore something like the regime of Monsieur Thiers.[9]

The reign of Pope Pius X is probably the most graphic illustration of how a Pope's personality can influence political life. Where Leo had been conciliatory and diplomatic, Pius X saw all politics in a dogmatic religious perspective. The contrast between the two leaders is most graphically illustrated in the attitudes of Pius X and the French bishops toward the newly-voted separation law. The Pope would make no compromise with the satanic law, while the French bishops, appointees of Leo XIII, suggested that the French Church make the best of the new situation.[10]

The Pope's rigid political outlook seemed to lead at times to inconsistencies. He condemned the left-wing *Sillon* but he also tacitly approved condemning the right-wing *Action Française.*[11] He bitterly opposed the separation, but not the Republic. He approved this description of his activity: "As public opinion became more and more committed to the Republican form of government, the Holy See tried to stop the Catholic opposition to the Republic in the name of religion."[12] In his Encyclical *Gravissimo*, the Pope was even more indignant: ". . . certain enemies of the Church are trying to persuade the people . . . that the Republican form of government in France is odious to Us. . . . With all Our indignation, We denounce these remarks as false. . . ."[13] The Pope's opposition to the separation was made not on doctrinal political grounds but because he believed that the separation would result sooner or later in a full-scale oppression of the Church.[14]

[9] Barbier, *op.cit.*, p. 468.

[10] Barbier, *op.cit.*, Vol. IV, pp. 147-183.

[11] The condemnation of *Action Française* was not made public until 1926. See Adrien Dansette, *Histoire Religieuse de la France Contemporaine* (Paris: Flammarion, 1951), Vol. II, pp. 563-613.

[12] *La Séparation de l'Eglise et de l'Etat en France: Exposé et Documents* [Vatican White Paper] (Rome: Typographie Vaticane, 1905), p. 60.

[13] Quoted in J. de Narfon, *La Séparation des Eglises et de l'Etat: Origines, Etapes, Bilan* (Paris: Alcan, 1912), p. 84.

[14] The Pope also said in *Gravissimo* the following: "If any state is

Pius X reigned at the blackest hour for the French Church. As a reaction against the separation, he and some of the more conservative elements of the French Church urged French Catholics to unite in a great Catholic Party to defend the interests of the Church.[15] But because of the intransigence of the Pope and the unrealistic nature of this scheme, many French Catholic groups refused to commit themselves to it.

The intransigence of Pius X did nothing to solve the grave crisis brought on by the separation and even threatened to split Catholic forces themselves. And yet a more moderate Pope might have supported the French bishops in their desire for conciliation, and speeded up the process of Church-state reconciliation by a decade. At the end of the First World War the new Pope, Pius XI, finally did accept the separation. But the tactics of Pius X had cost the Church a large part of its land and other capital.[16]

B. THE FRENCH CLERGY

Under the Concordat both secular and regular clergy were closely controlled by the state, which paid all parish priests and bishops. In fact, it took over thirty years for the Republic to pass the Separation Law from the time it was first introduced, because many *laïques* believed that the clergy would do more harm if left uncontrolled. Before the separation itself most re-

---

separated from the Church, but allows the Church to benefit from the same freedom as everyone else and the free disposition of its property, the state has doubtless—and on more than one account—acted unjustly. But it cannot be said that the situation of the Church is completely intolerable. Unfortunately, things are quite different today in France: There, the authors of this unjust separation law really wanted to create a law of oppression." Quoted in G. Bonnefous, *Histoire Politique de la Troisième République* (Paris: Presses Universitaires de France, 1956), Vol. I, p. 31. See also Barbier, *op.cit.*, Vol. IV, pp. 147-183, for an extended discussion of relations between Pius X and the French bishops over the separation question. See also Dansette, *op.cit.*, pp. 333-372.

[15] At this time the Vatican was also being pressured by a conservative secret society known as *La Sapinière*, which probably had the ear of Pius X. See Dansette, *op.cit.*, p. 466.

[16] Church property which had been disposed of by the state between 1906 and 1924 was lost to the Church. See Dansette, *op.cit.*, p. 510.

ligious orders were expelled from France. Even after the separation, the orders were not allowed to return, and were specifically forbidden to teach, even in private schools.[17] State control even violated canon law in attempting to take from the bishops certain powers to dispose of Church property in a diocese.

The separation impressed the whole Church with the necessity of coordinating its forces. On the eve of the separation all the French bishops met in plenary assembly for the first time in over a century, to determine what their policies would be in the face of the crisis. There were three such meetings in a year and a half, as the French bishops tried to reconcile their views and the demands of the Vatican with the laws of the French state.[18] The majority of the French clergy was willing to accept *in extremis* a modification of Church-state relations, provided that the rights of the Church were strictly guaranteed. But an intransigent position was finally forced on all bishops by the Vatican and a conservative minority among the bishops themselves.

Before the separation all the French cardinals had written a collective letter to the President of the Republic, urging that any modifications in the Concordat be made by mutual consent, and adding these words: "If the Concordat ceased to exist we would be duty bound to demand for religion its freedom and the respect of its guaranteed rights. Our claim for such treatment is indisputable, unless the rules of justice and equality are to be suppressed with respect to the Church."[19] All the

[17] Most of the religious orders probably deserved sanctions for their extreme anti-Republicanism. The Assumptionnists, publishers of *La Croix*, and the Jesuits seem to have been the worst offenders, combining anti-Semitism with their anti-Republicanism. It is hard to prove what influence the orders had. Experts, however, are agreed that they were intemperate. See François Goguel, *La Politique des Partis sous la Troisième République* (3rd ed.; Paris: Editions du Seuil, 1958), p. 108. See also Thibaudet, *op.cit.*, p. 46.

[18] Dansette, *op.cit.*, pp. 333-372. In these pages Dansette discusses in detail the events surrounding the three plenary assemblies of the French Church.

[19] Letter found in *Archives Nationales*, F[19] 1980.

clergy of the Toulouse area wrote to their deputies asking them to respect the desires of the "majority of electors" and vote against separation. There was an implied threat to their message too: ". . . we ourselves will not hesitate, at the proper time, to exercise quite freely the duty imposed on us by our positions as defenders of the Church in the parishes given to us."[20]

At election time, then as now, the Hierarchy advised Catholics on the principles they should keep in mind when voting. However, the separation crisis elicited from the Hierarchy much more specific advice than usual. Just before World War I, for example, Cardinal Dubillard wrote this to Catholics: "The only candidates for whom Catholics can and should vote are those pledging formally to uphold religious interests and who will accept the following program. . . . If any candidate publicly accepts this program and promises to defend it, vote for him no matter what his party affiliation (Republican, Royalist, Imperialist). But firmly refuse to vote for any candidate who will not subscribe to our legitimate demands, even if he calls himself liberal, moderate, or antigovernmental."[21]

The French clergy did not have the same political importance throughout France. According to Siegfried, the influence of the clergy was especially predominant in certain areas of the West. As late as the separation crisis the areas of clerical influence coincided with the bastions of anti-Republicanism. "When one is really attached to the priest, when one fears his disapproval, one does not resist him in any realm. Thus, the most Catholic regions of the West are at the same time those where the clergy makes itself not only a moral pastor, but also a political guide. . . . The strongholds of clericalism are virtually the same as the strongholds of the adversaries of the Republic, or more exactly the Republican spirit. Although Catholic activity is not necessarily anti-Republican or anti-

[20] Letter reported in *Express du Midi*, Toulouse, May 1905. In *Archives Nationales*, F[19] 1970.

[21] Quoted in Brugerette, *op.cit.*, Vol. III, p. 84.

democratic, this is the kind of coincidence where we can confidently expect to find a cause-effect relationship."[22]

On the other side of the political fence, a handful of so-called *abbés démocrates* were wholeheartedly committed to the Republic, and even were glad that the Church was now "poor but free." However, these priests did not counterbalance the vast majority of the Church; their newspapers, like Naudet's *Justice Sociale* and Garnier's *Peuple Français*, were never widely read. One of their representatives, Abbé Lemire, sat in the Chamber of Deputies throughout the separation crisis, but was denounced by his own bishop.[23] Now the position which they espoused has been accepted by the majority of French Catholics; their own ineffectiveness highlights the profound evolution in Catholic thought since the separation.

The separation was a great test and a great lesson for the French clergy. The test was to see whether a Catholic political force, backed by the clergy, could be created that would undo the laws of 1905-1906. Although the clergy exerted its utmost energy, it failed the test, for by World War I its political impact did not seem significantly increased.

The clergy learned its lesson well: to protect its own interests, national institutions had to be established for the French Church. A beginning was made with the plenary assemblies of bishops, and other organisms were to follow just after World War I. The clergy was preparing for what it thought would be a protracted political struggle to regain its legitimate place in society. Who would have predicted on the eve of the separation that only thirty years later most of the clergy would be far removed from partisan politics? The pendulum of Church-state relations, which had swung far to the side, would soon reach a new moderate point of equilibrium.

[22] André Siegfried, *Tableau Politique de la France de l'Ouest* (Paris: Armand Colin, 1913), pp. 393 and 400.

[23] Brugerette, *op.cit.*, Vol. III, pp. 323-327.

C. CATHOLIC LAYMEN'S GROUPS

At present there are innumerable distinctions among Catholic lay groups, for each differs in its closeness to the Hierarchy and its political responsibilities. At the turn of the century these distinctions did not exist. The Church was fighting for its life, and no group of active laymen could afford the luxury of being merely a "pious union." Just like the monarchists, the groups mainly interested in defending the Church found themselves opposing the established political order. Thus, in studying the various activities of Catholic lay groups we should remember that this is a "crisis situation" for them too. They had to exert their maximum effort; and it can be assumed that in the political realm Catholics did everything at this time which they could do.

From the turn of the century until the First World War, a Catholic political party existed in France—the *Action Libérale Populaire*, or ALP. The ALP is all but forgotten today, although at its height before the 1906 elections it had 78 supporters in the Chamber of Deputies.[24] It was a center party, neither anti-Republican nor progressive in the sense of the *abbés démocrates.*

The ALP considered itself more than just an electoral machine. It was to be the central political agency for all Catholic groups: diocese organizations, Catholic women's organizations, the clergy, and so forth. All were expected to call on the ALP when they needed something done in parliament or the administration.[25] Because of the politico-religious crisis at hand, the ALP was closer to Catholic institutions than later parties, including the MRP.[26] A large Catholic women's group, the *Ligue Patriotique des Françaises*, was virtually its feminine affiliate.[27] It is not surprising therefore that the ALP found most

[24] Eugène Flornoy, *La Lutte par l'Association: L'Action Libérale Populaire* (Paris: Lecoffre, 1907), p. 32.

[25] *ibid.*, pp. 60-61.

[26] The MRP declines modestly to call itself "Catholic," and has no structural relation to Catholic Action or the Hierarchy. See Chapter Seven.

[27] The *Ligue* was the direct antecedent of the women's division of General Catholic Action today. See Barbier, *op.cit.*, Vol. II, p. 514.

of its electoral strength in the areas where Catholic groups had the highest support and notably in the clerical areas of the West.

As a fully Catholic group, not just "of Catholic inspiration," the ALP tried to appeal to all Catholic moderates, whether of the moderate left or the moderate right. In this, it followed the pattern of the "Catholic party" which Albert de Mun had attempted to found in 1885.

Though the ALP was far more successful than any of its predecessors, its appeal finally waned. By the First World War the ALP had virtually disappeared. There are many reasons why it failed to capture a permanent audience. First, it tried to be all things to all men. It was officially "Republican," but it advocated "the defense of religious, civic, and economic freedom, endangered by the Masonic, Jacobin and Socialist tyranny."[28] But more important was the absence of groups such as Catholic Action. Today, Catholic Action gives an educated, dedicated following to the MRP; at the turn of the century the *ad hoc* Catholic groups existing with the ALP were not able to perform this function.

Rather than its own policies or its desires to further the goals of the Church, the chief importance of the ALP lies in the groups which evolved from it. Many of its leaders formed the *Parti Démocrate Populaire* after World War I, and the latter group, in turn, became the main nucleus of the MRP.

Calls for unity of all Catholic laymen are nothing new, but the separation crisis saw an unusually large number of attempts to create other coordinating organizations outside the ALP, which all Catholics could enter. Many of these attempts were instigated by the Vatican or the French clergy, rather than Catholic laymen themselves. The pattern had been set by Albert de Mun, who attempted, and failed, to set up a large Catholic Party based on the nonpolitical Catholic social and economic groups that existed around 1885.[29]

[28] Flornoy, *op.cit.*, p. 1.

[29] See Henri Rollet, *Albert de Mun et le Parti Catholique* (Paris: Boivin, 1949).

After de Mun's failure, the *Union de la France Chrétienne*, formed at the suggestion of Cardinal Richard, attracted representatives of most moderate Catholic forces.[30] The Union was officially neutral in the political realm, but tacitly favored the Royalist cause. As it developed, its counterrevolutionary form became more and more apparent, and soon such leaders as de Mun left. Only a few months after the foundation of the Union, the rallying call of Leo XIII caused its demise.[31]

In 1898 the Vatican sponsored an electoral federation which was just as unsuccessful as the Union mentioned above. Again members of Catholic groups such as the *Association Catholique de la Jeunesse Française*, the writers for *La Croix*, and the social Catholics Harmel and de Mun joined the electoral group. But Catholic forces failed to gain ground in elections and the federation was short-lived.[32]

Between the separation and World War I the Vatican tried to develop still another Catholic political group. The Pope called for a union of all Catholics, regardless of ideological preferences, under the authority of their local bishops. A number of "diocese unions" were formed to follow the Pope's advice. But like so many other attempts at Catholic unity, these unions soon took on a conservative or reactionary shade. Liberal Catholics, and this time even *La Croix*, opposed the unions, and the initial enthusiasm of their organizers was soon dispelled. By the war only twenty-one unions had been set up.[33] The unions were the last formal attempt to unite lay Catholics around the Church Hierarchy for partisan political goals.[34] Like all previous attempts the unions failed to achieve a great political

[30] Among its members were Albert de Mun, representatives of publications like *La Croix* and *Univers*, delegates from *Jeunesse Catholique*, and from many other groups.

[31] For a description of the Union see Barbier, *op.cit.*, Vol. II, pp. 301 ff.

[32] See Barbier for a description of the federation. *ibid.*, p. 471.

[33] Brugerette, *op.cit.*, Vol. III, pp. 77 ff.

[34] Even if a group were officially nonpolitical, according to Dansette it could not help exerting political influence during these troubled times. ". . . the state of mind of Catholics was such that any initiative, even one unrelated to the regime question, would be inevitably directed against the regime." Dansette, *op.cit.*, Vol. II, p. 382.

impact because of the conflicts among the various Catholic laymen's groups.

The most important Catholic laymen's groups at this time were neither run by the Hierarchy nor designed to attract all Catholics. They reflected the desires of specific social or ideological subgroupings within French Catholicism. Perhaps the most famous example of these, destined to have a profound effect on future generations of French Catholics, was the *Sillon* of Marc Sangnier.[35]

The *Sillon* was one of the first successful attempts to dissociate the Church from the doctrines of the right, and is thus one of the forerunners of the working-class apostolic movements which will be studied in later chapters. Sangnier and his followers in *Sillon* were profoundly attached to the Republic, which they considered the "most Christian" of political institutions. Unfortunately, they did not know how to distinguish partisan activity in support of the policies of the regime in power from religious activity in support of the humanitarian ideas in Catholic dogma. *Sillon* attempted to combine religious and political action, and confused the two. This confusion ultimately brought the dissolution of *Sillon* in an evident use of a double standard, for the Hierarchy tolerated political activity by more conservative Catholic groups.

Despite its failure to distinguish between political and religious activity (in this it reflected the spirit of the time) and despite its relatively few adherents, *Sillon* has made a lasting imprint on French Catholicism.[36] Such eminent Catholics as Cardinal Feltin, Archbishop of Paris, are former *Sillonistes.* After *Sillon* was dissolved its leaders formed the *Jeune République*, a political group that tried to carry on much of the work of *Sillon*, and which also contributed much to the foundation of the MRP.

[35] *ibid.*, pp. 397-436. Dansette devotes an entire chapter to the *Sillon.*

[36] At the height of its power, *Sillon* had only around 20,000 members. See Henri Rollet, *L'Action Sociale des Catholiques en France, 1871-1914* (Bruges: Desclée de Brouwer, 1958), Vol. II, p. 25.

The period before World War I saw the foundation of the first Catholic Action group, the *Association Catholique de la Jeunesse Française* (ACJF). Founded by Albert de Mun, the ACJF was a well-organized movement, ready to fight for the interests of the Church by the time of the separation crisis. However, in its first years, the ACJF was more a pressure group than the apostolic movement it was later to become; it could not help being so, considering the temper of the times. Although much ACJF activity around the time of separation is forgotten, it certainly used its 140,000 members to advantage.[37] Barbier mentions a number of conferences and meetings sponsored by the ACJF to drum up opposition to the Separation Law as well as various campaigns of information throughout France. A petition against the proposed law which was circulated by the ACJF received, according to Barbier, over 3,400,000 signatures.[38]

None of the Catholic groups mentioned here can be considered politically successful in the long run. One indicator of the failure of Catholic groups to support the cause of the Church effectively is the steady decline in votes for Catholic parties from 1900 to World War I. According to Brugerette, the votes for Catholic candidates in parliamentary elections were as follows: in 1889, 3.4 million; in 1893, 1.3 million; in 1914, 0.8 million.[39] According to Jacques, Catholics lost one third of their electorate between 1906 and 1910.[40] Catholic political ineffectiveness is corroborated by the Papal Nuncio himself: "Political action by Catholics is zero. Almost all the Catholic Deputies belong to the nobility and are far inferior in their

[37] In analyzing the ACJF, Barbier comments on "the daring of its social theories which, in many important areas, rival the theories of the most progressive Christian Democrats." Barbier, *op.cit.*, Vol. III, pp. 68-69. A more concrete indication of ACJF effectiveness is noted by Barbier: the ACJF was actually made a constituent element of the ALP political party. See Barbier, *op.cit.*, Vol. IV, pp. 89-90.

[38] *ibid.*, p. 34.

[39] Brugerette, *op.cit.*, Vol. II, p. 364.

[40] Léon Jacques, *Les Partis Politiques sous la Troisième République* (Paris: Sirey, 1913), p. 438.

moral value and in their talent to their colleagues in the Chamber."[41]

There are a number of reasons for Catholic political ineffectiveness in this period. First, as has been mentioned, it is always difficult to bring all Catholics together for a common political purpose. Second, most Catholic groups were not organized for effective political pressure on the government, but only for vague "social action." The social Catholic movement of the late nineteenth century was extraordinarily active, as the masterful studies by Duroselle and Henri Rollet attest,[42] but its work was limited to social welfare and economic improvement rather than partisan political activity. Finally, Catholics never succeeded in dispelling completely the myth that Church groups were in league with the Monarchists, bent on overthrowing the Republic. Thus they automatically lost much support from more moderate segments of society.

D. THE CATHOLIC PRESS

In France the press has always reflected the opinions of the various "tendencies" into which society is divided. Each main current of thought and all the subgroups as well will have a magazine or review to spread ideas throughout France. For Catholics, too, the press has offered the best vehicle for spreading ideas throughout the Catholic elite and into the French masses.[43]

Lack of adequate source material makes a complete coverage of the pre-World War I Catholic press impossible. For many ephemeral publications records are virtually nonexistent, and

[41] Letter from Mgr. Montagnini to Cardinal Merry del Val, quoted in Mgr. Montagnini, *Les Fiches Pontificales* (Paris: Nourry, 1908), p. 168.

[42] Rollet, *L'Action Sociale des Catholiques en France*, Vol. II, *passim*. Jean-Baptiste Duroselle, *Les Débuts du Catholicisme Social en France*. (Paris: Presses Universitaires de France, 1951).

[43] Most Catholic publications were read only by an elite—usually the people who were already convinced of the particular ideas held by the paper. For example, *Ere Nouvelle*, the spokesman of the Catholic avant-garde in the Second Republic and one of the most famous Catholic newspapers of the Nineteenth Century, had a circulation of barely 20,000. See Duroselle; *op.cit.*, p. 304.

in most instances the circulation figures are unavailable. Certain publications of Catholic groups, such as *Etudes*, the Jesuit monthly, or *Annales de la Jeunesse Catholique* of the ACJF were already being published before 1914. And there were innumerable regional publications more or less tied to Catholicism, whose obscurity makes any assessment impossible. Even concentrating on newspapers, it is often hard to discover, beneath the polemics of the day, which are "Catholic" and which are not.

Is there any key to distinguishing a "Catholic" publication in this period from one which is "Monarchist"? Did Catholic newspapers contribute any more to the political impact of Catholicism than the Monarchist press? These questions are difficult because ecclesiastical approval of the press as we know it today was not practiced at the time of the separation. The only newspapers that had a special place with reference to the Church were *La Croix*, published by the Assumptionnists, and *Univers*, a Catholic-oriented paper already over a half-century old. Thus, for the moment any newspapers which might have contributed to the political impact of Catholicism must be included with the "Catholic" press, even though by today's standards they could be put in another category.

As might be expected most Catholic and associated newspapers at the turn of the century were conservative or reactionary. The times were not propitious for extensive development of the Catholic left.[44] Some of the publications were downright extremist. The most striking are the violently anti-Semitic *Libre Parole* and the archlegitimist *Gazette de France*. These publications also extolled the interests of the Church, and in return most other Catholic publications showed no love for the French Jews.

The "moderate" press was dominated by *La Croix*. Today, *La Croix* has prestige and influence among a French elite, but little mass influence. But at the turn of the century it was big:

[44] Most of the press of the *abbés démocrates* did not survive World War I.

local editions of the paper were set up throughout France, and numbered over one hundred just before World War I.[45]

At the time of the anticlerical crusade *La Croix* could not have remained as objective politically as it claims to be today. Along with most Catholic groups, it conducted a bitter campaign against Freemasonry, and was not at all well disposed toward the regime of Monsieur Combes.[46] Yet *La Croix* was ready to submit whenever the Church issued a statement—in this it was more Catholic than the extreme-right papers. For example, *La Croix* never criticized the foundations of the Republic after Pope Leo's call for Catholic support. It supported the ALP (just as it has often supported the MRP tacitly today) because it was considered the "most Catholic" political party.[47] Even after the Separation Law, *La Croix* prudently awaited the decision of the Pope before taking a stand.[48]

The Catholic press, whether extreme or moderate, seems to have had a negligible political impact in France in the years around 1905. It could not swing public opinion away from the *laïques* at elections and it failed to curb anti-Catholic sentiment just before the separation. This is difficult to understand since all Catholic publications (except certain ones of the extreme left) were united against the projected legislation.[49] One explanation is that the Catholic press consisted of a multitude of small, uninfluential papers. According to one estimate, in 1913 there were ninety-six Catholic publications in Paris alone![50] Another explanation is the disagreement on a positive

[45] See Jacques, *op.cit.*, pp. 423-424. Also Barbier, *op.cit.*, Vol. IV, pp. 39-45.

[46] French *Archives Nationales* has a collection of clippings and evaluations of these newspapers during the separation crisis (1879-1908): F[19] 1966-1971.

[47] Barbier, *op.cit.*, Vol. IV, p. 115-116. In *La Croix* for April 29, 1902, the editor called Jacques Piou of the ALP "our leader."

[48] "We shall not take a stand either for or against the law . . . silence will be the rule until the Pope has spoken." *La Croix*, quoted in Brugerette, *op.cit.*, Vol. II, p. 568.

[49] The same publications had been against Dreyfus too, but this did not prevent Dreyfus from receiving a pardon. See Dansette, *Histoire*, Vol. II, p. 281.

[50] Jacques in *Annuaire de la Presse Française et Etrangère et du Monde*

alternative to the Combes version of the French Republic. Papers like *La Croix* wanted a more tolerant Republic, while other publications helping the Catholic cause were Royalist. All of these difficulties within the Catholic press reflect one central fact: the political sphere is not the most effective place for Catholics, through coordinated effort, to make their impact felt.

There is prima-facie evidence for concluding that the various Catholic "actors" at the turn of the century completely misjudged the temper of the times. Their verbal aggressiveness and cooperation with conservative forces did not woo any of the *laïques* away from anticlericalism; rather, anticlerical forces grew constantly during the period.

The end of tensions was not brought about by deliberate policies from Catholic groups but by the fraternity of all World War I combatants for France. And after the war, as Catholics appeared to prefer piety to politics, they felt more and more "at home" in the French regime. Indeed, in the years since separation Catholic political effectiveness has certainly increased, as Catholic groups have become used to working within the laic Republic instead of spending their time in a sterile and futile struggle against it.

III. Catholic Institutions Between the Two World Wars

The interwar period is a halfway point for the Church. The struggles of the Combes era were finished but the bitterness remained, with a resurgence of "laic" or "clerical" reflexes from time to time. The new forms of Catholic Action were just emerging, and the Hierarchy had not yet defined the relations between political activity and religious status. In short, this is a period of rapid evolution, which can shed light on the transition between Catholic excesses of the separation, and our own times.

Politique, 1913, pp. 944 ff. The 1954 edition of the same *Annuaire* listed over 100 Catholic publications in Paris. See pp. 498 ff.

HISTORICAL SKETCH

A. THE VATICAN

The interwar period was dominated by the personality of Pope Pius XI. Three key events marked his pontificate, each of which reflected Pius' state of mind. First, Pius XI called for organized apostolic work in various dechristianized social classes, thus beginning Catholic Action as we know it today. Secondly, the Pope brought the Church much closer to accepting the laic Republic. He tried to liquidate the smouldering political quarrels with the regime by accepting with modifications the provisions of the Separation Law for the disposal of Church property.[51] Diplomatic relations between France and the Vatican were reestablished in another gesture of good will. Also, the Pope finally made public the condemnation of the anti-Republican *Action Française*. The condemnation, issued under Pope Pius X, had been kept secret over a decade for political reasons.[52] Another main goal of Pius XI was to remove the Church from the political realm as much as possible. This was one of the reasons for channeling Catholic energies into Catholic Action apostolic work. But here the Pope was not immediately successful, for Catholic groups could not in a short time be completely removed from the French political scene.

B. THE FRENCH CLERGY

World War I changed the attitudes of the French clergy and of their critics. For the first time in a generation, the war pushed all internal political differences into the background. Priests served with distinction in the army, and many of the religious orders which had been expelled from France returned to volunteer their services. After the war, a return to the prewar pattern of violent quarrels between Church and state was unthinkable. This was doubly true since the laic side, having achieved its main goal of Church-state separation, was now willing to accept the *status quo*.

Just after World War I the French clergy began applying

[51] See Dansette, *Histoire*, Vol. II, pp. 509-510.
[52] *ibid.*, p. 579.

some lessons learned during the separation crisis. In 1919, the first national institution of the Hierarchy was established: the Assembly of Cardinals and Archbishops. Shortly after, a National Secretariat was organized to coordinate the activities of all Catholic laymen's groups. With these institutions the French Hierarchy for the first time had valid spokesmen for its interests both in the French government and in the Vatican.

Between the French clergy and the Pope there was a difference in perspective similar to the differences during the separation crisis. But this time, the Pope was progressive and willing to compromise with the Republic, while the French bishops, most of them appointees of Pius X, were more conservative.[53] However, there was less danger that the aftermath of separation would have untoward political consequences, because the Pope's new policies restricted the political activities of the clergy. The international situation also helped limit the political impact of the clergy. Starting in the 1930's world affairs once more took the spotlight away from the still-smouldering Church-state issue inside France.[54]

Nevertheless, one political question in the interwar period involved most of the French clergy, despite the wishes of Pius XI. Most of the French clergy had been favorable to *Action Française*, and remained so even after publication of the Papal condemnation.[55] The same is true of most Benedictines, many Jesuits and Dominicans, and many secular priests.[56] Therefore, just thirty years ago large segments of the French

[53] The French cardinals were "unanimously agreed to resist respectfully" the Vatican policy of compromise on the question of Church property. See *ibid.*, pp. 506-507. Mgr. Marty, Bishop of Montauban, ordered Catholics not to vote for those who favor or even tolerate the principle of *laïcité*. *Ibid.*, p. 535. The most significant thing about this statement is that it was made just thirty years ago; today it would be impossible to find a statement of this type from a French bishop.

[54] Cf. Frederick Russell Hoare, *The Papacy and the Modern State* (London: Burns, Oates and Washbourne, 1940), p. 268.

[55] Dansette quotes the Archbishop of Aix as saying that eleven of the seventeen French cardinals and archbishops favored *Action Française* even after the condemnation. Dansette, *Histoire*, Vol. II, p. 599.

[56] *ibid.*, p. 600.

clergy were so bitterly against the regime that they could not adhere wholeheartedly to the decision of the Pope himself! The chapters to follow will point out the profound evolution by the French clergy in recent years away from such extremism.[57]

One of the great unsettled issues of the interwar period was the place of religious orders in France. The anticongregation laws of 1901 and 1904 remained on the books, so most orders were not legally allowed in France. But the era of good feelings during World War I brought a climate of tolerance in which the orders were allowed to return and the law was unenforced. However, not until the Vichy regime were the anticongregation laws officially modified.[58]

C. CATHOLIC LAYMEN'S GROUPS

As the interwar period was a transition, it is not surprising to find two different political opinions among Catholics. Some looked back to the prewar struggles and inclined to extremism, and some deemphasized political activity in anticipation of a new era of toleration. The former were most likely to join *Action Française*, in which was concentrated most of the conservative, antiregime sentiment after World War I. But *Action Française* was not really a Catholic institution, as the Papal condemnation made plain to all. After the condemnation, when a great many Catholics became disenchanted with the activity of Maurras and his friends, Catholic Action received a great influx of members.[59]

Catholic Action illustrates more moderate reactions of Catho-

[57] This period seems to have marked the extreme limit of the "rightward swing" in the French Church. Many analysts think that French Catholicism is now in a "leftward swing" that has already taken much of the clergy further to the left than the Socialists—especially on colonial and Algerian policies. See Duverger in *Le Monde*, March 26, 1959, p. 1.

[58] Laws of September 3, 1940; Law No. 505, April 8, 1942; No. 1115, December 31, 1942. These laws are still in force. See Dansette, *Histoire*, Vol. II, p. 510.

[59] *ibid.*, pp. 563-613. Dansette makes a good general survey of the relations between the Church and *Action Française*.

lics in the interwar period. The first groups of Catholic Action were youth groups, notably the ACJF from before the war. In the late 1920's a Catholic group for young workers, the *Jeunesse Ouvrière Chrétienne* (JOC), was established in Belgium, and soon came to France. The JOC had a new formula of trying to convert a social class by using members of that class. It renounced political activity entirely, in favor of pursuit of its apostolic goals. This formula soon was generalized to all Catholic Action groups, and became the dominant pattern among Catholic laymen just before World War II. As a reaction against the too-political orientation of Catholicism during the separation crisis, the new Catholic Action was perhaps too far from the field of temporal activity, at least down to World War II. Since the war and down to the present day, Catholic Action has once more been increasing its political activity.[60]

Along with Catholic Action, the interwar period saw the rise of other types of Catholic groups, which would soon become institutionalized within French Catholicism. An important group was the *Fédération Nationale Catholique,* of General de Castelnau. It arose to combat the anticlerical action threatened by the *Cartel des Gauches* in 1924, and its effectiveness is attested by the failure of the *Cartel* to achieve any of its aims.[61] It had no general philosophy of action, however; in this the *Fédération Nationale Catholique* was different from the Royalist or anti-Semitic groups which flourished before World War I.

The *Fédération Nationale Catholique* was the first mass social Catholic movement for men. Two years after its foundation it had reached over 1.8 million members.[62] In its early years it had perhaps a latent hostility toward the Republic, but

[60] "It is very significant to compare the orders of the Assembly of Cardinals and Archbishops in 1936, forbidding active Catholic Action members from serving a function in a political party, with the orders of 1950, which call for workers to join Workers' Catholic Action, provided they serve in other organizations!" Adrien Dansette, *Destin du Catholicisme Français, 1926-1956* (Paris: Flammarion, 1957), p. 422.

[61] See Dansette, *Histoire,* Vol. II, p. 519.

[62] *ibid.*

gradually moved away from political preoccupations, and now the *Fédération* (under the name of *Action Catholique Générale des Hommes*, or ACGH) is an integral part of Catholic Action.

In the interwar period important women's organizations worked parallel to the *Fédération Nationale Catholique*. Some of these groups soon formed the *Ligue Féminine d'Action Catholique Française* which is now the Catholic Action counterpart of ACGH, under the name of *Action Catholique Générale des Femmes* (ACGF). The *Fédération* and its women's counterpart both based their activity on parishes and dioceses, in close cooperation with the clergy. Another group of women, the *Union Féminine Civique et Sociale*, also organized in the interwar period and still exists in basically the same form today. However, the latter group is much more independent of the Church Hierarchy than the successors of the *Fédération* and the *Ligue*.

Along with the *Fédération* and the women's groups, other social action organizations were developing throughout the interwar period. The *Semaines Sociales*, established before the war, increased in vitality and influence.[63] The CFTC, still closely connected with the clergy and other Catholic groups, took an increasingly important place in the growing social Catholic movement.[64]

Partisan political activity like that of the ALP and the *Sillon* also continued in the interwar period. A political party, the *Parti Démocrate Populaire*, and a group called *Jeune République*, carried on the traditions of the two prewar organizations. Neither was important numerically; the Popular Democrats never had over eighteen deputies, while the left-oriented *Jeune République* was even weaker. But together they form the link between the earlier ALP and *Sillon*, and today's MRP.

In the interwar period for the first time there was a structural difference between Catholic parties and other Catholic groups, the parties calling themselves "of Catholic inspiration," and

[63] See Chapter Five. [64] See Chapter Seven.

breaking all formal ties with the Hierarchy.[65] This organizational pattern was carried on by the MRP. The MRP also found indispensable the experienced personnel (at least those who had not compromised themselves with Vichy), the youth organization, the special sections dealing with particular social classes, the international coordinating group, and other elements of the Popular Democratic Party which were incorporated directly into the MRP.[66]

The MRP now has a greater political impact than the Popular Democrats ever did, for a number of reasons. Perhaps most significantly, the MRP has been able to add elements from Catholic Action, from social Catholic groups, and from other elements of the Catholic left to the nucleus of Party cadres. Virtually every moderate or left-wing group mentioned in this chapter has given some members to the MRP. This in itself makes these groups politically significant. Later it will be shown that almost all the top MRP leaders were once active in one or another of the interwar Catholic groups.

In the interwar period changes in the Catholic press paralleled the evolution of Catholic groups just mentioned. New publications emerged and old ones were revamped to reflect the more spiritual, less politically-inclined principles of contemporary Catholics. It was during this period that *La Croix*, under the direction of Father Merklen, lost most of its political partisanship. At the same time, however, more than just a vestige of the old partisan Catholic press remained. In fact, important new partisan Catholic publications were formed. *France Catholique*, still today a spokesman for conservative Catholic forces, was founded in a spirit of near-hostility to the Republican regime. *Ouest-Eclair*, with its 250,000 to 400,000 circulation, carried the message of Christian Democracy to the masses in western France, while the intellectual bulwarks of Christian Democracy were being laid by the newly-founded *Aube, Vie Intellectuelle*, and by *Sept* and its successor *Temps Présent*.

[65] Dansette, *Histoire*, Vol. II, p. 547. Cf. Louis Biton, *La Démocratie Chrétienne dans la Politique Française* (Angers: Siraudeau, n.d.), p. 59.
[66] *ibid.*

And dynamic French Catholic forces on the far left launched *Esprit*. At this time there even existed a review, *Terre Nouvelle*, which attempted to find a synthesis between Communism and Catholicism.[67]

The center of gravity of the Catholic press moved significantly to the left in the interwar period. This was due to two factors: first, the extremist publications of the right virtually disappeared. Royalism was no longer taken seriously; anti-Semitism had diminished greatly, and after 1926, the publications of *Action Française* began to lose their appeal to Catholics. Also at the same time the number of publications representing the Catholic left flourished.

After this brief analysis of Catholic groups before World War I and in the interwar period, it seems probable that, compared to Catholic groups today, those in preceding eras should be judged less dynamic and politically less effective.[68] They were never masters of the political situation, but always had to react to a *fait accompli.* Their extremes were politically ineffective, though they are quite understandable during the time when they faced bitter foes who held the reins of government. It would have been noteworthy if Catholic groups under these circumstances had not been extremist.

It takes time for groups which have been decades under state control and tutelage to acquire the proper attitude toward political life. The separation removed state control (and state subsidies) from Catholicism; the proper political attitude was achieved only after World War II. The quarrels which plagued France down to the 1920's (and which still survive in the school

[67] For a detailed study of the Catholic press in the interwar period, see René Rémond, *Les Catholiques, le Communisme et les Crises, 1929-1939* (Paris: Armand Colin, 1960).

[68] We cannot be sure of the political impact of Catholic groups before World War II because sufficient information is not available on their activity, their membership, and so forth. The histories of French Catholicism that have appeared have dealt with the political ideas of selected Catholic groups, but have not considered questions of political impact. One of the purposes of this book is to provide surer indications of the political impact of Catholic groups today.

problem) made it harder for Catholics to acquire a healthy respect for France's political institutions. Even now, Catholic groups have not yet put into universal practice the formula—discussed in the next section—which they have found for balancing temporal and spiritual activity. This will not be done and Catholics will not achieve a permanent, healthy relation to other French political forces until certain outstanding questions such as the school problem are permanently removed from the center of the political stage.

IV. The Development of the Laic State in Theory and Practice

A. DEFINITIONS

The key issue facing Catholic groups throughout the past half-century has been the relationship between Church and state. The struggles between the two since the French Revolution have inspired leaders of both sides to draw up what they considered the ideal relationship between the Church and state. Most suggestions can be reduced to three basic types: *cléricalisme*, *laïcisme*, and *laïcité*. The French forms are used because the concepts have quite different connotations in Anglo-American experience. The French have fought for decades over these three concepts, and it seems useful to see precisely what they mean and how they have been applied in practice up to the present time.

Cléricalisme and *laïcisme* both imply an interpenetration of politics and religion. *Cléricalisme* has been defined as follows: "I shall call *cléricalisme* the system which makes a political weapon out of ecclesiastical authority. People are *cléricales* if they accept or undergo both religious control and political control from the clergy. . . . In general, people who are very Catholic, or if you will, very respectful of the clergy's religious influence, are at the same time inclined to *cléricalisme*."[69] "*Cléricalisme* as defined by some people is supposed to be the

[69] André Siegfried, *Tableau Politique de la France de l'Ouest*, p. 392.

tendency of a spiritual society to interfere in the political domain of the State. This is contrary to the authentic thinking of the Church."[70]

Laïcisme is practically the reverse of *cléricalisme.* The ACA seems to have best described it in these terms: ". . . . A philosophical doctrine which contains a whole materialist and atheistic conception of human life and of society . . . a system of political government which imposes this conception on civil servants even in their private life, on state schools, on the entire nation."[71] *Laïcisme* has been further defined as follows: ". . . The negator of Catholicism and the propagator of a rationalist religion which puts man in the place of God."[72] ". . . Justifies all despotic excesses and leads straight on to dictatorship. It brings us back to the pagan conception of the State from which Christianity freed us, when all the progress of modern law works to limit the absolutism of the State."[73]

Laïcité is more difficult to define, although in all acceptable definitions it includes the separation of spiritual matters from the competence of the state—and thus a limitation of the power of the state. The most recent and most authoritative statement of *laïcité* was given by Cardinal Gerlier at Lourdes in August, 1958: "*Laïcité* of the state can have quite varied meanings. If it concerns an affirmation of the sovereign authority of the state in its domain of the temporal order . . . this doctrine is fully in accord with the doctrine of the Church. . . . If *laïcité* of the state is to mean that, in a country of many religious beliefs, the state should allow each citizen to practice freely his religion, this second meaning, if correctly understood, also conforms to Church doctrine. Of course the Church is saddened by this

[70] Cardinal Gerlier, speech at Lourdes, quoted in *Cahiers d'Action Religieuse et Sociale,* Vol. 262, September 15, 1958, p. 498.

[71] Statement by the cardinals and archbishops of France, November 13, 1945, quoted in *Informations Catholiques Internationales,* February 1, 1956, p. 14.

[72] Dansette, *Histoire,* Vol. II, p. 316.

[73] Cardinal Gerlier at Lourdes, quoted in *La Croix,* August 23, 1958, p. 1. Clearly, *laïque* as we have described it denotes a partisan of *laïcisme.*

division of religious beliefs. But it wants the act of faith to be made freely."[74]

This conception of *laïcité* resembles the philosophy of relations between equal states in the international realm: complete freedom of each in its own realm and noninterference in the internal affairs of the other.

B. CHURCH AND STATE IN PRACTICE

The quarrel over definitions reflects the historical pattern of Church-state relations even before the separation crisis. During the *Ancien Régime*, Church and state were intimately related, though neither *cléricalisme* nor *laïcisme* existed in a pure form. The Church was one of the pillars of the kingdom, with immense power in local political affairs. The king had important religious prerogatives, including the nomination of bishops. For a short time during the Revolution, especially between 1791 and 1795, with the "Constitutional Church," a *laïcisme* akin to persecution prevailed. In neither the *Ancien Régime* nor this reaction to it can we find the idea of Church-state separation, however.

During most of the nineteenth century, even under the Republican regime, there seemed to be little enthusiasm for separating the Church and the state. Lamennais, who dared to preach "freedom" for the Church, was expressly refuted by the Pope in the encyclical *Mirari Vos.* Many politicians of the left wanted to continue the Napoleonic Concordat as the best means to control the Church. Even as late as 1901, when a law was voted giving freedom for private associations to organize, religious congregations were in practice excluded.[75]

Despite Catholic protests, the separation of 1905 established the legal basis of Church-state relations that has lasted down to the present. Of course, the new formula of separation was

[74] *ibid.*

[75] Dansette, in *Histoire*, Vol. I, has a good general treatment of Church-state relations down to the Third Republic. For an analysis of the effects of the 1901 law on religious orders, see Dansette, *Histoire*, Vol. II, pp. 304-306.

violently criticized by Catholic groups. However, by the 1930's neither extreme *laïques* nor extreme *cléricaux* could possibly change the law. In a very brief space of time—about five years—the Jesuits of *Action Populaire*, the Dominicans of *Vie Intellectuelle*, the Assumptionnists of *Bonne Presse*, and many lay Catholic intellectuals all decided to accept the modus vivendi which had been established and which was close to Cardinal Gerlier's second definition of *laïcité*. At the present time almost all Catholics have joined the pioneers in accepting *laïcité*. However, it is something quite new in French history, and only time will tell whether it will remain the keystone of Church-state relationships.

Even now Church-state relations are being modified. Within the framework of the 1905 separation a sort of "positive neutrality" is being created, which has more in common with certain American practices of Church-state cooperation than with French historical tradition.[76] Local communes can pay the curé as "guardian of the church," if his church is a public monument.[77] Catholic missionaries in underdeveloped lands have always been supported and recognized as in the "public interest." And the Concordat of 1801 is still valid in Alsace-Lorraine. These ties with the state do not compromise the independence of the Church. They reflect a more enlightened view of positive freedom, following a formula that "the State cannot witness the disappearance of that which deserves to live."[78] Thus, since French society needs a healthy Church, many feel that the state must provide money and other aid to keep the Church healthy when it lacks such funds itself.

[76] At present, the state subsidizes various Catholic Action youth groups, as well as the Catholic scouts. Interview with M. Etcheverry, in charge of liaison with private youth organizations at the High Commission for Youth and Sports, Paris, June 9, 1959. Unless otherwise noted, interviews were held in Paris.

[77] Canon Kerlévéo, "Le Régime de l'Eglise en Droit Français," in V.-L. Chaigneau, *L'Organisation de l'Eglise Catholique en France* (Paris: Spes, 1955), p. 55.

[78] Quoted from René Rémond, "L'Evolution de la Notion de Laïcité entre 1919 et 1939," in *Cahiers d'Histoire*, Vol. IV, No. 1 (Lyon: 1959), p. 85.

To a great degree the triumph and consolidation of this positive neutrality between Church and state depends on the school question. A new school law voted in December 1959 indirectly recognizes that Catholic schools perform a public service by paying the salaries of most teachers in such schools, including teaching members of the clergy. Many people are fearful that this law could destroy the legal bases of separation altogether, so obviously there is still too much passion involved in the school question for an effective solution without much more hard bargaining. If in the long run the new school law leads to a permanent relaxation of tension and a new spirit of mutual comprehension between *cléricaux* and *laïques* it will be one of the best guarantees that the Fifth Republic will continue secure and strong.

The Ecclesiastical Nucleus

I. The Basic Teachings of the Church

A. INTRODUCTION

In certain respects French Catholic institutions resemble our solar system. Lay Catholic groups gravitate around a central element or "sun," some being quite close to it while others are in orbits farther removed. The "sun" in this case comprises the totality of ecclesiastical institutions—in Rome as well as in France itself.

Because this cosmological image must be considered in a political sense, it is greatly complicated and thereby loses much of its orderliness. In the first place, the ecclesiastical nucleus of French Catholicism has no single, unified political behavior pattern. Secondly, political activity seems to increase as one moves away from the ecclesiastical nucleus. It is greatest among political parties, none of which is explicitly Catholic. Finally, the "gravity," or the force holding all elements of French Catholicism together, cannot be fully grasped with the tools of political analysis used in this book. This force is faith, and it, rather than any political considerations, explains the stable structure of French Catholicism.

But despite the limits to a thorough understanding of the structure of French Catholicism, much can be learned from studying each of its major elements in turn. The ecclesiastical nucleus is particularly significant indirectly, for it provides keys to the political behavior of the groups "in orbit" around it. It directs some of them; others it coordinates, and still others it merely advises.

The ecclesiastical nucleus can also have a direct political influence through declarations, announcements, and articles issued by priests and bishops or other dynamic clerical leaders.

These representatives of the Church seldom engage in such obvious partisan activity as did their forebears a half-century ago, although this may still happen from time to time. Often, however, a spiritualistic platitude may be only a thinly-veiled call to action, understood by the faithful who share a common vocabulary.

B. THE SOCIAL DOCTRINE OF THE CHURCH

In the Church an uncounted mass of documents, from the Vatican as well as from individual clergymen, from the present as well as from past centuries, concerns man in society. The most noteworthy documents are called collectively the "social doctrine of the Church." Unfortunately, no one has ever accurately defined just what the "Church social doctrine" is. It seems unlikely that anyone will ever do it, for a definition would render static what has historically been a body of teachings evolving along with society.[1]

Although the Church social doctrine cannot be defined precisely, its main constituent elements can be easily found. It consists of the body of recent Papal pronouncements (formal or informal) related to economic, social or political questions, plus certain long-accepted Church principles (e.g., the dignity of man, which makes him a subject rather than the object of social action). It does not ordinarily include comments or exegeses on these principles by others outside the Vatican: "Thus, two aspects must be carefully distinguished: on one hand, the authentic social doctrine of the Church; on the other hand, applications of principles and conclusions from them by theologians, sociologists, schools and movements. The work, the research, the positions of these Christian economists and these schools do not constitute Church social doctrine itself."[2] It is important to distinguish between the Church social doctrine and

[1] Note two of the key books on Church social doctrine published in France: Mgr. Guerry, *La Doctrine Sociale de l'Eglise* (Paris: Bonne *Presse*, 1957); Cardinal Richaud, *Annexe au Directoire Pastorale en Matière Sociale* (Paris: Bonne Presse and Editions de Fleurus, 1955).

[2] Mgr. Guerry, *op.cit.*, pp. 15-16.

commentaries on it, because only the doctrine itself theoretically is binding on all Catholics.

Must one consider commentaries or declarations by his own bishop as part of the Church social doctrine? This is a question fraught with difficulties, for the moment unanswerable.[3] At any rate, even as defined above, the social doctrine of the Church can vary and even show inconsistencies. Thus, the social spirit of *Rerum Novarum* is far different from that of Pius the Ninth's *Syllabus*.

In what form is the Church social doctrine stated? It is usually vague and imprecise, with many shadings of meaning capable of varied interpretations. At times a Pope speaks out clearly, as did Pope Pius X in refusing to accept the solution to the separation crisis proposed by France and tacitly accepted by progressive bishops. But even when the Pope speaks clearly, the well-informed Catholic will look carefully to see if the Pope demands any positive reaction from him.

In practice, the Church observes a distinction between authoritative pronouncements that are to be obeyed in all circumstances, and others which can be modified if necessity demands it. The first group represents *theses*; the second, *hypotheses*. The thesis includes principles in all their dogmatic rigidity; the hypothesis includes the softened, less rigid principles which are practiced in everyday life. To illustrate the difference, the Church generally insists on the necessity of giving children a Catholic schooling. The principle is rigid and universally binding on Catholics. But by tolerating the existence of "neutral schools" in France, the Church is accepting a hypothesis.

In any case, the Church social doctrine seldom requires a specific political action from an individual. "The Church constantly proclaims that it does not intend to make rules for the practical or purely technical levels of social organization."[4]

[3] As we shall see below, especially in the concluding chapter, many Catholics find ways of interpreting their bishops' declarations as they desire in any case.

[4] Mgr. Guerry, *op.cit.*, p. 19. Many other quotations can be cited to show that the Church does not want to meddle in partisan politics; it

C. POLITICAL QUESTIONS INVOLVING THE SOCIAL DOCTRINE OF THE CHURCH

Obviously, the Church social doctrine is much too variable and complex to be summarized in one short, coherent section. Books on it have been written by different Church leaders, including Cardinal Richaud, Mgr. Guerry, the Jesuit Father Villain, and the Benedictines of Solesmes, and each of these books seems to emphasize a different "tendency" of the Church social doctrine.[5] For a clearer picture of the intricacies of Church social doctrine it is useful to indicate the political problems which most often draw responses from the Hierarchy in doctrinal terms. This will at least show the political categories in which the Church feels particularly involved.

On questions concerning the religious structure of the Church

---

has learned its lesson from the crisis at the turn of the century. For example, according to Deroo, "We remain *as a Church* in the religious sphere, outside of any partisan politics, regardless of the appeals that might be made to us, from one side or another." André Deroo, *L'Episcopat Français dans la Mêlée de son Temps* (Paris: Bonne Presse, 1955), p. 109. We have already seen in the preceding chapter how *cléricalisme* was denounced by the Hierarchy itself. But this does not mean that the Hierarchy cannot comment on political questions. As Pope John XXIII stated, "the Church has the right and obligation not merely to guard ethical and religious principles but also to intervene authoritatively in the temporal sphere when it is a matter of judging the application of these principles to concrete cases." Encylical *Mater et Magistra*, quoted in *New York Times*, July 15, 1961, p. 8.

It is interesting to compare the Papal encyclical to the tone in an article in *La Croix*, dated September 12, 1951. This is the day after the *Loi Barangé* was passed by the National Assembly, which is certainly no coincidence: "Of course the Church concerns itself with politics. . . . It is concerned with the political activities of the citizen as with all human activities, to regulate them and to direct them. It is concerned with politics as a lighthouse is concerned with a ship. The lighthouse does not replace the captain; it does not grasp the rudder or give orders to the crew. Rather, it points out the reef, the channel and the port. The captain cannot dispense with the lighthouse nor can he refuse to do his own job. In this same way, the Church reveals the final goal for men and lights their way; but it asks them to do their jobs, in the light that it brings them."

[5] Mgr. Guerry, *op.cit.*; Cardinal Richaud, *op.cit.*; Father Villain, *L'Enseignement Social de l'Eglise* (Paris: Spes, 1954); *Les Enseignements Pontificaux*, collection published by the Monks of Solesmes (Paris: Desclée et Cie., 1952).

itself or of institutions connected to the Church, the ecclesiastical nucleus is naturally quick to defend its interests. This explains the quarrels over the Concordat at the time of separation of Church and state in France. It explains the particular importance of the schools question, for Catholic schools are considered in certain respects part of the Church apparatus. Questions such as the special Concordat status of Alsace-Lorraine, military and high-school chaplains, and so forth are of the same order.

Related to the first category are questions which affect the ability of the Church to survive and expand. Among such questions, modern war is the most important and also the most difficult to analyze. The Church is obviously for peace—and not just because peace offers the Church the best opportunities for expanding its missionary activities. Yet military chaplains often serve on both sides in a war, and do not campaign for immediate cessation of hostilities. Since all the religious forces of the world seem to be on the same side of the cold war fence at present, a more carefully-defined Church doctrine of war is not unlikely.

The Church is firmly opposed to any form of *laïcisme* as it was defined in the last chapter. This opposition is based on a certain self-interest, since the Church feels that a state formally denying God's existence may soon become a persecutor of religion.[6] The laic state is accepted only when it declares itself incompetent to consider the spiritual sphere at all.[7]

A certain rudimentary desire for survival is one of the main determinants of the Catholic attitude toward Communism. Since the formal condemnation by the Holy Office of July 1, 1949, the Church has progressively tightened its attitude on collaboration in any form with Communism.[8] This condemnation is made in particularly energetic terms in a more recent

[6] Cf. Guerry, *op.cit.*, p. 36.

[7] See the definition by Cardinal Gerlier of *laïcité*, in *La Croix*, August 23, 1958, p. 1.

[8] The condemnation is reported in *Documentation Catholique*, July 31, 1949, column 961-962.

interpretation by the Holy Office forbidding Catholics even to vote for sincere Christians if they cooperate electorally with Communists.[9] An even more far-reaching condemnation (though without the force of a Vatican pronouncement) is made by Mgr. Guerry: "Even if Marxism were perfect from a worldly standpoint, even if it assured peace and prosperity to men and nations, even if it suppressed all earthly injustice, the Church would maintain its absolute condemnation."[10]

The Church is also interested in questions involving social and moral activities which it has traditionally exercised: these include determining standards of public morality in all mass communications, lifting the level of public morals, stimulating institutions of charity, and so forth. Of course, certain moral principles can ultimately lead to partisan stands.

There are social and even political areas in which the Church historically has been interested, which remain important areas of concern for it today. The maintenance of private property as a general rule is one of them.[11] Other questions include harmonizing social classes, protecting and encouraging family stability, opposing more lenient divorce laws, and encouraging

[9] This represents a hardening of the Church's attitude, for just ten years earlier, Cardinal Suhard had said that he could tolerate a certain cooperation between Catholics and Communists for "precise and limited objectives," so long as the cooperation was not "habitual or profound." Comment made January 31, 1949. Cf. *Documentation Catholique*, March 13, 1949, column 328.

[10] Commission Episcopale du Monde Ouvrier, *Engagement Temporel* (Paris: A. C. O., no date), p. 53.

[11] Of course, private property can be used in immoral ways, and the well-being of the worker is more important even than the perpetuation of the Capitalist system, according to *Rerum Novarum*. However, the French Church points out the dangers of modifying the Capitalist system: "Nationalization potentially has all the dangers of statism, and runs the risk of favoring too much industrial concentration. The common good requires that private property remain the general rule. However, higher motives could legitimize nationalizing a particular source of production. . . . The priest in this circumstance will not fail to observe that lack of political responsibility by citizens is often the cause for measures of state control." From *Directoire Pastoral en Matière Sociale à l'Usage du Clergé* (Paris: Editions Fleurus, 1954), p. 44. Cf. Guerry, *op.cit.*, pp. 133-134. Pope John XXIII reaffirms these views in his encyclical *Mater et Magistra*. See *New York Times*, July 15, 1961.

better housing conditions. The Church also preaches obedience to the state itself, and this remains as fundamental for the faithful in Red Poland as for those in Franco Spain.

D. OBEDIENCE TO THE CHURCH SOCIAL DOCTRINE

There are wide variations in the attitudes of the Catholic world toward the social doctrine of the Church. In the first place, it is not clear exactly what must be obeyed. The range of Vatican decisions which are absolutely binding on individuals has never been carefully defined, and for good reason. The Vatican would not want to lose the fine art of framing statements that allow for the widest possible interpretation. But interestingly enough, unofficial Vatican observers seem to judge the scope of binding statements to be much wider than do observers in France.[12]

There is clearly an obligation for the believing Catholic to obey the formal pronouncements of the Pope: "Like every general doctrine of the Church, the social doctrine requires the approval of all Catholics, in its essential elements, and as it follows from authentic, authoritative teachings."[13] Papal radio-messages and discourses before various groups in Rome do not, obviously, have the same authoritative quality as encyclicals, and are not presented in the same terms. This differentiation allows the Pope and other Church officials to speak out on civic or even partisan political matters while still leaving a certain freedom to individual Catholics. All they need to do

[12] In *Osservatore Romano*, for January 6, 1951, Mgr. Pietro Parente wrote the following: "First of all, a general reminder that even the ordinary teachings of the sovereign pontiffs are obligatory for all Catholics in their entirety, without distinguishing between essential principles and particular statements. No Catholic is permitted to consider a Papal document out of date because the circumstances that fostered it have changed. Only the Church can make such a judgment." Quoted in *Documentation Catholique*, May 6, 1951, column 524. However, Mgr. Guerry is not so categorical. He speaks of different attitudes toward different Papal documents. One can treat them with "respect, prudence, delicate and docile attention," or a "favorable predisposition." (Guerry, *op.cit.*, pp. 172-173.)

[13] Mgr. Dell'Acqua, official of the Vatican Secretary of State's Bureau, in preface to Guerry, *op.cit.*

is put their ideas in terms of "suggestions" rather than "commands."

The mass of Catholics who ignore Church social doctrine (as they ignore most of the dogma of the Church) cannot be expected to obey all Church teachings. Even those acquainted with the Church social doctrine do not always follow it. Mgr. Guerry himself admits that one of the gravest problems faced by the Church at present is the disdain or ignorance of Church social teachings. He repeats a Papal quotation that the excesses of Capitalism and Communism should "convince everyone, especially priests," to accept the social doctrine of the Church.[14]

The problem of obedience to the Church social doctrine differs between fully Catholic groups and groups simply of Catholic inspiration. Most fully Catholic groups have a major goal of propagating Church social doctrine in their milieu and undertake to obey not only the formal pronouncements of the Vatican but also the specific instructions given them by the Church Hierarchy and local bishops in France. Certain groups of Catholic inspiration also claim to reflect faithfully the social doctrine of the Church, but these groups (and certain "Catholic" groups of the extreme right) often pay only lip service to the terminology used by the Pope and give the Church social doctrine their own particular interpretation.[15]

Church social doctrine plays a certain role in the political activity of Catholic groups and individuals, but its role must not be overestimated. As will be shown, most Catholic political activities, even those of Catholic Action groups, do not directly or logically follow from the principles of Church social doctrine.

[14] Guerry, *op.cit.*, p. 10.

[15] Groups of "Catholic inspiration" are much freer and more autonomous than "Catholic" groups. A good example of the difference can be seen by comparing two groups of Marc Sangnier's. The *Sillon* claimed to be Catholic, but its ideas did not harmonize with those of the Vatican and it was condemned. From it arose *Jeune République*, which had the same basic ideals but which did not call itself Catholic. It could not be condemned in the same way *Sillon* was.

II. Vatican Leadership and French Politics

A. CENTERS OF VATICAN LEADERSHIP IN THEORY AND PRACTICE

It would be impossible to give an exhaustive account of Vatican influence in French society; too many facts about the behavior of Vatican officials toward key political issues are lacking. Nevertheless, given the Vatican's obviously essential political role it is indispensable to make a general inventory of the chief Vatican actors and their roles.

Since the main focus must always be on French political life, the Vatican often must appear as an "offstage actor," less important than the Church in France. In this case it should be understood that the Church is being viewed in a functional and political manner, not from a spiritual or religious perspective. In many instances the French Church would claim its complete dependence on Rome in social as well as spiritual matters. But in actual fact, the French Church makes most temporal decisions without recourse to Rome. The Vatican usually intervenes only when a question seems to have an overriding international significance. In such cases, as will be shown below, the Vatican has complex but efficient machinery to control the French Church.

It is not necessary here to elaborate the position held by the Pope within the Church.[16] His powers are administrative and doctrinal as well as strictly ecclesiastical: the Pope is a "second bishop" for each Catholic, with immediate power over individual Catholics throughout the world. He is the administrative head of the Church apparatus; the Sacred Congregations and other institutions of the Vatican Curia are agencies acting for him. Their most important decisions are always approved by the Pope. Religious orders throughout the world and movements of laymen that are specifically "Catholic" are in many ways dependent on the Pope. No bishop may exercise his episcopal prerogatives without confirmation by the Pope. The Pope

[16] See Mgr. Van Lierde, *Derrière les Portes Vaticanes* (Paris: Mame, 1958).

is the source of much Church social doctrine, and must personally approve and promulgate any dogma which a Catholic is bound to believe. He has also a negative doctrinal control since he can denounce any ideas that he deems unsatisfactory to the Church. Finally, the Pope is the supreme appeal for cases of canon law and for any other subjects of dispute in the Church.

This theoretical position of the Pope is basic to any understanding of the structure of the Church, but in the perspective of this study it is more useful to delve a bit below the formal structures.

With certain exceptions, political questions concerning the Church in French society cannot be studied in detail by the Pope, who is a very busy man.[17] However, a number of Vatican institutions can keep the Pope briefed on matters relating to France. The Sacred Congregations are especially important both in matters of organization and dogma. For example, the Holy Office has almost unlimited discretion in matters affecting faith and morals (for the Church a very large category indeed!). The Holy Office, particularly its administrative chief, Cardinal Ottaviani, had a major role in the suspension of the French worker-priest movement in 1954. The Consistorial Congregation, which acts as a kind of "ministry of the interior," obtains detailed reports from every bishop in the Catholic world every five years, concerning the state of individual dioceses. Propagation of the Faith is concerned with missionary and other activities in underdeveloped areas, including most of the French Community.[18]

A few cardinals stationed in Rome direct the Sacred Congregations. These "Curia Cardinals" play a very important

[17] It should be noted in this connection that the American Institute of Organization published an "efficiency report" on the Church in which it suggested that Pope Pius XII worked too hard by himself, not depending enough on teamwork. Reported in *Information Catholiques Internationales*, February 1, 1956, p. 27.

[18] For descriptions of these congregations and their duties see Van Lierde, *op.cit., passim*, and Jean Neuvecelle, *Eglise Capitale Vatican* (Paris: Gallimard, 1954).

role in the temporal and spiritual life of the Church.[19] Another important Vatican institution is the semiofficial newspaper, *Osservatore Romano*. It frequently takes editorial stands on political affairs in France and other countries. Formally, these stands do not commit the Church, but they give a good indication of the sympathies and perhaps the future actions of Vatican leaders.

B. THE ROLE OF PERSONALITIES IN MAKING VATICAN DECISIONS

One of the striking things about many highly-centralized human groups is the dominant role of the leaders' character traits, personal habits, etc. This is true in the French Church, and it is even more important in the Vatican itself. The preferences, even the personal fancies of a Pope can have a profound effect on Catholic policies, as has been already seen in Chapter Two. Undoubtedly, the reign of Pius XII was among the most "personalized," and a careful study would certainly reveal effects of the Pope's personality on many aspects of French social life. A much greater knowledge and appreciation of France by John XXIII will certainly have its effects too.

In addition to the Pope himself, the personalities of other Vatican dignitaries—notably the Curia Cardinals—are felt in France. It has been said that Cardinal Ottaviani of the Holy Office emphasizes too much the archaic details of Canon Law and does not emphasize sufficiently the "hypothesis" in his decisions. This helps explain the abruptness of the decision in 1954 curtailing the worker-priest experiment.[20]

C. THE CHIEF MEANS OF VATICAN INFLUENCE IN FRENCH SOCIETY

The Vatican can choose among a wide number of means for

[19] See *Informations Catholiques Internationales* (hereafter also called *I.C.I.*), November 1, 1958, pp. 24-26.

[20] Description of Cardinal Ottaviani from private conversation with an informed church official, Paris, April 1959. The Vatican, of course, is more concerned with the thesis than the hypothesis. The Pope, as the pontiff, must define the thesis; hypotheses would generally come from local clergies, and would be merely tolerated by Rome. Ottaviani, however, seems to lack much ability to tolerate in this way.

exerting influence in French society. For the clergy, the most militant Catholics, and lay groups integrally part of the Church, the Vatican disposes of particularly strong controls: encyclicals, letters of condemnation (*Sillon* in 1910; *Action Française* in 1926), condemnations of certain political theories (Communism is the most notable). The list of encyclicals with political overtones is so long that it would be impossible even to list the most critically important ones.[21] Even if the politically-significant Papal documents could be subjected to content analysis and other forms of evaluation, it would be difficult to know how these documents affect individual Catholics.[22]

The Pope's administrative powers over the clergy provide still other ways for the Vatican to influence French society. In addition to exhaustive reports on the state of their dioceses, all bishops make periodic *ad limina* trips to Rome to consult with the Pope. Bishops with special functions in the Church (most cardinals, for example), make the trip more frequently than the required five-year interval. No meeting of bishops of a particular country can take place without the approval of the Pope. Decisions reached on behalf of all bishops of a country must be submitted to the Pope for his comments and suggestions. The Vatican Hierarchy can also control the activities of religious orders in France and elsewhere through the heads of these orders, who generally reside in Rome.

Although the analysis of Vatican influence is by no means complete two observations seem clear. The Vatican most often intervenes in the affairs of the French Church when questions of international significance are at stake. And the Vatican, with

[21] Among the most socially significant encyclicals are *Rerum Novarum* of 1891, *Divini Redemptoris*, where Pius XI condemned the satanic plague of Communism, the 1864 *Syllabus* of Pius IX, which is a "Magna Charta" for the Catholic extreme right, the Christmas, 1944 radio message of Pius XII, where the Pope defined the healthiest form of democracy, and *Mater et Magistra*, the social doctrine of John XXIII. See also Cardinal Richaud, *op.cit.*, *passim*.

[22] It seems likely that the ordinary Catholic "man in the street" is not even aware of most Papal pronouncements; their attentive audience is probably limited to the clergy and really active laymen.

its centralized administrative structure, could conceivably orient the French Church toward the Pope's own opinions on social and political questions. Whether or not such an orientation occurs today will be discussed below.

D. THE PAPAL NUNCIO IN FRANCE

The Papal Nuncio is a special link between the Vatican and French society. The Nuncio is first of all a diplomatic representative of the Vatican in France: he represents the Pope and the interests of the whole Church.

But the Nuncio has many special attributes that make him different from the normal ambassador. First of all, he is the middleman between the Pope and the French clergy. A bishop sometimes works directly with the Vatican, but in general the Nuncio is consulted first. Thus, unlike any other ambassador, he has a special, direct relationship with Frenchmen outside the government. In fact, he has a mission of surveillance, of observation, and of reporting on the general condition of the Church in France.

Some of the prestige of the Pope naturally is transferred to his Nuncio. A recent Nuncio in France (who now happens to be John XXIII himself) liked to quote from Pius XI: "Honor and love Our representative: may he truly be for you the eye, the heart, the hand of the Pope."[23]

Unfortunately, it is not possible to present an objective view of the actual activities of the Nuncio. Outside of unsupported polemics and relatively unimportant narrative, little information is available. It is known that the Nuncio suggests to the Pope names of possible successors when a bishop's seat is vacant. The Nuncio can set limits on the functions of Catholic Action groups. He exercised an important role in the worker-priest controversy. However, it does not seem that the Nuncio has the time or the staff to investigate all organizational aspects of the French Church and to report them fully to the Pope. This function must logically be done by local bishops them-

[23] Quoted in *Semaine Religieuse de Périgueux*, July 14, 1951, p. 209.

selves. The Nuncio must concentrate only on important questions of general policy.[24]

Without more systematic information, it seems impossible to generalize further on the role of the Nuncio in French political life.[25]

E. DOES THE VATICAN GIVE A POLITICAL ORIENTATION TO FRENCH CATHOLICISM?

At the end of World War II, the French clergy and other Catholic groups realized the necessity of improving the Church's appeal to the working class. Many Church leaders wanted to associate the Church more closely with "progressive" forces in France, to convince the masses that the Church was no longer an institution of the French bourgeoisie. Many of these reforms and innovations bore fruit, in such organizations as the *Chrétiens Progressistes*, in such publications as *Quinzaine*, and in apostolic movements such as the worker-priest experiment. These three endeavors all developed close ties with "progressive" or Communist forces in France, and subsequently all were discontinued because of Vatican pressure. This naturally leads people to wonder whether the Vatican is consciously orienting the French Church in a particular political and social direction.

Other facts would seem to confirm the hypothesis that the Vatican is pushing French Catholicism in a certain political direction. The French Hierarchy was in its majority favorable to continuing the worker-priest experiment, and tried to present its opinions to Cardinal Ottaviani. The latter, refusing the dossier, said, "Unnecessary, I have my own."[26] The year following

[24] Confirmed in interview with Canon Berrar, Curé of St. Germain-des-Prés, April, 1959.

[25] The role of the Nuncio as revealed in the notes of Mgr. Montagnini should not be applied to the present political scene. In the past fifty years there has been a complete change in the position of the Church in French society. See Mgr. Montagnini, *Les Fiches Pontificales* (Paris: Nourry, 1908).

[26] Quoted in Petrie, *The Worker Priests* (London: Routledge & Kegan Paul, 1956), p. 64.

the end of the worker-priest experiment (at least its formal end), the Holy Office condemned *Quinzaine*, which immediately ceased publication. The following year, the Provincial of the Dominican order stopped the French Dominican publication *Vie Intellectuelle*, which represented an even more moderate tendency than *Quinzaine*. It was feared that the Holy Office itself would bring a formal condemnation against *Vie Intellectuelle* if it were not stopped by the Dominicans themselves.[27] Finally, on March 25, 1959, the Holy Office forbade Catholics to vote for those who are allied with or favor the cause of the Communists, even though these people might themselves be Catholics.[28]

It would be rash to conclude from the events presented above that the Vatican is deliberately planning to isolate the French Church from all the left-wing forces in French society. But officials like Cardinal Ottaviani will accept no compromise with the Reds, and are prepared even to sacrifice Catholic institutions to maintain the Church's rigid stand against Communism in Western Europe.[29]

There are other realms where the Vatican seems to be orienting French politics in a controversial direction. For centuries the Church has encouraged the evangelization of underdeveloped areas; only recently it has become aware of the movements for self-government arising throughout Asia and Africa. In recent years it has accepted these movements and even tried to encourage them, in a way that has not always pleased colonial powers. For example the Vatican has been developing as fast as possible a native clergy, including native bishops, and the latter often give valuable support to native independence

[27] Information from private conversation with Georges Hourdin, Director of *Informations Catholiques Internationales* and *Vie Catholique Illustrée.* May 5, 1959.

[28] *Le Monde*, April 15, 1959, p. 3. Although this decision was prompted by a local situation in Sicily, the Holy Office and the Pope have given it a universal validity. This should be contrasted with the earlier statement made by Cardinal Suhard. See this chapter, footnote 9.

[29] Idea from an interview with a high church official in Paris.

or autonomy movements.[30] This attitude probably contributed to and facilitated the recent breaking of colonial bonds between France and her African territories.

The Vatican also has helped mould French political life on the school question. The tactics of French leaders of Catholic school organizations were approved, and often instigated, by the Vatican.[31] Certain statements in *Osservatore Romano* during the consideration of the Barangé Law in 1951 seem downright extremist. In an article published in *Osservatore Romano* on January 6, 1951, Mgr. Pietro Parente concluded thus: "Even admitting the possibility of a neutral State school, openly laic, neutrality (which often is a deception) would soon be only a weapon to direct children along a certain path, more harmful than any confessionalism. . . . The Church condemns without distinction *laïcisme* and *laïcité*."[32]

Many leaders of the French Hierarchy would object to this statement. In the Vatican itself many officials would object to its tone, and even Pope Pius XII had praise for the public school in France.[33]

The Vatican is universal in its activities, but it is also immersed in the habits and customs of the country where it is located. Inevitably there is a certain "Italianization" of Vatican ideas, especially outside the purely sacred realm. This Italian

[30] Cf. this statement of the Pope himself: "To one side We said, 'do not refuse or obstruct just and progressive political freedom for the peoples who want it.' To the other side We gave this warning: 'give Europe credit for your advancement. Without Europe's influence in every domain, you could be swept up by blind nationalism and thrown into chaos or slavery.' " From the French translation of Pius XII, in *Documentation Catholique*, May 12, 1957, column 584.

[31] The former deputy Michel Raingeard seems to have been an important intermediary between Rome, French Catholic school groups, and the French National Assembly when the Barangé Law was being considered. At least, this is what he admits. Interview with Raingeard, January 8, 1959. In fairness to Rome, many responsible Vatican officials disapproved of some tactics from the extreme right on the school question.

[32] *Documentation Catholique*, 1951, column 525.

[33] Note his speech to a delegation of public school teachers, reported in *Documentation Catholique*, April 8, 1951, column 388.

perspective is reflected in Vatican statements that are often quite unsuitable to the French political scene. The Vatican tries at times to direct political groups of Catholic inspiration, forgetting that these are independent of any Catholic direction in France. The French political climate could not support a single Catholic political party as virtually exists in Italy. The situation of the MRP was misunderstood, with important repercussions, by a writer for *Osservatore Romano*, who differentiated between the MRP and the RPF before the 1951 elections as follows: "Surely it would be unsatisfactory (*pénible*) for a fraction of Catholic voters to prefer a vague, right-wing transformism of the right to the Popular Republicans. The Popular Republicans, despite their drawbacks, are determined to follow a well-defined program, and their sincere effort in placing France on the road to a better future deserves our esteem. On the other hand, the right wing transformists [e.g., the Gaullists in the RPF] would most likely slip down the steep slope of intransigence."[34]

III. Institutions of the French Church: National Level

A. INTRODUCTION

In a centralized state like France, the social and political problems on the national level interest Catholics most. But from a religious standpoint—which is the fundamental viewpoint for French Catholicism—the life of the Church is centered on the diocese, the parish, and Rome. It is not on the national level; national Church institutions have no canonic value. Nevertheless, in the past half-century, unofficial national institutions have slowly been added to the fabric of the Church in France. Their social and political importance now surpasses other levels.

[34] Alessandrini in *Osservatore Romano*, May 25-26, 1951, reported in *Documentation Catholique*, 1951, column 680. *La Croix*, in commenting on this partisan opinion, underscored that it does not *oblige* a Catholic to take a particular political stand or vote for the MRP. See *La Croix*, May 31, 1951, p. 5.

The true picture of interrelations between the Vatican, national, and local units of the Church is very complex. For certain social matters with dogmatic or spiritual content, the national institutions of the Church could play only an intermediate role. Examples were given earlier in this chapter. But for most social and political questions concerning France, the national institutions are far more significant than the Vatican or the individual dioceses. On such questions the Vatican gives the national Church bodies great freedom.[35] The autonomy of the national Hierarchy is not always apparent because French bishops have the habit of explaining or justifying decisions in terms of the social doctrine of the Church or other statements by the Pope. However, decisions in these terms have not been determined by Church social doctrine; this doctrine is so varied that it is easy to justify or condemn any predetermined position.[36]

On the national level, the main concerns of the French Hierarchy can cover a wide range of topics, some only incidentally germane to this book. There seems to have been an evolution in the nature of problems considered since World War I. Before 1914, problems of a highly partisan nature were treated in a

[35] The worker-priest experiment would probably have been regulated by the French Hierarchy if its importance had been limited to the Church in France. But the experiment was closely watched in South America and Spain, where many considered it a dangerous compromise with Communism. Cardinal Ottaviani in the Vatican acted because of the international repercussions of the problem, rather than because of its internal social repercussions in France. The worker-priest question can be contrasted with the Algerian War or the recent danger of unemployment in France. These were serious problems too, but had much less religious significance outside of France. Therefore, the Vatican left to the French Hierarchy the initiative for acting on them.

[36] In commenting on the Algerian situation before 1960, the French Hierarchy could have used the principles from the Papal Encyclical *Fidei Donum* to justify independence for the territory. Most chose instead to concentrate on the Church doctrine toward torture and psychological warfare. In their analysis of the new Constitution the cardinals and archbishops minimized the absence of all reference to God and stressed that the Church is not opposed to a certain conception of *laïcité*. They could have been much more intransigent with different, but no less orthodox, interpretations of Church doctrines.

highly partisan manner, for the Church was allied with the "Party of Order." Since World War II, the Church Hierarchy has deemphasized these partisan questions. The deemphasis is related to the general movement toward understanding between *laïques* and *cléricaux* in the past few years; but more important, it reflects the desire of the national Hierarchy to remove the Church from any suspicion of affiliation with one party or tendency in French politics. Such affiliation, even when very subtle, offers no permanent political gains for the Church. This was proved during the separation controversy and again in Vichy France.

The main aim of the Hierarchy at present is to "universalize" the Church throughout French society, notably in the dechristianized proletariat.[37] The other principal interest of the national Hierarchy is closely related to the first: missionary work in underdeveloped areas.

The political questions with which the national Hierarchy is most concerned now follow from its apostolic interests: evolution of the French Community, the economic situation in France, social justice for the working class, and so forth. Also it is interested in questions such as the school problem, where vested interests of the Church are at stake, and in matters where the existence of France herself may be at stake—the Algerian war being the best example. All these questions are now considered in an atmosphere of calm; compromise is generally emphasized. The national Hierarchy seems to have learned since the 1920's that all-out partisanship is not an effective means of attaining any of its goals.

B. ADMINISTRATIVE ORGANS

The most important administrative organ for the national Hierarchy, and indeed for the entire French Church, is the Assembly of Cardinals and Archbishops. In France, it is called simply the ACA. Formed of all French cardinals and arch-

[37] The 1960 plenary assembly of French bishops considered the "evangelization of dechristianized milieux." See *I.C.I.*, May 15, 1960, pp. 5 ff.

bishops (eighteen to twenty in all), the ACA was first organized in 1919. It generally meets twice a year, for short periods only. A Permanent Secretary (Mgr. Guerry) has a certain weight in the Church, though he seems to be limited in the initiatives he can undertake.[38] Mgr. Guerry, all the cardinals, and three archbishops form a Permanent Commission which prepares the agenda for the full ACA meetings and makes decisions on behalf of the ACA when it is not meeting. Technical questions are decided by the ACA on advice from one of the specialized episcopal commissions, which will be described below. At times, when crucial national problems call for an immediate statement from the Church, the French cardinals alone will make the statement. They probably will have discussed the subject beforehand with their colleagues on the ACA.

Since the episcopal commissions and the Permanent Commission of the ACA meet only at set intervals, someone must carry on policy decisions for the ACA on a permanent basis. The job has been given not to Mgr. Guerry, but to Cardinal Feltin himself. It is logical for the Archbishop of Paris to have this keystone role, since so much in France is centralized in the capital. Still, this post has raised Cardinal Feltin's prestige and importance a notch above his fellow members of the ACA (canonically all archbishops are equal).[39]

Unable to meet more than a few days every six months, with many subordinate groups doing specific work in its name, the ACA concentrates on major policy decisions and statements of general orientation for the French Church. Where it is possible to prepare them in advance, it often issues statements on political issues. These statements represent in the public mind the "view of the Church" on an issue, though Catholic groups do not necessarily all agree with the ACA.

[38] *Informations Catholiques Internationales*, April 15, 1957 has a description of the ACA and its Permanent Secretary. See pp. 17-19.

[39] If Feltin or the Permanent Commission of the ACA make important decisions, these must be formally ratified at the next ACA meeting. See Dansette, *Destin*, pp. 74-75.

The ACA has close contacts with all the bishops of France, but its actual relationship to them is a matter of speculation, since so much is kept strictly secret. The ACA can recommend policies to individual bishops; such recommendations are probably followed where a bishop cannot fully inform himself. However, ACA declarations or confidential statements do not "bind" bishops. Each bishop is supreme within his diocese.[40]

The subjects on which the ACA can speak cover the whole gamut of politics. For example, before important elections there is always a statement by the ACA on the duty of Catholics to vote. Before really crucial elections there are often more specific declarations.[41] When the Algerian conflict engendered tortures by both sides, the ACA did not spare its criticisms of the French Army: "It is never permissible to use intrinsically bad means, even to serve a cause that is just."[42] This simple, though vague, statement inspired countless pages of commentary throughout France.

ACA control over Catholic laymen's groups is often far-reaching, though it does not have direct control over groups of "Catholic inspiration." The ACA must approve all national chaplains and lay leaders of Catholic Action groups. It must give a formal mandate to a group before it becomes a part of Catholic Action. If a group seems to be deviating from its assigned goals the ACA can modify its activities. For example, a former official of a Catholic Action youth group, Georges

[40] A bishop may publish in his own name "his version" of an ACA communication, and this may have a certain national impact. See the tactic of Cardinal Richaud with an ACA declaration on the Catholic press, Chapter Six. But no bishop's interpretation has the value of a statement by the ACA itself. In turn, the ACA can use only moral suasion in dealing with bishops. The ACA can take no sanctions against renegade bishops.

[41] Thus, before the recent Constitutional Referendum, the cardinals of France issued a joint declaration in which they rejected the argument that one should vote "no" because the Constitution omits reference to God. Neither the presence nor absence of God, they said, can "hinder a Catholic from speaking out freely on the proposed text. This text must be judged in its entirety, taking into account the present situation of the country and the common good." See *La Croix*, September 18, 1958, p. 1.

[42] Quoted in *Chronique Sociale*, Vol. 65, No. 3, May 30, 1957, p. 234. Cf. *Informations Catholiques Internationales*, April 1, 1957, p. 6.

Suffert, who had been made administrative director of the Catholic publication *Témoignage Chrétien,* fell into disfavor with the ACA and was forced to resign. This could be interpreted as a warning that a Catholic magazine must not go too far, even in its nonspiritual opinions.[43] The ACA can do much to limit the sale and influence of the Catholic press by controlling its dissemination in Churches and in parish press groups. Thus, quite recently an ACA declaration forbade the sale of all but strictly "religious" Catholic literature inside Churches.[44] Finally, the ACA can even create new lay organizations. The adult workers' Catholic Action group was basically a creation of the ACA to further Church work in the French proletariat.

A word of caution must end the section on the ACA. It should not be inferred that the ACA has no power over the diocese because it lacks formal competence to discipline bishops. Catholic clergy and laymen are too used to obedience in the Church not to follow the recommendations of their mightiest ecclesiastical authorities even if they are just "recommendations." Among the most devout Catholics, even a vague suggestion can be extremely effective; those who do not follow it probably would rebel even if the clergy issued a morally-binding command.

Two organizations which are closely connected to the ACA must be briefly considered. Eighteen episcopal commissions advise the ACA on all kinds of technical problems, both spiritual and temporal. Each of the following subjects forms the work for one episcopal commission: missionary work inside France, General Catholic Action, the working class, the rural world, the middle-class world, teaching, and information.[45]

Each commission is presided over by an archbishop or cardinal who is considered particularly qualified in the matter

[43] For an interpretation by *laïques* of the Suffert affair, see *France Observateur,* September 25, 1958, p. 24.

[44] For further discussion on this point, see Chapter Six.

[45] It should be noticed that many of the commissions are concerned with particular social classes or categories. These latter are very important bases for organizing and recruiting laymen.

studied by the commission. Every bishop in France is on at least one commission. Secretarial functions for all commissions are handled by the Secretariat of the Episcopate or the Secretariat of Catholic Action; the commissions have no permanent secretariats themselves. And since the full commissions meet only four or five days per year, the two secretariats just mentioned carry out most of the routine work for them.

The most important tasks of the commissions are usually parcelled out among bishops, so the work of each individual bishop is more important than the work which the commissions themselves have time to do. Actually, the commissions themselves are largely devoted to study and meditation. At any rate, all their recommendations must be submitted to the ACA for final clearance.[46] The episcopal commissions reflect power more than they create it. They give bishops with special social competence a framework in which they can have power over Catholic groups without being totally responsible for them.[47]

The last important administrative organization of the national Hierarchy is the plenary assembly of bishops. When organized in 1951, the assembly was considered a revolutionary institution, since it comprised all the bishops of France. The previous plenary assemblies had been held more than forty years earlier, in the separation crisis described in Chapter Two. Some feared that all the bishops meeting together would be tempted to follow a "national" course of action which would resemble the old bugaboo of Gallicanism.[48] However, despite

[46] See Chaigneau, *L'Organisation de l'Eglise Catholique en France,* Chapter v, pp. 87-92, for details on episcopal commissions. The judgments about the commissions come from interviews with Catholic Action officials, each of whom was asked about the importance of the commissions for his group. The consensus was that they had very little importance. See list of interviews for Chapter Four.

[47] See *La Croix,* May 16, 1951, p. 4. Cf. interviews with Mgr. Foucart, Associate Secretary of the French Episcopate, December 16, 1958, and with Mgr. Ménager, Auxiliary Bishop of Versailles and Secretary of Catholic Action, January 8, 1959.

[48] The very existence of the plenary assemblies shows a significant evolution in the attitudes of French Catholics. For a century and more each diocese in France jealously guarded its independence in social and

the potential importance of the assembly, it has remained until now much less active than the ACA. The main reason is the difficulty of frequent meetings. Since 1951, the assemblies have met every three years, but since each meeting must be approved by the Pope, there is no guarantee that others will follow. However, the practice of meetings every three years is now fairly fixed.[49] Another reason why the assemblies have remained ineffective is their lack of a permanent secretariat or steering committee. Secretarial tasks are handled by the ACA and its subgroups.

The main duty of the plenary assemblies is to consider major innovations and general policy statements for the Church. For example, the pastoral letter on Church social doctrine published in 1954 appeared with the approval of the 1954 plenary assembly.[50] Any statements made in this context carry great weight because (unlike statements from the ACA) they have always received the endorsement of all French bishops.[51]

Since the first meeting in 1951, the plenary assemblies have developed a tradition of issuing declarations concerning major social problems confronting France. After every meeting since 1951 a declaration on the school problem has been issued. The Plenary Assembly of 1951, which met just before the Barangé Law was voted, declared that only the Catholic school is "fully satisfactory." But at the same time, it recognized that large numbers of Catholic children go to public schools, and said that this would be tolerated, if it were approved by the local bishop

---

temporal matters. Bishops accepted superiors in Rome, but not in Paris. This state of mind has gradually given way to cooperation and coordination through national institutions, where Church problems can be most effectively considered.

49 See Chaigneau, *L'Organisation de l'Eglise Catholique en France*, p. 71.

50 *Directoire Pastorale en Matière Sociale au Service des Prêtres* (Paris: Editions Fleurus, 1954).

51 Even though all bishops approve a program, it is not formally binding on the whole French Church. As Cardinal Liénart said, "The decisions which we shall take in common will not have the force of law, because our assembly is not a Council and each of us remains the judge of what should be applied to his own diocese." See Chaigneau, *loc.cit.*

involved.[52] The vagueness of this declaration shows that the French bishops collectively were much more moderate in their school position than were such organizations as the APEL, for example.[53] The same vagueness appears in the 1954 and 1957 declarations: "only the Christian school is fully satisfactory for the Christian," and "the Christian school is the normal place of education for Christian children." The 1960 Plenary Assembly, commenting on the 1959 school law, was more explicit. It ruled out any "integration" of Catholic schools into the public school system, since the special features of the former would be lost, but it also pledged to cooperate loyally with the new law.[54]

C. SPECIALIZED SECRETARIATS

The national Hierarchy is assisted in its administrative work by four specialized secretariats: the Secretariat of Catholic Action, the Secretariat of the Episcopate, the Secretariat for Catholic Schools, and the Secretariat for the Working Class. All but one of these have been established since 1945. They are all specialized in activities crucial for the entire French Church. Their development is one more indication of the empirical manner in which the national Hierarchy is organized. The Secretariats are not formally of equal importance nor do they deal with similar problems; but in each case they represent the response of the French Hierarchy to a particular national problem.[55]

The Secretariat of Catholic Action was founded in 1931, when Catholic Action groups were first developing in France. Officially this Secretariat is a coordinating agency for all Catholic lay groups mandated by the French Hierarchy. In practice,

[52] See *Documentation Catholique*, April 22, 1951, columns 455 ff.

[53] See Chapter Eight.

[54] See *France Catholique*, May 6, 1960, p. 1; Chaigneau, *L'Organisation de l'Eglise Catholique en France*, p. 76; *I.C.I.*, May 15, 1957, p. 5.

[55] The different ranking of the secretaries indicates the inequality of the secretariats. The Secretaries of Catholic Action and of the Episcopate are bishops; the Secretary for Catholic Schools is a monseigneur; the Secretary for the Working Class is only a canon.

its work is very limited, since the Secretariat is largely a one man affair. Mgr. Ménager, the Secretary, has no staff whatsoever.[56]

The functioning of the Secretariat of Catholic Action quite naturally reflects the conception that Mgr. Ménager holds of Catholic Action. For him, Catholic lay groups should first and foremost develop the leadership potential of young Catholics. The brightest *militants* should be allowed to develop their own programs of action, hence Catholic Action should be given as much freedom of movement as possible. The Secretariat itself does not meddle in the daily affairs of Catholic Action groups.[57]

Mgr. Ménager has an interesting conception of how Catholic laymen should influence French temporal affairs. He would favor the "Christian nucleus" formula: the truly exemplary leaders developed by Catholic Action should be encouraged to enter already-established "neutral" organizations such as trade unions, family groups, political parties, etc. There their already-proven leadership will give them places of responsibility, from which they will try to permeate the group with the spiritual ideals learned in Catholic Action.[58]

The Secretariat of the Episcopate serves only clerical groups,

[56] The description by Jean Meynaud seems to reflect the theoretical state of the Secretariat rather than its true position. See Jean Meynaud, *Les Groupes de Pression en France* (Paris: Armand Colin, 1958), pp. 87-88.

[57] Even on a matter like the school question, Mgr. Ménager did not try to control the activity of Catholic Action groups: his conception of his job would not allow such control, and he believed the whole working-class apostolate might have been compromised by a rigid position on an issue which was completely misunderstood in the working class.

[58] Many of these ideas were described by Mgr. Ménager himself, in a private conversation with the author on January 8, 1959. Note that the Secretariat is not the only means by which the Hierarchy can control or supervise lay Catholic groups. Each Catholic Action group is supervised by one bishop who is supposed to be a specialist in its activity. Usually he is selected from a relevant episcopal commission. He generally limits his activity to advice on spiritual questions, but on certain occasions he can intervene, when he believes that a policy is not in accord with Church thinking. These supervisory bishops seem to act quite independently of Mgr. Ménager, and bypass him when they contact their colleagues about problems in other Catholic Action groups. See Chaigneau, *Les Ouvriers dans la Moisson*, p. 88.

just as the Secretariat of Catholic Action considers only lay groups. The Secretariat of the Episcopate was formed in 1945, reflecting the need for linking individual bishops more closely to the national activities of the Church. The Secretariat is small: Mgr. Villot as Secretary and his assistant Mgr. Foucart employed only five research experts. But the duties of the Secretariat are large, for it performs most of the purely "secretarial" work of the ACA, the plenary assemblies, and the episcopal commissions. Agendas for meetings of these groups can be revised by Mgr. Gouet, the present Secretary, or by Mgr. Foucart, although they do not select the main themes to be discussed.

The most significant temporal job of the Secretariat of the Episcopate is providing each bishop with selected items of information—on French political and social life, or on the international situation, for example.[59] In many provincial centers the bishop will lack the means of getting this information himself, so the Secretariat can help him form his judgment on temporal questions. Does the Secretariat orient his information in any direction? This is impossible to say, because all the information it sends out is confidential. At any rate it seems clear that bishops have the opportunity to become well-documented on any question whatsoever, thanks to their "information service" in Paris. Furthermore, the two monseigneurs in the Secretariat of the Episcopate have access to the innermost workings of the Church Hierarchy, and can keep each bishop carefully informed on the work of the ACA, other groups, and individual prelates.[60]

59 The information includes published articles in magazines or scholarly publications, as well as confidential impressions gleaned by Church officials. The institutions of the Church and those of the state are both centered in Paris; there is certainly contact between officials of the two, and thus there is opportunity for the Church to obtain much political information not known to the general public. This information is then passed on to all bishops by the Secretariat.

60 Though it does not do so frequently, the Secretariat can speak for the French Hierarchy, in certain cases where Church doctrine is clear and when the ACA or a plenary assembly are not meeting. Thus, in

The two remaining secretariats are concerned with much more specific questions. The Secretariat for Catholic Schools has a twofold job: first, it coordinates the administration of all the Catholic schools in France and represents them before the public; second, it works to promote effective state support for all private education, and for Catholic schools in particular. In the interests of logical presentation, these activities will be discussed in Chapter Eight. Here the place of this secretariat in the national Church organization will be briefly indicated.

The Secretariat for Catholic Schools is responsible to the Episcopal Commission on Education, and acts on behalf of the Commission's presiding bishop, Cardinal Roques. It is in close contact with the directors of parochial schools on all levels, especially for the dioceses. The fact that there is a secretariat dealing only with the school problem indicates the importance of schools for French Catholicism. They are by far the biggest "business" of the Church, and at the same time they are an important force for safeguarding and developing the vitality of the Church. The material conditions of the Secretariat (headquarters building, layout of offices, number of researchers) seem far better than those of the other secretariats. Such material conditions, by the way, go far in showing the real importance in temporal matters of each secretariat.

The Secretariat for the Working Class (*Secrétariat Nationale de la Mission Ouvrière*) was created by the ACA only in March, 1957. It has not yet achieved a permanent form. Up to now it has been another "one-man orchestra," in the person of Canon Bonnet, its secretary.[61]

February 1956, when *laïques* in parliament attempted to repeal the Barangé Law, the Secretariat of the Episcopate warned publicly of "religious freedom in jeopardy" and a "campaign undertaken against the Church." See *Documentation Catholique,* February 19, 1956, column 218. It should be noted that Mgr. Villot was chosen in 1960 to be Coadjutor Bishop of Lyon. His successor as Secretary of the Episcopate was Mgr. Julien Gouet.

[61] Bonnet, one of the dynamic young men in the Church, is being increasingly relied upon by the Hierarchy in view of the final elimination of the worker-priest movement.

The existence of this secretariat again illustrates the empirical procedures of the Church Hierarchy. Within the French working class there is a tradition of solidarity among all groups that truly represent the workers. If the Church is to extend its influence into the proletariat it must develop Catholic organizations composed *of* workers, and concerned *only* with workers. Many such groups now exist, but until now they have not been coordinated in a working-class atmosphere. Such coordination is the prime duty of the new secretariat.

The secretariat is an unusual case, since it practices a vertical coordination which cuts across the line separating "Catholic" from "neutral." For example, Canon Bonnet has frequent contacts with leaders of the CFTC and of non-Catholic family groups as well as Catholic groups such as the ACO.[62] All forces that can cooperate with the Church, whether part of Catholic Action or not, are mobilized in certain "missionary sectors" which the Church is attempting to evangelize in an all-out effort.[63]

Canon Bonnet is especially important as an intermediary between the ACA and the French working class. He passes directives from the ACA to Catholic working class groups, and he also explains to the Hierarchy the workers' viewpoint on temporal questions. Thus, he has been active in presenting to the Hierarchy the working class opposition to any state aid to private schools that might seem to discriminate against workers' salaries. The moderate position of the Hierarchy on the school question before the 1959 law may in part have been due to Canon Bonnet's activity. Bonnet also is responsible for recent declarations by high French prelates on the unemployment situation in France. On issues such as these, French bishops are certainly dependent on someone like Canon Bonnet, and he can perhaps make his own ideas prevail in such circum-

[62] The contacts with the CFTC, of course, are unofficial.

[63] A description of the missionary areas can be found in *Témoignage Chrétien*, May 15, 1959, "Dossier de la Semaine." Here can be found also a good description of the organization and goals of Bonnet's secretariat.

stances as the "opinion of the Church." Finally it should be noted that the superior to Canon Bonnet is not Mgr. Guerry, head of the Episcopal Commission of the Working Class, or Cardinal Liénart, head of the *Mission de France*, but rather Cardinal Feltin himself. This shows once more the importance of the Archbishop of Paris in the organization of the Church.

The chaplains or ecclesiastical advisors who are assigned to every Catholic institution complete the picture of the national Hierarchy. Like the Secretariat of Catholic Action, these chaplains are important only as their groups have political significance. In most Catholic Action youth groups and also in certain adult groups the chaplains contribute much to the functioning of the organization. However, in the most dynamic adult Catholic Action groups they have little importance. There are ecclesiastical advisors, similar to chaplains, for most Catholic publications.[64] They approve the presentation of articles on religious subjects, but never have any policy-making functions. Neither they nor the chaplains of Catholic Action are independent, for they are responsible to Mgr. Ménager, the local bishop specially concerned with their group, and the bishop in the diocese where they are residing.

At this stage in analyzing the national level of the Hierarchy, two conclusions are evident. First, though the Hierarchy has relatively little to do with specific day-to-day decisions of adult Catholic groups, it is always ready to give advice and corrections if necessary—on its own accord in the spiritual realm, and on request in the temporal realm.[65] Secondly, one must not project into the future the structures of the past. Both Catholic

[64] The advisor to *Témoignage Chrétien* was removed by the ACA.

[65] However, the ACA has severely judged the temporal policies of a group like the *Mouvement de Libération du Peuple*—so much so that the MLP was excluded from Catholic Action by the ACA. See Dansette, *Destin*, pp. 375-376. The control of the Hierarchy over Catholic Action youth groups has, logically, been stronger than over the adult groups. Thus, when various Catholic Action youth groups quarreled over the exact political content of their movements and the extent to which they should be centrally coordinated, the quarrel was settled by the ACA. See Dansette, *Destin*, pp. 401-406.

Action and such groups as the ACA and the specialized Church secretariats modify in a certain way the traditional organization of the Church, which was based on the independence of dioceses. The new groups may in turn become modified if more effective organizational principles are found.

IV. Institutions of the French Church Below the National Level

A. THE STRUCTURE OF THE DIOCESE

The diocese is the living core of the Church. From a canonic viewpoint the diocese forms a "church" in itself, under the higher authority of Rome. Though many temporal problems cannot be considered within the framework of the diocese, its historically predominant position makes it indispensable in the temporal actions of the Church.[66] The bishop has the right to exclude any temporal group—even if it advertises itself as "Catholic"—from his diocese. He sometimes exercises this right, though only when extremist positions are involved.

It must not be inferred that the dioceses are the remnants of an ancient past destined to disappear as the Church adapts itself to the modern world. On the contrary, recently there has been a constant development of diocese organizations which work actively in temporal affairs. Every diocese has a semiofficial publication, usually called *Semaine Religieuse*, which presents the views of the bishop and his collaborators on a broad range of questions, from spirituality to practical politics. The *Semaines Religieuses* are hardly read outside of the Hierarchy, the local clergy, and the most devout Catholic laymen, but in other publications they are widely quoted and commented on.[67]

All Catholic Action groups are organized in diocese federa-

[66] In France most dioceses coincide with departments. The fortunes of the two are linked.

[67] At the library of the *Union des Oeuvres*, a valuable index of articles from all French *Semaines Religieuses* is kept. The index, while not exhaustive, offers some indication of the political themes in these diocese publications.

tions, whose officers receive a mandate from the bishop. This allows the organizations to share in the apostolic work of the diocese. It also means that the bishop has a control over the "tendencies" within Catholic Action. The bishop can withdraw his mandate and suspend the operation of any Catholic Action group in his diocese. He appoints and can dismiss the diocese chaplains of Catholic Action groups. The bishop also sets the duties and coordinates the activity of all chaplains through the Diocese Direction of Works. In this group chaplains from all Catholic organizations in the diocese regularly meet (there is no equivalent of this for laymen). Although their concern is mainly with spiritual problems and they are not organized efficiently in all dioceses, Diocese Directions of Works could well originate more effective apostolic programs and carry out other work of social or civic importance in the diocese.

There is one sector between the diocese and the national levels where organizations are needed: the regional level. Many problems are not common to all of France but exceed the limits of a department: the school problem is the best example, for it is really serious only in Western France and a few departments of the Massif Central. Regional economic problems raise similar organizational difficulties. A solution has been proposed which would increase the powers of archbishops over their dependent bishops, but nothing definite has yet been decided.[68]

The Diocese of Paris and its archbishop occupy a special place in French Catholicism, and must not be considered on the same level with the other bishops. Cardinal Feltin finds virtually all the important national Catholic groups in his diocese. He delivers sermons at parliamentary sessions; he is the chief chaplain for the armed forces; and he is the caretaker of the interests of the ACA. Only a prelate with exceptional qualities of leadership would be chosen for Paris in the first place.[69]

[68] See Dansette, *Destin*, p. 457.

[69] Cardinal Feltin, before coming to Paris, was Bishop of Troyes and Sens, and Archbishop of Bordeaux.

B. THE POLITICAL IMPACT OF BISHOPS: DECLARATIONS ON POLITICAL SUBJECTS

Bishops, more than any other members of French Catholicism, exert political influence through public declarations. A declaration has the weight of a bishop's ecclesiastical position plus his own local prestige behind it, so is often given careful attention by wide segments of the public.[70] The best way to illustrate the political role of bishops is by presenting sample declarations on timely topics: the Algerian conflict, the development of the Fifth Republic, national elections, the school issue. The quotations that follow are among the most interesting statements by bishops on these issues, though they are by no means "typical," nor are they all-inclusive. Bishops vary so much in their preferences, their capacities, and their notions of the temporal world that no general conclusions on their political tendencies should be drawn from these quotations. Nor do these quotations give a complete view of bishops' political activity, since there are other ways to exert political influence. But the declarations are the most accessible indications of political activity.

Statements on the 1958 referendum

Some statements in 1958 were impartial; most were vague but favorable, while a few were much more positive. All were preoccupied with the word "laic" in the Constitution. The bishops also had to reply to extreme right Catholics who had waged a strong campaign to reject the Constitution because of its *laïcité* and its failure to mention God.

Mgr. Lefebvre, Archbishop of Bourges: "Without doubt, even in a country with varying beliefs, the State should normally recognize, in the simple light of reason, the rights of God, on which natural law and all the rights of man are based.

[70] According to the Sondages Poll, when voting, 24 percent of the French electorate take "some account" of Church principles, while 16 percent do so "a great deal." "Le Catholicisme en France," in *Sondages*, Vol. XIV, No. 4, 1952, p. 25.

. . . Those who would require the faithful as a duty of conscience to abstain or to vote *no* in the referendum simply because the word "laic" exists in the Constitutional project are mistaken."[71]

Mgr. Guerry, Archbishop of Cambrai: "For all practical purposes you must ask yourself two questions: First of all, does the Constitution guarantee in the proper amount a strong authority which will serve the common good? . . . Secondly, does the Constitution guarantee sufficiently the freedoms and rights of the human being, the family, associations, trade unions, and intermediary bodies? Does it guarantee religious liberties? For the overseas countries does it bring an advanced status conforming to France's vocation and the legitimate aspirations of the overseas populations? . . . If, for example, rejecting the Constitution would have the country run the risk of civil war or political anarchy, obviously those whose vote contributes to such a national misfortune would incur a heavy responsibility."[72]

Mgr. Richaud, Archbishop of Bordeaux: "A text of this kind should be evaluated in its entirety and not just on one word. . . . Abstainers should weigh the immediate, disastrous consequences of this act for the entire country, even for the world equilibrium. Catholics will appreciate the phrase of Article Two guaranteeing, in the Fifth Republic, respect for beliefs. It is fortunately quite like the declarations of Cardinal Gerlier at Lourdes on the question of *laïcité*."[73]

Mgr. Chappoulie, Bishop of Angers: "In Anjou, I imagine that many of you will vote *yes*. Is this not the advice which you will get from the political groups which the majority of you usually vote for?"[74]

Mgr. Rupp, Auxiliary Bishop of Paris, talking to immigrants: "You must vote. How? The Church, which guides and frees human consciences, proclaims that it is permissible to vote *yes*.

[71] *La Croix*, September 16, 1958, p. 5.
[72] *La Croix*, September 21-22, 1958, p. 3.
[73] *La Croix*, September 16, 1958, p. 5.
[74] *Documentation Catholique*, September 14, 1958, p. 1201.

You love France. Your work demonstrates it. Think of her primary interests when voting. The Christian world, all free consciences, put great hopes in the French revival."[75]

Mgr. Rastouil, Bishop of Limoges: "The point is not to vote in favor of a political party, but to give at last to France a new Constitution, desired by the immense majority of Frenchmen, forever promised and forever held up. . . . Can one vote *yes*? Nothing opposes this choice. . . . If the groups which have decided to vote *no* are considered, one must admit that most of them oppose giving Catholics equality in rights and freedoms. Therefore, in conscience Catholics can vote *yes*. They are even allowed to think that they must vote *yes*."[76]

"Mgr. Le Bellec, Bishop of Vannes: "The faithful in our diocese will easily understand that, in the present disunited situation, there can be no hesitation. At an hour obviously decisive for the destiny of France, there is a very clear duty to vote *yes*, en masse."[77]

Statements on recent parliamentary elections

Certain general themes are repeated by bishops at every election: voting is a duty, there is no excuse for abstaining, one cannot vote for Communists or others who oppose Christian notions of morality. One more specific idea has been reiterated in every election since 1951: one must vote for the candidate favoring a just solution to the school problem. Many declarations make the point more specifically—for example, they ask Catholics to vote for the candidate favoring state aid to private schools *and* who is in the strongest electoral position. The declaration of Mgr. Cazaux is a case in point.

Although each bishop is free to make the declarations he desires, themes are practically identical throughout France. For example, everywhere the school problem was emphasized more in 1951 than in 1956.[78]

[75] *La Croix*, September 23, 1958, p. 3.
[76] *Le Monde*, September 20, 1958, p. 5.
[77] *La Croix*, September 23, 1958, p. 3.
[78] The election statements of Cardinals Feltin, Gerlier, and Saliège

Interestingly enough, it seems that there is no correlation between support for private schools and their existence in an area. Bishops of dechristianized areas without Catholic schools were just as firmly for the principle of state aid as the bishops of Brittany. This illustrates the fact that these declarations represent "theses" rather than "hypotheses."

Again, these quotations presented here are not representative; they are designed to show the most interesting and most extremist episcopal positions.

Mgr. Cazaux, Bishop of Luçon: "Luckily, all the candidates who favor the triumph of school justice in our region have pooled their lists. We are very happy about this, because, while your free choice is safeguarded better than with a single list, your vote has a greater effectiveness. . . ."[79]

Mgr. Théas, Bishop of Tarbes and Lourdes: "It is a duty of conscience to refuse to vote for candidates who advocate a doctrine condemned by the Church—the Communists for example—or for candidates who do not accept the essential Christian freedoms, especially for schools. We want not only a formal freedom for the school, but also the practical, normal means to exercise this freedom."[80]

Mgr. Pirolley, Bishop of Nancy and Toul: "Vote for candidates considered most qualified to safeguard and promote the rights of religion and at the same time serve the higher interests of the country and the working classes. Among these rights effective school freedom is in the foreground. This means giving all families, even the humblest, the possibility of choos-

in 1956 did not mention the school problem at all. Cf. *Documentation Catholique*, December 25, 1955, columns 1619-1620. In general the Hierarchy was more reticent to take political stands in 1956 than either before or after. See Goguel, "Note Complémentaire," in Association Française de Science Politique, *Les Elections du 2 Janvier, 1956* (Paris: Armand Colin, 1956), p. 422.

[79] *Semaine Religieuse de Luçon*, June 9, 1951, p. 274. This is the diocese with the largest percent of Catholic school children in France—well over half the school population are in Catholic schools.

[80] *Le Monde*, November 15, 1958, p. 3.

ing the school for their children, by a just distribution to them of public funds."[81]

Mgr. de Provenchères, Archbishop of Aix-en-Provence: "Choose those who . . . seem able to base their actions on the principles of the Church social doctrine, especially in matters of family rights, the education of children, peace among social classes, and religious freedoms. You must make your vote count, especially on the second round."[82]

Declarations on the Algerian conflict

Before the summer of 1958, frequent declarations from French bishops deplored the tortures, killings, and other injustices in Algeria—whether inflicted by the rebels or by the French themselves. When certain bishops also attempted to apply to Algeria the Church's liberal stand on national aspirations of peoples prelates like Cardinal Saliège vigorously protested, and the Church came into conflict with conservative groups that historically had been the bulwarks of French Catholicism.[82a] After the crisis of 1958, when the Algerian situation became even more linked with the question of a new regime, some bishops seemed less outspoken. But most refused to let political changes deter them from deeply-felt moral principles. The bishops with special interests in Algeria have remained particularly outspoken: the Algerian bishops themselves, Cardinal Feltin, who is the Chief Chaplain of the French Army, Cardinal Liénart, head of the *Mission de France*, and Mgr. Ancel, Auxiliary Bishop of Lyon, among others. It is significant that the bishops with the most personal interest in the

[81] *Le Monde*, November 16-17, 1958, p. 3.

[82] *Témoignage Chrétien*, March 6, 1959, p. 11. This declaration concerns recent municipal elections in France.

[82a] In early 1958, a rightist student group in Algeria warned the Algerian bishops: "Excellencies, make no mistake. In France as in Algeria, Catholic opinion is breaking away from the Hierarchy, whose attitude seems too often anti-French. As for the Catholics of Algeria, they want to remain both good Christians and good Frenchmen. It is to be hoped that certain of their priests will demonstrate both qualities also." Quoted in Pierre Houart, *L'Attitude de l'Eglise dans la Guerre d'Algérie, 1954-1960* (Brussels: Le Livre Africain, 1960), p. 56.

Algerian war were quite divided in their interpretations of it. Cardinal Liénart and Mgr. Ancel let it be known that the Church could not positively condemn the struggle of the Algerian rebels, while Cardinal Feltin often praised the work of French troops in Algeria. At times the Algerian bishops concentrated on the benefits brought by France to Algeria, but Archbishop Duval of Algiers also spoke courageously for greater justice to the Algerian masses.

Cardinal Liénart, head of the *Mission de France* and Archbishop of Lille: "Reliable information given us by local soldiers who have returned from Algeria and confirmed by much authoritative evidence, reveals the use in Algeria of a whole series of inhuman procedures: arbitrary arrest, physical and psychological torture, execution without trial, massacre of civilian populations, wholesale roundups of suspects, executions of prisoners, killing of wounded men. . . . But denouncing tortures must not be a means of concealing terrorism [of the nationalists]. The one and the other are equally unjustifiable."[83]

Mgr. Ancel, Auxiliary Bishop of Lyon: "For an insurrection to be legitimate, three conditions must be present. First of all, a people or a national minority (I use this second expression for those who consider Algeria a part of France; in this case, Algeria would be a national minority) must be seriously and unjustly oppressed and must have tried every means short of force to remove the injustices. If, in spite of these efforts, the people or national minority cannot eliminate the unjust oppres-

[83] *Documentation Catholique*, April 27, 1958, cols. 554-556. In 1959, Cardinal Liénart endorsed a vigorous condemnation, published by the *Mission de France*, of torture and other injustices which both sides committed in Algeria. The text actually says that it would be better for France to lose the war than to continue immoral violence. See *Les Evêques face à la Guerre d'Algérie* (Paris: Editions du *Témoignage Chrétien*, 1960), p. 41. In October, 1960, the Assembly of Cardinals and Archbishops was just as forceful: "Whatever their source, acts of terrorism, outrages against human beings, violent procedures to extract confessions, summary executions, attacks on the innocent as a means of reprisal, are all condemned by God. Even to take advantage of legitimate rights or to insure the success of a cause considered just, it is never permitted to use intrinsically perverse methods, for they degrade one's conscience and their only sure result is continually to set back the hour of peace." *ibid.*, p. 66.

sion, it can resort to insurrection, provided the other two conditions have been realized. Secondly, for a legitimate insurrection to be undertaken, the grave consequences which always follow (think of the number of dead, the destruction, etc.) must not be worse than the consequences of the injustice before the insurrection. Thirdly, for an insurrection to be legitimate, there must be a moral certainty of success. . . . There is no right to begin an insurrection which is obviously destined to fail.

"The judgment which must be made on these three conditions is not simply political. It is also a moral judgment. Consequently, the Church may intervene. But in fact, as far as Algeria is concerned, the Church has not intervened. . . .

"Given these reflections, it does not seem possible for us as Christians to take the responsibility of judging the moral value of this insurrection. We cannot positively affirm that it is legitimate; neither can we condemn it as if it were illegitimate."[84]

Common declaration of the Algerian bishops: "We shall escape from the impasse only by seeking loyal relations and dialogues with the most varied social groups . . . with a view to mutual understanding and constructive collaboration."[85]

Mgr. Guerry, Archbishop of Cambrai: "[In Algeria] as everywhere throughout the colonial world the winds of independence are blowing. . . . We must understand the suffering of Moslems facing the contempt of certain Europeans. We must also understand the Moslems' humiliation to feel in tutelage and to be considered naturally inferior. They yearn to be respected as men and to have their claim to form an Algerian nation recognized. A national conscience is awakening in them."[86]

[84] *Documentation Catholique*, June 21, 1959, cols. 811-812. The *Mission de France*, with Cardinal Liénart's endorsement, said in April 1959, "If we Frenchmen wish to be patriots we must recognize the right of the Algerians too to love their country." *Les Evêques face à la Guerre d'Algérie*, p. 11.

[85] *Documentation Catholique*, April 13, 1958, column 460.

[86] Quoted in Houart, *op.cit.*, p. 23.

Mgr. Duval, Archbishop of Algiers, speaking after the military revolt of April 1961 had been crushed: "I am happy and proud . . . that, in spite of the tragic circumstances and dangerous temptations, the misled people ready to use any means at all were but a feeble minority. In general, you have persevered in the way of Christian duty. . . . It is brotherly love which will enable you to be of service to Algeria, which needs you. The best guarantee of your rights is your will to cooperate in the building of Algeria.[86a]

Mgr. Lacaste, Bishop of Oran, observing that the Algerian rebels fight "a subversive war, caused by blind hate": "The army pursues its task of moral education among the immense crowd of humble people . . . entrusting themselves to the army in a moving gesture of simplicity. . . . May the State, the head and heart of the nation, soon be worthy of such an army, and may the army, in turn, remain worthy of such a State."[87]

Cardinal Saliège of Toulouse, in a joint declaration with a number of partisans of *Algérie française*, 1956: "Who wants to drive us from this land linked to us by 125 years of civilization? Alongside the perennial outlaw leaders, the merciless assassins, and the pitiful hostages of terror, there are impatient souls, blinded by propaganda. They call themselves patriots and are made the instruments of panarabism, an imperialism which is theocratic, fanatical, and racist. . . . Are we going to deliver to the worst possible tyranny the million Frenchmen with roots in Algeria and the millions of Moslem French who have spilled their blood side by side with us on all our battlefields? . . . Our conviction is absolute. *Yes, it is just and proper to use French power to protect all people against terror.*"[87a]

[86a] *La Croix*, April 29, 1961, p. 1. During the revolt all six French Cardinals agreed on a joint declaration pledging to do all in their power to avoid civil war and to concentrate on achieving the common good, "which is assured first and foremost by the legitimate government in power." See *Le Monde*, April 27, 1961, p. 3.

[87] Quoted in *France-Monde Catholique*, No. 182, July, 1958, p. 5.

[87a] *Documentation Catholique*, June 24, 1956, cols. 804-805.

Declarations on the school question

Among the countless declarations on the school question published in election periods or at other times, there are just a few basic themes which appear constantly: Only public support of Church schools gives parents the real freedom to choose a school for their children, and this liberty is the foundation of all liberties in the state. A Catholic education is a sacred right and duty for all Catholics. Private schools perform a public service which the state is unable to perform fully itself. Private school teachers will become a "subproletariat" unless paid adequately by the state. Catholic parents pay taxes two times for two education systems, and so forth.

These themes (which will be discussed in Chapter Eight) generally indicate a moderate, rational approach to the school question. However, more stringent measures are sometimes taken in certain dioceses. For example, in the Diocese of Vannes, a family sending children to a public school was threatened with excommunication by the bishop.[88] This could happen only in an area where the majority of children went to Catholic schools.

The place of the school problem in national elections can be shown briefly in the following quotations from French bishops. The first two quotations concern bishops' views of the parliament of 1946-1951, which considered the school question on many occasions. The last quotation shows that at times the "hypothesis" on the school question comes close to being advocated by bishops.

Mgr. Feltin, Archbishop of Paris, to Catholic legislators, end of 1950: "Catholics, when you hesitate before decisions which might determine peace or war, public order or disorder, education or moral degradation of a whole people, you realize what are fear, anguish, scruples of conscience. . . . Supporting the common good, the claims of the rights of God, and the dig-

[88] See *Le Monde*, November 23, 1950.

nity of man have not given you in the past and will not give you in the future easy successes, Gentlemen."[89]

Mgr. Cazaux, Bishop of Luçon, talking about the "laic Deputies": "These gentlemen are fixed, rigid, hardened. Only one thing matters: it must be made impossible to teach religion, even to those who want it. This is the meaning of their 'freedom,' that deceitful and bloody freedom, the same freedom which produces today outcasts in the Western World and martyrs in the East. . . . And many would willingly underscore these words from a deputy, perhaps the most significant in all the debates: 'if this Chamber cannot grant justice, it should disappear!' "[90]

The "Lyon Theological Committee" (approved by Cardinal Gerlier): "The neutral school can be suitable for religiously-divided regions when, because of economic or geographic circumstances, it seems to be the only solution which does not hurt any spiritual family, or again in areas of religious indifference where practicing Catholics could not furnish school children enough to justify the existence of a Catholic school."[91]

If the preceding statements seem to indicate a certain reticence to speak out on political issues or a desire to be purposefully vague, this is not surprising. Many factors can curb to some degree bishops' political activity. First, the French Government has the right to question on political grounds any bishops nominated by the Vatican. If there are political objections to the prospective bishop, the Vatican will generally nominate someone else.[92] In Alsace and Lorraine, where the 1801 Concordat is still in effect, the two bishops are directly proposed by

[89] *Semaine Religieuse de Paris*, December 2, 1950, pp. 1112-1113.

[90] *Semaine Catholique de Luçon*, March 31, 1951, pp. 156-157.

[91] *Documentation Catholique*, April 14, 1957, column 481. This statement originally appeared in the *Semaine Religieuse de Lyon*, the official publication of the diocese. Thus it must have had the approval of the Archbishop of Lyon, Cardinal Gerlier.

[92] See J.-M. Fison, "L'Organisation Administrative de l'Eglise Catholique en France. La Nomination des Evêques," *Revue Administrative*, No. 9, May-June 1949, pp. 234-245. See also "Rôle du Pouvoir Civil dans les Nominations Episcopales en France," *Le Monde*, June 29-30, 1958, p. 13.

the French Government. Bishops are also limited in effect by what the ACA or the plenary assemblies have said. No bishop would want to break the unified front which they try to show to the world. Finally, the tradition of obedience in the Church also creates a habit of assenting to things even though one may not always approve them fully. So a national-level declaration of the Church or a declaration by an especially well-qualified bishop in a political field will usually not be challenged by the other bishops.

Certain bishops could even be victims of their dioceses instead of leaders of them. There are certain regional peculiarities which no bishop could change. For example, the Vendée region of the West is still traditionalist or even Royalist, and insists on the strongest possible Church position on the school problem, while frowning on rapid Church innovations in any field. The Bishop of Luçon could not go against these trends. Around Limoges or in most of the south of France, dechristianization is so widespread that the bishop is practically a "man alone." In such cases, where he cannot stimulate vital and influential Catholic lay groups and where social custom takes no notice of him, the bishop cannot hope to have much temporal importance.

C. LOCAL LEVELS

In the local parish the everyday life of the Church is carried on. The parish priest is officially the agent of the bishop, under his control and supervision, but in many everyday activities he has much freedom of action. In certain regions of France parishioners ask the priest whom to vote for. Sometimes priests run for office themselves, though in this case each must have his bishop's approval.[93]

[93] In Marseille, during the November 1958 elections, a priest ran on a Poujadist ticket without the bishop's permission. He was denounced, but it is not known if other sanctions were taken. See *Le Monde*, November 16-17, 1958, p. 3. The *Doyen d'âge* of the French National Assembly is now Canon Kir, Deputy and Mayor of Dijon. Abbé Pierre, once a deputy, switched from the MRP to a small extreme-left political group, on his own

A recent public opinion poll indicates that a great many people consider the parish priest active—too active—in the political realm. Forty-two percent of those polled thought that the priest was too active in politics, forty-six percent "just right," and only five percent "not enough."[94]

Usually the parish priest is the sparkplug of local Catholic Action groups, though in exceptional conditions dedicated laymen have the key role. The priest usually determines the success or failure of such groups by his ability to arouse interest in them. Often the choice of Catholic groups in a parish depends on his own personal preferences: some priests will be attracted to general Catholic Action groups because they are more closely attached to the parish, while others will favor some specialized Catholic Action groups because of their dynamism. Few groups could become solidly implanted in the parish if they did not have the wholehearted approval and preference of the curé.

A good part of the Catholic press also depends on the parish priest. Most leading Catholic weeklies and monthlies are distributed by parish press committees outside of Paris. If a priest is committed to the progressive views of *Témoignage Chrétien* or to the conservative views of *La France Catholique*, one or the other will see its circulation rise in the parish.[95]

The parish differs widely in importance throughout France. In the country the parish is generally an important social entity, while it is not in the large city. In the traditionally pious areas of Western and Eastern France the priest enjoys all the influence that comes from a position with prestige, even with charisma. In very small or very poor parishes, the priest, even

---

volition. This is another indication of the temporal freedom of action of a priest in public office. However, in a clear example of conflict between temporal and religious duties, Mayor Kir was forbidden by his bishop to receive Khrushchev at Dijon.

[94] A recent poll of the *Institut Français d'Opinion Publique*, reported in *I.C.I.*, December 15, 1958, p. 18.

[95] All officials of Catholic publications interviewed agreed on the importance of the parish priest in the circulation of the Catholic press.

though he is greatly respected, will be able to develop little lay Catholic activity.

The role of chaplain or ecclesiastical counsellor in Catholic lay groups on the local level is often given to the parish priest. He is supposed to be just a spiritual guide, but often he feels the necessity of more positive leadership. For example, in groups of young Catholic girls, the chaplain is the only adult, the only mature, experienced person, and the only man! It would be unrealistic to think that he would not be a temporal as well as spiritual leader in such a group.[96]

The local levels of the Church are so vast and so diversified that few generalizations about their direct political role can be made. It seems fairly sure that parish priests, lacking the ecclesiastical authority of a bishop but much closer to the people, will use personal contacts and friendships much more than published declarations to make political ideas known. Of course, such influence cannot be easily examined by an outsider. More tangible evidence of the political role of the local clergy will come in the chapters on Catholic Action and the press, for parish priests and local members of religious orders are usually the advisors to such groups.

D. RELIGIOUS ORDERS

As yet very little is known of the actual importance of religious orders in France. The majority of them probably have no political significance whatsoever. However, Jesuits, Dominicans, and to a lesser extent Assumptionnists, *Fils de la Charité*, Benedictines, and *Petits Frères de Jésus* play a certain temporal role in French society. These orders are almost completely independent of the French Hierarchy in their spiritual activities. They have their own hierarchy going back to Rome, and their own traditions of obedience—very strict for the Jesuits, freer for the Dominicans. In the temporal sphere religious orders are

[96] The Jesuits freely admit providing Catholic Action youth groups with their own conceptions of social action. Cf. interviews with Father Robinot-Marcy and others at *Action Populaire*.

formally under the control of the local bishop and the ACA just as all other Catholic groups are. But of course, their direct connections with Rome can permit certain orders to have a freedom of action which would not be possible for an ordinary secular priest.

The most striking way for religious orders to influence directly French political life is through their publications. Jesuits, Assumptionnists, Dominicans, and *Fils de la Charité* all control important printing houses and reviews; the Assumptionnists direct *La Croix*, the only Catholic daily newspaper of national significance in France. Some of these publications are spokesmen for a religious order; others are simply owned or managed by an order. In the interests of clarity, all will be presented in detail in Chapter Six.

In addition to their direct political activities, many of the orders have a very substantial indirect political impact, through serving as chaplains for various Catholic groups. Thus, until recently Jesuit chaplains served the *Association Catholique de la Jeunesse Française* and the youth groups that had sprung from it, as well as *Témoignage Chrétien*, which they founded. The *Fils de la Charité* served the JOC. Dominicans advise the Catholic employers' group (CFPC) and take an active part in the operations of *Vie Catholique Illustrée.*

Religious orders also staff other social institutions with temporal importance. *Economie et Humanisme*, an important center of economic and social thought, is directed by Dominicans. *Action Populaire*, directed by the Jesuits, has the best documentation on Catholic social institutions in France, and tries to stimulate the work of Catholic lay groups wherever possible. The *Fils de la Charité* control the *Union des Oeuvres*, a well-to-do publishing concern which puts out many Catholic reviews and has close connections with various Catholic children's movements. These various social activities will be presented in more detail in Chapter Five.

It would be difficult to say that religious orders represent any one "tendency" in French Catholicism. True, the Benedictines of Solesmes are connected with the right-wing *Verbe*, and Jesuits founded the left-wing *Témoignage Chrétien.* But there are differences within every order. As Neuvecelle rightly says, this holds for even the most "monolithic" ones: "The Dominicans include among their eminent members men of the extreme left and of the extreme right, from rock-ribbed conservatives to flaming radicals. Though it might seem startling, it is the same for the Jesuits, despite their strong internal cohesion."[97]

In recent years there have been signs that Rome and the French bishops want to remove the orders from what they would consider a too openly political role in French society. The Jesuits have been removed from advisory positions in national and diocese Catholic Action groups and from *Témoignage Chrétien.* The Dominicans were forced to abandon *Vie Intellectuelle.*

Is this the prelude to a general "detemporalization" of religious orders? Certain diocese officials would not be unhappy at this, since there is often rivalry between regular and secular clergy. But restricting the orders in this fashion would probably not be in the interest of the Church as a whole: "The great renovations in Christianity have always been the work of religious orders . . . and one wonders if, today still, the regular clergy are not better armed than the seculars, by their more rigorous discipline, to undertake experiments as arduous as the working-class life for a priest."[98]

It is fitting to end the chapter on the ecclesiastical nucleus of French Catholicism with the problem of the worker-priests. Creating the worker-priest movement is one of the progressive actions of the French Church to win back the working class to the faith. It is not this, nor the structure of the *Mission de Paris* and the *Mission de France*, which will be studied here,

[97] Jean Neuvecelle, *Eglise Capitale Vatican* (Paris: Gallimard, 1954), pp. 105-106.

[98] Adrien Dansette, in *Destin*, p. 461.

but rather the political influence which the worker-priests developed.[99]

The priests in the *Mission de Paris* found it necessary, if they were to be accepted as fully proletarian, to undertake certain temporal activities. For example, most worker-priests joined trade unions, generally the CGT. But some soon found themselves accepting full-time responsibilities in a trade union, to the detriment of their on the job contact with the workers.[100] This gradual assumption of temporal activities can often end in extremes. Thus two worker-priests took part in Communist-inspired riots protesting the arrival of General Ridgway as NATO commander in France: "Ridgway in France means war. We don't want war. Ridgway, go home!"[101] They were subsequently put through the third degree by the French police, and published an account of their treatment, which did not win the love of the police for them.[102] But more consequential than these particular incidents of political activity is the state of mind which worker-priests seemed to develop about the working class, the bourgeoisie, and the Church. If we are to be punished for political activities, they said, what about the "bourgeois" priests? "When the worker-priests make propaganda in favor of the Peace Movement or demonstrate against sending the general commanding American troops to Europe, everyone becomes indignant. But it seems quite natural for a monk to conduct military expeditions, for a bishop, taking judicial powers into his own hands, to criticize the verdict in the Oradour affair, and for a prince of the Church to speak over Strasbourg radio in favor of a pro-American Europe. The

[99] The *Mission de Paris* was the organization of priests working full-time in factories and living like the workers around them, founded by Abbé Godin in the 1940's. It was curtailed by Rome in 1954 and ended in 1959. The *Mission de France* is the organization directed by Cardinal Liénart to supplement priests in "dechristianized" dioceses with other priests, specially prepared for apostolic work. It is concerned with all classes outside the Church, not just the industrial proletariat. It is still flourishing, with the blessings of the French and Vatican hierarchies.

[100] Dansette, *Destin*, pp. 198-199.

[101] Quoted in Petrie, *op.cit.*, p. 134.

[102] *ibid.*, pp. 133-137.

worker-priests think that there is only one real scandal: the way that the bourgeoisie treats the working class."[103]

Among the worker-priests a class consciousness was very acute: "Only through the truth of our proletarian existence can our priesthood show itself to this world little by little, and can we live within this new humanity. . . . The priests who persist in taking part in the classic forms of priesthood are simply trying to adapt to the workers the bourgeois expression of religion."[104]

We shall see in Chapter Four the same sort of class consciousness in Workers' Catholic Action (ACO), but tempered always by a certain piety. The worker-priests seemed to lack this piety, in their almost pathological fear of betraying the working class. One can already advance the hypothesis that the lay Catholic workers in ACO have a more realistic attitude toward their class. But certainly all members of the French working class have a deep-seated feeling of being exploited by the other classes in French society; this is why workers hang together more than other social groups.

Worker-priests often developed hostile attitudes toward the other apostolic activities of the Church and toward certain temporal organizations of Catholic inspiration. They feared even that other working-class Catholic groups had been tainted by bourgeois values from the Church: "Not only do they reject any ties with the parish, Workers' Catholic Action, or the CFTC, they even ignore these groups systematically. When they meet them, they are especially careful to affirm their total independence from them. . . . After they were, for valid apostolic reasons, detached from Church institutions and linked with working-class institutions dominated by the Communists, the worker-priests in their majority finally rose up against the few working-class institutions attached to the Church, such as the CFTC and Workers' Catholic Action."[105]

In 1954 the Vatican ordered the worker-priests to abandon

[103] Dansette, *Destin*, pp. 191-192.
[104] *ibid.*, pp. 243-244.
[105] *ibid.*, pp. 193-194, 241.

any responsible positions they may have held in trade unions or other temporal groups and to cease full-time factory work. Such work could not consume more than three hours per day. Also, all priests connected to the working-class apostolate were to reside in religious communities, rather than by themselves. On the surface, these orders were strict. In reality, however, they were understood to be "theses" rather than "hypotheses," and for long months a handful of worker-priests continued to work a normal factory schedule and to participate in the CGT and other proletarian groups. The worker-priest experiment was not finally stopped until 1959, when Cardinal Pizzardo of the Vatican Holy Office declared that factory work is incompatible with the life and obligations of the priesthood.[105a]

If the worker-priests inspired controversy in France and throughout the Catholic world, it was because of their political activities and their potential significance for the Church, rather than their actual numerical importance. There seem to have been fewer than a hundred worker-priests throughout France at the height of their activity.[106] The groups which have succeeded the worker-priests in evangelizing the proletariat, such as *Mission de France* or the *Petits Frères de Jésus,* are much larger numerically, but seem to reject any overt political activity.[107]

105a Cardinal Pizzardo, the author of the statement, also noted that the priest in a factory could be tempted to join fellow workers "in the class struggle." See *Témoignage Chrétien*, September 18, 1959, p. 15. Cardinal Feltin had previously recommended the continuation of some worker-priest activities. See *New York Times*, September 15, 1959, p. 3.

106 Dansette says that there were ninety worker-priests of the *Mission de Paris* in 1951. See Dansette, *Destin*, p. 179.

107 According to *Le Monde* there are over 400 priests and seminary students working in the *Mission de France. Le Monde*, May 20, 1959, p. 9. On the activity of the *Mission de France*, see *Etudes*, Vol. 299, No. 11, November 1958, p. 253 ff. Inadvertently, two priests of the *Mission de France* became involved in the Algerian controversy, when they were arrested because their apostolic activity among North Africans looked suspicious. This followed an earlier incident involving a Prado priest of Lyon who also seemed to be inadvertently helping the Algerian rebels. See *Le Monde*, December 28-29, 1958, p. 4.

E. CONCLUSION

The ecclesiastical nucleus is an inexhaustible source of information and speculation for the social scientist, even when he concentrates just on the political activity of French churchmen in the past decade. From the facts thus far assembled, there seem to be two different perspectives from which to judge the political impact of the ecclesiastical nucleus: the *actual* examples of influence, direct and indirect, and the *potential* or *theoretical* influence of particular Church groups. To illustrate the difference, the Pope could have condemned the right-wing Catholic groups which advocated rejecting the new Constitution on religious grounds. Potentially, the Pope has this power, but his judgment dictated a different course. Bishops potentially can allow in their dioceses only the Catholic groups pleasing to them. Seldom do they act as arbitrarily as this. Thus, studying the theoretical powers of Church groups does not indicate what their real political impact is. The latter must be studied empirically, through analyzing all the information on Church social activity to which a layman has access.

Generally, when Church leaders forbear from applying their potential powers to the fullest extent in the political realm, this indicates a desire to leave temporal action in the hands of the laymen, and usually reflects a satisfaction with the Church-state relations of the moment. For example, if one compares the difference between potential and actual influence now with what it was during the separation controversy at the turn of the century, when virtually all bishops opposed the regime, clearly the ecclesiastical nucleus has removed itself from the partisan sphere in many areas. Now, Church-state relations in France are more and more cordial. They seem to be moving toward the *modus vivendi* that we know in the United States. If this comes, it will be a healthy development for French politics. It will come, provided both sides can remain moderate and tolerant on the last great issue of controversy between clerical and laic forces: the school problem.

It is a temptation, judging the distance between potential

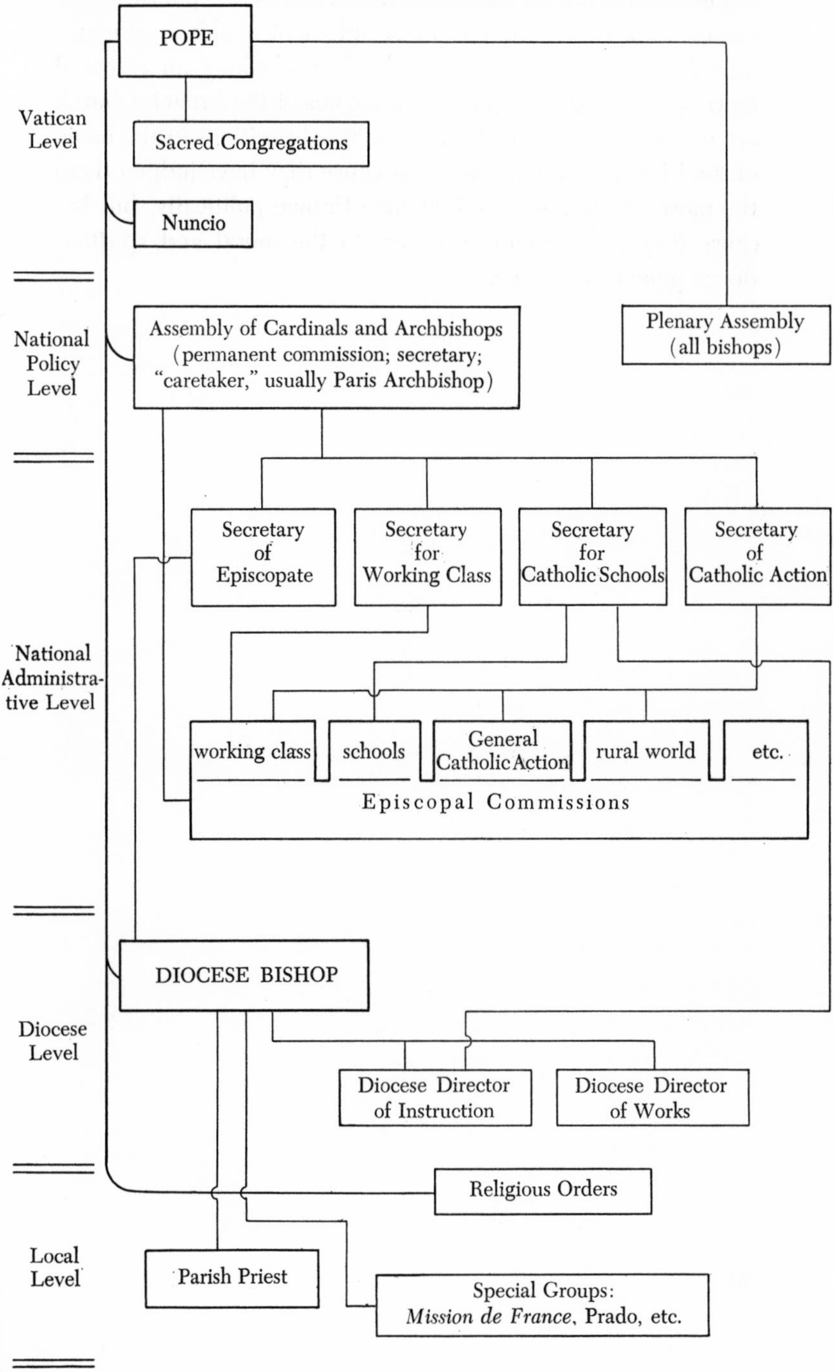

FIGURE 1. Chart of Principal French Ecclesiastical Groups and Their Interrelations

influence and actual influence, to evaluate the "political efficiency" of French Catholicism. A judgment of this kind might be valuable; but it runs the risk of overlooking an essential fact: the *raison d'être* and the main goals of the French Church are not political. If prelates take political positions in the name of the French Church, it is not because they have judged them the most effective way to influence France politically, but because they judge them necessary to the moral and spiritual development of France.

Catholic Action: The Auxiliary to the Hierarchy

I. General Characteristics of Catholic Action

A. THE DUTIES OF CATHOLIC ACTION AND RELATIONS TO THE HIERARCHY

Catholic Action comprises all laymen's groups which are formally mandated by the Hierarchy to aid it in its apostolic function. Not all Catholic groups are in Catholic Action, since not all of them receive the formal mandate. Catholic Action groups are all organized on national and diocese levels, following the Hierarchy which controls them, while other Catholic groups may have quite different organizational bases. These differences plus divergent political perspectives justify treating Catholic Action in a chapter by itself.

Catholic Action is mandated to carry on one basic purpose only: to further the apostolic work of the Church. In France, the term *apostolat* contains two different ideas. Primarily it means bringing non-Catholics into the Church through conversion. But it also means stimulating those who are already formally Catholics to perfect their faith and to become "Christian witnesses" to the society around them.[1]

As has been already noted, the apostolic activities of all

[1] This is the author's own definition, since the notion of *apostolat* in France is taken for granted and seldom defined. This definition has been approved by Church and academic authorities in private conversation. It should be noted that certain apostolic groups are outside Catholic Action. Recently the Vatican, through Cardinal Pizzardo, recommended that a new form of apostolic action be undertaken among workers and other social classes. Secular institutes would be formed, with both clergy and lay members. The clergy would keep the spiritual purity of the secular institutes while the lay members, working full time in factories or offices, would try to bring their fellow workers closer to the Church. See *France Catholique,* September 18, 1959, p. 2.

CATHOLIC ACTION:

Catholic Action groups are directed and coordinated by a Secretary of Catholic Action, representing the whole French Hierarchy. Moreover, each Catholic Action group is "watched over" by one bishop from the proper episcopal commission. Chaplains advise Catholic Action groups on all levels and are especially important in local groups and among youth, where they are the only adult, experienced participants in the group. The Hierarchy must approve the national officers and chaplains of all Catholic Action groups, and on the diocese level the local bishop also must give his "mandate" for Catholic Action groups to participate in the life of the diocese.[2] Rome is by no means absent from the picture; each Pope since Pius XI has defined the scope of Catholic Action. John XXIII seems particularly interested in the latest Catholic Action evolutionary patterns.

Originally the apostolic activities of Catholic laymen were carried on individually. Around the turn of the century the first organized apostolic groups arose in France; the work of the ACJF during this period is especially noteworthy. Finally, in the interwar period Catholic Action apostolic work was organized within social classes: Catholic workers grouped together to convert non-Catholic workers, Catholic farmers to convert non-Catholic farmers, and so forth.[3] This milieu principle still governs most Catholic Action groups today.[4]

[2] "Within the particular church with which he is entrusted, the bishop alone has the power to approve a movement." Mgr. Guerry, "Action Catholique," in G. Jacquemet (ed.), *Catholicisme: Encyclopédie* (Paris: Letouzey et Ané, 1950), Vol. I, pp. 98-99. The nature of the mandate is clarified in this "doctrinal note" from the ACA: "The mandate is given to a movement. It gives it a field of action within which laymen are fully responsible for seeking the necessary means to accomplish their apostolate. The Hierarchy judges, from a spiritual viewpoint, the value and the spirit of these methods, as well as their consequences. But the Hierarchy has confidence in the laymen, and leaves them responsible for their action." Quoted in *Documentation Catholique*, July 21, 1946, columns 743-744. Cf. Mgr. Garonne, *L'Action Catholique* (Paris: Arthème Fayard, 1958), p. 50.

[3] Interpretation from René Rémond, in a private talk.

[4] It should be clear that the reason Catholic Action groups were established in various social milieux—the reason they exist at all—is their apostolic role. If Catholic Action has a political impact in a milieu or in

More and more Catholic Action groups have been pursuing their goal of conversion indirectly. They have tried especially to convince non-Catholics of the moral effectiveness of Catholic Action, hoping that an appreciation of the organization would soon develop into a conversion to the faith. This "presence" of Catholic Action seems to suit the French context better than Billy Graham-style "crusades," and enables Catholic Action to broaden both its religious and its temporal effectiveness.

As officially-mandated Church groups, all Catholic Action organizations commit the Church by their apostolic activity. Their temporal activities also commit the Church in a certain way. In fact, all the Catholic Action activities to be described here plus those noted in the preceding chapter form the basic Church political impact on France.

Where Catholic Action groups differ on a problem, it generally reflects a difference of opinion within the Hierarchy as well. Where there seems to be a wide consensus, as on the Algerian problem, the activity of Catholic Action groups strengthens the position of the majority of the Hierarchy in France (and its notoriety among certain people).[5]

Although in certain respects Catholic Action has strengthened the position of the Hierarchy with regard to French social life, it seems to have affected some of the Hierarchy's leadership within French Catholicism. The local Catholic Action group rather than the parish, the national group rather than the diocese, have become for many Frenchmen the real centers of moral and spiritual principles: "Today the devoted Catholic rarely expects guidance from his bishop; he gets information and a judgment on events from a newspaper. He receives his instructions from a national movement. This is a very profound transformation in the conditions which contribute to the formation of Catholic opinion. It is the equivalent for

---

French society as a whole, this is only a by-product of its essentially religious *raison d'être.*

[5] See Meynaud, *op.cit.*, pp. 87-89.

religious society of the appearance of organized parties for the political society."[6]

The Hierarchy recognizes Catholic Action's influence, and has attempted over the years to decrease the influence of Jesuits and other regular clergymen who were chaplains of many Catholic Action groups. For example, chaplain positions in all youth groups except the JOC were at one time monopolized by the Jesuits. In recent years most Jesuit chaplains seem to have been removed from national positions, being replaced by the secular clergy. This seems to indicate that the French Hierarchy wants to assure its own preeminence as spiritual leader for Catholic Action—a task that was perhaps too neglected in the past.

B. CATHOLIC ACTION AND THE INDIVIDUAL

To help perfect their own Catholicism, all members of Catholic Action groups are supposed to participate in an activity called *revision de vie.* This entails trying to apply Christian principles to all the events of one's daily life. An individual will meet with fellow members of a local Catholic Action group and review his recent behavior patterns. Any activities not in keeping with Christian principles will be pointed out. The local chaplain participates in this meeting and evidently has a key role, since he points out the Catholic dogma applicable to a given action. Psychologically, the practice of *revision de vie* has some relation to Catholic confession and to Communist indoctrination techniques.[7] The goal is to make it a *habit* for the individual to apply Catholic principles to his daily life—to

[6] René Rémond, "Droite et Gauche dans le Catholicisme Français," *Revue Française de Science Politique*, Vol. VIII, No. 4, December 1958, p. 811.

[7] There is no published description of *revision de vie* outside of mimeographed brochures put out by and for Catholic Action members. However, the principle has been publicly endorsed by all the Hierarchy. For example, Pope John XXIII in the encyclical *Mater et Magistra* stated that "Christian education . . . should strive to implant and foster among the faithful an awareness of the obligation to carry on in a Christian manner their economic and social activities." See *New York Times*, July 15, 1961, p. 8.

have him act on the street, in the factory, in the shop not as a worker or student or farmer, but as a Catholic. In this respect *revision de vie* has important political consequences.[8]

It is quite difficult to appreciate the importance of *revision de vie* within Catholic Action groups. Its psychological impact on individuals would seem to be considerable, if it were practiced as it is ideally set forth, by all participants in Catholic Action. But at present it is impossible to find out how many people actually do participate in regular Catholic Action meetings.

However, certain Catholics are profoundly influenced by the methods of Catholic Action. They are so stimulated by the religious principles taught in Catholic Action that they work tirelessly to apply them to all facets of life around them. Some enter other Catholic groups in the political or social realm; others become active "Catholic nucleii" in neutral organizations. In both cases a large number assume posts of responsibility and leadership.[9] Thus, a great number of MRP leaders of today spent their early years with Catholic Action. There they developed a need for commitment in the social and political spheres, which was nourished and oriented by *revision de vie.* Eventually they found satisfaction through their work in the MRP. This is even clearer with the young Catholic Action leaders who developed the *Rassemblement des Forces Démocratiques,* to be discussed in Chapter Seven.

[8] Of course, *revision de vie* does not fully succeed in making a man "think Catholic." Many millions of Catholics have never attended a session or even heard of the practice. Furthermore, it is practiced a little differently in some milieux than in others: bourgeois sessions tend to be more theoretical than farmers'. (Interview with Jean Villot, MFR official, March 3, 1959.) Some Jesuits are concerned that the practice has become less "spiritual" since they left Catholic Action chaplaincies.

[9] This is part of the purpose of Catholic Action. "Catholic Action does not have to organize the temporal world; it must respect the autonomy of temporal institutions, but it must develop its members to live an incarnate Christianity, real and concrete. By its organization, Catholic Action must christianize institutions and social life in passing on to them the Christian spirit." Quoted from André Deroo, *L'Episcopat Français dans la Mêlée de son Temps* (Paris: Bonne Presse, 1955), p. 191. Cf. Mgr. Guerry, "Action Catholique," p. 99.

CATHOLIC ACTION:

In its ideal form, Catholic Action seems to have two different effects on an individual's patterns of loyalty. Specialized Catholic Action, working in the milieu, seems to strengthen the ties between the individual and his associates; one cannot convert his fellow workers unless he is like them.[10] But on the other hand, *revision de vie* also tends to dissociate some of the class-based thinking habits (especially those of workers) in favor of a more "Catholic" approach to life. In this way the Church tries to hasten the *rapprochement* between social classes and milieux which most French workers think is still unrealistic.

But the ideals of Catholic Action should not be allowed to conceal social reality. Out of the whole adult working-class population, only a few thousand have ever practiced *revision de vie*: the membership of Workers' Catholic Action plus a handful of workers in other Catholic Action groups. Of course, influence is not just a matter of number. An important elite has grown up within Catholic Action; as it has matured, it has changed many aspects of French Catholicism. This elite is of great significance for the Church, though it is no substitute for converting an entire social class.

Even if they escape from all the consequences of *revision de vie*, the rank and file members of Catholic Action are profoundly influenced by Catholicism, for a deep faith is the *sine qua non* of membership in Catholic Action. Whether one has learned it in Catholic Action, in catechism, or just in Catholic surroundings, one accepts the discipline of the Church; one does not quarrel with the religious views of his bishop or other Church authorities. Interestingly enough, Catholic Action furnishes a sizeable number of religious vocations from its membership.

[10] The national officials of Catholic Action youth groups spend several years working in the Paris Headquarters of their movement, but all of them consider this a temporary assignment. They do not generally become white-collar workers afterwards, but return to their work in the farm or the factory. Of course, those with proven ability may rise to other positions later, as did Paul Bacon and Joseph Fontanet, both former members of Catholic Action youth groups and both cabinet ministers in the Debré Government.

It has been estimated that 1,000 of the 2,500 new nuns every year come from Catholic Action.[11]

C. CATHOLIC ACTION AND THE POLITICAL SOCIETY

The Hierarchy has often made it clear that in theory it disapproves of all partisan activity by Catholic Action. As early as 1936, the ACA decreed that "leaders and active members of Catholic Action will not be at the same time directors, representatives or propagandists of a political party."[12] The present philosophy of the Hierarchy is summed up in this quotation from Mgr. Guerry: "The Hierarchy has recalled many times the imperious necessity of political action and civic or social action. . . . But as necessary as this action is, the Hierarchy has always clearly distinguished it from Catholic Action."[13]

However, the Hierarchy is careful to avoid a too-rigid distinction between spiritual and temporal. Catholic Action has temporal implications and inevitably has a social importance: "Catholic Action, though it does not engage in partisan politics, wants to prepare people to participate in worthwhile and honorable policy-making. It wants to prepare citizens politically, and even in this field, educate them as Christians and as Catholics."[14]

Through its members' activities in other groups, Catholic Action will have great temporal significance, according to Mgr. Guerry: "Catholic Action could not be disinterested in the organization of the temporal world. It must even give it vitality from within by the personal action of its laic members, who live as Christians in the temporal society. For this end, it prepares its members to carry on temporal activity in different organizations, under their own responsibility as citizens."[15]

[11] *Monde Scolaire*, No. 1, December 1958, pp. 26-27. The same reference breaks down a sample of 2952 nuns from Catholic Action as follows: from JACF, 1165; JECF, 941; JOCF, 640; JICF, 360 (some were in two or more groups).

[12] Quoted in Dansette, *Destin*, p. 92.

[13] Quoted in *La France Catholique*, No. 488, April 6, 1956, p. 5.

[14] Pope Pius XI, quoted in *La Croix*, May 18, 1951, p. 1.

[15] Mgr. Guerry, *Action Catholique*, p. 99.

Pope Pius XII is even more explicit on the "political" role of Catholic Action: "Political, in the highest sense of the word, means simply collaboration for the welfare of the City. But this welfare has a broad meaning, and thus it is on the political level that laws of the highest importance are debated and decided: laws such as those concerning marriage, the family, the child, the school, to name only a few. Are not these questions just the ones that interest religion particularly?

"Catholic Action must not enter the battles of partisan politics. But . . . it would be at fault if it left the field free for the unworthy or the incapable to direct the affairs of state. To what point can and should the apostle keep himself away from these limits? Here it is difficult to formulate a uniform rule for everyone. Circumstances and mentalities are not the same everywhere."[16]

If Catholic Action groups are examined descriptively rather than theoretically their political impact seems even more significant. This has been underscored by many French students of Catholic Action. For example, according to Professor René Rémond (once Vice-President of the ACJF), all Catholic Action groups represent a particular social "tendency"—the moderate left philosophy of Social Catholicism.[17] As the Pope himself hinted, Catholic Action organizations have not been afraid to take positions on political questions where the Church social doctrine seemed to apply. Virtually all Catholic Action groups protested a recent government austerity measure cutting down the amount of social security reimbursement for medical expenses. All favor an increase in family allocations and more imaginative policies in the field of housing; all are against birth control, and so on. The success of such measures as the expanding housing program or the reinstatement of full

[16] Pius XII to the World Congress of Laic Apostolate, quoted in *Cahiers d'Action Religieuse et Sociale*, No. 113, November 15, 1951, p. 611. We must note that circumstances and mentalities are especially different between French Catholic Action and Italian Catholic Action.

[17] See Rémond, *loc.cit.*

social security coverage for medical expenses in 1959 is probably due in part to behind-the-scenes activity of Catholic Action groups.

However, no responsible Catholic official believes that Catholic Action groups should intensify their direct pressures on the government: this would be betraying their own goals. But even more important, it would be ineffective because of the inherent mistrust most Frenchmen have toward the Church's meddling in politics. Thus, when the 1958 crisis brought sharply into focus the need for a healthier relationship between state, intermediate groups, and the individual, Catholic Action groups were most concerned with increasing their "civic education" activities. They did not appreciably increase more partisan activity. This seemed to be a realistic tactic since their future political effectiveness will come mainly from inculcating members with the values and doctrines of Catholicism and urging them to form "Christian nucleii" within political groups.[18]

The most dynamic Catholic Action groups work in specific social milieux, despite the imposing membership figures of parish-based General Catholic Action. Within each milieu, the style of Catholic Action differs somewhat. In fact, one can have a preliminary idea of the nature of the major French social classes in comparing the behavior of Catholic Action in each of them. There is also a difference between youth and adult Catholic Action. Youth groups must be concerned with the general upbringing of their members, and so must necessarily be less rigid in distinguishing spiritual from temporal activity. In each milieu Catholic Action has developed with different degrees of success. Rural Catholic Action has an immense impact among the agricultural elite and rural masses. In the working class Catholic Action is dynamic but still pitifully small in num-

[18] In 1960 and 1961 the Algerian crisis brought forth exceptionally strong reactions from Catholic action youth groups: see below. See Michael Fogarty, *Christian Democracy in Western Europe, 1820-1953* (South Bend: University of Notre Dame Press, 1957), Chapter XXIII, for a description and evaluation of "Christian nucleus" action.

bers; the "middle classes" also are difficult to organize into Catholic Action groups.[19]

These differences in milieu are among the chief stumbling blocks to effective coordination of various Catholic Action groups. Differences are most evident when politics is discussed. Thus, youth groups find no difficult working together where political questions do not arise to emphasize their different social perspectives.[20] But where political considerations enter the picture, even youth groups find it hard to cooperate for any common policies. With adults the situation can be worse.

The most graphic illustration of dissensions among Catholic groups due to class differences is the ACJF crisis, which will be briefly analyzed. The *Association Catholique de la Jeunesse Française* or ACJF, founded over a half-century ago, formed the nucleus which gave rise to the specialized Catholic Action youth groups that we know today—with the exception of the Young Christian Workers (JOC). After World War II, the ACJF became a disembodied coordinating organization consisting of the Young Christian Farmers, Workers, Students, and Independents (JAC, JOC, JEC, JIC), but without any members of its own. In the late 1940's, a great effort was made to give predominant expression to the "mass milieux" of workers and farmers represented by the JOC and JAC. At the same time, however, the ACJF leadership decided to increase its coordinating activity and to issue political statements in the name of ACJF constituent groups. Ecclesiastical approval for this was given by the Secretary of Catholic Action.[21]

In 1949 the ACJF leadership created an executive commission, whose essential task was to elaborate common policies for all its groups, ". . . to give to all members of the different

[19] Cf. Joseph Folliet, "Difficultés de l'Action Catholique," in *Présence de l'Eglise* (Lyon: Editions de la Chronique Sociale, 1949), pp. 103-133.

[20] The *Patronages*, or Church clubs, for example, are often very successful on the parish level in uniting all Catholic Action youth groups around the curé.

[21] Mgr. Courbe, then Secretary of Catholic Action, praised the ACJF for its work with public authorities. See his article in the Catholic Encyclopedia, in Jacquemet (ed.), *op.cit.*, p. 103.

movements a common formation and information in the economic, social, and political realms."[22] By 1952, ACJF leaders were commenting unfavorably on the possibility that military service would be prolonged, and making other comments that did not seem quite in keeping with ACJF religious bases.[23]

Starting in the early 1950's the JOC began to question the new political role of the ACJF. The quarrel had several dimensions. The JOC, jealous of its autonomy, feared that the ACJF would dictate to it a bourgeois line of action.[24] Also, the JOC was largely made up of young boys without intellectual training who feared that they would be dominated by members of the other groups. But most important, the JOC feared the consequences of any political action on attitudes of Catholics in the working class. As the evolution of the *Mouvement de Libération du Peuple* and the worker-priest affair show, there is always a danger of the workers being seduced by Marxism and the Communist Party once they start thinking in theoretical terms about political problems. Thus, the JOC wanted to keep Catholic Action on a strictly apostolic basis. None of the other groups feared this taint by Marxism, and were willing, therefore, to consider political questions. Paradoxically, however, the JOC has often taken many remarkable political stands itself.[25]

The ACJF crisis reflects a fundamental misunderstanding among French social classes themselves. It was finally submitted to the Hierarchy, which supported the JOC contention that each movement in the ACJF should be autonomous. This provoked the resignation of the head of ACJF and the virtual disappearance of the ACJF itself. So even today class consciousness is so strong that Catholic groups from different milieux cannot work in a climate of complete mutual trust. As this

[22] Quoted in Dansette, *Destin*, p. 403.

[23] See *Recherches*, A 19, January 1952, pp. 16-17.

[24] See *Actualité Religieuse*, January 15, 1955, p. 9, and *I.C.I.*, October 1, 1956, pp. 15 ff. See also René Rémond, "L'ACJF et la Jeunesse Ouvrière," in *Vie Intellectuelle*, Vol. XXVII, No. 3, March 1956, pp. 26-41.

[25] See Dansette, *Destin*, pp. 398-400. See also next section of this chapter.

chapter unfolds and milieux are successively studied, the differences in their "climates" will be even more apparent.[26]

As each group is examined in detail, it will become clear how difficult it is to give a thorough political account of Catholic Action. Without many costly psychological and sociological studies, it will not be possible to give a completely accurate picture of the Catholic Action impact on individuals and on French political life. The positions taken by Catholic Action groups on the chief political issues at the end of the Fourth Republic show the official views of these groups, but much guesswork must be used to evaluate the real political importance of these formal statements.

II. Catholic Action in the French Working Class

A. ORGANIZATION AND PHILOSOPHY OF ACTION

The working masses have always been the hardest for French Catholicism to penetrate. This is especially true of factory workers, who are considered the nucleus of Catholic Action in the working class.[27] The working class developed as a major social force in France at the time when opposition to the Church was widespread, because of the Church's connection with the aristocratic, pre-Revolutionary vestiges of French so-

[26] Catholic Action youth groups still have friendly cooperative relations, and have found that some limited political cooperation is still possible. All collaborate in sending *Entraîneur*, a newsletter, to their members in Algeria. All the important youth groups published this statement on Algeria: "It is no longer possible today for young Christians to ignore the Church doctrine on the legitimate aspirations of peoples." See *I.C.I.*, September 15, 1955, p. 5. All Catholic Action groups also cooperate in the semigovernmental *Conseil Français des Mouvements de Jeunesse* (which includes laic youth groups too, but no Communists). All Catholic Action youth groups, incidentally, are approved by the Ministry of Education, and most receive subsidies from the state for their "educational" activities. See *La Route*, April 1959, pp. 16-24. Cf. *Conseil Français des Mouvements de Jeunesse, Presence de la Jeunesse* (Toulouse: 1955). Cf. Interview with M. Etcheverry, *Haute Commission à la Jeunesse et aux Sports*, June 9, 1959.

[27] The term *Action Catholique Ouvrière* signifies that the emphasis is on the industrial proletariat (*ouvrier*), rather than a broader mass of workers (*travailleurs*).

ciety. Most workers, along with the bourgeoisie, joined in the opposition. The workers continued their opposition when the Church and the bourgeoisie again became reconciled.

The full realization that the working class was profoundly "dechristianized" did not come to the Hierarchy until the interwar period, when many important structural changes were occurring in French Catholicism. At that time, along with the tiny professional and political worker groups under Christian influence it was decided to create groups wholly spiritual, but at the same time run by the workers themselves. This spiritualist principle—the principle of Catholic Action—gradually spread into other milieux as well.

Of the present Catholic Action organizations, the oldest is the *Jeunesse Ouvrière Chrétienne* (JOC). The JOC was founded in Belgium in 1925 and introduced into France the next year. Under the sponsorship of the Hierarchy and the parish clergy, JOC was soon flourishing. Within a decade it had 1,000 sections and a membership of over 65,000, had engendered its own feminine auxiliary, the JOCF, and was in large measure responsible for the growth of similar youth organizations in other milieux.[28]

The JOC was most interested in piety. It tried hard to exclude all political and temporal considerations from its major activities. Its idea that a Church organization should stay outside the bounds of politics seemed novel at first, but it was gradually accepted by all the groups which followed the JOC. However, most of the latter developed a greater understanding of social realities than did the JOC.[29]

In the course of its rapid prewar development, the JOC also fostered adult groups, the *Ligue Ouvrière Chrétienne* and the *LOC Féminine*, which were formed in part by former *Jocistes*. These two groups had a certain importance before the war. Their publication *Monde Ouvrier* had around 90,000 circulation

[28] See Dansette, *Destin*, pp. 92-102.

[29] Interpretation from interview with Jean Mazeaud, national officer of the JOC, March 16, 1959.

in 1937, and immediately after the war it reached an even larger public. But the LOC and LOCF, dissatisfied to be merely "adult appendages" of the JOC, gradually changed their style of action. They emphasized more and more the political aspect of problems, coming to the point where they wanted to engage in frankly political action. By this time their ties with the Church had been strained so much that the groups were formally excluded from Catholic Action.[30] What was left of these adult Catholic worker groups, now totally outside the Church and strongly anti-Capitalist, seems to have merged into the *Union de la Gauche Socialiste*—one of the small left-wing non-Communist political groups—and later into the *Parti Socialiste Unifié*. Along the line of this evolution a certain number of *ex-Jocistes*, dissatisfied with the political orientation that these groups were taking, formed the *Mouvement de Libération Ouvrière*, which devoted itself primarily to family affairs. Though the MLO is not officially a part of Catholic Action, it is favorably considered by most Catholic laymen and the Hierarchy.[31]

Having seen how easy it was for Catholic workers' groups to evolve toward political action, the Hierarchy decided to create an adult group firmly within Catholic Action, where a climate of Church orthodoxy and apostolic purpose would be insured. This new group, founded in 1950, was called *Action Catholique Ouvrière* (ACO).[32] So now, there are three working-class

[30] By this time the groups had formed an organization called *Mouvement de Libération du Peuple*. Cf. Maisie Ward, *France Pagan? The Mission of Abbé Godin* (New York: Sheed and Ward, 1949), p. 18. See also Dansette, *Destin*, pp. 372-378.

[31] The Hierarchy has never formally condemned the evolution of former *Jocistes*. On the contrary, it encourages Catholic workers already in Catholic Action to enroll in "friendly but neutral" political groups like the *Union de la Gauche Socialiste*, or the MRP, if it is not too conservative for their tastes. However, neither these parties, nor the MLO, lacking the official mandate of the Hierarchy, can be considered within the Catholic Action complex.

[32] Officially, the ACO is the "organized apostolate of working-class laymen, called to participate in the apostolic mission of the Church, to evangelize the common people." *Cinq Ans d'ACO: Hommes et Femmes*

groups that are members of the Catholic Action family: the JOC, JOCF, and ACO. Whether individually, cooperating with one another, within the Secretariat of Canon Bonnet, or within the larger framework of the Church, they constitute the "presence of the Church" among French workers.

In the range of their activities, the ACO and JOC differ considerably. Whereas the ACO is concerned primarily with spiritual considerations and theoretically rejects partisan political action, it is difficult for the JOC to observe such distinctions. It is hard for boys still in their teens, who have not been to school past the age of fourteen, to understand the difference between spiritual and temporal in all its subtle ramifications! They may want to consider only pious questions, but for most *Jocistes* the JOC serves a spiritual and a temporal purpose: it strengthens their Catholic faith and it opens up the outside world to them. On the other hand, members of the ACO, who must be participants in other groups and already be familiar with the world, can devote their time to what they feel are religious considerations.[33] Even the ACO in practice exerts a certain political impact, as will be shown shortly.

Like all Catholic Action groups, JOC and ACO are limited to Catholics; but only a nominal adherence to the Church is required.[34] In addition, no one can join the ACO unless he is first an active member of some temporal group. This seems to be a very judicious way of limiting the natural desire of adult workers—even in a Catholic group—to take stands on concrete political issues. It also stimulates the creation of "Christian nucleii" in such organizations as the family movement or political formations such as the *Parti Socialiste Unifié.* However,

---

du Peuple devant le Message Chrétien (Paris: Editions ACO, 1955), p. 13.

[33] One of the goals of ACO is to give its members a "spiritual armament" against the temptations of the world around them: "ACO gives to its members who belong to organizations that could be morally and spiritually dangerous, the support which they need to act always like Christians." Commission Episcopale du Monde Ouvrier, *L'Engagement Temporel* (Paris: ACO, no date), p. 57.

[34] Dansette, *Destin,* p. 95.

this double requirement also limits the ACO to only the most active *militants*.[35]

Since its formation the ACO has been constantly increasing its membership. The JOC membership, in contrast to that of the ACO, seems to be declining since the war.[36] There are many reasons to explain the loss of dynamism of the JOC. The most important is probably the long military service which French youngsters have performed under trying conditions in Algeria. The veterans coming back from the war are in no condition to continue acting in a youth organization. So the average age of the JOC is surprisingly low—around 18, it is generally estimated.[37]

The members of ACO must be active in other groups, as was already observed. But not just any group; they must be in organizations which actively work for the betterment of the proletariat. The Communist Party and the "parties whose positions are contrary to Christian morality and the teachings of the Church" are out of bounds to ACO members.[38] The Hierarchy has given "suggestions" which are quite revealing on the most appropriate organizations to join.

"A worker may be called committed when he acts in a working-class or general-interest organization for the collective advancement of the working-class world. Among the workers' organizations trade unions must be mentioned first (CFTC,

[35] At present its membership is around 25,000. But this is sizeable for a group just recently formed. Membership figures from a talk by Félix Lacambre, President of the ACO, March 1, 1959.

[36] From 65,000 members in JOC and JOCF in 1937, the movements have dwindled to around 5,000 active members each, according to Jean Mazeaud, JOC official, in interview, March 16, 1959. The circulation of the main JOC publication, *Jeunesse Ouvrière*, has declined from 270,000 in 1937 to below 30,000 today. See Dansette, *Destin*, p. 97.

[37] Mazeaud interview. Cf. Dansette, *Destin*, pp. 397-8. Without the Algerian situation and other wars that France has been fighting continuously for twenty years, could the JOC hold on to more young workers and assure that a larger percentage go on to ACO? Perhaps not; but interestingly enough both Italy and Belgium, countries without foreign wars, have succeeded in establishing mass Catholic Action movements for the working class. See Fogarty, *op.cit.*, p. 216.

[38] See *Témoignage Chrétien*, April 24, 1959, p. 9.

CGT, FO, autonomous). Then movements such as the *Mouvement de Libération Ouvrière,* family organizations such as the *Associations Familiales Ouvrières,* the *Associations Populaires Familiales,* and political parties. There is no one political party exclusively reserved for workers; there are workers in many political parties—for example, in the *Jeune Republique,* in the MRP, and the *Mouvement de Libération du Peuple.*"[39]

These "suggestions" are not binding, but anyone familiar with the vocabulary of the French Church will see that as written they have a definite slant. The Hierarchy, while preferring the CFTC, gives formal consent to joining the CGT. The only important party mentioned is the MRP—the RPF was moribund in 1957 and the UNR had not yet arisen—so when other bishops at elections advised "voting usefully," ACO members must have felt almost forced by the Hierarchy into the ranks of the MRP.

Both the ACO and the JOC have extremely close ties to the Hierarchy, from the Episcopal Commission for the Working Class down to local chaplains. The ACO has deliberately been developed in a spirit of clerical paternalism, as was noted above.[40] For the JOC it is easy to see how the clergy, especially the local chaplains, could influence young workers without higher education and with little knowledge of the world at large. The Hierarchy for its part has been accused of a "workers-can-do-no-wrong" policy, as when the Hierarchy preferred the JOC thesis to the positions of other youth groups in the

[39] *Engagement Temporel,* p. 11. The book has the approval of Mgr. Guerry, Archbishop of Cambrai and President of the Episcopal Commission for the Working Class.

[40] The ACO National Bureau meets three times a year with the Episcopal Commission for the Working Class, headed by Mgr. Guerry, to give progress reports to the Hierarchy and to hear the judgments of the Church. All manner of questions are discussed: strikes, relations with the CGT, the worker-priest problem, the question of Catholic schools, among others. See *Cinq Ans ACO,* p. 35. In the diocese, ACO teams also report to their local bishop. *ibid.,* p. 122. Chaplains of ACO local sections are in constant touch with lay members and with the Hierarchy. And finally, Mgr. Ménager, Secretary of Catholic Action for the Hierarchy, supervises ACO and JOC as all other Catholic Action groups.

ACJF crisis. But from the doctrinal standpoint the Hierarchy is just as demanding on the workers as on other social classes. Thus the policies of the Hierarchy on the school question have been carefully explained to the ACO and the latter is expected to uphold them among fellow workers.[41]

Relations with the Hierarchy are not simply in one direction. Significantly, ACO keeps the Hierarchy informed and up-to-date on all matters of interest to the French working class: "It is the role of ACO members, in daily contact with the mass of workers, to alert the bishops on the significance of their activity for the working class. It is the role—and the grave duty—of ACO members to tell their bishops what clarifications and additions would have made it easier for workers to understand and accept that activity."[42]

In 1959 a delegation from ACO met with a number of influential bishops to tell them that most workers objected to bringing up the school question at a time when the workers' living standard had declined. And ACO members as well as their national chaplain, Canon Bonnet, have been keeping the Hierarchy, notably Cardinal Feltin, advised on how different kinds of apostolic movements might be received among the workers.[43]

If the JOC and the ACO have certain peculiarities that distinguish them from the other Catholic Action groups, it is largely due to their social context. The French working class retains in 1961 many of the anti-Capitalist and "proletarian" reflexes that characterized most Western workers' movements a century ago. The strength of class consciousness among French

[41] *Engagement Temporel,* p. 25. Cf. Interview with Canon Bonnet.

[42] *Correspondance des Aumôniers ACO,* No. 72, November 1958, p. 15.

[43] ACO members are not averse to criticizing bishops either; sometimes this spirit even extends to the ACO chaplains! For example, *Correspondance des Aumôniers ACO, op.cit.,* pp. 3-7 reports that many ACO members were indignant over the activity of certain bishops before the latest referendum. "Isn't it true that one feels bullied, treated like a little child, when a bishop takes a political decision in our place? . . . We must recognize that the bishop makes blunders, and we must go on working, knowing that he makes blunders."

workers brings a certain dilemma to the ACO: they must embrace this class consciousness in order to be fully accepted members of the working class, and at the same time they must try to change it by introducing Christian moral principles.[44] The JOC, facing a similar dilemma, often disappointed many of its older members by refusing as a general rule to take partisan political stands. However, at the same time, often in spite of itself, the JOC found itself making statements which it considered spiritual, but which had the highest partisan content.[45]

Given the circumstances of the working-class milieu, can a spiritually-oriented group such as ACO have any real mass influence? The President of ACO, Félix Lacambre, in a speech March 1, 1959, estimated that only one fifth of devout Catholic workers are now members of ACO, and practicing Catholic workers are themselves a minority of the working class. It seems likely that workers' Catholic Action could not reach the non-Catholic workers at all under its present goals. But the strict ACO formula is the only practical one for a working-class group that does not wish to run the risk of losing its Catholic status, as happened to the adult *Jocistes* before the war. Thus, the ACO and the JOC will probably not under present circumstances convert many non-Catholic workers; their potential strength lies in persuading the Catholics still outside their ranks to join them. In the distant future, if there is an evolution away

[44] "The first aim of ACO must be to educate the working class starting with the problems of life, so as to discover the Christian aspects in life." Deroo, *op.cit.*, p. 194. "The fundamental and definitive mission of the ACO is to make Jesus Christ known in the working-class manner, in the working-class situation (de faire connaître Jésus-Christ à la manière ouvrière, dans la condition ouvrière)." *Perspectives Apostoliques* (Paris: ACO, 1954), p. 14.

[45] Dansette describes the *Jocistes* as follows: "Under the pressure of their milieu and in the name of their religious convictions, they go from the absolute of faith to the absolute of politics: but sometimes certain of them begin to consider these political positions incompatible with the Church. . . ." Also it seems that a large number of former *Jocistes*, disappointed by the Church's apolitical stands, go over to the Communist Party. See *Destin*, p. 400.

from the present class consciousness of the French proletariat, the situation may change considerably.

B. ACTIVITIES OF POLITICAL IMPORTANCE

Spreading Christian ideals throughout the French working class, the prime aim of the ACO and JOC, is an act of political importance. Members of the ACO and JOC are made to feel a quasi-religious obligation to exert influence among their fellow workers: "A worker is obliged in conscience *to act,* and to act collectively, in the service of his comrades and of the entire working class. . . ."[46] Through sessions of *revision de vie,* militant Catholic workers are made to apply Christian principles to the reality around them. Thus, as with the Communist Party activists, an effective and disciplined elite is created which can extend its influence far and wide among workers. But all this is only an indirect way for the ACO to have political influence.

While they officially disclaim it, both ACO and JOC have direct political importance as well. The main centers of influence are their publications, which try to interpret in a spiritual sense the major political news of the day. The quotations given here indicate their positions on several questions of current importance.

On professional or moral questions the ACO and JOC have never been afraid to express their views, even when partisan politics was involved. So, in August 1954, during a series of worker protest strikes, the ACO published a communiqué: "For long years the working class has known only deception. It is becoming clearer and clearer that the present social, economic, and political structures are to a large degree responsible for social injustice, for an un-human economy, and for a class-based policy of the government which is against the very spirit of the gospel."[47]

[46] *Engagement Temporel,* p. 35.
[47] *Perspectives Apostoliques,* pp. 59-60.

After a recent national meeting, the ACO denounced many aspects of current French life in strong terms: "The evident decline of workers' buying power is a consequence of the economic recession; citizens' values lie dormant, and this contributes to depreciating the values of a true democracy; consciences are degraded because of the Algerian war, the use of immoral means, and racism."[48]

The membership of the JOC was seriously affected by the Algerian War, as was mentioned above. Thus, it is perhaps understandable that the JOC should take a strong stand on the conflict. In fact, wherever military service is an issue, the JOC makes known its ideas. "It was in the vanguard in 1950, fighting against military service for eighteen months, and in 1955-1956 it was for negotiations with the Algerian rebels."[49] In 1958, the JOC criticized the Algerian conflict in terms even more bitter: "There is a confusion and a feeling of impotence also before a public opinion almost amorphous, worked over even today by a cunning, insidious, and deceitful propaganda which does not hesitate to use all the modern means of information to form—or rather, to deform—public opinion and thus to paralyze in advance the possible reactions towards the Algerian drama. . . . In Algeria, the soldiers assimilate the effects of an efficient propaganda. Thus their faculty of judgment is annihilated."[50] Through this strong language the JOC is describing an event which is considered morally wrong and which deprives the JOC of older boys who would be otherwise its leaders.[51]

[48] Quoted in *Le Monde*, April 28, 1959, p. 12.

[49] Dansette, *Destin*, p. 399.

[50] *33e Conseil National de la JOC Française* (Paris: Equipe Ouvrière, 1958), p. 10 and pp. 51-52. In April 1961, the JOC, ACO, and most other Catholic Action groups issued a joint declaration firmly supporting de Gaulle's Algerian policy.

[51] The JOC also supports Church schools because of the large influx of members it receives from these schools. Those run by the teaching order *Frères des Ecoles Chrétiennes* have a particularly large working-class membership. Of these, the JOC says, "these fellows theoretically receive at the Catholic school a Christian upbringing which should prepare them even now to become active members of the working class and active Christians. . . ." *ibid.*, pp. 49-50.

The question of the regime itself seemed less important for the JOC than the Algerian issue. Still it judged favorably an anti-Gaullist demonstration on May 28, 1958. "That manifestation of unity in the face of the danger of dictatorship can be the prelude to a renovation of the Republic."[52]

The ACO presents a more logical and consistent evolution in its political sentiments over the past decade. In its beginnings, the ACO steered clear of political controversy. There is nothing, for example, in any of its publications before the 1951 elections that could be termed advice on how to vote. But as early as 1955 a certain change occurred. The ACO began to take obvious political positions, only thinly disguised in moralistic terms: "The ACO condemns as a supreme insult to God, Father of all men, the armaments race, source of misery . . . war in all its forms, the exploitation of colonial peoples and all personal or collective acts based on racial prejudices. The ACO denounces present-day society, based on profit which materialises man by making money his goal and the master of his fate."[53]

In 1958 the ACO made a valiant attempt to reconcile the personal views of its members with its Church purpose. Most of its comments on the Algerian situation, for example, are approvals of the attitudes of certain liberal priests or bishops. Thus, in May 1958 ACO presents with its approval the letter of a missionary priest concerning the Algerian situation: ". . . it is a duty to accede to the just aspirations of a people toward

[52] *Jeunesse Ouvrière*, No. 179, June 1958, p. 2. The JOC recommended that its adherents read several publications to keep abreast of the latest political happenings. Those cited were *Le Monde, Témoignage Chrétien, Express*, and *France Observateur*. All these papers are of the "left" or "extreme left"; only *Le Monde* was for the new Constitution. See *JOC, Lettre aux Fédéraux*, No. 87, September 1958, p. 3. The Republic, whether the Fourth or the Gaullist one, gives about two million old-style francs a year in subsidies to the JOC, through a front organization known as *Associations de Services Populaires*. (Interview with M. Etcheverry, Office of *Haute Commission à la Jeunesse et aux Sports*, June 9, 1959.)

[53] Declaration of April 6, 1955, quoted in *Cinq Ans ACO*, p. 136.

a political independence which constitutes for it a true moral and spiritual good. This means that Christians, anxious to abide by their beliefs, must recognize the existence of a political problem in Algeria and must work to bring a solution on this level."[54]

In the crisis of 1958, ACO was quite cautious. The slightest hint of approval for de Gaulle or the military leaders who brought him to power would be harshly judged by many workers, while an open condemnation of the new regime did not reflect the ideas of the Hierarchy. The declarations of the JOC could be attributed to the awkwardness of youth; ACO members were responsible adults. So the main theme in mid-1958 was that the working class, along with the rest of the French nation, had failed to show a true civic consciousness before the plots and counterplots of various private interests. Complacency, egoism, materialism seemed to be widespread vices among the French citizenry, and ACO leaders felt clearly a failure on the part of the working class.[55] Once the de Gaulle regime was established, the ACO, fearing that one man could destroy the basis of democratic government, urged overzealous priests not to praise de Gaulle as the man sent by Providence, and not to be so obviously favorable toward the UNR and *Démocratie Chrétienne* among the political parties. This makes the apostolic work of the ACO more difficult by increasing worker resistance to the Church.[56]

The school question was not much emphasized by the ACO for reasons already seen. Yet, the ACO National Committee

[54] Father Voillaume, quoted in *Témoignage*, No. 68, May 1958, p. 8. These words, presented as a Christian imperative, are close to what until recently would have been called sedition!

At the end of 1959, *Témoignage* quoted a church official as follows: "The church admits that a people's aspiration to independence is legitimate. But the church does not say whether one is conscience-bound to favor granting independence immediately to Algeria." See *Témoignage*, No. 83, Dec. 1959.

[55] *ibid.*, No. 70, July-August 1958, p. 6.

[56] *ibid.*, No. 81, October 1959, and No. 75, February 1959, p. 1.

followed the Hierarchy to the letter in setting forth the "essential freedoms" which all must respect: ". . . trade-union freedom, freedom of opinion and of the press, school freedom, and religious freedoms."[57]

C. POLITICAL EFFECTIVENESS OF WORKING-CLASS CATHOLIC ACTION GROUPS

It is striking that neither ACO nor JOC, aside from publishing statements, engages in concrete activities of political importance.[58] Their political impact largely consists of the opinions in their publications or their declarations at national conferences. This abundance of words and scarcity of action is not limited to Catholic Action groups; it is one of the constants in French political life.

But the political impact of JOC and ACO does not come merely from what they say. Members of these groups learn to evaluate politics from a new perspective through *revision de vie*. This is especially important in the working class, for a worker's perspective is often based on a very particularistic conception of the world. Through the values of Catholicism, the worker in ACO or JOC has his horizon broadened. Thus these groups create an elite—small in number but high in apostolic zeal—which has a broad view of the needs of the working class based on an appreciation of the desires of other classes as well. This elite (which in certain respects resembles the elite in the Communist Party) is encouraged to take positions of leadership in the working class. It hopes to be the nucleus of

[57] *ibid.*, No. 67, April 1958, p. 1. Later, *Témoignage* took to task the APEL for its "stupidities," in giving the impression that the school question was the only criterion for voting. *ibid.*, No. 74, January 1959, p. 3. However, once the new school law was passed, ACO opposed attempts by *laïques* to repeal it. *ibid.*, No. 86, March 1960.

[58] The closest they come to this is the yearly theme which most Catholic Action members use as the basis for social investigations and propaganda. The themes vary from year to year and from one Catholic Action group to another. They never have a partisan context, but, for example, the theme of the JAC and JACF for 1959 was "the politician."

an authentically worker-based Christian community which would dispel the latent anticlericalism in certain worker milieux.

The success of these goals is extremely hard to assess, but it would seem that they have borne fruit. Very little active hostility to the Church can be found in the working class (it is now found mainly among the intellectuals, especially school teachers!). The success of the CFTC among industrial workers probably is due in some measure to the work of the JOC in getting Catholicism accepted in the working class. Finally, certain individuals have been stimulated by the JOC to attain positions of leadership. One is a government minister, Paul Bacon; another founded a publishing house, *Les Editions Ouvrières*, and the list could be extended.[59]

A few Catholic Action successes must not obscure the great amount of work still to do among French workers. The working class offers no end of peculiarities which complicate the task of Catholic groups. It has its own customs, its own moral standards, its own way of life. In the working-class scheme of things, the Church has not yet been fully accepted. Catholic Action must dispel worker prejudices before it can think of creating a mass force within the French proletariat. It could not succeed by itself in such an enormous undertaking. This was obvious to the Holy Office when, in the decree forbidding full-time factory work for priests, it urged the creation of Secular Institutes to evangelize the working class. Such institutes would be obviously outside the ACO framework.[60]

[59] M. Villette, publisher of *Les Editions Ouvrières*, stated in an interview that he could not have advanced to his present position if the JOC had not "opened his mind" to the world. Interview, June 25, 1959.

[60] See *Témoignage Chrétien*, September 18, 1959, p. 15.

Catholic Action groups themselves realize the enormity of their task, especially the difficulty of coping with the particularistic "working-class way of life." This quotation will illustrate the extent of the problem: "Long before entering the factory, the youngster from the working class is already marked by conditions outside himself. He enters this workers' life from the first moments of his existence. . . . Work schedules often do away with any normal family life. The home is marked by the consequences of a working existence with insufficient wages . . . at school the kids encounter other schoolmates who are not 'quite the same as they are.'" *33e Conseil*, p. 100.

III. Catholic Action in Rural France

A. ORGANIZATION AND PHILOSOPHY OF ACTION

If the working class is further from the Church than any other French social group, many areas of rural society have retained their ancestral faith in all its orthodoxy. Paradoxically, it is in the "Catholic" rural world that Catholic Action groups are freest from Church controls, for there is less danger that they will be dechristianized by the customs of the milieu. For example, the ACO was founded by the Hierarchy itself, while its rural equivalent, the *Mouvement Familial Rural* (MFR) was founded by laymen and is the only Catholic Action movement energetically recruiting nonpracticing Catholics. The other two groups of interest here, the *Jeunesse Agricole Chrétienne* (JAC) and its feminine counterpart, JACF, have always been the most successful Catholic Action youth groups because of the wide areas in rural France receptive to Catholic ideas.

JAC and JACF were born in the great upheaval of Catholic Action in the early 1930's. The MFR originated during the war when older members of JAC realized that an adult, family-based organization was needed.[61]

All three of these groups are organized on regional and national levels paralleling the institutions of the Church. The most important groupings appear to be federations, correspond-

[61] A movement for children is closely related to rural Catholic Action. Called *Coeurs Vaillants-Ames Vaillantes,* it prepares boys and girls for activity later in Catholic Action youth and adult groups. Over a million children take part in this movement, most of whom later join or become sympathizers of rural Catholic Action groups. The children's group is part of the powerful and rich *Union des Oeuvres,* which will be discussed in Chapter Six. It also receives aid from the French Government through the Ministry of Education and from some localities through the Barangé Law. This law supports it as an "educational movement," while the Ministry of Education sees it as a guarantee against the communization of French youth. Interviews with M. Etcheverry, June 9, 1959, and M. de la Potterie, head of Document Service, *Union des Oeuvres,* March 24, 1959. Cf. *Annuaire Services Généraux de l'Episcopat* (Paris: Action Catholique Française, 1955), p. 60.

ing to dioceses or Departments. Certain local sections lead precarious lives, due to a scanty population or lack of enthusiasm among a local populace, or even less-than-wholehearted cooperation from the local curé. However, in many areas local groups can be extremely dynamic.

Both the adult and the youth Catholic Action groups are divided into a number of branches. The JAC is divided into various age categories (the oldest group, including young adult farmers up to age 25 or 30, is politically the most interesting). Specialized groups and a number of commissions handle the difficult problems which the JAC faces. Among them is a commission on soldiers, which has some political importance.[63] The MFR has a similar organizational structure, having groups concerned with technical and professional problems faced by the rural family, the situation of the farmer, and rural-based factory workers. For the latter, the MFR and the ACO work closely together.[64] A civic commission in the MFR has an important role in distributing to members material designed for "civic education." These local units seem to have more political significance for the MFR than for the youth groups. For JAC and JACF, the chaplains and the national leaders seem to be politically the most significant elements.

The rural Catholic Action organizations have far more members than specialized Catholic Action groups in any other milieu.[65] The exact membership figures, however, are hard to find. Having grown up empirically in a tolerant atmosphere, the JAC-JACF and the MFR do not have strict criteria for active membership. Hundreds of thousands of young farmers participate in their activities and are influenced by their ideas

[62] Cf. Marcel Faure, "Action Catholique en Milieu Rural," in Fauvet and Mendras, *Les Paysans et la Politique* (Paris: Armand Colin, 1958), pp. 345-360.

[63] *ibid.*, pp. 346-347.

[64] Interview with Jean Villot, Chief of Agricultural Workers' Section, MFR, March 3, 1959.

[65] It is paradoxical that the "individualistic French peasant" should have fostered a truly mass organization, while the Catholic working-class groups are quite small in numbers.

without being formally enrolled; the line between "militant member," "ordinary member," and "sympathetic bystander" has never been clearly drawn. However, there are indicators which will give some idea of the strength of rural Catholic Action. A JAC national congress in 1939 attracted 20,000 participants, while a series of regional congresses in 1954 was attended by 350,000.[66] JAC officials claim that the JAC and JACF together count 300,000 members.[67]

There are notable differences between the behavior of members in the JAC and the JOC. Former *Jacistes* who have completed their military service and return to their farms generally rejoin the youth group or the MFR; many attain positions of importance in the JAC. Thus, the leadership of JAC is older and the average age of its members is higher than in the JOC. Also the JAC is more independent of the Hierarchy than the JOC, although the difference is not so great as with the adult organizations. Finally, the JAC has more cordial relations than the JOC with its Catholic cousins. The quarrel over the ACJF outlined earlier embittered relations between the JOC and all other Catholic Action youth groups.

The MFR cooperates with the ACO to a greater degree than the youth counterparts. For example, there is a common effort to increase Catholic impact among rural factory workers. But the MFR is not a "class" movement like ACO; it is not limited to farmers. In the 1951 MFR conference, representatives from all rural groups were present: ". . . the small farmer of the

[66] Dansette, *Destin*, p. 100 and p. 389.

[67] Interview with Henri Catherin, head, older members' branch, JAC, February 23, 1959. *I.C.I.*, January 15, 1956, claims that the two groups include between 350,000 and 400,000 (p. 7). If the JAC and the MFR seem impressive in size, here, as in all Catholic Action groups, the most important element is still the local *militant* who can attract a following and channel it toward Catholic Action. This kind of *militant* will probably become a member of the "rural elite" and thus will spread even further the aura of Catholic Action. See Faure in *Paysans et la Politique*, p. 357 *et passim*. The number of these *militants* cannot be accurately ascertained, but over 18,000 subscribe to the JAC magazine for "leaders," and over 20,000 to the JACF magazine for "leaders." *ibid.*, pp. 309, 348. *Annuaire, Services Généraux de l'Episcopat*, p. 68.

West met the 'boss' of a large farm of *Ile de France*. The artisan met the insurance agent, the agricultural worker talked to the factory worker, the doctor with the school teacher. . . . And the dialogue continued among the rural civil servant, the notary public, the pharmacist, the social worker, the family worker, and many others."[68]

The main means of "action" for the JAC-JACF and the MFR are their published statements. The publications which have a wide audience can help spread Catholic values, or at least make the rural public better-disposed toward the Church. Each of the rural Catholic Action movements publishes a number of reviews, but few have political value. For the JAC the only significant publication is *Jeunes Forces Rurales*, the mass paper. The JACF has a very successful mass paper called *Promesses*; but it has no political value. None should be expected from young rural girls. The MFR has two publications of interest: *Foyer Rural*, the mass paper, and *Mon Village*, for *militants*.[69] *Clair Foyer*, the giant of all rural publications in circulation, takes no partisan stands. It represents the pious family-oriented elements in the MFR.[70]

Outside of their publications, the rural Catholic Action organizations deal very little with political events. Their activities are almost all concerned with technical problems in rural life. Very few official declarations on general social problems are made by MFR leaders, but they are frequently made by the ACO. This probably is another indication that MFR is not required constantly to reemphasize its loyalty to the Church and its milieu, as is the ACO.

The rural Catholic Action organizations have essentially the

[68] *Foyer Rural*, No. 201, August 31, 1951, p. 1. The JAC also wants to expand its appeal to all "classes" living in the country. See Father d'Haene, *La JAC A Vingt-Cinq Ans* (Paris, Collection Semailles, 1954), p. 110. But it seems to be based largely on small farmers. See Faure, in *Paysans et la Politique*, p. 348.

[69] *Foyer Rural* is not openly confessional, so is formally outside of Catholic Action. But the difference is more apparent than real. See J. Mondange, *La Presse d'Aujourd'hui* (Paris: Hirondelle, 1951), p. 134.

[70] Circulation figures are given in the chart at the end of the chapter.

same relations to the clergy as the JOC or ACO. Once again a special place must be reserved for the local group chaplain, who can greatly influence rural youngsters, both through his maturity and through the process of applying "Catholic solutions" to their problems.[71] For the youngster in Catholic Action the local group may become more important than the parish itself; the formal institutions of the Church lose some of their attraction when one can act within the Church while not leaving one's social milieu. This explains why there is some opposition to rural Catholic Action groups among the "traditionalist" clergy of the West.[72]

Because so many in the rural milieu retain their Catholic faith, the Church has paid less attention to the rural Catholic Action organizations than to those in the worker milieu.[73] On every level, the rural Catholic Action organizations have had more freedom of choice and activity than worker groups. But absence of Church control did not diminish the spiritual impact of rural Catholic Action. It has certainly had a wider impact than worker groups, because of its larger numbers and wider acceptance in its milieu.

B. THE POLITICAL ACTIVITY OF RURAL CATHOLIC ACTION

As with the JOC and ACO, rural Catholic Action groups have an indirect political impact on their milieu and also take particular political stands. The indirect impact, a by-product of the apostolic purpose of Catholic Action, will be considered first.

[71] See *Pour Comprendre la JAC, par un Groupe de Dirigeants* (Paris, JAC, 1945), pp. 40-41.

[72] "The dioceses are furrowed with Catholic Action chaplains. . . . Not only does the curé constantly see his active colleagues crossing his parish horizon, he also sees ardent apostles rising among his flock, whose forming is to some degree out of his hands." *Les Paysans et la Politique*, p. 514.

[73] "The JAC had the great advantage of having been left to itself by thinkers and clergymen, at a time when the latter concentrated on the working class. . . . It was never encumbered by theories of apostolic activity from clergymen. . . . It could forge its doctrine itself—a doctrine of laymen." *Ibid.*, p. 350.

Like other Catholic Action groups, the JAC-JACF and the MFR have three goals of apostolic action: to extend the domain of Catholicism in the milieu; to encourage a benevolent attitude toward the Church by all organizations in the milieu; and to create an elite permeated by Catholic values and aspiring to leadership in the milieu. The apostolic activity among the rural masses tends more to have them "think like Catholics" than to have them adopt the external practices of the Church.[74]

Apostolic action aims to create a psychological change in the young farmer. He should stop thinking and acting as a farmer, relating everything to his particular social context; he should start thinking and acting like a Catholic, relating everything to higher Christian values. In rudimentary form, this is similar to the *revision de vie* principle. It is designed to combat the class particularism that exists to a degree among farmers—though not as strongly as among workers.

This apostolic activity is perhaps more geared to producing a Christianized elite than influencing the entire rural population.[75] This elite is designed to "think Christian, judge Christian, act Christian, starting from problems of life."[76] It is not too concerned with forming a "Christian community" in rural France, because the environment is not hostile in the first place. Rather, elite members of Catholic Action want to enter neutral farm organizations as Christian nucleii. They do not believe

[74] "The JAC does not try at first to bring young people back to religious practice. Instead, it (1) makes them discover the true Christian spirit; (2) helps them to *live* in a more Christian way; (3) leads them closer to Christ. . . . In the beginning, it takes youngsters just as they are, no matter how far from the desired goal, and asks of them only a *slight* progress. . . . Religious instruction (God, Christ, Christian truths) will be relatively slow: first the soul must be given the *thirst* to know. Above all, *religious practice*, even the most essential, must not be precipitated or desired with too much insistence." *Pour Comprendre la JAC*, pp. 5 and 98-99.

[75] Note the comment on the "nucleii of fervent Christians" produced by rural Catholic Action, in *Paysans et la Politique*, p. 514.

[76] A. Achard, *Vingt Ans de JACF, 1933-1953* (Paris: Editions JACF, 1953), p. 112.

in starting their own Catholic professional organizations, as was done in Belgium and Holland.[77]

During the Fourth Republic, the JAC-trained rural elite was very reluctant to enter the established political parties, although when voting it usually chose the MRP.[78] After the crisis of May 1958, a number of Catholic Action trained leaders, notably Michel Debatisse, former General Secretary of the JAC, formed a political tendency called the *Rassemblement des Forces Démocratiques* (RFD). The RFD, in many ways an extension of rural Catholic Action into the political arena, will be examined in Chapter Seven. The RFD is only the most obvious political consequence of Catholic Action in the rural milieu. On many individuals Catholic Action has a strong psychological impact, with political results which cannot be fully explained here.

The publications of rural Catholic Action furnish relatively few statements of an out-and-out partisan nature. On the Algerian question the MFR tried to steer clear of any political involvement, while the JAC took more open stands since many of its members were serving in the army. However, in its statements the JAC seems to be rather moderate on the Algerian question, close to the policies of de Gaulle.

"Algerian extremists . . . endanger the existence of democracy and good relations with the people overseas. This is sufficient for their activities to be ended."[79]

"But the Algerian war continues. Despite the offers of negotiation and the Constantine plan to develop Algeria, the rebels refuse to open negotiations."[80]

[77] Fogarty, *op.cit.*, p. 250. Often the JAC-trained elite is not enthusiastically received in farm groups, because it is suspected of being too "radical" and of having too little respect for the historic structure of French rural life. See *Paysans et la Politique*, p. 351.

[78] According to Fauvet, the young Catholic Action rural elite switched from the conservative biases of older generations and was ready to support the MRP. See *Partis Politiques et Classes Sociales en France*, p. 175. But a later judgment was that this elite did not desire to enter any specific party. See *Paysans et la Politique*, p. 509.

[79] *Jeunes Forces Rurales*, No. 304, February 15, 1959, p. 16.

[80] *ibid.*, No. 301, January 1, 1959, p. 16. Cf. *ibid.*, February 15, 1960, p. 16. Here the JAC recognizes that each side in Algeria has valid and

By and large rural Catholic Action groups have been favorable toward General de Gaulle since he reappeared on the French political scene in May 1958. Before he took office, the JAC had some reservations: "And if his past can inspire confidence in his respect of republican laws, there is room for doubt on the real intentions of Charles de Gaulle—and on his chances for success."[81] Later, however, the MFR was less reserved: "We need an arbiter with enough authority to impose his will on all. Clearly the great majority of Frenchmen puts confidence in de Gaulle to be that arbiter."[82] Both the JAC and the MFR seemed rather favorable toward the new Constitution: "A page in our history has just turned. Starting today, we must prepare a new form of democracy and create a truly modern state. . . . General de Gaulle has made it clear that he will not solve everything himself. He needs the help of every Frenchman. Especially the help of the young people."[83]

"Several authorities in the French Hierarchy have wanted to reassure their flock . . . that . . . the text of the Constitution sufficiently guarantees the rights of the human person, of the family, and religious freedoms. Therefore, the national interest requires that the voters respond en masse, in one way or the other. Ambiguity is no longer permitted."[84]

Like the Gaullists, the JAC and MFR are wary of the established parties in France. The Communists and forces associated with them are not treated kindly, either in France or in the international sphere: "The experience of the last six years seems to show that any agreement, any collaboration no matter how superficial, is impossible between Communist and non-Communist countries."[85] The Socialists are hardly treated with

---

just claims. Complete independence is feared, since it would probably result in partition. Once negotiations did start, all rural Catholic Action groups wished their success and condemned the reactionaries who tried to sabotage them.

[81] *Jeunes Forces Rurales*, No. 288, June 1, 1958, p. 16.

[82] *Foyer Rural*, No. 583, December 26, 1958, p. 1.

[83] *Jeunes Forces Rurales*, No. 289, June 15, 1958, p. 16.

[84] *Foyer Rural*, No. 570, September 26, 1958, p. 1. The "therefore" in this quotation makes it quite clear what the opinion of the MFR is.

[85] *En Equipe, JACF*, No. 24, October-December 1951, p. 18.

respect in recent issues of the Catholic Action rural publications. After the defeat in the legislative elections of November 1958, the Socialist Party seemed at a turning-point: "Is it harvesting the bitter fruits of its *embourgeoisement* and of its lack of doctrine and ascendency over the masses?"[86] The official doctrine of rural Catholic Action opposes any identification with a single political party, even with the "most Catholic" one: "Catholics of unimpeachable sincerity are found in almost all parties, from the Socialists to the extreme right. So much the better for the independence of the Church."[87]

On the school question there is little enthusiasm among JAC or MFR leaders. There are only a few indications of the "basic principle of educational freedom."[88] Even at the height of the school crisis before the passage of the Barangé Law no positive statement of support can be found in the rural Catholic Action press.[89]

The preceding quotations are by no means a cross section of what one generally reads in rural Catholic Action publications. There is information on political subjects, but it is usually presented in an unbiased form, which could hardly sway one's opinions one way or the other. For example, before an election, the platforms of the principal parties will be presented with brief sketches of the important figures running for office. During the May 1958 crisis a number of articles took the French people to task for their lack of civic responsibility, and pledged to increase the civic education activities of Catholic Action. But this is always in an unbiased spirit; it is politically significant only in that it helps to inform the rural population. *Jeunes Force Rurales* has well expressed the phi-

[86] *Jeunes Forces Rurales*, No. 300, December 15, 1958, p. 16.

[87] *Mon Village*, No. 82, August 1951, p. 1.

[88] See, for example, *Foyer Rural*, No. 195, July 20, 1951, p. 1. "For educational freedom to be real, there must be the means to exercise it."

[89] According to one MFR official the MFR cannot take a stand on this question because too many of its members are from areas where there are few Catholic schools, and they are not much desired—even by the local bishops! The question seems to be a regional one, even inside the MFR. Cf. *Les Paysans et la Politique*, pp. 505-506.

losophy behind this information: "*Jeunes Forces* does not play politics. But . . . it gives political information. This is something entirely different. . . . When we judge a political event, we do so only as young farmers and young Christians, conscious that everything happening in the world interests them and concerns their life and their future."[90]

The JAC and JACF have two other institutions of some political importance. They sponsor dozens of rural talent shows, which attract hundreds of thousands of youngsters. These are nonpartisan meetings (government ministers frequently attend), but they help further the "permeation" of the rural milieu by Catholic Action. The JAC and JACF jointly hold a "campaign of the year," as do most Catholic Action groups. The theme of the campaign for 1959 was "the politician." A meeting of JAC and JACF leaders at the beginning of the campaign was addressed by a veritable who's who of French Catholicism—at least of its moderate left wing. Among the speakers were Pierre Limagne, director of *La Croix*; Georges Hourdin of *Vie Catholique Illustrée*; Simonnet and Pflimlin from the MRP; Marcel Prélot, Maurice Duverger, Father Viau from *Economie et Humanisme*; Father de Soras from *Action Populaire*, and many others.

Although the MFR has no talent shows or yearly campaigns, it has interesting activities of its own. In rural areas where it is strong, it often holds "educational meetings" with local government leaders—mayors, general councillors of Departments, etc. The same thing occurs on the national level, although usually the MRP and the conservative deputies are the main participants in MFR briefing sessions. At any rate, the meetings can give the MFR much political significance in rural areas where it is strong. In certain areas of the West or South, a majority of local officials have seen it in their best interest to join the MFR. According to Dansette, in the single Department of Jura, 4,000 municipal officials and 800 mayors belong

[90] *Jeunes Forces Rurales*, No. 292, August 1, 1958, p. 3.

to or support the MFR![91] These activities give the MFR an added impact in French politics. But they are largely unstudied, and cannot be properly evaluated without more systematic research into local-level French politics.

C. POLITICAL EFFECTIVENESS OF RURAL CATHOLIC ACTION

It should be clear by now that the process of evaluating the effectiveness of rural Catholic Action groups is immeasurably difficult. These groups desire essentially to "condition" the rural masses through direct contact by a trained Catholic Action elite. This contact consists largely of local personal friendships which cannot be evaluated, though it is significant that the elite-directed magazines have upwards of 20,000 circulation for each rural Catholic Action group. The rise of the RFD in 1958 shows that the rural elite is not afraid of committing itself in the political field, although it will not do so in the name of Catholic Action, and it will prefer to form a new "tendency" rather than enter an older political party. But all these are only indicators, and cannot furnish the final evaluation of the political effectiveness of rural Catholic Action.

Even greater difficulties are encountered if one tries to evaluate the "pressure group" activities of the MFR, for one is bound to fall into the morass of local-level French politics. Obviously, politicians, including National Assembly deputies, would not become members of the MFR if this were a political liability. But the extent to which it is an asset remains largely a mystery.

The least significant activities of rural Catholic Action often are easiest to evaluate. Opinions on partisan matters—which are often few and played down by Catholic Action leaders themselves—indicate that these groups belong to the Catholic center and are quite a bit more moderate than working-class Catholic Action. Even their refusal to take political positions is a kind of "centrist reflex." And recently, indications would seem to show that little attention is given to statements pub-

[91] Dansette, *Destin*, p. 389. Cf. Also interview with Jean Villot.

lished by the MFR or JAC. The rural population is coming to have the same political reactions as the rest of French society.[92]

Perhaps the greatest obstacle to judging the impact of rural Catholic Action is the Catholic character of many rural areas in France—at least of those areas where Catholic Action has been able to develop most rapidly.[93] A worker who joins a Catholic Action group is choosing to be "different" from the mass of his coworkers and so will stand out. But this is not true in the rural areas where the majority is still actively Catholic. Here joining Catholic Action is a normal thing to do, and may reflect very little personal conviction.

IV. A Note on Catholic Action in the Bourgeoisie

A third "milieu" in which Catholic Action is organized is the French bourgeoisie. But Catholic Action has a very minor role in the bourgeoisie, despite its general adherence to religion. Paradoxically, Catholic organizations other than Catholic Action find easy access to the bourgeoisie, and have multiplied there. Perhaps this is because certain Catholic publications or groups of "Catholic inspiration" seem to be more in harmony with the middle-class environment than the Catholic Action formula. Also, the apostolic needs of the bourgeoisie are less apparent (though probably no less real) than the needs of the working class. Insofar as Catholic Action in the bourgeoisie does exist, it will be interesting to compare its form with the form of Catholic Action in other milieux. This will indicate something about the nature of the milieux and the ability of Catholic Action to conform to different social contexts.

The most characteristic feature of bourgeois or middle-class

[92] Farmers read the same periodicals as other social groups, according to *Les Paysans et la Politique*, p. 303. Their voting habits, outside of extremist parties, follow the habits of other groups. *ibid.*, p. 49.

[93] The MFR is strong in Catholic areas, but not in all of them. Why there should be Catholic areas where the MFR is weak is not entirely clear. A rock-ribbed traditionalist clergy might offer some obstacles, as noted before. See the maps at the end of the book.

Catholic Action is its extreme variety—reflecting the diversity of the milieu. There are a number of professional groups more or less attached to Catholic Action (groups for engineers, doctors, lawyers, etc.) none of which has any political value. The main Catholic Action youth organizations and the main adult group are both divided into various subgroups depending on "social nuance." Thus, young people from the aristocracy, from the upper bourgeoisie, from the professional classes, from the "shopkeeping middle class" will each have their separate local organisms. Their "nuance," of course, depends on the social position of their parents. Furthermore, the main adult group has separate local units for men and women; it does not emphasize the family as much as the MFR.[94] These divisions seem to corroborate the impression that the French bourgeoisie and middle classes are really a number of distinct "milieux" without any common feelings binding them closely together.

A second distinguishing characteristic of the main Catholic Action groups in the bourgeoisie is their philosophy of action. Activities are almost wholly pious; temporal action, even the harmless-sounding "civic education," is rejected as a major goal.[95] Furthermore, there is no attempt to organize any mass action; all the emphasis is on individual contacts and conversion of friends and associates by the active Christian witness.

The middle-class orientation of Catholic Action is reflected in the membership of the two main youth groups, *Jeunesse Indépendente Chrétienne* (JIC) and JICF, and in the adult group, *Action Catholique Indépendente* (ACI). There is no mass following for any of these groups; everyone is considered a *militant* or active member. The ACI includes 30,000 active members, or about the same as the ACO.[96] The JICF, which is the oldest of the three and the "parent" of the other two, now includes around 8,000 members, while the JIC, perhaps

[94] *L'ACI à Lourdes* (Paris: ACI, 1958), p. 116.

[95] *ibid.*, p. 109.

[96] Interview with Michèle Lesoeur, national officer of the ACI, March 17, 1959.

because it seems like the boys' auxiliary to the JICF, is barely alive, with a small membership, little enthusiasm, and no social significance.[97]

Almost in spite of themselves, bourgeois Catholic Action groups often incur difficulties from the local clergy. In many areas the curé believes that separate ACI or JICF groups merely weaken the structure of the parish without bringing much in the way of positive results. Furthermore, General Catholic Action, which is largely middle-class, is much more successful than ACI, and is based directly on the parish.

As might be expected, relations between the ACI and General Catholic Action are often less than cordial. But on the other hand there are rather close ties between ACI and Worker Catholic Action. One reason is that between ACO and ACI there is no competition for the same clientele. There are frequent meetings between ACI and ACO leaders, and between those of JOC and JIC. In its publications the ACI shows a great deference toward ACO and toward the working class in general. In this sense, ACI seems to embody the best of the nineteenth-century Catholic Social movement, without indulging in its paternalism. However, this has probably made ACI penetration into the French bourgeoisie more difficult, since many more conservative members of this class do not understand the close ties with worker organizations.

It would be hard to find much politically-important activity in the JIC-JICF or the ACI. Thus, these groups can be given a summary treatment. There are neither the many direct statements of political importance characteristic of the JOC nor the indirect importance that large size and enthusiasm give to the MFR. The publications of each group are not read outside the confines of the group and contain little political news of importance. There is not even any encouragement to participate in temporal organizations as a "Christian nucleus." This is something that is tolerated but not emphasized.

[97] Interview with Marguerite Guilhem, national officer of the JICF, March 18, 1959.

CATHOLIC ACTION:

One exception to the apolitical behavior of bourgeois Catholic Action groups is *Recherches*, the publication of older boys in the JIC. From time to time one finds articles on political events, although they are never much emphasized. With some exceptions, articles seem progressive in tone. Nevertheless, during the May 1958 crisis, *Recherches* criticized the Deputies: "They only know how to jabber, compromise principles, dodge issues, and delay decisions." In the face of this, "the young people in general . . . would not have opposed a mild dictatorship."[98] Between the Korean War and 1956 there was much criticism of the international posture of the United States; in one issue, a writer thought the U.S. was "sliding down the fatal slope that leads irresistibly to war with the U.S.S.R."[99] In internal politics, *Recherches* criticized certain organizations of the right wing, even those which were Catholic: "*Homme Nouveau* . . . constantly confuses the cause of God with an extremist and intransigent traditionalism. . . ."[100]

The JIC-JICF and the ACI are not politically effective groups. But their milieu is as difficult to work in as the working class. The French bourgeoisie lacks a strong tradition of organized action and thus cannot undertake the activities of a JOC or an MFR. And there are too many other Catholic groups which a bourgeois would feel more at home in. Why should a bourgeois bother with the piety of the ACI *Courrier des Militants*, when *France Catholique* will give him all the news of the world in a Christian perspective and better defend his own middle-class values? Why encourage youngsters to join the JIC when the Catholic scouting movement, with hundreds of thousands of youngsters, mostly from middle-class families, will also inculcate Christian values? Fogarty shows that in Holland and Belgium the middle classes have succeeded in fostering active Catholic Action groups.[101] In France, the diver-

98 *Recherches*, June 1958, p. 4.
99 *ibid.*, April 10, 1951, p. 9.
100 *ibid.*, February 25, 1951, p. 17.
101 Fogarty, *op.cit.*, pp. 260-261.

sity of the bourgeoisie and the existence of a large "traditional" element that prefers more orthodox Church activity seem to doom the future evolution of bourgeois Catholic Action groups.[102]

V. General Catholic Action

A. INTRODUCTION

French Catholic Action operates on two basic principles: action within a milieu, and unspecified, or "general" action. The two General Catholic Action groups are the "giants" of all Catholic Action: *Action Catholique Générale des Hommes* (ACGH), and *Action Catholique Générale des Femmes* (ACGF).

The differences between specialized and General Catholic Action are both structural and apostolic. The heart of General Catholic Action (ACG) is the parish, rather than a local milieu or professional group. Working in the parish, with people who are already Catholic, ACG's role is to strengthen the Christian community rather than extend it through "missionary" activities. The idea is to make the parish a more attractive institution for lukewarm Catholics and to make it more hospitable to the new dedicated Catholics attracted to the Church by specialized groups.[103]

The parish focus of ACG does not in itself limit its political impact. If all practicing Catholics in France were to be forged into a "community," with standardized "Catholic" reactions to temporal events, this would be the most important political force in France. However, as we shall see, ingrown dissensions among Catholics and the limited goals which ACG has set for itself make this potential impact unattainable.

B. ORGANIZATION AND PHILOSOPHY OF ACTION

Both ACGF and ACGH evolved from Catholic pressure groups of the interwar period. ACGH came from the *Fédéra-*

[102] Cf. Folliet, *Présence de l'Eglise*, pp. 108-109.
[103] Cf. *De la Ligue à l'ACGF* (Paris: ACGF, 1954), *passim.*

tion Nationale Catholique, formed by General de Castelnau in 1924 to combat the laic policies of the newly-elected legislature. The group continued to take an active part in political events down to World War II. By its origins it was definitely on the conservative end of the political spectrum. It is claimed that over three million Catholic men joined its ranks, and were the principal cause for the defeat of Herriot's laic policy toward Alsace Lorraine.[104] In 1945 the ACA decided to remove the Federation from the partisan arena while keeping its organizational setup and bringing it in line with the older specialized Catholic Action movements.[105]

For a certain time the newspaper *La France Catholique* was the spokesman for the ACGH. But its partisan stands were incompatible with the Hierarchy's conception of ACG activity. *France Catholique* was useful to French Catholicism, however, so it was not discontinued—merely made "independent" of the ACGH.[106]

ACGF can trace its lineage back to the Catholic women's organizations established at the turn of the century to fight Combes and the other champions of *laïcisme*. "There was an evolution from the attitude of necessary resistance, to a constructive attitude of being present, as witnesses, in the community."[107] Thus, both the General Catholic Action groups have a common heritage of political activity in defense of the threatened Church. Once the threat of *laïcisme* disappeared, the Hierarchy decided to transform existing groups into more pious and apostolic auxiliaries to the clergy.

General Catholic Action has been established in most parishes of any size. ACGF claims to exist in no less than 28,000, or over nine tenths of all French parishes. ACGH claims

104 *France-Monde Catholique*, No. 189, April 1959, p. 2.

105 Cf. Brochure, *A la Decouverte de l'ACGH* (Paris: ACGH, 1959), p. 9.

106 However, the positions of *France Catholique* still parallel those of the leaders of ACGH. The Editor of *France Catholique*, Jean le Cour Grandmaison, is also the Honorary President of ACGH, and both organizations share the same building.

107 *De la Ligue à l'ACGF* (brochure).

7,000 parish groups. However, there are no stringent rules governing membership; in many of the 28,000 parishes the curé has simply asked a group of pious women to pay for a subscription to *Echo des Françaises*. In each parish a chaplain guides the activity of the Catholic Action group. Generally it is the curé himself. In those parishes where there are active laymen, ACG is further divided into "teams." For ACGH these teams deal with information and publicity, distribution of Catholic publications, liturgy, Catholic schools, and other tasks of little political significance. The ACGF teams deal with family instruction, library service, charitable aid, and civic education. Some of these teams are quite important and will be dealt with in the next section. All the teams depend on the active members of ACG, stimulated in the first instance by their curés. There seems to be little positive role for the hundreds of thousands of nominal members of ACG.

If it lacks wide enthusiasm and dedication, ACG does have very impressive membership figures. According to ACGF, there are over two million women affiliated with the organization. The mass publication, *Echo des Françaises*, now prints around 2,100,000 copies per month. This makes the ACGF the largest organization in France and gives *Echo des Françaises* the largest circulation of any French publication![108] ACGH, according to Dansette, has around 600,000 members.[109] However, the mass publication of ACGH, *France-Monde Catholique*, which theoretically should go to all members, has a circulation of around 260,000.[110] Even this is a very respectable figure.

The ACGF has made an interesting breakdown of its membership by social class. According to its figures between 50 and 75 per cent of its members are either in a farming or in a working-class family. Another ACGF study shows that most members come from the North, the Northeast (including areas like

[108] Chaigneau, *Les Ouvriers dans la Moisson*, p. 99.

[109] Dansette, *Destin*, p. 413.

[110] Interview with M. Lecomte, editorial writer of *France-Monde Catholique*, March 17, 1959.

the Marne Department, outside the deeply Catholic area of France), and scattered Departments of the Northwest and the South.[111] There are some "Catholic" areas where the ACGF has not taken root, notably Côtes-du-Nord and Haut-Rhin. The reason for this, confided an ACGF official, is the animosity of certain traditionalist priests who object to any laymen's initiatives, as well as hostility from some dynamic priests who would prefer such Catholic Action groups as the MFR.

To interpret membership figures properly at least two facts must be kept in mind.

First, as indicated, most members of ACG are simply "dues-paying," and do nothing more than receive the monthly publications. The publications themselves have to describe the basic aims and activities of the organizations for the many members who ignore them.[112]

Second, the membership figures, although large, could actually be evidence of stagnation. The ancestor of the ACGH is said to have had three million members soon after being founded in 1924.[113] And the precursor of ACGF was already vaunting its two million members in the 1930's.[114]

To have a more reliable idea of the strength of these organizations, the publications destined for active members only must be examined. *Militantes ACGF* (formerly *Notre Tâche*) has a circulation approaching 160,000 according to ACGF files. The ACGH publication *Animateurs* has 10,000 circulation. Though these figures are not large compared to the mass ACG membership, they indicate nonetheless a substantial core of active parish workers. This core is still among the most impressive social groupings in France today, at least in numbers. Nor is it unimportant to have over 10,000 parish priests working to recruit ACG members among the faithful in the parish.[115]

[111] Information from private files of ACGF.

[112] Cf. *Echo des Françaises*, November 1958, p. 8.

[113] *France-Monde Catholique*, No. 189, April 1959, p. 2.

[114] According to *La Ligue en Marche*, undated brochure, there were 1.8 million in 1933.

[115] *Courrier des Aumôniers*, newsletter for ACG chaplains, has a circulation of 10,000.

The main goal of ACG is to make the parish into a "living community." This is the Church's attempt to renovate a structure which in many cases seems out of tune with modern life.[116] Because ACG is working toward this goal, it must be satisfied with less freedom of action than its cousins of specialized Catholic Action. The latter are best judges of the requirements of their milieux. But in the parish, the leader and the best judge is bound to be the priest himself.

C. ACTIVITIES OF POLITICAL IMPORTANCE

Like other Catholic Action groups, ACGH and ACGF have an indirect political significance through giving their members a "Catholic perspective" on life, and a direct significance through other activity and published opinions. However, the structure and goals of ACG have modified both its direct and its indirect political value. Though the practice of *revision de vie* is supposed to be carried out by all ACG members, in practice only a small minority ever participates in *revision de vie* sessions. The minority is certainly no larger than the circulation of the ACG active member magazines.[117] It is expected that some members will be stimulated by their experiences in ACG to engage in social and political activity; but such activity is not made a prerequisite for joining ACG, as it is for ACO.[118]

The politically-important activities of General Catholic Action have a different focus from those of other Catholic Action groups. Being based on the parish, which usually is the same as a local commune, ACG groups naturally are interested in the activities of local government. The social, medical, and other activities carried on in French local government are all fair game for ACG comments and criticism, especially since these areas are generally outside the bounds of virulent partisanship.

Local ACG activities can be put under three headings. First,

[116] Mgr. Ménager, *Mandat de l'ACGF: Ses Exigences* (brochure) (Paris: ACGF, 1958).

[117] Confirmed by Mlle. des Gachons, head of civic education, ACGF, in an interview, March 19, 1959.

[118] Cf. *A la Decouverte de l'ACGH*, pp. 3-4.

the active ACG members usually organize a propaganda and information team in the parish which distributes tracts, puts up posters, and even goes door-to-door working for "Catholic" causes. One of its chief jobs is disseminating information on Catholic schools, for which ACG works closely with the APEL.[119] Tracts are always distributed before all elections, local or national, recalling to the general public that they should vote only for candidates inspired by the Catholic social doctrine, that a Catholic cannot vote for a Communist, etc.[120]

The second local ACG activity occurs only in parishes where there are particularly dynamic members. In such parishes, an information center is established, whose main task is distributing publications of Catholic inspiration. These centers are supposed to distribute all such publications without discrimination. However, groups sometimes refuse to distribute certain left-wing magazines, notably *Témoignage Chrétien*, because of their views on Algeria.

The third activity is a general effort toward civic education. This is carried on primarily by the ACGF, while the information centers are usually staffed by ACGH members. ACGF members themselves are a prime audience for material from various Catholic agencies specializing in political and social information.[121] Complete dossiers of civic material are sent from these agencies and from the ACGF national office to members in all parts of France, with the hope that this material will filter down to the mass of ACGF women and will influence parishes where the Church has remained strong.[122]

Seldom do general Catholic Action groups act directly as pressure groups on the national level to influence legislation. However, in a truly exceptional move, the head of ACGF, Vicomtesse de Curel, wrote to René Pleven, head of govern-

119 See Chapter Eight.

120 See the ACGH tract on the 1958 elections, "Partis, Programmes, Candidats," distributed in all parishes by the ACG and by other groups, including the APEL.

121 See Chapter Five.

122 Information from interview with Mlle. des Gachons.

ment in 1951, to urge state aid for Catholic schools: "Families have an inalienable right to choose their school. The State has the duty to make this choice materially possible. . . . Well, then, why so many interminable debates? . . . Is this not a contrivance unworthy of a democratic country? Our elected representatives must realize that we Catholic women and mothers, particularly the younger among us, have firmly decided to demand this fundamental liberty: the practical possibility to raise our children in schools of our choice, where the education is infused with our own convictions. . . . In the name of the 2,200,000 women of the LFACF, and their 5,000,000 children."[123]

The published statements of ACG on political subjects differ somewhat from those of ACO or the MFR. General Catholic Action groups have not completely lost the habits of their predecessors; they are more anxious to defend all interests of the Church that seem menaced by government or private groups. ". . . The ACGF alerts public opinion on today's main problems: the school, the family, youth, and when certain religious or family freedoms are menaced, it intercedes, in the name of all its members, before public authorities."[124]

Certain articles in ACG publications refer to elections of national importance. For example, in 1946 the main ACGF publication, *Echo des Françaises*, bitterly opposed many principles in the first version of the Fourth Republic Constitution, subsequently rejected by French voters. Omitting explicit reference to freedom of education was termed "an intolerable blow to the inalienable rights of families."[125] "France is the country of liberty," wrote *Echo des Françaises* in 1946; "she proved it May 5 in defeating the Constitution."[126] However nothing was said about the next draft of the Constitution, which the French electorate approved. For the 1958 referendum the comments of ACGF and ACGH seemed quite moderate and circumspect,

[123] *Echo des Françaises*, October 1951, p. 1. LFACF stands for the former name of the ACGF.

[124] *ibid.*, November 1958, p. 8.

[125] *ibid.*, April 1946, p. 2.

[126] *ibid.*, June 1946, p. 1.

with only the slightest hint of partiality toward the new Constitution: "We deplore that the proposed Constitution does not mention anywhere GOD. . . . However we note with satisfaction that the definition, taken from the preceding Constitution, of the "Republic indivisible and laic" is now modified by the following two phrases [Constitution quoted]. . . . None of the *principles* of the proposed Constitution being against Church doctrine, Catholic voters can accept it if the means that it provides seem to correspond to the present needs and permanent necessities of France. . . ."[127]

The following editorial from *Echo des Françaises* is a marvel of subtlety, but probably put its readers in a psychological state to approve the 1958 Constitution: "By our vote we shall help establish the destiny of France, our living conditions and those of our children. . . . To make this choice, let us go beyond, if necessary, our personal preferences. Let us consider at stake the future of all who live in our parishes, in the towns and villages of France and the overseas territories. Let us not stop at our own self interest but let us seek the common good of the whole country, even though this might require certain sacrifices from us."[128]

In the legislative elections of 1958 the national ACG publications were generally moderate and nonpartisan, though readers were reminded that not only Communism but also "Marxism" had been condemned by the Church.[129]

But on the school question ACG does not compromise. *Echo des Françaises* urged Catholic women to join the APEL at the time the Barangé Law was being considered.[130] At times a "thesis" position is presented, which would seem to forbid Catholic students in the public schools: ". . . Justice, equality, and liberty demand that parents have at their disposition schools reflecting their convictions: neutral if they are nonbe-

[127] *France-Monde Catholique*, No. 183, October 1958, p. 4.
[128] *Echo des Françaises*, October 1958, p. 1.
[129] *ibid.*, November 1958, pp. 2-3.
[130] *ibid.*, November 1951, p. 1.

lievers, confessional if they are religious."[131] Generally, after the Barangé Law, ACG put less stress on the school question, but many times before the 1959 school law it referred to principles of "effective freedom" which can be guaranteed only by more state subsidies of Catholic schools, so poorer families can have Catholic school tuitions reduced.[132] However, the public school is not maligned. The "hypothesis" that Catholic children patronize state schools is recognized. The Bishop of Arras himself, in an ACGH-sponsored brochure, recognized that "toward public school children we have duties also."[133] ACGH urges Catholics who send their children to public schools to support them loyally, and make sure of their religious neutrality.[134]

In balance, the published statements of ACG seem perhaps a bit more conservative than those of specialized Catholic Action groups. In any case, it seems hard to support the contention of a recent French study: "It is a fact that the League [e.g. ACGF] is actively engaged in the struggle against Communism, Socialism, and Radical-Socialism—thus in the political struggle. Whatever its protests of neutrality, let us recognize that these protests would in any case be impossible to hold. Every action on the social level has necessarily a political significance."[135]

This description seems more appropriate to the prewar ancestor of ACGF than to the present-day organization. Recently ACGF has made very few anti-Socialist or anti-Radical statements, and they are always in general and moderate terms. Its anti-Communism is no worse than that of many other moderate groups.

[131] *France-Monde Catholique*, No. 104, November 1950, p. 1.

[132] See for example *France-Monde Catholique*, No. 184, November 1958, p. 4, and *Echo des Françaises*, November 1958, pp. 2-3.

[133] Mgr. Perrin, *Directives Catholiques en Matière Scolaire* (Paris: FNAC, 1953).

[134] *La FNAC à l'Oeuvre dans le Domaine de l'Ecole* (brochure), (Paris: FNAC, 1953).

[135] Mattei Dogan and Jacques Narbonne, *Les Françaises Face à la Politique* (Paris: Armand Colin, 1955), p. 128.

Outside the strictly political sphere, the economic doctrines of ACG also have a certain interest. ACGH particularly is committed to an enlightened classical liberalism which seems quite close to the views of Antoine Pinay, former Economics Minister in the Debré Government. It also coincides with the economic views of *La France Catholique*, and of the French bourgeoisie in general: "The strict reorganization of our finances and our budget . . . reflects a firm desire for realism, courage, national economic health, and lastly morality, by the return to a franc which really is a franc."[136]

D. THE POLITICAL EFFECTIVENESS OF GENERAL CATHOLIC ACTION

ACGH and ACGF have the largest membership of any Catholic organization. Yet even compared to other Catholic Action groups their activity in the partisan political realm seems almost negligible. *Echo des Françaises* and *France-Monde Catholique* do not lack articles on current events, but no partisan implications can be found in most instances. When an election occurs, there are articles explaining that Catholics must vote but not even suggesting which parties seem "best." The Algerian crisis evoked the necessity of praying for peace. The events of May 1958 inspired articles on the crisis of French civic consciousness, but, unlike other Catholic groups, ACG drew no partisan conclusions from these events. ACGH protested mildly against the army uprising in Algeria in April 1961, but ACGF did not do even this.

The most important reason for the lack of political effectiveness is the position of ACG in the Church, under the wing of the parish priest. In part also the ineffectiveness is due to the decentralization of ACG into practically autonomous local units. Finally, ACG groups are more completely "ecclesiastical" than other Catholic groups. They exist to perfect the local unit of the Church, not to influence any particular social class.

[136] *France-Monde Catholique*, No. 187, February 1959, p. 1.

VI. Miscellaneous Catholic Action Groups

A. IN THE ACADEMIC WORLD

Certain professional groups are well-suited to the Catholic Action formula. However, in most professions, even when the Catholic element has a predominant place, Catholic Action groups are generally small and without political significance. Certain groups, however, especially those in the academic world, should be briefly mentioned.

French students are served by two Catholic Action groups. The *Jeunesse Etudiante Chrétienne* (JEC) is much like the other specialized youth groups already considered. However, the JEC is the smallest of these groups and the one which seems the least able to fulfill its apostolic goals. From its creation in the early 1930's down to World War II it seemed dynamic; but since the war the JEC has declined, both in activities and in numbers. At present the JEC magazine for university students has only 1,000 circulation.[137]

The *Fédération Française des Etudiants Catholiques* (FFEC) was organized in 1922, before the Catholic Action movement was started. It is not a homogeneous group, but a loose federation of Catholic student clubs from both public and private schools. Each club has great independence of action; many antedate the FFEC itself and none depends on the FFEC to attract its students. Each has its own particular activities. This independence is probably the reason why the FFEC and the JEC have not merged. The newer, more hierarchical Catholic Action principle would not be accepted by most constituent elements of the FFEC.

Before the war there was a sizeable difference in behavior between the two groups. The JEC represented the socially-minded avant-garde of students while the FFEC was more

[137] JEC seems more dynamic among secondary school pupils. It has been estimated that its total membership is 50,000, and undoubtedly most of these are from the secondary level. See *I.C.I.*, June 1, 1957, p. 6.

spiritually oriented.[138] Since the war this distinction has largely disappeared, as the JEC devotes more of its time to spiritual activities. The main difference in goals now seems to be that the JEC emphasizes converting non-Catholic students, while the FFEC concerns itself with students who are already active participants in the life of the Church.[139]

One of the peculiarities of the student environment is its rapid turnover rate. If JEC establishes a "Christian nucleus" in a certain classroom or field of study, in two years all the members of the group will have left and all the work must be begun again. The JEC staff suffers yearly crises as its most experienced members graduate and leave. So each year the organization has slightly different methods of working. In addition, there seems to be an inherent instability in the student environment. As Dansette says, "The student world is fickle, unstable, permeated with ideological and sentimental currents which die as soon as they are born. It is not astonishing that the history of the JEC does not enjoy a continued development like that of the JAC."[140]

The political activities of the FFEC are virtually nonexistent. The JEC acts within the French national students' union, in constant (and it appears cordial) relation with the Communist student organization, among others. This has been condemned in some quarters, but the directors of the JEC seem undisturbed by this proximity to the devil.[141] The Communists do not control the policies of the national student group; in fact, the latter seemed willing to compromise with certain Catholics on the school aid controversy.[142]

The JEC long had a policy of taking sides on issues, even those of political significance, for the value that this "commit-

[138] Dansette, *Destin*, pp. 101-103.

[139] Interview with Jean Bize, General Secretary of the JEC, March 18, 1959.

[140] Dansette, *Destin*, p. 103.

[141] See Claude Sales, *Où Va la JEC?* (Paris: Editions de l'Epi, 1954), p. 55. In 1960, Communist and Catholic youth organizations issued joint appeals for ending the Algerian war.

[142] See Chapter Eight.

ment" gave students: "The positions taken have a teaching objective: to develop in young people a consciousness of all their responsibilities. . . . The Movement chooses a certain problem, on which it publicly proclaims its opinion, to give members the habit of judging problems in reference to Christianity, and not to impose on them a doctrine for the question."[143] This is a rather mystifying philosophy: take a stand not because you firmly believe in it, but because it will give valuable experience —for taking stands in the future! It reflects a certain tendency of French intellectuals to "commit themselves" verbally to positions that they would never think of defending by actions.

At any rate, the JEC commits itself on issues from time to time, hoping that most people take it seriously. However, except for the Algerian problem, the JEC tries not to pick the most controversial political issues. During the debates preceding the 1959 school law the JEC was quite cautious. It regretted the fact that a "solution" had not been found, but did not advocate any specific measures itself.[144]

The JEC might seem at first view to have no political importance and little organizational effectiveness, but like all Catholic Action youth groups, it trains youngsters for positions of leadership as adults, and trains them in applying Catholic principles to their lives. From the JEC will come many of the future leaders of the entire French society, rather than leaders of a particular milieu.[145]

Teachers also have their Catholic Action movements; in fact there are two principal ones, just as there are two CFTC teachers' unions, one dealing with private school teachers and the other with those in public school. *Paroisse Universitaire* is the main group representing public school professors. It has enjoyed a steady growth as the Christian spirit advances in the state schools. The private school group is *Les Enseignants Chrétiens*. It is naturally interested in the question of aid to Catholic

143 Claude Sales, *op.cit.*, pp. 52 and 53.

144 *Action Catholique Etudiante*, February 1959, p. 12.

145 The JEC has furnished more than its share of leaders in the ACJF, and many top officials of the MRP. See Chapter Seven.

schools, but all other civic and social questions seem outside its scope of interest.

The presence of an official Catholic group in the public schools is recognition of the "hypothesis" in the school question mentioned in Chapter Two. The Church does not just tolerate Catholics in the public schools, it encourages them (now professors, perhaps later students). Pope Pius XII himself confirmed this in a talk to Catholic public school teachers: "Courage, confidence, perseverance! Your task is too fine, too obviously blessed by God. . . . May you gain sympathy for your work from many of those who, in good faith, still consider it with a certain mistrust and reserve. This is one of Our most earnest desires."[146]

The Church gives its official blessing to the double apostolic goal of *Paroisse Universitaire*: respect for the Christian faith and respect for the public school. However, the temporal positions of *Paroisse Universitaire* members often conflict with the aims of major Catholic groups. Many of its members are in the laic teachers' union which opposed the principle of the Barangé Law and the 1959 school law.

B. "PAX CHRISTI"

Founded in 1952, *Pax Christi*, a unique organization even closer to the Hierarchy than Catholic Action, includes clergymen as well as laymen in its ranks. All Catholic Action is based on social structures; *Pax Christi*, however, has a functional basis: it is concerned solely with questions of peace. Its members come from all walks of life and all countries. It was founded on the initiative of Cardinal Feltin, who is now the international president. In France there are only 20,000 in its ranks, but among them are many influential individuals, including bishops and heads of lay Catholic groups.

Pax Christi, according to one interpretation, was started to channel Catholics away from the Communist-inspired peace movement which in the early 1950's attracted a wide audience

[146] Quoted in *Le Monde*, April 4, 1959, p. 6.

in France.[147] It seems to have a "progressive" outlook itself; the two vice presidents of *Pax Christi* are Joseph Folliet and Maurice Vaussard, both close to *Témoignage Chrétien.*

In discussing political questions *Pax Christi* limits itself to statements already made by bishops or clergymen, and comments on these statements. Taking advantage of the wide diversity of opinions within the Hierarchy, *Pax Christi* seems to select those statements which back up its own view of political reality. For example, on pages eight and nine of *Pax Christi,* Number 71, June 1959, a number of episcopal statements on Algeria are presented. One statement criticizes the French and Moslem extremists who "call on passions and violence." Another justifies a priest aiding a wounded rebel: "Every priest has the right and the duty to give aid and assistance to the sick or wounded, whoever they may be." Two statements from Algerian bishops are presented. One states ". . . we shall get out of the impasse only by seeking loyal relations and dialogues in the most diverse groups and at all levels of responsibility." The other urges ". . . accepting contacts, a dialogue always to be taken up again because it is never achieved. . . ." These statements had considerable political value before de Gaulle formulated his "three choices" for Algeria's future. Through its quotations, *Pax Christi* seems to have favored autonomy or even independence for Algeria long before they became official government policies. It quotes a priest who favors, ". . . the fundamental right of any people with the proper means, to guide itself to independence while considering the national and international common good."[148]

During the May 1958 crisis, *Pax Christi* distributed 1,500,000 tracts urging all Frenchmen to pray for peace.[149] Aid in spreading the message was given by all Catholic Action and Catholic social groups, whose leaders in Paris were all in touch with

[147] *La Nef,* January 1954, pp. 102-103.

[148] *Pax Christi,* No. 61, July 1958, p. 5.

[149] However, the average circulation of *Pax Christi* is around 14,000 per month. Once a year a special edition has much wider circulation. See OJD *Officiel,* 130, October 1959, p. 25.

Cardinal Feltin. Once the de Gaulle government was in power, *Pax Christi* did not object to it. It quoted Cardinal Liénart: "We must pray God to give those who hold the responsibility of power the necessary courage and lucidity to maintain unity among all Frenchmen."[150]

Pax Christi might be one of the "waves of the future" for French Catholicism. If a lowering of attachment to social or professional milieux in France should develop, the *Pax Christi* functional formula could be substituted for the Catholic Action formula. But for the present, it is more an instrument for increasing the audience of the French Hierarchy, or at least of those officials whose views are similar to the "line" of *Pax Christi*. It is also an attempt, albeit ineffective, to coordinate all the Catholic organizations on questions of world peace.

The Hierarchy could have left the initiative of *Pax Christi* wholly to laymen. The fact that priests have associated themselves with its work might indicate that the problem of world peace is exceptionally vital for the French bishops. Or it might indicate their displeasure with some of the political ideas of certain Catholic Action groups—which, it should be recalled, also commit the Church to a certain degree.

Though their main goals are apostolic and nonpolitical, Catholic Action groups can make their views felt on many temporal issues. Through their position within French Catholicism they have access to a widespread audience for all their actions, whether temporal or spiritual. However, it cannot be said that Catholic Action has one single political impact on French life. Many members of Catholic Action simply do not care about political matters; these are not what attracted them to the Church. Furthermore, the various Catholic Action groups have not wanted to create an interrelated elite with common religious-based political reactions. Each group needs its elite for its own purposes. Finally, no single political impact has been

[150] *ibid.*, p. 2. During the crisis of April 1961 Pax Christi reminded Frenchmen of their "duty to obey only the legitimate authorities, guardians of the common good." See *La Croix*, April 26, 1961, p. 4.

possible because no political question is viewed in exactly the same way by all Catholic Action groups. In its reactions each group reflects its particular milieu.

TABLE 1

The Chief Catholic Action Publications and Their Circulation

GROUP	PUBLICATIONS FOR MASS (PLUS CIRCULATION IF KNOWN)	PUBLICATIONS FOR LEADERS (PLUS CIRCULATION IF KNOWN)
(Working Class)		
JOC	*Jeunesse Ouvrière* 30,000	*Lettre aux Fédéraux*
ACO	*Témoignage*	*Courrier des Responsables*
(Rural World)		
JAC	*Jeunes Forces Rurales* 66,000	*Militant à l'Action* 18,000
JACF	*Promesses* 90,000	*En Equipe* 20,000
MFR	*Foyer Rural* 130,000 *Clair Foyer* 250,000	*Mon Village* 30,000 *Construire* 2,000
(Bourgeoisie)		
JIC	*Jeunes Equipes*	*Recherches*
JICF	*Jeunesse et Présence*	*Aux Responsables*
ACI		*Courrier des Militants*
(General)		
ACGF	*Echo des Françaises* 2,000,000	*Militantes ACGF* 160,000
ACGH	*France-Monde Catholique* 230,000	*Animateurs* 10,000
(Miscellaneous)		
FFEC	*Bulletin Mensuel d'Informations*	
JEC	*Action Catholique Etudiante* 1,000	
PAX CHRISTI	*Pax Christi* 14,000	

(For Circulation: Office de Justification de la Diffusion, *Officiel*, 1957-1960. *Annuaire, Services Généraux de l'Episcopat*, 1955. *I.C.I.*, May 15, 1960, p. 20.)

FIGURE 2. Chart of Main Catholic Action Groups

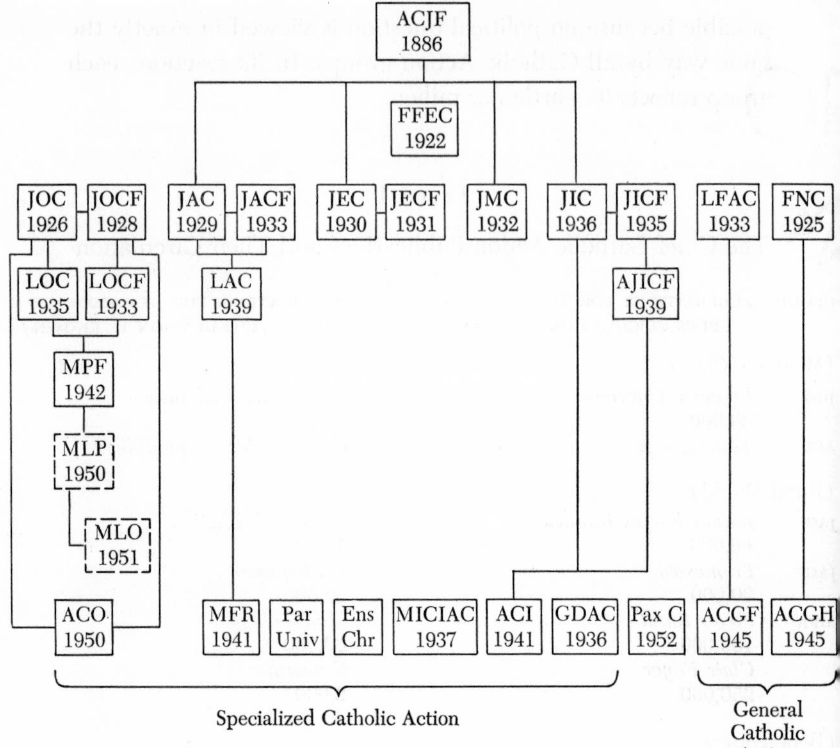

Source: Dansette, *Destin du Catholicisme Français*, pp. 86-87. Simplified and revised.

Abbreviations (see also List of Abbreviations at the beginning of the book):

AJICF	*Anciennes de la Jeunesse Indépendente Chrétienne Féminine*
ENS. CHR.	*Les Enseignants Chrétiens*
FNC	*Fédération Nationale Catholique*
GDAC	*Groupements Diocésains d'Action Catholique*
JMC	*Jeunesse Maritime Chrétienne*
LAC	*Ligue Agricole Chrétienne*
LFAC	*Ligue Féminine d'Action Catholique*
LOC	*Ligue Ouvrière Chrétienne*
MICIAC	*Mouvement d'Ingénieurs et de Chefs d'Industrie d'Action Catholique*
MLO	*Mouvement de Libération Ouvrière*
MLP	*Mouvement de Libération du Peuple*
MPF	*Mouvement Populaire des Familles*
PAR. UNIV.	*Paroisse Universitaire*
PAX C.	*Pax Christi*

FIGURE 3. Main Hierarchy Controls over a "Typical" Catholic Action Group

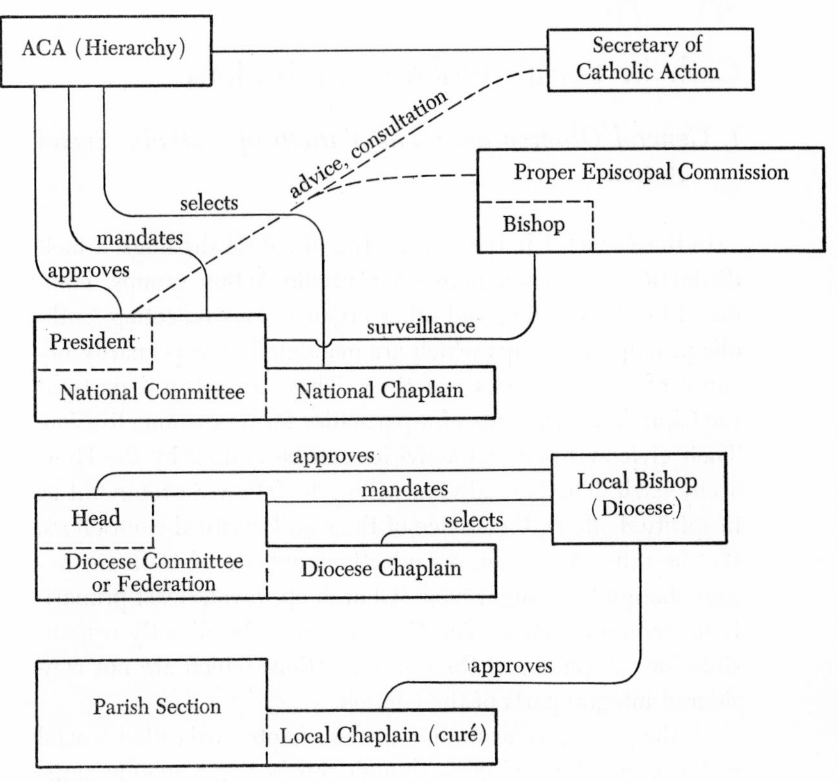

Catholic Social Action Organizations

I. General Observations: The Variety of Catholic Social Action

In the French Church, always full of subtle shadings, a tacit distinction has arisen between Catholic Action groups, mandated by the Church, and other organizations reflecting Catholic principles. Groups which are mandated exist primarily because of their religious functions. They are integral parts of the Church, instruments of a particular form of evangelization. Their civic and political activities can be limited by the Hierarchy itself. They are always willing to follow, in temporal as in spiritual affairs, the advice of their ecclesiastical counsellors. On the other hand, the organizations outside of Catholic Action, though they might have "Church approval," exist primarily for temporal action. The Church cannot be directly responsible for the actions of these organizations which are not considered integral parts of the Church.

All the groups to be studied in this chapter are called "social action organizations" even though this is not a wholly satisfactory term. However, the term is the one which is most often employed in France, and no more convenient one can be found.[1] Catholic social action organizations date for the most part from the era when Church and state were in active conflict. Their primary goal was to support the interests of the Church in what seemed like a life-and-death struggle. As the years passed, the growth of mutual tolerance and the appearance of Catholic Action groups which are even closer to the

[1] See, for example, Henri Rollet, *Sur le Chantier Social: L'Action Sociale des Catholiques en France (1870-1940)* (Lyon, Editions de la Chronique Sociale, 1955). See also Chaigneau, *Les Ouvriers dans la Moisson*, chapter VIII, "Institutions et associations pour l'action sociale."

Hierarchy modified the structure of certain social action groups. New groups arose which reflected new social problems, so "Catholic social action" gradually became a residual term which included all Catholic groups not formally mandated by the Church but still closely related to it. Now the widest possible organizational types are represented in this broad category, with many different aims. The only thing in common is their distance from the Hierarchy: a "middle distance," between Catholic Action and Catholic inspiration.

Since the Hierarchy in normal situations is forced to ignore these organizations officially, they have a wide latitude in the positions which they can adopt. The Church cannot restrict their political activity as easily as it could that of Catholic Action. This activity by social action groups does not firmly commit the Hierarchy, but it is not wholly unrelated to the Church, either. The heritage of past history often creates unclear situations like this.

Many of the groups to be considered can, in fact, trace their beginnings back to the nineteenth century, and most were originally carriers of the social Catholic doctrines of nineteenth-century men such as de Mun and Harmel. Later generations have considered that these early Catholic social thinkers confused paternalism with economic justice, and the political realm with the religious realm. Such ambiguities also are part of the heritage of the groups considered here.

II. Occupational or Milieu Groups

One major division of social action organizations includes those groups representing a particular milieu or social category. Among them are the Catholic family association, the Catholic scouting group and its adult extension, the Catholic employers' association, and Catholic groups for intellectuals and women. Interestingly enough, the first three are parts of larger groupings without direct Catholic attachment. The family and scouting groups both have a special relation to the state and receive sizeable subsidies from it. All three groups are in social climates where the Church is accorded a benevolent tolerance, and in this sort of atmosphere it could be possible for Catholic groups to engage in some political activity without incurring mass hostility.[2]

The groups considered in this section all represent particular social categories, very much like the specialized Catholic Action groups. However, all are much further from the Church, and their activity has entirely different purposes. Technical and social activity is performed in and for itself, not as a means to a higher apostolic end.

A. "ASSOCIATIONS FAMILIALES CATHOLIQUES"

The major Catholic groups looking after the needs of the family in France are in a federation known as the *Associations Familiales Catholiques* (AFC). With around 50,000 members, AFC is an integral part of the semipublic National Union of Family Associations. Departmental units of AFC are integral parts of the National Union's departmental federations. The semipublic groups have very important advisory powers whenever matters concerning the family are considered by the French administration or by Parliament. But the AFC is not limited to a role within these groups. It can also act directly on behalf of its own members. Indeed, this is necessary, for on such questions as divorce or parochial school attendance semipublic bodies are forced to be neutral while Catholic doctrine would seem to indicate a firm position.

The AFC has never been given a mandate by the Hierarchy and has never claimed to act as an agent to convert non-Catholics. However, AFC activities have been approved on many occasions by the Pope and the French ACA. Pius XII himself

[2] As noted in the preceding chapter, in the working class "Catholic" and "political" seem to be mutually exclusive. Perhaps this explains why no groups of social action, where temporal and spiritual are often confused, have got a foothold in the proletariat. Groups which are successful there, the CFTC for example, must divorce themselves from the institutions of the Church and call themselves merely of Catholic inspiration.

wrote to the President of AFC, ". . . without excluding the worthy action of other Christian inspiration groups, required at times by varied conditions of milieu to take less firm stands, the Holy Father cannot but wish the continued development of your Catholic associations."[3]

One reason that stronger ties with the Hierarchy have not been established is the political role of the AFC. Another might be that, while AFC claims to represent all Catholic family interests, until recently certain Catholic family organizations from the working class have chosen not to affiliate with the AFC because of its conservative tendencies.

On the national political scene the AFC has worked in several fields. The divorce laws now on the statute books in France have been consistently opposed, as has any tendency to treat the head of a large household on the same economic or tax footing as the single person.[4] The AFC has been particularly active in fighting for the cause of Catholic schools. Members are told that they must vote for only Parliamentary candidates formally pledged to support Catholic schools. They must also give active support to the electoral campaigns of such candidates.[5]

The AFC was supposed to specialize in matters affecting Catholics in the public schools, to avoid any duplication of effort with the APEL.[6] But the AFC has not emphasized this goal. The main reason seems to be the character of AFC members. They are not the kind who would ordinarily send their children to public school in France, so they should not be expected to be very good supporters of the public school cause.[7]

The neutral, semipublic family organization has many individual Catholics in it, including its principal national officials. Since the latter decided not to join the AFC, they evidently put

[3] Quoted in *ACCF*, undated pamphlet, p. 11. ACCF stands for *Associations Catholiques de Chefs de Famille*, former name of AFC.

[4] *ibid.*, p. 3.

[5] *Tâches Familiales*, suppl. to No. 83, July-August 1958, p. 1.

[6] See Chapter Eight. Cf. *Annuaire Catholique, 1958-59*, p. 800.

[7] Cf. exhortations in favor of Catholic schools, *Tâches Familiales*, No. 86, May-June 1959, pp. 2-3.

family matters in a different category from their Catholicism. So the people who do join the AFC by choice are generally those who are most conscious of their religion and who extend it furthest into all spheres. More than likely they are drawn toward the right wing in politics. This quality was especially apparent during the Barangé controversy in 1951. The AFC sent to each "Catholic Deputy" a letter stating the following: "We reject the materialist, brutal adventures of the Marxists; we disapprove certain of our present laws, which are excessively individualistic; we ask for the abrogation of the statist laws which tend toward Socialism and misunderstand the higher ends of the family and its head. . . . We rebel against the secularization of a society from which God is excluded; we do not accept the present divorce legislation . . . we do not agree that single men should be given the same civic rights as fathers of families."[8]

At the December 1951 meeting of the AFC it was not surprising that one of the speakers was Pierre Lemaire, director of *Paternité-Maternité*, one of the most extreme right-wing Catholic publications. The above quotation, from the AFC official publication *Tâches Familiales*, shows that the AFC has not advanced very far from its position before and just after World War I, when it was anti-Masonic and an active supporter of General de Castelnau. However, there is something unpredictable about the political activity of the AFC. After its extremism during the 1951 school crisis, AFC uttered not a single partisan word on the great crisis of 1958.

The importance of the AFC should not be exaggerated. Its membership figures were already over 50,000 in 1912; officially they are the same today, though this figure could well be too optimistic. The unchanging figure seems to reflect an inability to attract a large mass of Catholics, and in view of the AFC's tendency toward extremism this is not unusual.

AFC impact on political life would seem to be rather slight, either on its own or within the larger family group. Within the

[8] *Tâches Familiales*, No. 53, July 1951, pp. 2-3.

latter, its policies are circumscribed and it is clear to all that it cannot speak for "Catholicism." On its own, the AFC has freedom of political action, but its extremist orientation limits the breadth of its appeal.

B. THE SCOUTING MOVEMENT

The French Catholic scouting organization is an integral part of the general French scouting movement, and is responsible to the larger movement for its civic and temporal activity. Scouting groups are considered nonpolitical, mainly because they are heavily subsidized by the state, which asks in turn that their work be noncontroversial in nature.[9] Like scouting groups everywhere, the French scouts inculcate ideals of patriotism and service to the country, acceptable to all shades of opinion.

The whole French scouting movement is dominated by the Catholic scout group, which has almost seven times as many members as the next most important group.[10] Scouting in France seems to have little appeal to the working-class youth, so there is very little Communist penetration. There is rather a bourgeois flavor about the entire movement, which makes it all the more understandable why Catholic scouts should attract a majority.

The crisis of May 1958 coincided with a national scout encampment. This was an ideal time for the Church advisors to the movement to set forth the political usefulness of scouting and to indicate some of the principles which a regime should encompass and which a scout should desire. In short, if ever there were a time for a political "call to action," this was it. An examination of what scouts at this encampment were told will show just how far the movement dared to go.

The political struggles under the Fourth Republic were not

[9] State subsidy was over 200,000,000 old francs per year, said M. Etcheverry, of the French education ministry, interviewed June 9, 1959.

[10] Figure from Michel Rigal, General Commissioner of Catholic Scouts, in interview, March 23, 1959. According to Dansette there are now 100,000 Catholic scouts in all categories. *Destin*, p. 424.

spared criticism at the encampment. The Archbishop of Marseille wrote this to the meeting: "It is not simply the struggle among parties and political passions which slowly ripened today's crisis; it is also an imperfect knowledge of men and of situations; it is a collection of legislative texts which make it impossible to govern the country. . . . The scouts themselves cannot build the City. . . . As a Church movement, scouting can tell you in certain cases that a political stand is more in accord with the demands of Faith or incompatible with them. But scouts must remember that there is often more than one Christian solution to a civic problem. Outside Marxism, many truly free opinions present themselves, and we must carefully refrain from sanctifying or repudiating them in the name of the Church."[11]

At the encampment a lay scout leader stressed other failings of the regime: "Young people repudiate the parties that seem to seek power, not to accomplish something, but to stop others from getting power. . . . Today we are in a regime where everyone is theoretically free to do what he wants. But who can say that everyone has true freedom, for example the economic freedom to make of his life what he wants?"[12] These general, moralistic statements show that scouts usually maintain a nonpartisan attitude, even during grave social crises.

Like Catholic Action youth groups, the French scouts aim to produce a certain psychological impact on their members which will have results in their later life. In practical terms, this impact is limited to older scouts—primarily to those over eighteen, in the *Routier* organization, the equivalent of our Explorer Scouts. In the past there have been 10,000 to 15,000 *Routiers*, but recently membership has declined. Scout leaders were dismayed at the left-wing political views of some individual members, which seemed to be cultivated in local *Routier* study groups. A grave incident occurred when the *Routier* magazine, *La Route*, published eyewitness accounts of atroci-

[11] Quoted in *Le Chef*, No. 339, July-August 1958, p. 5.
[12] Quoted *ibid.*, pp. 80-81.

ties committed by the French army in Algeria. The eyewitness, Jean Muller, a *Route* leader, was killed in the war, but his accounts were well documented by others. This criticism of the Algerian situation by a Catholic scout was not well received by many conservative Church officials, and the Hierarchy eventually forced the *Route* leaders to resign.[13]

The *Routier* organization aims to create a community spirit among its members which will transcend differences in occupation or milieu. In particular, middle-class members are encouraged to try to understand the workers around them. There seems to be a certain rivalry with Catholic Action youth groups; though the *Routiers* do not try to convert, many of their other activities are paralleled in the JAC, JOC, and other groups of Catholic Action.

Scout life leaves a permanent impression on its most active members. This can be demonstrated by studying the positions of *Vie Nouvelle*, an organization set up by former *Routiers*, among others.

Vie Nouvelle includes only about 5,000 members, but it seems to have a certain influence because of the quantity of material which it publishes. Its membership comes largely from the middle class, as do the scouts themselves.[14] However, its goal is activity which can encompass all classes. It is frankly intellectual, even though it admits that its growth in the working class is inhibited by its emphasis on reflection rather than action. It has been recognized officially that "The *Vie Nouvelle* movement at present is 80 percent from a bourgeois-type milieu."[15] *Vie Nouvelle* officially calls itself a Catholic movement and has chaplains, but has not been mandated by the Church Hierarchy.

In its social ideas *Vie Nouvelle* seems quite close to the magazine *Esprit*. It favors the development of each person within a community of adherents, borrowing ideas from the

[13] See Georges Suffert, *Les Catholiques et la Gauche* (Paris: François Maspero, 1960), pp. 114-117.

[14] *Vie Nouvelle*, supplement, June 1957, p. 21.

[15] *ibid.*, p. 19.

personalist philosophy of Mounier and the Catholic principle of social solidarity.[16]

One of the goals of *Vie Nouvelle* is to bridge the gap between social classes in France; its aim is to approach the ultimate goal of a "classless society." This is a desirable end because then, ". . . all men, ex-bourgeois or ex-proletarians, will have the chance to become fully men, and an economy of needs will be substituted for an economy of profit."[17] While waiting for the ultimate goal, *Vie Nouvelle* aims to give to workers ". . . . a political culture which teaches one not to confine his activity merely to the ordinary people; a general political orientation really tending toward the liberation of the working class. . . . *Vie Nouvelle* helps workers to find a religious perspective in accord with contemporary thought."[18]

Despite its middle-class base, *Vie Nouvelle* has reached far to the left in many of its political statements. For example, it came out in unmistakable fashion against the Constitution of 1958: "We believe that those who favor the Constitution cannot decently pronounce anathema on those who reject it, and vice-versa, as long as everyone justifies his choice on hopes and demands going back to the same values. However, it seems to us, the writers of this article, more honest to take the responsibility of making a conclusion. We do so in voting 'NO.' "[19]

In addition to these positions, *Vie Nouvelle* publishes a certain number of documents, most of which are mimeographed and for use only by members, on problems of political theory, of Communism in the modern world, on the Algerian question, etc. Usually the viewpoints are similar to those of *Esprit*.

In most of its pronouncements, *Vie Nouvelle* appears to consider political life from a very abstract standpoint. There is no

[16] See Chapter Nine. Cf. Discussion on "Communities," *ibid.*, February 1959. Some *Vie Nouvelle* members even pool part of their income for joint social welfare projects. See *Témoignage Chrétien*, May 12, 1961, p. 19.

[17] *Vie Nouvelle*, February 1959, p. 10.

[18] *ibid.*, p. 21.

[19] R. Pucheu and A. Cruziat, in *Vie Nouvelle*, No. 7, September 1958, p. 5.

indication of any action being taken by the group, apart from the effort necessary to prepare pamphlets and brochures.

It is significant that scouting can inculcate in many of its members a desire to remain "in the Catholic family" as adults even when one is quite far to the left on the political scale. So scouts seem to contribute to building up a particular psychological frame of mind in which Catholicism permeates one's whole existence. This, it will be recalled, was also one of the prime aims of Catholic Action. In addition, *Vie Nouvelle* seems to push its adherents into the left fringes of French politics, thanks to its particular conception of political problems. It might be argued that the French government indirectly encourages this evolution by its subsidies of the Catholic scouting movement.

C. THE CATHOLIC EMPLOYERS' ORGANIZATION (CFPC)

The CFPC (now officially called the *Centre Chrétien des Patrons et Dirigeants d'Entreprise Français*) is a Catholic group of businessmen within the larger *Confédération Nationale du Patronat Français.* But unlike the scouting movement, the CFPC is only a small minority in the larger group. The membership figure is said to be only 5,000.[20] This evidently does not mean that the French employers are less Catholic than the scouts; more likely the Church deems it more important for scouts to belong to a group with a clearly Catholic atmosphere than for employers to organize along Catholic lines.

The CFPC aims to apply the social doctrine of the Church to the economic and social life of France.[21] It has no apostolic functions; small Catholic Action professional groups already accomplish this. It has ecclesiastical counsellors who for the most part are Dominicans.[22] Through these advisors, the explicit encouragement it gets from the Hierarchy, and the social role it wants to fill, the CFPC has a niche among the Catholic

[20] See *Témoignage Chrétien,* March 13, 1959, p. 15.

[21] Cf. *Etudes,* Vol. 289, No. 6, June 1956, p. 440.

[22] The Dominican Order also controls *Economie et Humanisme* and the publishing house *Les Editions du Cerf,* both of which are in the vanguard of social and economic research.

social action groups. Recently it seems to be loosening some of its ties with the Church, but it still is much closer to the French Catholic ecclesiastical nucleus than its working-class counterpart, the CFTC. The difference in distance is probably due to the different significance workers and employers now attach to the Church in France.

The CFPC does not aim to engage in any political activity outside its field of competence. It feels qualified to make judgments on the economic philosophy of the present government, but it does not criticize other questions. Within its sphere of competence, however, the CFPC is a leading spokesman for the progressive *Rerum Novarum* conception of economic and social life. It is interested in associating workers with the management of enterprises; doubtless it has played a part in the Fifth Republic's increased emphasis on this phase of employer-employee relations. It has helped form a committee to interest employees in the productivity of industry (CADIPPE) which receives government support.[23] It is hostile to Marxian economics, but not necessarily to the principle of nationalizations. Thus, in a recent meeting of CFPC an industrialist claimed that the foundations and fundamental characteristics of our modern civilization ". . . are structurally incompatible with the liberal, capitalist civilization in the pure state. . . ."[24]

The CFPC as a Catholic group is also interested in the traditional questions of family, housing standards, minimum wages, and so forth. But unlike its social Catholic predecessors of the nineteenth century, the CFPC does not seem paternalistic. Interestingly, the principles of the CFPC are widely accepted among French business groups. In the future, therefore, the CFPC must develop new and original types of activity if it is to survive as an autonomous group, independent of the larger businessman's organization.[25]

[23] Brochure, *CADIPPE*, October 1957.

[24] Quoted in *Etudes*, Vol. 239, June 1956, p. 443.

[25] According to Henry Ehrmann there is little essential difference between the goals of the CNPC and the activities of the *Confédération Nationale du Patronat Français.* See *Organized Business in France* (Princeton: Princeton University Press, 1957), p. 205.

It is hardly necessary to describe certain very small Catholic-inspired business groups such as *Jeune Patron*, which have on a reduced scale much the same ideology and the same kinds of activity as the CFPC, though they are perhaps more progressive.[26]

Two self-imposed limitations detract from the CFPC's political impact. First, it limits its published comments to technical economic questions. Secondly, it is designed more as a club for practicing Catholic businessmen than as a real action group. The CFPC has neither the proselytizing zeal nor the incidental psychological impact of Catholic Action. Perhaps it would be most accurate to consider the CFPC essentially a pious group designed to strengthen the faith of its members rather than a dynamic, outward-facing pressure group.

D. CENTRE CATHOLIQUE DES INTELLECTUELS FRANÇAIS (CCIF)

In recent years the number of French intellectuals—professors, writers, journalists, and so forth—who practice the Catholic faith has increased enormously. "In our day, Christian intellectuals are everywhere. They can be found in faculties, academies, scientific societies, research centers. By its numerical strength as well as its quality, this spiritual rebirth was obviously destined to show more explicitly the vitality of the Church. To make the rebirth more fertile, it seemed necessary to create a group which would allow it to fulfill its promise."[27]

So, the CCIF has been created to meet the needs of the new generation of Catholic intellectuals. The CCIF is not only a club where Catholic intellectuals can meet, but also an important service group for the Church. Intellectuals have a special role in applying the dogma of the Church to social realities. Pope Pius XII himself has affirmed this: "The CCIF would fulfill its vocation if . . . it showed each day more fully that being faithful to the Church and to the Gospels stimulates reason and freedom. . . . More specifically, you accomplish this service to the Church by contributing to Christian thought your

[26] For these groups see *ibid.*, p. 118 and pp. 200 ff.
[27] *CCIF*, undated brochure.

experience and your culture. Today theologians must be able to count on Our sons who are scholars or technicians, philosophers or jurists, historians, sociologists or doctors, to base theology on time-tested secular attainments."[28]

There is also a desire to convert other intellectuals: "Gentlemen, continue this research and this effort. The possibility for many of our colleagues to accede to the Faith depends on the work which you are accomplishing."[29]

The CCIF is one of the key elements in *Pax Romana*, the international Catholic intellectuals' and students' organization, but this affiliation seems to have no important repercussions on French political life.

Interestingly enough, the CCIF includes all "tendencies" among Catholic intellectuals: on its directing committee, for example, can be found Georges Suffert who was editor of *Témoignage Chrétien* before being dismissed by the Hierarchy because of his leftist views. There are also men like Jean de Fabrègues of *La France Catholique*, Gabriel Marcel, Joseph Folliet of *La Chronique Sociale*, François Mauriac, Georges Hourdin of *Vie Catholique Illustrée*, Professor Duroselle, Henri Rollet, President of ACGH, and many others. The General Secretary is Etienne Borne, who is also on the MRP national committee. The wide variety of tendencies represented should not be surprising, considering the diversity of the "intellectual milieu." But as a consequence, the CCIF cannot take any political stands on touchy issues, for its members would surely be divided.

As befits a group of intellectuals, the CCIF sponsors a number of lectures on religious, literary, economic, and social themes. However, subjects concerned with the French political crisis have been largely bypassed. The problem of Berlin was discussed, as were French economic ties with Europe and Africa, but nothing was mentioned on the Algerian question. The CCIF publishes a quarterly review, *Recherches et Debats*,

[28] Message to Catholic Intellectuals, November 1950, quoted *ibid.*
[29] Cardinal Feltin to CCIF, quoted *ibid.*

which discusses a specific problem in each issue. Here again, economic and political questions, when considered, are of a very general nature. The issue which appeared between May 13 and the constitutional referendum in 1958 dealt with "Aspects of Negro Culture." Finally, once a year the CCIF sponsors a "Catholic Intellectuals' Week," organized around a particular theme. A recent conference considered Catholic reactions to various sorts of nationalism. In these conferences, non-Catholics generally participate actively.

In none of its activities does the CCIF try to take decisions or even arrive at specific conclusions. It aims, through comparing various viewpoints, to clarify issues. This spirit of tolerance and even non-sectarianism gives the CCIF an important place within the French intellectual elite, around which so much of French political life revolves. But the CCIF does not appear to have a direct political impact itself.

E. THE "UNION FÉMININE CIVIQUE ET SOCIALE" (UFCS)

The *Union Féminine Civique et Sociale* is one of the organizations in France developing civic interest and knowledge among women. It does not represent a particular social class, nor is it formally Catholic. It is one of those "borderline cases" which could as well be included under the heading "Catholic inspiration" as in the present chapter. It is put here because its links to the Hierarchy are actually much closer than those of the MRP or CFTC. Confusion is caused by the fact that the UFCS was founded in 1925, before the present specialization of Catholic groups. At that time its aim was to work for a "Christian social order," and it considered itself "apostolic."[30] Though its aims are no longer formally bound up in the Church, the Hierarchy has often in recent years given it official encouragement. As Cardinal Feltin said, "The Commission of Cardinals and Archbishops has defined the specific domain of UFCS activity, which is distinct from that of Feminine Catholic Action. The Sovereign Pontiff has many times sent the UFCS

[30] Cf. Rollet, *Sur le Chantier Social*, p. 54.

his blessings, his congratulations, and his encouragements."[31]

The place of Catholicism in the activities of the UFCS had been defined by an eminent Jesuit theologian, Father Bigo, as follows: "Obviously, the reference to a Christian conception of man and society cannot suffice as the doctrine of a temporal movement, for the temporal domain puts into play techniques which are unrelated to the doctrine of the Church. Therefore, the *Union Féminine* must undertake on its own responsibility a great deal of civic, economic, and social analysis. But in this work the *Union Féminine* has a great force if it relies on the notions of the Christian conscience in social matters."[32]

The UFCS has no chaplains, but it has three official advisors from the Church, who help it set its broad lines of activity. They include Father Villain of *Action Populaire*, and Mgr. Blanchet, Rector of the Catholic University. The UFCS, though still closely linked to the Hierarchy, seems gradually moving in the direction of the CFTC and the MRP, though it still has far to go before it is completely deconfessionalized.

The UFCS aspires to being a "mass" organization, but it seems limited to a certain elite, and has no more than 15,000 or 20,000 active members at present.[33] The UFCS finds it relatively easy to contact public officials because it is recognized by the Government as being "of public usefulness"—the only women's social organization in this category. This recognition is another assurance that the UFCS will keep its distance from the Hierarchy, because neither religious nor political organizations in the strict sense get the special Government recognition.

There is a certain rivalry and overlapping between the UFCS and the ACGF. The latter is a "mass organization" with primarily an apostolic function, but which engages in some political activity. The UFCS also accomplishes an important work

[31] In *Semaine Religieuse de Paris*, May 19, 1951, p. 482.

[32] Talk June 25, 1957. From UFCS private files, obtained from Mlle. Thérèse Doneaud, April 7, 1959.

[33] Interview with Mlle. Doneaud.

of political education, despite its small size, but now disclaims any direct apostolic function. The UFCS would prefer that the ACGF in turn abandon civic education activities, since, it says, it can do this job more effectively. The ACGF, it believes, should keep to the spiritual realm. However, as has been often noted, the distinction between spiritual and temporal is difficult to maintain; ACGF publicizes Church social doctrine, while the UFCS shows what political positions follow from this social doctrine. Certain political consequences are clear to any layman in either case.

Over the years the political views of the UFCS have greatly evolved. This becomes clear if one examines positions which the organization has held on certain political problems. In 1946, when the first Constitutional project was submitted to the people, UFCS, like ACGF, recommended that it be turned down.[34] But by 1951, when the Barangé Law was being considered, the UFCS very carefully avoided partisan comments before the law was passed. Its national congress before the 1951 elections made no mention at all of the school question. After the law was passed, the UFCS published a justification for it, but in rather moderate tones.

In the 1958 crisis the UFCS did not forsake its prudence. There is no partisan use of Algerian or political crises inside France. Just before the 1958 Constitution was presented to the voters, the UFCS came out with a reasoned pronouncement, quite different from its negative stand in 1946. But this statement is not completely nonpartisan; any women who believed it would probably approve the Constitution: "Each of us is free to be a Gaullist or not. Gratefulness or admiration for the man who pulled France from a bad scrape can facilitate one's voting and dispose one to trust, but these feelings should not replace reason and destroy our freedom. . . . Let us try to realize what rejecting the Constitution would mean for metropolitan France, Algeria, overseas territories, and international opinion.

[34] *Françaises Face à la Politique*, pp. 129-130.

Its success would bring a government with important powers, which could lead us to hope for more continuity and cohesion in our country's politics, but perhaps with the risk of opening a pathway to extremes."[35]

By 1959, in common with most Catholic left and center organizations and many non-Catholics as well, the UFCS protested against the draconian economic and social policies of the Debré government.[36] However the UFCS continued to support the Algerian position of General de Gaulle. The instigators of the 1960 insurrection against de Gaulle's moderate Algerian policies were strongly criticized in the UFCS newspaper, which further pledged "confidence in President de Gaulle as he applies the policy which he has elaborated and which the immense majority of the country approves."[37]

If the political ideas of the UFCS easily class it with the Catholic organizations in the middle of the political spectrum, it is more difficult to estimate the real significance of its political influence. A number of debates and meetings are held during the year in Paris and some provincial cities on social or political questions, under the auspices of the UFCS. But they have little impact; the UFCS does not have the intellectual prestige of the CCIF, for example. On the other hand, UFCS members may be able to use some political notions acquired in their organization to expand their influence in local affairs.[38] Also, profiting from its character "of public usefulness," the UFCS is a member of certain public or semipublic groups connected with social, educational, or moral matters.[39]

Like all Catholic groups, the UFCS has been forced during the past decade to specify its role in French political life. The

[35] *La Femme dans la Vie Sociale,* No. 290, September 1958, p. 1.

[36] *ibid.,* No. 294, February 1959.

[37] *ibid.,* No. 301, January 1960. During the crisis of April 1961 the UFCS assured de Gaulle that they endorsed his "energetic action to maintain national unity." See *La Croix,* April 26, 1961, p. 3. At this time ACGF refused to support de Gaulle publicly.

[38] See *Françaises Face à la Politique,* pp. 129-131.

[39] *ibid.*

UFCS like the CFTC has become less confessional. But at the same time it has become less actively committed to partisan positions. With certain exceptions, the UFCS now takes a stand only on those questions where the social doctrine of the Church indicates a specific choice. Where the doctrine cannot be used to justify one course of action more than another, the UFCS is satisfied in appearing "objective."[40] This self-imposed restriction diminishes the political importance of the UFCS more than any other. It puts the UFCS on the same level of political impact as ACGF; indeed, ACGF seems in balance to have even more political importance.

III. Non-Specialized Social Catholic Groups: Secrétariats Sociaux, Semaines Sociales, Chronique Sociale

The rich historical tradition of social Catholicism is represented in France today by three overlapping organizations: the *Secrétariats Sociaux*, the *Semaines Sociales*, and the *Chronique Sociale.* The *Secrétariats Sociaux* are a group of loosely-connected research agencies located in major French cities. Every year they sponsor national study sessions, called the *Semaines Sociales.* The latter deal with a different theme of French social life each year. During their half-century of existence they have become respected in France and abroad. The *Secrétariat Social* of Lyon, the original one, edits one of the oldest reviews in France, the *Chronique Sociale,* founded in 1892. The *Chronique* is the unofficial spokesman of all *Secrétariats Sociaux* and of their brand of social Catholicism.

Like most of the groups in this chapter, these Social Catholic organizations retain certain ties with the Church Hierarchy. There has never been a clear distinction between priests and laymen in these social Catholic groups; priests work on technical matters where they are qualified, in addition to giving spiritual advice within the *Secrétariats Sociaux.* The *Semaines Sociales* are attended by laymen and priests, the latter as tech-

[40] Interpretation confirmed in interview with Mlle. Doneaud.

nical experts as well as exponents of the Church social doctrine. At the *Semaine Sociale* of 1959, more than one fourth of the 2,000 participants were priests. Very recently an official of the *Semaines Sociales* restated his group's ties to Catholicism: "As a Church institution, the *Semaines Sociales* are somewhat analogous to Catholic Action groups, though the two are not precisely the same. Certainly, the *Semaines Sociales* do not formally commit the Church. . . . They have the right to the freedom of research given them by the Church, but every precaution must be taken to prevent this freedom from degenerating into a series of blunders. The right to blunder varies according to the group: the Catholic press has a greater right to blunder than Church organizations themselves. But even within these limits, it would be hard to say that *Témoignage Chrétien* always says what it wants, when it wants, and how it wants. It follows, then, that others should not be blamed for having limitations that are the normal consequence of attachment to the Church community."[41]

The *Semaines Sociales* have also been called "a laic institution in the Church, controlled, guaranteed, and sanctioned by the authorities of the Catholic community."[42] According to Pope Pius XII, the *Chronique Sociale* should ". . . make known and propagate the traditional teachings of the Papacy related to the person, the family, the profession, the state and international relations."[43]

Since the end of World War II the social Catholic groups have been more and more preoccupied with technical economic and social questions, rather than those which are partisan or apostolic.[44] By sticking close to technical analyses these groups

[41] From *Témoignage Chrétien*, November 6, 1959, p. 2.

[42] Quoted in *Chronique Sociale*, Vol. LXII, No. 3, May-June 1954, p. 235.

[43] Pope Pius XII to Joseph Folliet, published in *Chronique Sociale*, Vol. LX, No. 3, June 1952, p. 254.

[44] "On the political level, the *Semaines Sociales* are tied to no party, not even to those whose program is closest to their thinking. Excluding any partisan position, they proclaim their respect for the established regime and responsible governments. But this does not stop them from giving to one and all the criticisms and suggestions which they believe are well-founded." From *Chronique Sociale*, Vol. LXII, No. 3, May-June 1954, p. 226.

have thus far been able to avoid the choice which most Catholic organizations must make: if they remain closely tied to the Hierarchy their fundamental goals cannot be political. If they insist on being "political" they must dissociate themselves from the Church by becoming of Catholic inspiration only. Though there is an apostolic flavor in the work of these groups, it comes only through technical work; none of the three engages in the open campaign for conversion practiced by Catholic Action groups. For this reason, social Catholic groups find it possible to avoid making a sharp distinction between priest and layman, as Catholic Action must do.

The political impact of social Catholic groups is felt in several ways. The *Semaines Sociales*, by studying technical problems and applying to them the social doctrines of the Church, help indicate to participants how they should act as individuals and as Catholics.[45] Local *Secrétariats Sociaux*, which largely consist of active members from other Catholic organizations, can put pressure on local authorities, and the national *Secrétariat Social* also puts pressure on the government in technical questions where partisan principles are not important (for example, housing policy and family allowances).[46]

The *Secrétariats Sociaux* have encouraged the foundation and expansion of many other Catholic groups, including the JOC and *Pax Christi*.[47] In return, certain well-to-do Catholic groups, notably such publishing houses as *Bonne Presse, Vie Catholique Illustrée,* and *Union des Oeuvres,* have contributed to the research activities of the *Secrétariats Sociaux*. Their money has enabled the *Secrétariats* to expand their civic education work—to be described below—and to strengthen ties with the *Semaines Sociales*.

The directors of the *Secrétariats Sociaux* are active in other Catholic groups. The president, Charles Flory, and one of the secretaries, Georges Hourdin, are leaders of the MRP. Hourdin

[45] *ibid.*, p. 229.

[46] Interview with Henri Théry, official of *Secrétariats Sociaux*, March 20, 1959.

[47] *Chronique Sociale*, June 1952, p. 277.

is also the president of the publishing company *Vie Catholique Illustrée*. Social Catholics in large number are attracted to the moderate political forces in French politics, and particularly to the MRP.

"There are no organic ties between the *Semaines Sociales* and the MRP, but in practice there are close relations. When social Catholicism sought the political embodiment of its views it scarcely had a choice outside of Christian Democracy. One can regret this, but that is the way things are. . . ."[48]

However, there are representatives of all "tendencies" of Catholicism on the governing board of the *Semaines Sociales*, just as there are for the CCIF: Mgr. Bruno de Solages; the Gaullist Marcel Prélot; Rémy Montagne, the man who unseated Mendès-France in the 1958 general elections; "leftists" such as J. Lacroix or Maurice Vaussard. This illustrates the evolution of social Catholicism from a "left-wing tendency" of French Catholicism in prewar days to a doctrine acceptable for all Catholics today.

After the crisis of May 1958, the Catholic social action groups were all profoundly shocked. The crisis demonstrated a fundamental lack of civic consciousness among the French people and a refusal by social groups to take responsible political action. It seemed that the events of May threatened social and economic as well as political life. The *Secrétariats Sociaux* greatly intensified their civic education activities and their contacts with other Catholic groups, to help remedy these deficiencies. A political information and civic education service (SIPEC) was established by the *Secrétariats Sociaux* in cooperation with many other Catholic groups to bring various Catholic leaders together to discuss problems relating to civic education. In a recent meeting to discuss the Parliamentary elections, civic education officials were present from all major Catholic Action groups. It is not clear what the SIPEC meetings can do, but here is at least the possibility of coordinating the entire Catholic Action complex for a political purpose.

[48] *Témoignage Chrétien*, November 6, 1959, p. 2.

Except for their attempts to attack civic irresponsibility, social Catholic groups now stay far from partisan politics. The material which SIPEC sends out to all Catholic and Catholic-inspired groups contains no recommendations expressed or implied.[49] A special issue of the *Chronique Sociale* dealt with the Christian attitude toward brainwashing and other aspects of psychological warfare.[50] But the psychological work of the army in Algeria was not considered! This "oversight" was justified as follows: "But Algeria? Psychological action in Algeria? It is true, we have not spoken of it, and deliberately. First, to eliminate any political tone and any polemical bitterness to our investigations. But also because value judgments on psychological action in Algeria presuppose factual judgments which we are not capable of making."[51]

At the 1959 *Semaine Sociale*, the theme was education. But nowhere does one find a direct statement in favor of state aid to Catholic schools. The conference did not even discuss the dangers of laic opposition to state aid for Catholic schools.[52] At the end of the study, the participants hoped that a durable solution to the school question could be found, but made no specific recommendations themselves. The publication *Servir*, of the *Secrétariat Social* of Paris, followed this nonpartisan trend in its special issue on the 1958 Referendum. There are references to practically all the historic Church pronouncements on civic questions, but no political stand is taken.[53]

From what has been analyzed there seem to be three ways in which social Catholic groups might have political impact: direct pressure on government and on elites; influence over the masses; influence through coordinating other Catholic groups. Their philosophy limits the first to purely technical and highly abstract questions. Their impact on the mass of

49 Information from files of *Union Nationale des Secrétariats Sociaux*, Paris.

50 *Chronique Sociale*, Vol. LXVII, Nos. 2-3, April 15, 1959.

51 *ibid.*, p. 184.

52 Semaine Sociale de Versailles, 1958: *Enseignement, Problème Social* (Lyon: Editions de la Chronique Sociale, 1958).

53 *Servir*, No. 128, September-October 1958.

lukewarm Catholics is so limited that they cannot have much influence this way. Finally, the coordination of Catholic groups is also unrealistic, because of the way each Catholic group jealously guards its own autonomy. Ties go vertically up to the Hierarchy, without passing through any social Catholic groups. This is why, without minimizing the role of the *Semaines Sociales* or of technical studies or the *Chronique Sociale*, certain Catholics have called the social Catholic formula "the product of a bygone generation."[54] The nonpartisan character of these groups was tested during the crisis of May 1958 and held firm. It is still unclear whether any tactical changes after May will eventually lead to a change in this position.

In concluding this section, we should reemphasize the evolution that has taken place in Catholic thought, which deprives the social Catholic tradition of the progressive flavor it had in the past. Social Catholic ideas formulated in the nineteenth century have long become too tame for the Catholic left, and even the right-wing *intégristes* try to adopt as their own many social Catholic principles. Like virtue itself, these principles are accepted by all. The right would go no further, while the most progressive elements of the Church would advocate many more guarantees of real social equality for the economically disfavored.

IV. Religious Orders and Social Action

A. ACTION POPULAIRE

Religious Orders direct two important social action organizations: the Jesuits at *Action Populaire* and the Dominicans at *Economie et Humanisme*. Like social Catholic groups, both are primarily concerned with studies of economic and social phenomena, and both do a certain amount of research on behalf of other Catholic organizations. *Action Populaire* has the finest collection of current Catholic reviews and newspapers in

[54] This expression from an official of *Témoignage Chrétien,* in an interview.

France—a collection which is invaluable to any scholar writing on contemporary French Catholicism.

Action Populaire was founded with an aim of mass propaganda, at a time when religious quarrels were still of prime political importance.[55] But since then its influence has been largely the result of its technical studies and of its impact on Catholic priests and lay groups. Officially the present aims of *Action Populaire* are as follows: "Make men conscious of their responsibilities in the face of social injustice and economic disorder; promote a transformation of economic, social, and international structures; help the worker and rural masses to better themselves collectively; accomplish these tasks on the level of thought, stimulation, and organization, *according to the demands of the Gospels and the Church*."[56]

Action Populaire publishes two reviews, the *Revue d'Action Populaire*, and the *Cahiers d'Action Religieuse et Sociale*. Both analyze current economic, social, and moral problems. They do not usually take sides in these matters and cannot as a general rule be considered partisan. Of the two, the *Revue* is more concerned with nonpolitical technical questions, especially in the social and economic spheres. The *Revue* is tolerant of certain points in Marxist economic doctrine, without subscribing to its other ramifications. It favors the development of all social structures (including political parties) which authentically reflect the interests of the working class.[57] On the Algerian question the *Revue* at times broke its nonpartisan tone, especially when important moral questions were involved. For example, in 1956 the *Revue* urged negotiations to end the unjustifiable tortures of the war: "Frenchmen and Algerians each defend legitimate values."[58]

55 Henri Rollet, *Sur le Chantier Social*, pp. 62-64.

56 Italics in Original. This motto appears on the cover of many issues of the *Revue d'Action Populaire*.

57 *Revue d'Action Populaire*, No. 52, August 1951, pp. 498 ff.

58 *ibid.*, No. 99, June 1956, p. 646. The frequent political crises since 1958 have led the *Revue*, the best known publication of *Action Populaire*, to increase its political coverage. But the emphasis is on analysis of problems rather than taking firm stands on controversial issues. Thus, de

The *Cahiers d'Action Religieuse et Sociale* contain more political information than the *Revue*. The information is not designed to influence, but to fill in readers on the course of events. Mass influence would be difficult anyway, because both the *Cahiers* and the *Revue* have circulations of only a few thousand, confined to Catholic circles and the French political elite.

Although both these publications are further from the Church nucleus than *Etudes*, the official publication of the Jesuit Order in France, they are no more openly partisan. It seems likely, in fact, that a subdued article on a question like Algeria in *Etudes*, with the weight of the Order behind it, would have more impact in France than a more direct article appearing in an *Action Populaire* publication.[59]

Much more significant than the publications of *Action Populaire* is the impact of the organization on other Catholic circles. A whole generation of young priests received much social and economic education in their seminaries based on the ideas of *Action Populaire*; this has made them receptive to working-class grievances and able to understand for themselves contemporary economic problems.[60] These priests and those who staff *Action Populaire* have been particularly active as chaplains in Catholic Action youth groups. All such groups (except the JOC) were staffed predominantly or even exclusively by Jesuits as chaplains. Recently, quarrels with the Hierarchy over the spiritual activities of these groups resulted in a mass exodus of Jesuits from their posts. As a consequence, most Catholic Action youth groups now allow more initiative from their members, and

---

Gaulle's proposed referendum on Algeria in January, 1961, brought this comment from the *Revue*, January 1961, pp. 2-3: "Although we can see good reasons for supporting General de Gaulle's Algerian policy . . . we could be induced to reconsider our support if this policy would change the form of the regime. . . . However, at present nothing justifies this suspicion. Certain attitudes of the government may irritate; they do not constitute the will to change the regime."

[59] *Etudes* was long considered the right-wing Jesuit publication, and the *Action Populaire* reviews the left-wing ones. Now there is little difference in political orientation among them.

[60] Cf. Interview with Father Robinot-Marcy at *Action Populaire*, May 12, 1959. Cf. also Rollet, *Sur le Chantier Social*, p. 63.

their spiritual activities seem more self-directed. According to the Jesuits at *Action Populaire*, where many of the former chaplains are now living, this change has resulted in a membership loss for all Catholic Action youth groups.[61]

B. "ECONOMIE ET HUMANISME"

Economie et Humanisme, a Dominican-sponsored research group, has many features of an American economic study organization. It examines technical economic questions just as *Action Populaire* does, but it has none of the other characteristics of the Jesuit group. *Economie et Humanisme* represents a certain school of economic thought in France: economic questions are evaluated as they affect the development of the human being, rather than in and for themselves.[62]

The research methods perfected by *Economie et Humanisme* have no direct partisan influence but they have oriented a number of priests and laymen toward a certain conception of the economic situation which naturally would lead them to sympathize with the political parties of the left.

Just after the May 1958 crisis *Economie et Humanisme* published an article which probably expressed the political views of its collaborators, though these views are not often expressed so clearly: ". . . these revolutionary days carried along the best and the worst. The best was the will to have done with the regime which, according to Mendès-France, could not resolve any problems confronting it. . . . The least pure was that Algerian minority which . . . after having dominated nine million Algerians, succeeded in imposing its will on 44 million metropolitan Frenchmen. The least pure was also the army's revolt against civil power. . . . The army seems to make and unmake the governments."[63]

Again in 1960 *Economie et Humanisme* gave one of its rare

[61] From an interview with an official of *Action Populaire*.

[62] Cf. "Pour une Démocratie Economique," in *Economie et Humanisme*, No. 111, May-June 1958, p. 1.

[63] *Economie et Humanisme*, No. 112, July-August 1958, p. 193.

partisan opinions, concerning the nature of de Gaulle's Republic: "De Gaulle's Gaullism, when it deals with the French people, ignores the state. The Power appears. . . . When he comes from his village, one *adheres.* This adherence comes 'from the depths of the country,' 'from the instinct of the country,' and it is 'confirmed by general agreement.' It is this general agreement which gives Gaullism its legitimacy. This whole picture is incomprehensible for a democrat. If it is not antidemocratic, it is at least ademocratic, since the connection between The Power and the French population belongs to the mythical universe of heroes—to the world of emotion and of the irrational. . . . The Power is not an arbiter, but a mediator. . . . De Gaulle's function is to charm and to seduce, for 'these people must be led with dreams.'"[64]

Since both *Action Populaire* and *Economie et Humanisme* are controlled by religious orders, there is always the possibility of the Hierarchy's curbing, censoring, or reorienting these groups. Naturally, in the technical fields with which they are most concerned these groups have autonomy. But if they should ever want to advocate a particular partisan viewpoint, they would run the risk of ecclesiastical sanctions. Perhaps it is this ultimate risk that has limited their partisan statements in number and in scope.

V. *Extremist Social Action Groups*

A. OF THE LEFT

Certain small Catholic groups of the extreme left or extreme right can be qualified as "social action organizations," if the term is loosely used. These groups are often related to the movements and publications of Catholic inspiration which will be considered in the two following chapters. They are put here not because there is anything particularly "Catholic" about their work, but because they call themselves Catholic and have

[64] *ibid.*, No. 124, March-April 1960, p. 38.

a close working relationship with certain members of the Hierarchy.

At present there is no group of this nature on the extreme left. Up to the mid-1950's, there was one, called *Jeunesse de l'Eglise.* It was committed to a left-wing personalism reminiscent of *Vie Nouvelle,* but it rapidly evolved toward a type of Marxian Christianity which could not be tolerated by the Hierarchy. Like many other Catholic groups, it did a lot of talking, a fair amount of publishing, but had very little real political impact. It finally died because of public indifference to it. The director of *Jeunesse de l'Eglise,* Father Montuclard, frustrated at difficulties with the Church Hierarchy, finally renounced his priestly status. Frustrated at his inability to attract an important working-class base, he left *Jeunesse de l'Eglise* as well.[65] The organization soon followed the extreme left *Chrétiennes Progressistes* (to be described in Chapter Seven) into oblivion.

B. OF THE RIGHT

The extreme-right groups, called *intégristes* in France, seem to be much more significant than the Catholic extreme left at present. All are inspired by a rigid view of their faith emphasizing the virtues of order and hierarchy in the political and in the spiritual realms. Their pet bugaboos are the "laic state," which, they say, will flourish as long as the Catholic school remains financially poor; religious experimentation and progressivism, exemplified by reviews like *Témoignage Chrétien*; and those who oppose the beneficial activities of the army, at home or abroad. Most of them explicitly or implicitly deplore the French Revolution and the Republics that have sprung from it.[66] These extremist views find little favor among the mass

[65] Cf. *Esprit,* Vol. xxv, No. 251, June 1957, p. 1025.

[66] See *Express,* February 19, 1959, p. 9. See also Rémond, "Droite et Gauche dans le Catholicisme Français," in *Revue Française de Science Politique,* VIII, No. 4, *passim.* In addition to the groups mentioned, other Catholic organizations of the extreme right should be noted in passing. A *Centre d'Etudes Politiques et Civiques* attracts some businessmen, while a small group coordinated by Pierre Lemaire concentrates on family

of French Catholics but, as will be seen in the next chapter, they find some support in the French Hierarchy and at Rome.

Perhaps the key men at present among the Catholics of the extreme right are Jean Madiran and Georges Sauge. Madiran will be discussed in the next chapter. Sauge, a former Communist Party member, has organized a "Center for the Advanced Study of Social Psychology," and a movement called *Force Psychologique.*[67] This movement seems to have a certain influence in the French army, which is greatly concerned with psychological warfare in Algeria. The main activity of Sauge is agitation against Communism, "Marxism," and left-wing Catholicism. Sauge has tried with little success to extend his influence into various center and right Catholic groups, especially the potentially powerful ACGF. Recently his importance has been enhanced by giving regular courses in psychological warfare to reserve army officers.

The views of Sauge are close to those of *Homme Nouveau*, which will be examined in the next chapter, but they are more concerned with the temporal activities that "necessarily" seem to follow from Catholic dogma. His doctrine is unimpeachable; but the activity which he tries to show as the "logical consequence" of this doctrine can be questioned. But because of this doctrine, Sauge has received support from such political figures as Georges Bidault, General Chassin, Poujade, and the corporatist Doctor Lefevre, as well as from some of the more rock-ribbed conservatives from among the Hierarchy. "Bishops or Prelates such as Msgrs. Marmottin, Morilleau, Rupp (auxiliary Bishop of Paris), Le Couédic, Bressoles, the Most Reverend Father de Fontgombault, do not object to hosting or expressing sympathies for Sauge's meetings. . . . 'Encouragements' even

---

affairs. The Joan of Arc Alliance, a group with Catholic overtones, has some influence among certain army groups.

[67] See *I.C.I.*, February 15, 1960 for a detailed study of Sauge and his activities. According to *Témoignage Chrétien*, over 10,000 people have studied at Sauge's "Center." December 11, 1959, p. 11. Cf. *Express*, December 3, 1959, p. 7. In 1961 the Center was established at Rome. See *Témoignage Chrétien*, May 12, 1961, p. 19.

come from Rome, from the pen of Mgr. Ottaviani, Secretary of the Congregation of the Holy Office."[68]

But these encouragements should not obscure the fact that most French Catholics prefer the conception of social action of the *Secrétariats Sociaux* or *Action Populaire*, where partisan political stands are generally avoided and where the legitimate aspirations of the working class are understood and encouraged. The danger from Sauge is not his attraction to the mass of Frenchmen. The danger seems rather to come from Sauge's appeal to a certain elite, which holds high posts in France's military organization. But even these military people, if they are devout Catholics, will see that Sauge has the approval only of individual bishops, while the more moderate social action groups have received the official approval of the ACA, on behalf of the entire French Church.

The essence of Catholic social action organizations is an interpenetration (some would say a confusion) between spiritual and temporal realms. In the nineteenth and early twentieth centuries this confusion was accepted as normal and most Catholic lay organizations during this period were of the social action type.[69] Now Catholic groups seek a clearer delimitation of spiritual and temporal activities, and Catholic social action organizations restrict more and more their partisan activity. At present their political influence is often less than that of Catholic Action groups themselves. Where they have kept both spiritual and temporal activities, the latter are not controversial and are limited to those milieux which are most benevolent to Catholicism.

Thus in comparing the political impact of social action groups with Catholic Action, it does not seem that further distance from the Hierarchy necessarily increases a group's po-

[68] *Express*, February 19, 1959, p. 9. Cf. *Témoignage Chrétien*, December 11, 1959, p. 11, and *I.C.I.*, February 15, 1960, p. 23.

[69] See Rollet, *L'Action Sociale des Catholiques en France*, Vols. I and II, *passim*, and Dansette, *Histoire Religieuse de la France Contemporaine*, Vol. II.

litical activity, even though the main goal of a group switches from religious action (conversion of non-Catholics) to temporal action (technical research and study). There are often more partisan political by-products of the former than of the latter.

The Catholic Press

I. General Characteristics

A. INTRODUCTION

The preceding chapters have distinguished among Catholic laymen's groups according to their distance from the ecclesiastical nucleus. The complexity of the Catholic press makes it necessary to include the major Catholic publications in one chapter, regardless of the distance a given publication may be from the core of the Church.[1]

The Catholic press comprises those publications which are approved by the Hierarchy. The ACA may approve a paper's editorial board. Or there may be recommendations by all bishops to subscribe (*La Croix* benefits from such recommendations), or sponsorship by individual prelates (this is the case with *Verbe*, for example). "Approval" can be expressed negatively, too, as in the criticism by bishops of certain activities of *Témoignage Chrétien*. It is usually, but not always, indicated by the appointment of a religious advisor to a publication.

Catholic publications exist in a surprisingly large number of fields; there is a bulletin for Catholic pharmacists, one for Catholic railroad workers, for sick Catholic children, etc. One of the unexpressed goals of French Catholicism is to extend publications inspired by Catholic principles to as many fields of human activity as possible. Although this chapter is concerned only with those Catholic publications that have political significance in the strict sense of the term, this attempt to

[1] In considering the press, this chapter is limited to national periodical publications and collections of Catholic books. Other media of mass communication, such as the cinema, radio, theatre, etc., will not be considered here. Catholic influence in these fields seldom has any political significance.

"saturate" society is itself politically significant and gives a political meaning to even the most pious review. The more that Catholic publications are read, the more society at large—or a particular milieu—becomes willing to accept all the doctrines of the Church. If one must be restrictive in choosing Catholic publications to examine, this general impact should not be forgotten.[2]

The Catholic publications to be considered fall into several different categories. There are the official and unofficial publications of religious orders. Among the laymen's publications, many were founded in a spirit of partisan politics and have since become more "spiritually minded"; some are still violently partisan and extremist. Mention must also be made of *Esprit*, which is in a unique position. Founded as an expression of Mounier's particular "personalist" philosophy, it has never claimed to be Catholic. But its major contributors are Catholics and its political position is very close to that of the Catholic left. In addition *Esprit* has had a decisive influence on an entire generation of left-wing Catholics.

Reflecting all the tendencies of French Catholicism, Catholic publications run the gamut from political extremism to pious moderation. To illustrate graphically their range in partisanship, the major Catholic publications can be put on a "partisanship scale" from the most politically involved to the most pious:

1. Publications with a well-defined political stand, a coherent view of life, and active supporters—that is, reviews which almost form movements themselves (*Esprit*, *Verbe*).

2. General reviews with a definitely partisan outlook which they admit, but without aspiring to direct action themselves (*Témoignage Chrétien* and *France Catholique*).

3. Technical or intellectual publications which are "slanted"

[2] The information in this part of the chapter has come primarily from a groundbreaking study on the Catholic press by Jacques Maître, "Le Fonctionnement de la Presse Catholique en France." Mimeographed study (Paris: Association Française de Science Politique, June 1957). The study was an invaluable introduction to the Catholic press, and made feasible a more detailed study than would have been possible otherwise.

and generally admit it (*Signes du Temps, Informations Catholiques Internationales, Cahiers d'Action Religieuse et Sociale, Revue d'Action Populaire, Economie et Humanisme, Etudes*).

4. General publications which are "slanted" and sometimes deny it (*Vie Catholique Illustrée, La Croix*).

5. Pious or technical publications with only residual political significance (*Pèlerin, Documentation Catholique*).[3]

The political significance of these categories will become clear in the sections to follow. But even now at least one observation can be made. The publications most closely related to the ecclesiastical nucleus are in groups 3, 4, and 5—that is, in the least political categories. The Hierarchy seems unwilling to let the clergy or the most trusted Catholic laymen go on political "crusades" as they did at the turn of the century.

B. HOW BEING "CATHOLIC" AFFECTS THE CATHOLIC PRESS

Like Catholic groups, the Catholic press is designed to further the interests of the Church in France. "General-interest" publications can permeate all levels of French Society, while more specialized publications can concentrate on a certain group or social category. Even in the latter case the requirements of the Church are put above the interests of the particular group.[4]

The notion of apostolic action is vague. Many attempts, therefore, have been made to clarify the purposes of the Catho-

[3] The French Catholic press differs greatly from the American Catholic press with respect to partisanship. A courageous and progressive stand such as Dorothy Day's in the *Catholic Worker* attracts very little notice here, while its French equivalent, *Témoignage Chrétien*, was the most popular Catholic weekly in France for a long time. This reflects differences in Church-state relations in the two countries: in France the society is permeated with Catholic influence while the Church in America is still struggling for a larger measure of social recognition. It cannot afford to be as free with its opinions as the Church in France.

[4] Cardinal Pizzardo emphasized this point a few years ago: "The mission of the apostolic press . . . is direct participation . . . in the apostolate of the Church. It is quite distinct from any other press, even of Catholic tendencies, which concentrates on specific political, economic, or social ends." Quoted in J. Mondange, *L'Information Catholique*, Vol. III, *La Presse d'Aujourd'hui* (Paris: Hirondelle, 1951), p. 114.

lic press. Some have considered that the Catholic press is primarily an instrument for the conversion of individual readers who are outside the Church.[5] Others have stressed creating a favorable atmosphere for spiritual values, so that Catholicism can eventually permeate all French society. "Catholic publications constitute one of the best means for making the Church's voice heard and for extending its teachings to the masses who are not generally reached either by Church works or by priests."[6] Another viewpoint stresses the need for providing a "Catholic explanation" to events: "There is a Christian view of the world and of history. . . . The Christian journalist will seek also a Christian explanation of group events."[7] Some Catholic publications, working within a particular milieu, hope to bring a more favorable attitude toward Catholicism in that milieu. This is notably the case for *Témoignage Chrétien*. Finally, another major goal is to provide information about the Church in as complete a form as possible. "Religion is a source of information as important as any other. . . . Only publications directed and edited by Christians, especially by Catholics—Catholics trained in the art of journalism—can give religion its proper place."[8] All of these goals are interrelated. All are present in some degree as motivations for every Catholic publication.

All Catholic publications differ in their goals from the "commercial" press such as *France-Soir, Paris Match, Elle, Figaro,* etc. The primary goal of the Catholic press is not to make money, nor is it to defend its temporal ideas. "If a Catholic en-

[5] See *ibid.*, Vol. I, *Une Industrie Nouvelle: La 'Fabrication' de l'Opinion Publique*, p. 89.

[6] Georges Hourdin, in *I.C.I.*, May 1, 1959, p. 2.

[7] Georges Hourdin, *La Presse Catholique* (Paris: Arthème Fayard, 1957), pp. 68-69. Related to this, some Catholics criticize the influence of the non-Catholic press in undermining the Faith: "The press . . . does not attack God, it respects religion. But it ignores the Faith. . . . A religion without a soul: this is what Christianity might become for the Catholic reader of the non-Catholic press. The latter doctors up religious news in its columns." Mondange, *La Presse Aujourd'hui*, p. 106 and p. 141.

[8] Georges Hourdin, *La Presse Catholique*, p. 14.

ters the publishing business to defend a political ideology or to earn money, his publication is not Christian."[9]

All Catholic publications treat the Church with great respect and try to give as broad a coverage of Church events as possible. The Church cannot be considered by any Catholic publication staff as merely another human social group.[10] Official decisions of the Pope are never directly criticized. The Catholic press is ready at all times to submit to the discipline of the Church; when a Catholic publication is condemned formally, it has no alternative but to stop publication.

Finally, there is a certain spirit of humility and mutual tolerance throughout the Catholic press, for everyone knows that his ideas are opposed by those of others who are just as good Catholics. "We do not pretend to bring anything else than a Christian testimonial. We do not impose our attitudes, our temperament, our style on anyone. We understand that all Christians have these same rights. We only ask them to recognize the same rights for us."[11]

In case certain Catholic editors or publishers might lack the required humility, the Hierarchy has prescribed rules of conduct toward all Catholic publications: "As long as papers or reviews . . . are not forbidden by the competent Church authority, no one has the right to oppose their sale. And in doctrinal or disciplinary matters, which are the exclusive concern

[9] *ibid.*, p. 62. Some publications come close to the borderline of temporal action. *Verbe* and *Esprit* exist more to defend an ideology than to defend the Church, so in this sense are different from all the other publications considered here. But a leftist magazine like *Témoignage Chrétien* affirms its Catholicism: "Our action always has been and remains spiritual above all. When we judge the temporal and when we take positions, we do so from a spiritual viewpoint." Georges Montaron in *Témoignage Chrétien*, April 17, 1959, p. 2.

[10] Cf. *Témoignage Chrétien*, November 6, 1959, p. 2, and *Chronique Sociale*, Vol. LXVIII, No. 3, May 15, 1960, p. 166.

[11] *Témoignage Chrétien*, April 17, 1959, p. 2. The same attitude was expressed, in interviews, by Jean de Fabregues, editor of *France Catholique*, and Abbé Richard, editor of *Homme Nouveau.*

of the Hierarchy, any accusation or condemnation by individuals without mandate must be considered as contrary to the constitution of the Church and bordering on insurrection."[12]

C. ECCLESIASTICAL CONTROL OVER THE CATHOLIC PRESS

All of the Catholic publications are "recognized as Catholic by the ecclesiastical authority."[13] This recognition implies a certain control as well. For many publications the control is exercised by the directors and editors themselves, since a great many publications are directly run by religious orders. For others the situation is more complex. Every Catholic publication has an ecclesiastical advisor who theoretically controls the content of the publication to make sure that it follows the principles of the Church. Actually, this control is exercised most sparingly and is always done after publication.[14]

In many Catholic communities parish press committees distribute much of the Catholic press. These committees usually reflect the views of the curé who heads them. If he prefers *France Catholique*, its circulation is likely to rise. Or if he is a partisan of *Témoignage Chrétien*, it will find favor with many parishioners as well. The temporal significance of these committees will be discussed below.

On the diocese level the control of the Church over publications often has a partisan character. The bishop can make known his own personal preferences, and can even cast doubt

[12] Cardinal Feltin, quoted in *I.C.I.*, October 15, 1956, p. 5.

[13] Father Gabel, quoted in *Guide Pratique des Catholiques de France*, 7th ed., Vol. I (Paris: Office Nationale de Propagande Catholique, 1958), p. 109.

[14] In an unusual move, the Hierarchy removed the ecclesiastical advisor from *Témoignage Chrétien* without replacing him. This seems like an exceptional act, perhaps taken as a disciplinary measure. However, it does not seem to deprive *Témoignage Chrétien* of its Catholic status. Georges Suffert, formerly the managing editor of *Témoignage Chrétien*, writes that in five years he was practically never told what to write by the Hierarchy and was censored only once. See Suffert, *Les Catholiques et la Gauche* (Paris: François Maspero, 1960), p. 29.

in the minds of the faithful on the Catholic status of a given publication.[15]

On the national level there are two potential centers of control: the Episcopal Commission on Information and the entire ACA. The Commission probably could have a certain influence over the positions of the Catholic press, but the bishops who compose it are divided on the proper function of the Catholic press, reflecting even sharper divisions among the Catholics of France themselves.[16]

The ACA exercises the most effective control over the Catholic press, since so much of the Catholic press is national in scope. For example, recently the ACA suggested that bishops stop permitting Catholic publications to be sold inside churches unless they have a "specifically religious character."[17] Usually the ACA need take no specific disciplinary actions itself; it suffices to recommend policies to each bishop, to publications, or to the faithful.

It is very rare that a Catholic publication incurs direct ecclesiastical sanctions. Indirectly, however, the Hierarchy can exert effective pressure. When a high prelate makes known to a Catholic publication the consensus of Church feeling, generally he will be respectfully followed. If the Hierarchy makes it known informally to a Catholic publication that it lacks the

[15] Cardinal Richaud forbade all "partisan" Catholic publications from being sold inside churches in his diocese, except *Courrier Français de Bordeaux, Panorama Chrétien, Pèlerin,* and *Vie Catholique Illustrée.* This gave the impression to his parishioners that these publications were in a "special category." This favoritism has not been endorsed by all the other bishops. See Jacques Maître, "Le Fonctionnement de la Presse Catholique en France," mimeographed study for the *Association Française de Science Politique,* June 1957, p. 5. Cf. *Le Monde,* April 5-6, 1959, p. 9.

[16] Cf. Maître, *op.cit.*, p. 15.

[17] See *France Observateur,* April 9, 1959, p. 4. If this directive is put into effect throughout France it will have a noticeable effect on the financial solvency of publications like *Témoignage Chrétien* which largely depend on sales in churches. Some have thought that *Témoignage Chrétien* was being "punished" by means of this pronouncement.

confidence of the Church, it is quite likely that the publication will stop its work. Such was the case, for example, with the Dominican Order's *Actualité Religieuse dans le Monde.* Excessive partisanship on issues such as the worker-priest affair brought an unofficial reprimand from the Hierarchy, and the Dominicans abandoned the publication.[18]

Up to now the French Church has lacked a policy on Catholic publications which would be valid for the entire country. Through declarations and encouragements or through reprimands, individual leaders of the Hierarchy can give their personal approval or disapproval to a Catholic publication, and this often brings dissensions among bishops to the public eye. All bishops have supported to some degree *La Croix.* But *Témoignage Chrétien* has had only the support of the more "progressive" bishops, notably Cardinals Gerlier and Liénart. It has incurred the opposition of Cardinal Richaud.[19] On the other hand, a publication which claims to be of "Catholic inspiration" like *Paternité-Maternité* has been approved by the Bishop of Reims, but severely criticized by most of the French cardinals.[20]

Both formally and informally the Church has been moderate in controlling the Catholic press. It has deliberately allowed a wide freedom of expression in the political and social realms and even allowed variations in the apostolic goals of the Catholic press. The Hierarchy, the custodian of the "thesis" that Catholics must read only the Catholic press, was wise enough not to emphasize unduly this impractical wish.[21]

[18] See the last issue of *Actualité Religieuse dans le Monde,* May 15, 1955, p. 1. The publication still exists, under the name of *Informations Catholiques Internationales,* but is run by laymen.

[19] From an interview with an official of *Témoignage Chrétien.* One of the reasons for supporting *Témoignage Chrétien* seems to be that it is the best way of keeping a certain group of "progressives" within the Church. See *I.C.I.,* March 1, 1956, p. 7, and July 15, 1956, p. 6.

[20] See *Actualité Religieuse dans le Monde,* January 1, 1954, p. 8. Cf. *I.C.I.,* February 16, 1960, p. 23.

[21] Few would follow the advice of *La Croix* that ". . . no conscientious Catholic has the right to buy or to read the 'worldly' press. . . . To each Catholic home a Catholic newspaper." *La Croix,* September 13, 1951, p. 4.

In this age of mass indifference to all that is religious, it might be more "efficient" for the Hierarchy to devise specific apostolic goals which all Catholic publications, no matter what their tendency, could follow. The Catholic press is a minority press, even among Catholic readers themselves; it will remain so until the nature of its apostolate is spelled out in more detail, and until a clear relation between its varied political positions and its apostolic goals can be seen. It is up to the Hierarchy to make the proper decisions in these matters.

II. The Organization of the Catholic Press

A. THE PRINCIPAL PUBLICATIONS AND PUBLISHING HOUSES

Dominating the national Catholic press are three "giant" publishing houses, each of which is responsible for several publications. These are *La Maison de la Bonne Presse, La Vie Catholique Illustrée*, and *L'Union des Oeuvres Catholiques de France*. Each was influenced by a religious order: *Bonne Presse* by the Assumptionnists, *Vie Catholique Illustrée* by the Dominicans of Paris, through the *Editions du Cerf*, and *Union des Oeuvres* by the *Fils de la Charité*.

The *Bonne Presse* was already thriving in the nineteenth century, and was active in the anti-Masonic, anti-Dreyfus struggles of the early 1900's. The *Union des Oeuvres* is a venerable service group whose publications, like those of *Vie Catholique Illustrée*, have been most notable since World War II.

Each of these publishing houses differs slightly from the others in its political orientations. *Vie Catholique Illustrée* is much more open in its political affiliations than the other two. Its director, Georges Hourdin, was until recently on the National Bureau of the MRP. One of its other directors, Robert Buron, is also an MRP leader. At the beginning of the Fifth Republic he was chosen to be de Gaulle's Minister of Public Works. *Bonne Presse* has often given tacit support to the MRP through *La Croix* and one of its directors, André Colin, is also on the MRP National Bureau. However, *Bonne Presse* cannot be too overtly partisan because of its ties to the Assumptionnist Order.

La Croix, published by the *Bonne Presse*, is the only Catholic daily newspaper of national importance in France. As such it has a semiofficial role in the Church and is always obliged to act "as if its attitude committed the reputation of the Church."[22]

The publications of *Union des Oeuvres* are much more pious in nature, tending more to create a Catholic atmosphere within certain groups than to take any political position. Thus, the mass-appeal monthly magazine *Panorama Chrétien* had no partisan articles at all during the crucial year of 1958. The children's magazines of *Union des Oeuvres—Coeurs Vaillants, Ames Vaillantes*, and *Fripounet*—pave the way for future adherence to Catholic Action.

All three publishing houses publish a popular magazine for the mass audience: the weeklies *Pèlerin* from *Bonne Presse, Vie Catholique Illustrée* from the publisher of the same name, and *Panorama Chrétien* which was already mentioned. The circulation for all three is about 1,300,000.[23] The children's magazines published by *Union des Oeuvres* and *Bonne Presse* reach 750,000 children regularly. These figures are very respectable, and compare favorably with the most popular non-Catholic publications in each category. Finally, it should be noted that all three publishing houses are making money, which is not always the case for the French press.

The *Bonne Presse* and *Union des Oeuvres*, still controlled by the orders which founded them, seem to be closer to the Church Hierarchy than *Vie Catholique Illustrée*, which is now "independent" of the Dominicans. But in fact, the officials of these three concerns consider one another equally "Catholic," or in other words the same distance from the Hierarchy.[24]

[22] Mondange, *L'Information Catholique*, Vol. I, p. 69.

[23] OJD *Officiel*, 1958, *passim*. Cf. Jacques Maître, *op.cit.*, pp. 6-9.

[24] Interviews with M. de la Potterie, head of documents section, *Union des Oeuvres*, Jean Pelissier, *Bonne Presse*, and Georges Hourdin, publisher of *Vie Catholique Illustrée*.

TABLE 2

The Publications of the "Big Three" Catholic Publishing Houses with Their Circulation

	Bonne Presse	*Vie Catholique Illustrée*	*Union des Oeuvres*
(daily)	*La Croix*[a] 150,000		
(weekly)	*Le Pèlerin* 580,000	*Vie Catholique Illustrée* 600,000	*Panorama Chrétien* (monthly) 180,000
(child)	*Bayard, Bernadette* 200,000		*Ames, Coeurs Vaillants, Fripounet,* etc. 600,000
(documentary)	*Documentation Catholique* 15,000	*Informations Catholiques Internationales* 18,000	
(other)		*Radio, Cinéma, Télévision*[b] 75,000	

[a] Sources for circulation figures: Jacques Maitre, "Le Fonctionnement de la Presse Catholique en France," mimeographed study for the *Association Française de Science Politique,* June 1957, pp. 6-9. See also *Echo de la Presse et de la Publicité,* No. 364, May 15, 1959, p. 19.

[b] Only the politically-significant publications have been included in this table.

B. "POLITICAL" CATHOLIC PUBLICATIONS, FROM EXTREME LEFT TO EXTREME RIGHT

Outside of the "Big Three" many independent Catholic publications express a particular political tendency. There are, or have been, Catholic publications representing every political shade of opinion from the extreme left to the extreme right. Generally there is one major review for each well-defined "tendency," although at present the Catholic extreme left is not represented. The Church has been very severe to publications in this category.[25]

[25] *Vie Intellectuelle, Quinzaine,* and *Jeunesse de l'Eglise* were all pressured by the Hierarchy to discontinue the dissemination of information which was considered too left-wing for the Church. A mimeographed sheet, first called *Le Bulletin* and later *La Lettre,* tried vainly to take on

Esprit has a certain attraction for the Catholic left. But it is now in the process of seeking a new ideological niche, with a changeover in its staff. At any rate, *Esprit* has always protested against being "Catholic," though accepting the term "of Christian inspiration." The directors of *Esprit* have usually been well-known Catholics, careful to avoid any explicit condemnation for "heresy" by the Hierarchy. Emmanuel Mounier, the founder and philosophical leader of *Esprit,* called it "a review confronting believers and nonbelievers, but in religious matters, we repudiate any syncretism."[26] Another important reason for including *Esprit* here is that the review is considered by many people as being Catholic: "To many people *Esprit* seems in fact to be a Catholic review, a review of the Catholic left."[27]

Témoignage Chrétien represents the progressive but not the extremist left in French Catholicism. Founded by a Jesuit, it has been forced to relinquish all ties with that order. The effectiveness of *Témoignage Chrétien* (or, as its supporters call it, T.C.) now seems to be declining. For example, its circulation figures have been dropping steadily for some years.[28] But individual supporters are capable of great devotion to the magazine—more, perhaps than any Catholics this side of the extreme right. There is even an organization of "friends of T.C." consisting of voluntary door-to-door distributors of the magazine.

Nevertheless, when a national magazine like T.C. declines to below 50,000 copies per week and is snubbed by major advertisers, its position seems precarious.[29] Sympathetic members

---

the role of *Quinzaine*. In recent months, a watered-down version of *Vie Intellectuelle* has been started by the Paris Dominicans.

[26] Quoted by Michel François, "La Revue qui a Formé une Génération Chrétienne," *France Observateur,* April 2, 1959, p. 12.

[27] *ibid.* Georges Suffert categorically denies that *Esprit* is a review of the Catholic left, yet he feels it necessary to analyze it in his book *Les Catholiques et la Gauche,* p. 123. The spiritual content of *Esprit* was a major factor in persuading the Archbishop of Paris to defend it against a possible Vatican condemnation. See *I.C.I.,* March 15, 1960, p. 20.

[28] OJD *Officiel,* No. 133, January 1960, p. 7.

[29] Maître, *op.cit.,* p. 19.

of the Hierarchy are aware of this problem and have recognized what a loss it would be if T.C. disappeared. But at the same time the Hierarchy has cast doubt as to the "orthodoxy" of T.C. by forcing its editor-in-chief, Georges Suffert, to resign, and by removing its ecclesiastical advisor.[30]

The opposite number of *Témoignage Chrétien* on the right side of the political spectrum is *La France Catholique.* Founded after World War II, *France Catholique* was originally the official magazine of the ACGH. It still shares the conservative political orientations of the Catholic Action group, and its editor is a director of ACGH. The two are located in the same building. However they are now formally distinct. *France Catholique* is much more partisan than *La Croix.* Yet many ordinary Catholics consider it the weekly complement to *La Croix*—that is, the "most Catholic" of all the national weeklies in France. This is actually not true, but *France Catholique* is unlikely to dispel the impression.

The most dynamic tendency in French Catholicism for the moment is the Catholic extreme right. Most of its publications and movements are increasing in circulation and influence. Among the national publications in this category are *Homme Nouveau, Pensée Catholique, Itinéraires, Verbe,* and *Documents-Paternité* (formerly *Paternité-Maternité*). The last-mentioned publication is not taken seriously and has been denounced by most leaders of the Hierarchy. *Pensée Catholique,* mainly an intellectual and doctrinal review, seldom speaks out on political issues, though when it does, it is with rare virulence. *Homme Nouveau* is the only publication of this group with ties to more moderate Catholic publications, as will be seen below.

The most interesting of the extreme right Catholic publications is *Verbe,* which sponsors a movement called *Cité Catholique.* It appears that the movement is more important than the review itself (which is not unusual in France; *Force Ou-*

30 See *L'Express,* September 25, 1958, p. 5.

vrière and *Reconstruction* started from reviews). *Verbe* and *Cité Catholique* seem to have strong support from the more traditionalist members of the French Hierarchy, and notably from Mgr. Marmottin, Archbishop of Reims. The Pope himself, when Nuncio in France, gave the movement his blessings. But neither *Verbe* nor *Cité Catholique* is mandated by the Hierarchy. *Verbe* is certainly much too extremist ever to receive such a mandate, for it considers itself "counterrevolutionary," rejecting the principles of the French Revolution, on which the Republic is founded.

As the embodiment of *Verbe*'s ideals, *Cité Catholique* has established "cells" among the French elite, especially within the army and among students. With bastions in the army it could become politically significant without compromising the purity of its doctrine or worrying about attracting the masses to its cause. Even now *Cité Catholique* can attract a respectable number from among the French elite. Over 1100 people attended its 1959 national congress.

Verbe emphasizes the dogma of the Church to a great degree—or rather, it emphasizes those encyclicals and teachings that support its own social and political teaching. Whether *Verbe* and *Cité Catholique* represent a "wave of the future" or a holdover from the prewar partisan Catholic leagues, is unclear at present, for it is still too early to judge their real political impact.[31]

None of these politically-oriented Catholic publications has received a formal mandate from the Church. All are controlled by laymen and the policies of none commit the Church as such. They have very modest circulation figures: together they would

[31] The best sources of information on *Verbe* are *I.C.I.*, February 15, 1960, pp. 17-25; Henri Fesquet, "Verbe, Revue de la *Cité Catholique*, renie les Principes de la Revolution," in *Le Monde*, July 9, 1958, p. 3; and J.-M. Le Blond, "Dangers Religieux de la Politique," in *Etudes*, Vol. 299, No. 12, December 1958, pp. 385-396, and Vol. 300, No. 2, February 1959, pp. 238-250. These, of course, are supplements to the magazine itself.

not publish 200,000 copies per issue—and half this figure is made up by T.C. and *France Catholique* alone. Low circulation figures give one indication of the political influence of these publications, though of course such figures are not the only criterion for judging influence.

C. PUBLICATIONS OF RELIGIOUS ORDERS AND CLERGY

A certain number of publications are neither part of the "big three" nor independent political organs. The most important are those belonging to religious orders. Jesuits, Dominicans, Benedictines and other orders print several technical and intellectual reviews, most of which have no political importance. But two should be mentioned because of their national influence and their concern with political problems. *Etudes* is the very respectable hundred-year-old organ of the Jesuit Order in France. The Dominicans of Paris are able once more to disseminate their rather progressive slant on political events through *Signes du Temps*, successor to the eminent *Vie Intellectuelle.*

Well over half the dioceses in France possess a local paper for temporal news, in addition to the official *Semaine Religieuse.*[32] These local papers are generally controlled by the bishop, though they are not formally tied to the Church. They usually have a small circulation, averaging not more than 15,000 per diocese. Few are partisan. However, they were politically significant in the past; their neutrality depends primarily on the views and desires of the local bishop.

Certain Catholic papers have several local editions. Those of the *Courrier Français de Bordeaux*, covering sixteen departments of southwest France, and the Sunday editions of *La Croix* are the prime examples.

[32] According to Mondange there are 73 of these weeklies in French dioceses. See J. Mondange, *Le Chrétien Devant l'Information* (Paris: CTIC, 1957), pp. 24-25. Hourdin counts 80, *La Presse Catholique*, pp. 106-111. This latter reference is the most authoritative statement on the local Catholic press.

D. CATHOLIC BOOK PUBLISHERS

Periodicals are not the only Catholic publications with political significance in France. A certain number of Catholic book publishers must also be mentioned. In France over 300 publishing houses have published "Catholic books" since 1951![33] Most of these organizations are not themselves Catholic; they simply have found it good business to publish Catholic books because they sell well. Only those publishers who specialize in turning out books of Catholic inspiration and whose work is imbued by the Christian spirit can be called "Catholic" book publishers.[34]

One major book publisher is controlled by the Paris Dominicans: *Les Editions du Cerf*. It published reviews like *Vie Intellectuelle,* and helped *Vie Catholique Illustrée* in the early stages of its development. *Cerf* recently published a study by Hubert Beuve-Méry, editor of *Le Monde,* on the causes for the collapse of the Fourth Republic. *Cerf* has also been quite interested in apostolic problems, especially in the attempts to convert the working class. It published the famous *France: Pays de Mission?* and recently Father Loew's *Journal d'Une Mission Ouvrière.*

Among other Catholic book publishers, *Editions Ouvrières* is closely connected with the JOC and with *Economie et Humanisme,* publishing many books on technical economic questions, on international affairs, and on religious sociology. *Editions Spes* was founded by Jesuits working at *Action Populaire,* but is now independent of them. It still publishes studies by

[33] See Syndicat des Editeurs de Paris, *Livres Catholiques 1951-1955* (Paris: Syndicat des Editeurs, 1955), *passim.* This booklet does not clearly define what a "Catholic book" is, since it includes those "susceptible to interest and to document the Catholic reader," as well as books on piety which have the Imprimatur. *ibid.*, p. 1.

[34] According to one estimate there are over 50 Catholic publishers, but only a handful deal with any politically significant books. See d'Arcier, *L'Information Catholique,* Vol. II, *Comment Diffuser la Pensée Chrétienne,* pp. 168-170. The *Annuaire Catholique de France* for 1958-59 lists 136 "publishers of Catholic books," though most of these are minor. See pp. 1277-1289.

Jesuits on religious sociology, on questions dealing with the proletariat, on political ideologies, and other social questions. Finally, certain "neutral" publishing houses have a policy of close cooperation with the Church, publish many books which receive the Imprimatur, and thus identify themselves closely with French Catholicism. One of the most ambitious collections of Catholic books is *Je Sais—Je Crois*, published by one of the "neutral" publishers, *Arthème Fayard*. When completed, this collection will comprise over 150 volumes.[35]

Catholic book publishers can be divided into "tendencies" which parallel the tendencies of Catholic periodicals. There are right-wing publishers, such as *Editions du Cèdre* (which publishes *Pensée Catholique*) or *Nouvelles Editions Latines*. Moderate or traditionalist publishing houses include *Arthème Fayard, Alsatia, Desclée*. Among publishers of the left are *Editions du Seuil*, publishers of *Esprit; Editions du Cerf*; and *Editions Ouvrières*. Of these publishers, the ones not controlled by religious orders have no direct ties with the Church and theoretically can publish any books they choose. Actually, a good number of their new books are of Catholic inspiration, so the publishing houses are at the service of the Church. The fact that they have influence within French Catholicism without much control by the Hierarchy raises some ill feeling among "controlled" publishers such as *Editions du Cerf*.[36]

The Church might possibly extend its control over publishers of "Catholic collections" in two ways. Most publishers of Catholic books have priests working with them as ecclesiastical advisors. At present these advisors receive no specific instructions from the Hierarchy and in fact soon become members of the

[35] Among the books in the collection are Georges Hourdin's study of the Catholic press, a book on Catholic Action by Mgr. Garonne, Archbishop of Toulouse, and future volumes which will study the relations between Christianity and Communism, and Christianity and colonialism.

[36] Interview with an official of *Editions du Cerf*. There is a Catholic Action committee dealing with the publishing profession and including 25 or 30 representatives of bookstores, writers, and printers "of Catholic inspiration." However, this group seems to have no direct political influence over its members. It meets only three times per year and is mainly interested in technical problems of circulation.

publishing team. But they could become more rigorous in their surveillance if asked to do so by the Hierarchy. The only other control by the Church is the Imprimatur. Now it is largely negative, implying that a book does not violate any doctrines of the Church. Perhaps it could be used more selectively to cull out the ideas disapproved of by the local bishop or the Hierarchy. It is, of course, quite unlikely that the Hierarchy would approve such methods in the near future.

As a net result of lack of control, some of the most influential centers of thought for French Catholicism exist independently of the Hierarchy. A publisher such as *Editions du Seuil,* which has a certain "Catholic aura" about it but no direct ties to the Church, has published most of the works of Mounier. In doing so it has contributed much to the evolution of the Catholic left without any approval or consent from the Church.[37]

E. OTHER STRUCTURES FOR THE CATHOLIC PRESS

The Catholic press has a financial independence far beyond the commercial French press because of its distinctive distribution system. Eliminating costly newsstand agents who take the middleman's cut of profits, most Catholic publications are distributed through parish press committees. Parish distributors, under the authority of the ecclesiastical and Catholic Action authorities, go from house to house in the parish, are present at public celebrations, and set up stands after Sunday Mass and on other occasions with a wide sampling of the Catholic press.[38]

The ACA has urged the press committees to distribute the totality of the Catholic press. But because of the personality of a bishop or of a local curé, many committees concentrate on selected publications. Certain distributors are active supporters of *Témoignage Chrétien,* or of *Vie Catholique Illustrée,* or

[37] Information from conversations with Professor René Rémond.

[38] For an authoritative treatment of press committees and financial independence of the Catholic press, see Maître, *op.cit.,* pp. 16-20.

France Catholique, and largely ignore the rest of the Catholic press. Few support the extremist Catholic publications, and it is not surprising that *Paternité-Maternité* called the press committees "crypto-Communist."[39]

The *Centrale Technique d'Information Catholique* (CTIC) is another technical press group, controlled by Mgr. Ménager and closely related to the parish press committees. The CTIC has a propaganda and public relations role in the Church. However, its propaganda does not usually relate to political subjects, with the exception of the school issue. Most of its work consists in posting placards and wall newspapers, designed to explain the basic dogma of the Church to the public at large. In this work the CTIC cooperates with the parish press committees. The CTIC has distributed many tracts and posters on themes such as "only the Catholic newspaper should be read in the Catholic home," or "parents must give their children Christian magazines." Analyses of the "neutral" press from a Catholic viewpoint are also made and widely distributed by the CTIC.[40]

The *Centre National de la Presse Catholique* has rather restricted duties, despite its title. It is formed of representatives from *Témoignage Chrétien, La France Catholique, Vie Catholique Illustrée, La Bonne Presse, L'Union des Oeuvres*, the MFR, the JAC, and *Homme Nouveau.* The Center is primarily concerned with technical questions: how to improve the distribution and increase the circulation of member publications; how to improve publicity for the publications; how to train local parish distributors to accomplish their task most efficiently. It has no control over the policies of individual members nor does it control local parish groups. *France Catholique* refused to join the Center for a number of years. It seems that it wanted to defer joining until it reached larger circulation figures.[41]

[39] *ibid.*, p. 17.

[40] For analyses of CTIC activities see CTIC: *Notre Courrier*, No. 114, July 1958.

[41] Interview with Jean de Fabrègues, editor of *France Catholique*. Cf. *France Catholique*, September 11, 1959, p. 8.

Another reason for moderate hostility from *France Catholique* is that the Center was founded by Mme. Sauvageot of *Vie Catholique Illustrée*, who had extremist political views before she converted to Catholicism.[42] But the spectre of Mme. Sauvageot did not delay *Homme Nouveau*, which is more traditionalist than *France Catholique*, from joining the Center.

The *Association Nationale des Périodiques Catholiques de Province* has a technical role similar to the Center. It has a Paris office supported from funds given by the *Courrier Français de Bordeaux*. From this office information on events in the Capital is sent to virtually all the local Catholic publications in France.[43] Such information can be invaluable, since so much of French life is centered in Paris. It seems to be objective and is not intended to sway the editorial policies of local papers. The Association, like the Center, is limited to the technical realm, helping to make the Catholic press as efficient as possible.

Cardinal Feltin, in cooperation with Protestant, Jewish and Moslem leaders, sponsors another press group, called *Les Informateurs Religieux*. The group comprises the professional journalists who write about religious events, though not necessarily of the Catholic faith themselves. Membership in the group makes the task of a reporter considerably easier: he is admitted to most meetings of Catholic organizations and is given some information not ordinarily available to the public. Even more important, the religious reporters for daily newspapers can serve as a sounding board for policies from the Hierarchy that might have public repercussions. This is especially true for a man like Henri Fesquet, religious reporter for the influential *Le Monde*. Most general Catholic publications have reporters accredited to *Les Informateurs Religieux*, but those of the extreme right, such as *Homme Nouveau* or *Verbe*, do not. The head of *Les Informateurs Religieux*, Jean Pelissier, is

[42] Mme. Sauvageot has been attacked by Jean Madiran in *Ils ne Savent Pas Ce qu'Ils Font* (Paris: Nouvelles Editions Latines, 1955).

[43] Hourdin lists 77 Catholic papers in metropolitan France which are members of the Association. Hourdin, *op.cit.*, pp. 108-110.

FIGURE 4. The Organization of the Catholic Periodical Press: Publications and Coordinating Groups

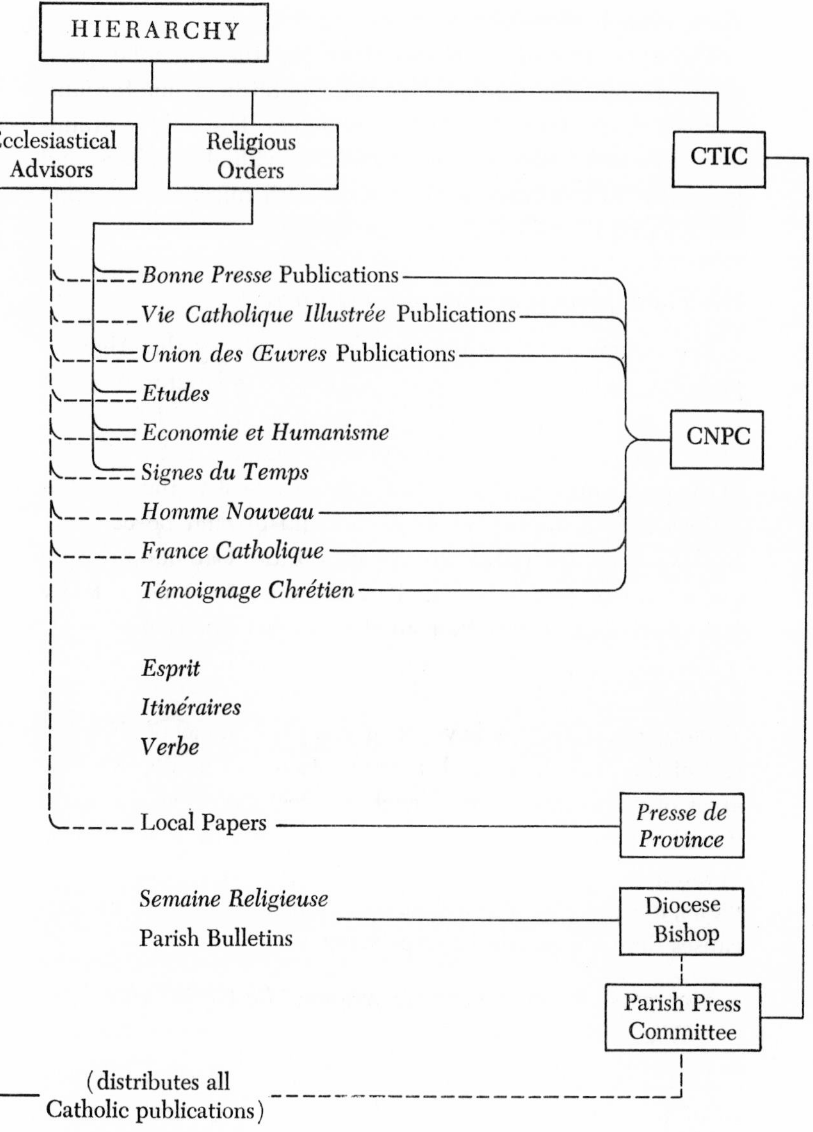

associated with the *Bonne Presse*, as is another principal advisor, Alfred Michelin.[44]

Three international organizations for the Catholic press should be noted in passing. One is for publishers, one for journalists, and one for publications themselves. These three groups have no control over policies of their individual members, and generally do not concern themselves with questions affecting the internal life of countries represented.

III. The Opinions of the Catholic Press

The nature of the regime, means for solving the Algerian problem, and state aid to private schools are keystones of the French political crisis. During the eventful year of 1958, when many feared a great disaster and others hoped that a solution to the problems was at last drawing close, most Catholic publications felt an imperative need to stand up and be counted. In this section the published opinions of the Catholic press on major political problems will be analyzed, to show more clearly just where each publication stood in a crisis situation.

The large publications with the most political significance, *La Croix, Vie Catholique Illustrée, France Catholique*, and *Témoignage Chrétien* have been analyzed in detail. For the rest of the Catholic press briefer mention will be made of the areas of preoccupation in French politics. *Esprit*, as was mentioned before, is a borderline publication. It will be interesting to compare its positions with those of the fully Catholic reviews, to see if a greater distance from the ecclesiastical nucleus causes different political perspectives.

A. THE GENERAL INTEREST PUBLICATIONS: "*La Croix*" AND "*Vie Catholique Illustrée.*"

La Croix was one of the leaders in the campaign for state relief to Catholic schools in 1951, when it generally stayed close to the APEL line. Often one could find in its pages articles

[44] Factual information from interview with Jean Pelissier, head of *Les Informateurs Religieux*, July 11, 1959.

explaining the basic doctrines of the Church on education. This was particularly true before the election in June 1951. At that time Church educational doctrine was supplemented with articles by French bishops on how Catholics should vote. In certain issues of *La Croix* just before the election, slogans favorable to school aid were put at the top of page one.[45]

As the "most Catholic" of all French newspapers, *La Croix* could give the impression that it spoke for the French Hierarchy on the school issue; this was particularly easy since there were no disagreements among French bishops on the propriety of aid to Catholic schools. Thus, before the 1951 elections, *La Croix* urged its readers as good Catholics to vote for "defenders of school freedom."[46] At times articles against the public schools appeared, though they were not the rule: ". . . The Communist Party is not complaining very much about our public schools; haven't they helped the Party to conquer one fifth of the voting public?"[47]

In its arguments justifying the cause of Catholic schools, *La Croix* was similar to the school pressure groups which will be examined in Chapter Eight. Unlike them, however, it did not consider the school question the only important electoral issue. Many other issues determined the common good, which deputies must work to better.[48]

In recent years, even before the 1959 school law, the school issue declined as more pressing social issues crowded the columns of *La Croix*. Before each election it is still mentioned, but generally *La Croix* uses vague terms like "school justice," without referring to the specific program of APEL or other groups.[49]

On the Algerian rebellion *La Croix* at first avoided a partisan interpretation of news. When bishops spoke up against

[45] See *La Croix* for January 3, January 5, January 6, May 16, June 2, 1951.

[46] See Father Gabel, "Notre Devoir," *La Croix*, June 15, 1951, p. 1.

[47] *La Croix*, September 8, 1951, p. 1.

[48] Father Gabel, "Pour Qui Voter?" *La Croix*, June 1, 1951, p. 1.

[49] See Father Wenger, "L'Oeuvre de la Justice," *La Croix*, November 22, 1958, p. 1.

tortures on one side or another, their statements were printed, but without much comment. In the early stages of the rebellion there were some articles defending certain types of colonialism.[50] But in more recent months *La Croix* has repudiated the extremist factions, especially those who favor integration at all cost: "Those who call ceaselessly for French Algeria have made the first step toward secession. . . . It must be concluded that there is a premeditated plot."[51] *La Croix* was not happy about the deputies elected from Algeria in 1958: "France has just suffered a setback in Algeria. We are menaced by the arrival in Paris of deputies who will weigh heavily on our metropolitan politics without helping as much as would be desirable for Algeria, to do the 'rest' which General de Gaulle has spoken about."[52]

La Croix repudiated any broad coalition of "anti-Fascist" forces including the Communists, that would try to put a quick end to the war. Referring to a meeting for peace in Algeria attended by François Mauriac, André Philip, and representatives of *Humanité*, *La Croix* called attention to a situation ". . . where the least success of Communists in France could push Western Europe over into the Soviet camp."[53]

Before such questions as negotiating with the Algerian rebels were within the realm of government consideration, *La Croix* refused to take a stand officially, because its position within French Catholicism might lead people to believe its stands were endorsed by the French Hierarchy. However, when negotiations were undertaken briefly in 1960, *La Croix* let it be known that it approved, and added this: "It is not possible for one million Europeans to dominate nine million Arabs much longer,

[50] See Father Ducatillon, in *La Croix*, May 29, 1956.

[51] *La Croix*, May 15-16, 1958, p. 1.

[52] Pierre Limagne, "De Gaulle ne se laissera pas enfermer dans une impasse," *La Croix*, November 12, 1958, p. 1.

[53] *La Croix*, April 1, 1958, p. 3. In 1961, *La Croix* repudiated the forces of the extreme right. During the abortive "revolt of the Generals" *La Croix* called de Gaulle's policies "the only way to peace" and urged everyone to cooperate in defeating the seditious army officers. See *La Croix*, April 25, 1961, p. 1.

just as it is out of the question for the nine million not to respect the rights of the minority."[54]

Similar factors gave *La Croix* a prudent reserve toward the floundering Fourth Republic until the great crisis of 1958 made everyone take sides. Then, *La Croix* became openly disillusioned with the Fourth Republic as it stood: "The French state is nothing more than a zombie. . . . The French state does not govern any more. Each day political reality shows this to us."[55]

By their Algerian policy after February 6, 1956, the Socialists more than any other group were blamed for the crisis of 1958.[56] When the Pflimlin government, inheriting the Socialist follies, came to power, *La Croix* was openly sympathetic. But even as Pflimlin tried to save the regime, *La Croix* saw the necessity of de Gaulle: "The common good demands, it seems, a renewal of the dialogue with Algiers. Doubtless de Gaulle is the only one qualified to undertake that task."[57] Until May 27, 1958, *La Croix* doubted that de Gaulle had a chance of coming to power. "For the time being, de Gaulle knows that, outside of a *coup d'état* little to his liking, he has no possibility of coming to power, in spite of what certain power-hungry pseudo-Gaullists may think."[58] On May 27, *La Croix* issued an agonized call for Pflimlin to decide on a definite course of action. By the following day, the negotiations between Pflimlin and de Gaulle were known and *La Croix* had already become more discreet. By May 29, it was speculating with the rest of the French press on the chances for a pro-de Gaulle majority in the National Assembly.

Since the May crisis, *La Croix* has retained a sympathetic view of the government. On the constitutional referendum it did not openly admit its preferences for a "yes" vote, but most of the bishops' pronouncements which it printed were favorable. The venerable columnist Pierre l'Hermite, much appreciated by his fellow clergymen, made no secret of his sentiments:

[54] *ibid.*, June 22, 1960, p. 1.
[55] Joseph Folliet, "Feu l'Etat," *La Croix*, March 9-10, 1958, p. 1.
[56] See editorial by Father Wenger, *La Croix*, May 17, 1958, p. 1.
[57] *La Croix*, May 20, 1958, p. 1.
[58] *ibid.*, May 24, 1958, p. 1.

"And you will vote YES?—Certainly!—You hear so many things, it's hard to tell right from wrong.—Talk is cheap, but when a boat is going to sink in a rough sea where there is only one life raft, do you go looking for added difficulties? You jump on till something better comes along!"[59]

However, the last editorial before the referendum seems quite objective: "Some fear that Fascism will triumph over democracy if the Constitution is approved. This is not just an illusion. Others firmly believe that rejecting the Constitution will cause the triumph of Communism and the ruin, before long, of all our freedom. In a world where international Communism is strong, this fear is not less justified."[60] The reticence of *La Croix* certainly reflects the desire of most French bishops not to take sides openly in the referendum. But it also seems that *La Croix* shared some of the reserves toward the new regime that can be found in *Témoignage Chrétien*. It certainly was not bothered by the term "laic" in the new Constitution, as was the Catholic extreme right.

Another recent question involving partisan politics on which *La Croix* took a firm stand was the Communist issue. During the 1958 national election campaign, it repeated anti-Communist themes which were surely familiar to its readers: "On November 30, the majority of Frenchmen will do their best to dam up the Communist tide in their voting districts. This will be necessary, but not very positive. . . . Actually, it is less important to defeat the men of the Communist Party than to defeat their ideas and to extirpate from France a very pernicious ideology."[61]

Unfortunately, none of the other Catholic publications can furnish the researcher with as much material as *La Croix*. Only a daily newspaper could follow the crisis of May 1958 in all its complexity. A few Catholic weeklies and especially monthly magazines must for technical reasons be made up days in ad-

[59] *ibid.*, September 13, 1958, p. 1.
[60] *ibid.*, September 27, 1958, p. 4.
[61] *ibid.*, November 20, 1958, p. 1.

vance. Thus they must limit their comments to the broad questions of long-term value in French politics. Furthermore, few other Catholic reviews attempt to exercise a mass influence. *France Catholique* and *Témoignage Chrétien* are the most successful exceptions. For most other Catholic publications there is no possibility of any mass influence.

Vie Catholique Illustrée resembles *La Croix* on most issues, although there are shades of difference in their emphases. For example, on the school issue *Vie Catholique* tended to subordinate specific remedies to the greater needs of economic and social justice. Also *Vie Catholique*, like the Dominican Order which founded it, has a special interest in converting the dechristianized masses: "As French Catholics become aware of the gravity of the apostolic problem confronting them, the problem of the private school tends to lose some of its importance."[62]

Vie Catholique Illustrée has not spoken out often on the Algerian rebellion or the political crisis of 1958, but its rare partisan declarations have often had wide repercussions. For example, in the issue of July 28, 1957 (pp. 7-11), a leading article describes the tortures inflicted by the French police in Algeria. The victims of these tortures were often Europeans who happened to have conciliatory views toward the Moslem nationalists, according to the article. This article inspired the Minister of Defense to forbid the distribution of *Vie Catholique* to military posts from October 1957 until early in 1958.

In the July 3, 1960 issue of *Vie Catholique*, Georges Hourdin seemed to modify the "progressive" views of his magazine when he recognized the permanent role of the army in Algeria: "We think of all our Algerian brothers of European origin, and demand that their rights and their property be defended. We ask the army, which today is winning an indisputable victory and without which nothing would have been possible, to remain on the scene."

[62] Georges Hourdin, owner and publisher of *Vie Catholique Illustrée*, writing in *Le Monde*, May 3, 1957, p. 5.

Turning toward French domestic policy, immediately before the end of the Fourth Republic Hourdin became exasperated with the moral state of the regime: "I do not need to insist on the necessity of a reform. It stands out before everyone's eyes. The fact that Parliament is neither capable nor worthy of accomplishing the reform itself leads us straight toward a dictatorship."[63]

Like *La Croix, Vie Catholique* blamed the Socialists for much of France's ills: "From the present crisis one Party comes out terribly diminished: the Socialist Party. Successive and contradictory Socialist errors have for a good part put France and Algeria in an explosive situation. At the last moment the Party recoiled before its responsibilities, either taking refuge in abstention or putting the burden on the shoulders of General de Gaulle. Except in Anglo-Saxon countries, will the destiny of Socialism always be to lay the groundwork sometimes for Communism, sometimes for Fascism, sometimes for authoritarian regimes?"[64]

But partisan statements are exceptional in *Vie Catholique.* Regularly only one page is devoted to political news each week —a page which is edited by Joseph Folliet of the *Chronique Sociale* and *Semaines Sociales.* The page probably escapes the average reader, and at any rate its material is usually quite objective.

The personal attitudes of the directors of *Vie Catholique* are even more partisan than these quotations would indicate. This is easy to prove, by comparing their style in *Vie Catholique* with another of their publications, *Informations Catholiques Internationales*, a review of information and documentation sent to specialists in religious and social questions. From the

[63] *Vie Catholique Illustrée,* April 27, 1958, p. 3.

[64] *ibid.*, June 15, 1958, p. 8. French Socialism does not seem capable of attracting many Catholics of any tendency: left-oriented Catholics are disappointed at its lack of dynamism, its petit-bourgeois base and its present leadership. Center Catholics do not mind cooperating with it from time to time, but prefer to vote for parties more favorably disposed to Catholicism, especially the MRP. Right-oriented Catholics are terrified by the Socialist brand of *laïcité.*

beginning of the rebellion, the latter has taken quite definite stands on Algeria: "The sins which are committed in Algeria by an unchecked police against Algerian nationalist militants are also our sins, insofar as we are journalists and can lift our voices or try to act in protest, but do not do so."[65]

"Algeria is not France. It has become little by little that stirring thing which is a nation in its beginnings. . . . However, it is not true, . . . that Algeria can completely dispense with France."[66]

"Present policy obstinately attempts to keep the *status quo* in Algeria and to reestablish it clandestinely in the rest of North Africa. It is insane."[67]

These quotations prove—and a personal interview confirmed—that Hourdin and his associates have definite, even impassioned views on political events. These views are not emphasized in *Vie Catholique Illustrée* because the latter aspires to remain in the "inner circle" of reviews closest to the Hierarchy. It has succeeded in its efforts, since it is one of the publications which Cardinal Richaud has allowed to be sold in churches. But unlike its sister reviews *Pèlerin* and *Panorama Chrétien*, *Vie Catholique* constantly risks reflecting too closely the opinions of its publisher.

B. THE NON-EXTREMIST PARTISAN PUBLICATIONS: *France Catholique, Témoignage Chrétien,* AND *Homme Nouveau*

The three publications to be considered in this section are designed primarily to increase the strength of Catholicism within a specific segment of political life. At the same time, none of these publications is an "outside instrument": they are wholly Catholic, and at the same time they all consider themselves integral parts of their political tendency. While trying to convert or improve the faith of left-oriented "progressives," *Témoignage Chrétien* sincerely shares their views, and it is the

[65] *Actualité Religieuse dans le Monde*, February 1, 1955, p. 1.
[66] *I.C.I.*, September 1, 1956, p. 4.
[67] *ibid.*, March 1, 1958, p. 4.

same for *France Catholique* among the *bien-pensant* moderates and *Homme Nouveau* among the authoritarian traditionalists.

France Catholique stresses the school question a great deal more than does *La Croix.* Its columns are frequently open to the chief Catholic school interests, and occasionally the public schools are criticized: "The laic school is either militantly atheist or areligious. . . . Inevitably the public schools have come to the point not so much that they suppress religion but that they attack it covertly or even overtly. . . ."[68]

At election time there was no secret which parties should be supported, since the criteria set forth by *France Catholique,* including support of Catholic schools, excluded all the parties of the left: "The Church does not engage in politics. There is not a Catholic party. Catholics can choose their deputies in different parties, but within the following limits: 1) You must vote for those who oppose Communism and collectivism. 2) For those who pledge to defend the family. 3) For those who pledge to defend freedom of education."[69]

On the Algerian question *France Catholique* has naturally taken a conservative position. In the early stages of the war it had spoken of an "Algerian fatherland," but it was violently against the Catholics who seemed to prefer the cause of the rebels over the work of the French army.[70] It favored a greater strengthening of the army in Algeria and was strongly against giving Algeria the possibility of choosing independence. Without Algeria, France herself might be pushed over into the camp of Moscow.[71] However, as the 1958 crisis drew near, *France Catholique* recognized that ". . . there is no 'Christian solution' which must be pursued in Algeria."[72]

France Catholique had little praise for the Fourth Republic, nor was it enthusiastic about de Gaulle's new Constitution.

[68] *France Catholique,* June 1, 1951, p. 4. [69] *ibid.*

[70] *ibid.*, January 13, 1956, and March 2, 1956, p. 1.

[71] *ibid.*, March 16, 1956, p. 1. But at the same time *France Catholique* also opposed the extremist wing of French settlers in Algeria. See *ibid.*, January 29, 1960, and Februay 5, 1960.

[72] *ibid.*, April 18, 1958, p. 1.

Political parties as they functioned under the Fourth Republic were denounced for their doctrinaire, theoretical, unrealistic behavior.[73] The pragmatic behavior of General de Gaulle during the May crisis—not committing himself to a particular policy before taking power—won the support of *France Catholique.* But the magazine warned against giving de Gaulle free reign. It saw the dangers of a one-man regime which many of its conservative colleagues were ready to follow uncritically. "More and more we have the impression that we are governed by anonymous committees. . . . Thus we slip down the hill toward a dictatorship which, though paternalistic, would be neither less dangerous nor more effective."[74]

On the Referendum of 1958 the "grand old man" of *France Catholique*, Jean le Cour Grandmaison, wrote, "Without enthusiasm and without illusions, but resolutely, I shall vote YES on September 28."[75] But at the same time he recognized the good reasons which could lead Catholics to vote against the Constitution. In more recent elections, *France Catholique* seems to have limited itself to giving information, without injecting its own opinions.

Témoignage Chrétien is the second important Catholic weekly review of political ideas. It takes more political stands than any other Catholic publication, and these positions are about as "progressive" as one can go and still remain within the Church. On the school question, however, T.C. was moderate. It was not against a certain state aid to Catholic education, but every article in its columns tried to conciliate the interests of public and private schools. It published with approval this statement from the *Secrétariat Social du Nord*: "Freedom of education should not be the only criterion determining how a Christian will vote. However, in certain circumstances it can constitute the essential criterion. . . . If the theoretical freedom of education is not gravely endangered for the moment, it has

[73] *ibid.*, May 2, 1958, p. 1.
[74] *ibid.*, April 1, 1960, p. 1.
[75] *ibid.*, September 5, 1958, p. 1.

not yet been made truly effective. All freedoms hang together, and to let one die endangers all the others."[76]

In 1951 T.C. hoped above all else that the school question would not disrupt the MRP-SFIO coalition. It was not especially pro-MRP, nor did it always view the Socialist Party sympathetically. However, it saw that if the MRP were deprived of Socialist cooperation it could only move toward the right, and this would give the right an overwhelming preponderance in the National Assembly. T.C. hoped that its plan of state payment for salaries of all teachers, public and private, would be the basis of an understanding between the MRP and the SFIO.[77] This was in line with the formula that private schools perform an irreplaceable public service and that thus they deserve some state financial aid.[78]

It is hard to specify the policy of T.C. on the Algerian question. Among its columnists have been men like André Mandouze, who was jailed by the French Government for his ideas in favor of Algerian independence. Long before de Gaulle, Mandouze came out for negotiating directly with the FLN.[79] He also criticized the conduct of the war by the French army. T.C. has even opened its columns to sympathizers or spokesmen for the rebel cause, much to the wrath of many moderate Catholics.[80] In Lyon and other regions of France in early 1958 certain distributors of T.C. near churches were assaulted by T.C.'s Catholic opponents. This episode brought support for T.C. from Cardinal Gerlier, its unofficial protector in the Hierarchy, and from all T.C.'s colleagues on the *Centre National de la Presse Catholique*.[81] Other statements in T.C. on Algeria have been more moderate in tone. Before the first elections of the Fifth Republic, T.C. called for a "development of the Algerian

[76] *Témoignage Chrétien*, June 8, 1951, p. 4.

[77] *ibid.*, July 27, 1951. The 1959 school law provides for state payment of private teachers' salaries. See Chapter Eight.

[78] *ibid.*, September 7, 1951, p. 1.

[79] *ibid.*, November 7, 1958, p. 16.

[80] See *Témoignage Chrétien*, March 14, 1958, p. 8. Also March 13, 1959, p. 20.

[81] *ibid.*, March 28, 1958, pp. 1 and 2; March 21, 1958, p. 1.

personality" without making these terms clear.[82] Such a phrase had clear partisan implications when it was uttered, a year before General de Gaulle made such phrases respectable.

As the silhouette of de Gaulle appeared on the political horizon, T.C. did not offer uncompromising hostility. One can even find some favorable comments to him just before he became premier: "General de Gaulle has spoken. We respect his person and his work. . . . Lately we have come to think that General de Gaulle could be, in such a tragedy, the man of national unity. We wish to write nothing that could aggravate the difficulties of the nation. In the coming days, the intervention of General de Gaulle could be the last recourse of the country."[83] But at practically the same time T.C. contains quite conflicting opinions: "By continuing to ask us for an act of blind confidence in his person, General de Gaulle appears to betray the very essence of what constitutes the democratic link between the people and power."[84]

Along with the rest of the French left, T.C. became suddenly attached to the Fourth Republic when de Gaulle seemed to pose a threat to its existence. This attachment was not without its dangers, for objective criticism of the Republic's faults might be neglected. A well-known professor of political science seemed to fall into such a trap, writing in T.C. just after the May 13 crisis: "The regime, thought by many to be nearing its end, is really one of the most robust of regimes, like those adolescents who seem destined to die at an early age but who live to be 100. . . . Politically the *coup de force* is, therefore, scarcely more conceivable than it is technically feasible."[85]

For the referendum, T.C. did not hide the fact that ". . . the great majority of the T.C. staff has firmly decided to vote 'no.' "[86] However, its columns were open to partisans of the new Constitution too.

[82] *ibid.*, October 31, 1958, p. 2.
[83] *ibid.*, May 23, 1958, p. 2.
[84] *ibid.*, May 30, 1958, p. 1.
[85] René Rémond in *Témoignage Chrétien*, May 16, 1958, p. 20.
[86] *Témoignage Chrétien*, September 26, 1958, p. 1.

Homme Nouveau is the spokesman for the *Mouvement pour l'Unité*, a once-flourishing group which favors a wide extension of activities controlled by the Church. It also has close ties with *L'Armée Bleue*, an international group with 90,000 French members devoted to Our Lady of Fatima and to the conversion of Russia as the most necessary step to building lasting peace. With such a background, it is not surprising that *Homme Nouveau* often confuses the spiritual and temporal realms. On the school question, *Homme Nouveau* presented all the arguments in favor of aid to Catholic schools, with a bit more vehemence and dogmatism than *France Catholique*.[87] The Algerian crisis has not much interested *Homme Nouveau*, and when it is mentioned, it is usually as a stepping stone to criticizing the regime.

Homme Nouveau has its real originality in criticizing the French Republican regime. The magazine favors a new religious-social order for France, in the best traditions of Catholic authoritarianism, but not wholly exempt of a certain puritanism as well: "It would be proper for France, first of all metropolitan France, to stop being tinged with atheism, immorality, and the tireless, creative voracity of unhealthy publications, bars, movie-houses, and night clubs. Only true Catholicism can restore France's youth and insure true human advancement."[88]

The main cause of France's instability is the heritage of the Revolution: "The cause of our instability . . . comes from the reversal of values which earned for the events of 1789 the name 'Revolution.' At that time law was proclaimed to be the expression of the general will. This general will became a god, and all references to a natural law linked to the will of the Creator were dispensed with. . . . The first thing to do is to repudiate frankly the atheism of the state, affirmed under the term *laïcité* in the preamble of the Constitution."[89]

An excess of liberal democracy is considered dangerous: "Any political system is abnormal if the head of state and the

[87] See *Homme Nouveau*, May 3, 1959. The issue is devoted entirely to the school problem.

[88] *Homme Nouveau*, January 24, 1957, p. 1.

[89] *ibid.*, April 27, 1958, p. 1.

representatives of the people are chosen exclusively by the votes of citizens taken as isolated individuals."[90]

The Communist Party is one of the bugaboos of *Homme Nouveau*, but the parties of the non-Communist left are also greatly suspected: "We should outlaw the legal existence of the Communist Party, insofar as it refuses to condemn expressly the crime of genocide committed in Hungary."[91] "To repudiate with the Communists: *Union de la Gauche Socialiste, Union des Forces Démocratiques*, and the *Parti Socialiste Autonome*. . . . These parties are even more dangerous than the Communists, when they include, or are helped by, so-called Christian elements."[92]

A schematic view of the principles of *Homme Nouveau* is provided in the issue before the 1958 national elections: "NO to atheistic, inhuman Communism. NO to the Socialist barracks. NO to king money. NO to school totalitarianism. YES to the inviolable rights of man, the image of God. YES to the state which fills all its place and nothing more. YES to an economy serving everyone. YES to a clean sweep in the street and elsewhere. YES to peace by the general control of disarmament."[93]

In contrast to its extreme-right brethren, *Homme Nouveau* came out in favor of the new Constitution in 1958. This indicates after all a certain tolerance and willingness to compromise in the political realm that most Catholic extremist movements lack. However, Jean Madiran, in an interview with the author, considered *Homme Nouveau* in the same category as his extremist *Itinéraires*.

C. PUBLICATIONS OF RELIGIOUS ORDERS

After examining the Catholic "mass influence" press and non-extremist Catholic publications geared to political tendencies, two organs of religious orders must be considered: *Etudes* and

[90] *ibid.*, July 20, 1958, p. 4.
[91] *ibid.*, January 24, 1957, p. 1.
[92] *ibid.*, November 16, 1958, p. 5.
[93] *ibid.*, November 16, 1958, p. 1.

Signes du Temps, the successor of *Vie Intellectuelle*. Ideas here are not presented in the same spirit as in publications treated earlier. These two publications do not pretend to influence opinion in general, nor to reflect specific temporal positions. They are more theoretical and technical; problems are treated in a more detached manner.

Etudes, as a Jesuit review, is very interested in the school problem. In a recent article on the school question, emphasis was laid on finding a "permanent solution." The intransigence of certain Catholic pressure groups was criticized, and Socialist support was deemed necessary for a permanent settlement of the school quarrel. "Any solution will remain unstable . . . if it has not the approval, at least tacit, of the Socialist Party and of the traditionally anticlerical left."[94]

On the Algerian problem *Etudes* devoted long and erudite articles to questions such as torture or psychological warfare from the Christian standpoint.[95] These questions are given an objective treatment although it is clear that in their extremes the Church opposes them.

On the referendum there is an interesting comment from *Etudes*: "In the present disunity . . . it is not unreasonable to try unity around one man as a path toward more mutual comprehension. One can believe that this man . . . seeks to persuade the French little by little to be on good terms with one another and to understand one another. It even seems that the attitude he maintains in the really ambiguous present situation, his care not to see conflicting groups harden their positions, even the ambiguousness that he tolerates . . . testify in favor of his realism and the honesty of his future choices. . . . One can reasonably think that the Constitutional text to be voted on in the

[94] *Etudes*, Vol. 301, No. 4 (April 1959), p. 109.

[95] Cf. *Etudes*, Vol. 293, No. 6 (June, 1957), pp. 445-447. Cf. also *ibid.*, Vol. 300, No. 2 (February 1959), pp. 185-202, and *ibid.*, No. 3 (March 1959), pp. 202-316. By 1961, Father Le Blond wrote that soldiers have no duty to obey their officers if these latter, through tortures, sedition, etc., disobey the government. See *Etudes*, Vol. 309, No. 6 (June 1961), p. 298.

referendum marks a progress on what preceded, and that finally, stronger than the fears or the prudence which one might have, a veritable hope is shining."[96]

Finally, *Etudes* has written two extremely unfavorable analyses of the *Cité Catholique* movement and *Verbe.* This is not unusual; the arguments used by *Verbe* abound in a rigorous doctrinalism for which the Jesuits themselves are noted—although the Jesuits keep their doctrinalism to the religious realm, while *Verbe* spills over into political questions. It was on this issue of religious doctrinalism as a basis for political judgments that the Jesuits criticized *Verbe.*[97]

Vie Intellectuelle, long the principal spokesman for the Paris Province of the Dominican Order, was forced to suspend publication at the end of 1956. But at the beginning of 1959 a new review, *Signes du Temps*, was started, to continue the basic line of *Vie Intellectuelle*. Thus, the latter can be considered still "alive." More than *Etudes, Vie Intellectuelle* takes specific political positions: before Hungary its foreign orientation verged on neutralism; its view of the school question was rather ambiguous; and in domestic politics it seemed to prefer the parties on the moderate left.

On the school question, *Vie Intellectuelle* was against the laic position, but was not wholly pleased with the Barangé Law: "It was imperative to stop the damage and ruin of an important part of our school patrimony, especially at a time where an abundance of children is coupled with a lack of schools and teachers. But the problem could have been solved more efficiently, in an atmosphere of calm, with another majority. The original sin of the Barangé Law is that it was the work of a right-wing majority, and so the left, religiously or superstitiously, considers it intolerable. . . . If having the Barangé Law voted by a partisan majority can be considered by many as a

[96] *Etudes*, Vol. 299, No. 10 (October 1958), pp. 6 and 17.

[97] Jean-Marie Le Blond, "Dangers Religieux de la Politique," in *Etudes*, Vol. 299, No. 12 (December 1958), pp. 385-396, and *ibid.*, Vol. 300, No. 2 (February 1959), pp. 238-250.

political error, abrogating it by an equally partisan majority would be another political error."[98]

Election pressures launched by the Catholic school pressure groups were roundly criticized: "Catholicism is not a political party. This is known theoretically, but all the consequences are not always drawn from this principle in the realm of public life: To elect a candidate simply and solely because he is Catholic, or to choose between two candidates equally Catholic the one whose faith is most obvious and most advertised, are serious deviations from correct civic consciousness. . . . There could not be any Church solutions to the school problem that could be called Catholic; the possible solutions are more or less democratic or republican; they would be Christian only incidentally, if they could be made to agree with the elementary demands of justice and freedom."[99]

Vie Intellectuelle had been suspended and *Signes du Temps* had not yet started during the 1958 political crisis. This is perhaps a blessing, since the reviews might have been tempted to take a partisan stand against the new Constitution and incur the wrath of many bishops. In the Fourth Republic *Vie Intellectuelle* was particularly hostile to the persistence of "clerical criteria" dividing left from right. This is why it was so opposed to the way the Barangé Law was passed. It considered that no constructive majority could be based on religious factors, and deplored the fact that some opposition to the Mendès-France government was based on such factors.[100]

D. EXTREMIST PUBLICATIONS AND *"Esprit"*

Recently the Catholic extreme right has developed new publications with gusto; at least three reviews representing this

[98] Editorial, "Un Nouveau Pont-Aux-Anes: La Loi Barangé," *Vie Intellectuelle,* Vol. XXVII, No. 3 (March 1956), pp. 1-3.

[99] *Vie Intellectuelle,* Vol. XXVI, No. 12 (December 1955), pp. 2-4. *Signes du Temps* questioned the feasibility of the 1959 school law. It did not actually oppose the new law, but feared that it would rekindle the intransigent opposition of anti-Catholic *laïques.* See *Signes du Temps,* No. 1, January 1960, p. 40.

[100] Cf. Editorial "Alerte au Clericalisme," *Vie Intellectuelle,* Vol. XXV, Nos. 8-9 (August-September 1954), pp. 1-4.

tendency now flourish. *La Pensée Catholique,* published by *Editions du Cèdre,* is said to have close ties with Cardinal Ottaviani and other Vatican personalities. Generally in recent years it has confined itself to abstract social or spiritual questions, following its aim to combat on the doctrinal level the movements of the Catholic left which might endanger the spiritual unity of the Church. But its true civic and political tendencies came to the surface during the 1958 crisis: "The Revolution builds in the place of the natural cadres willed by God an Administration which stifles humans. All democracies are forced to orient themselves toward totalitarianism or they will crumble. . . . Democracy substitutes the notion of party for the notion of country. It is a permanent state of civil war. . . . The men of the Revolution hold the soul of metropolitan France captive: France is no longer in France, but in Algeria!"[101] The review can really go to ridiculous extremes: "Thus . . . *Christ has chosen France to establish his Kingdom on this earth.* Such is the divine mission of our country, which constitutes—after the mission of the People of Israel and following in its stead—the most glorious and most transcendent privilege which has ever been accorded to a people. *Non fecit taliter omni nationi!*"[102]

Spain and Portugal, though poor, are envied because the temptations of a wholly secularized society do not exist. The Algerian war is viewed as "The Cross against the Crescent, brought up to the firing line by the masters of the Red Star, the hammer, and sickle."[103] Catholics share the blame for the perpetuation of the Algerian conflict: "In progressive Christian circles, as in French Communist circles, the leaders of the new war recruited their best fighters, more ardent and more effective than fanatics without a country and the fellagha."[104] The remedy for this situation is clear: outlaw the Communist Party, as a necessary condition for France to win the Algerian war.[105]

101 *La Pensée Catholique,* No. 56 (Summer 1958), pp. 59-61.
102 *ibid.,* p. 69. 103 *ibid.,* No. 54 (Spring 1958), p. 5.
104 *ibid.,* No. 49 (Winter 1957), pp. 4-5.
105 *ibid.,* No. 53 (Winter 1958), p. 53.

Pensée Catholique is important chiefly because of the strong support it receives from certain elements in Rome and the extreme right elite in France. The director of *Pensée Catholique,* Abbé Luc Lefèvre, spoke in the Invalides church on March 20, 1960 to commemorate the exploits of General Foch. Among those present were two Government Ministers and General Weygand. However, *Pensée Catholique* does not inspire any following among the ordinary people in France.

Quite different is the situation of *Verbe,* the organ of the young and dynamic *Cité Catholique.* A great many members of *Cité Catholique* are recent converts, some even from the Communist Party. They naturally seem to go to the "other extreme" on the political scale (some would argue that extreme left and extreme right are not far from one another). What they need most is careful training in the dogma of the Church, and this is what *Verbe* tries to provide them.

Verbe specializes in unearthing statements from reactionary bishops living before the *Ralliement* or at the turn of the century; these represent fairly well its current political and social ideas. *Verbe* seldom comes out with a definite political opinion; its views are well-concealed in theoretical and spiritual reflections and it is almost impossible to select specific quotations on any problems of current political interest.

Every issue of *Verbe* has on its frontispiece a quotation from Albert de Mun which gives the tone of the review: "The Revolution is a doctrine which pretends to base society on the will of man instead of the will of God. . . . The counter-Revolution is the opposite principle; it is the doctrine which bases society on the Christian law." If this does not clearly show *Verbe*'s attitude toward the principles of 1789, perhaps an editorial will clarify matters: "We are among those who think that the Revolution is a bloc, and that it is satanic. . . . From liberalism to communism there is, strictly speaking, no change of principles, but a succession of degrees. . . . There cannot be a full, entire counter-Revolution without an absolute, firm profession of

Catholicism."[106] On the Constitution of 1958, *Verbe* was equally intransigent. After noting the absence of any reference to God, *Verbe* wrote "God or anarchy. God or Communism."[107]

The newest addition to the arsenal of the Catholic extreme right is *Itinéraires*, a monthly review representing the ideas of Jean Madiran, one of the directors of *Nouvelles Editions Latines.* Like *Pensée Catholique, Itinéraires* has mainly an intellectual following. It does not direct a mass movement as do *Verbe* or *Homme Nouveau.* It is much more rational and well balanced than *Pensée Catholique*, although it uses the same themes as all other right wing Catholic publications, including *Pensée Catholique.*

The first important theme of *Itinéraires* is the temporal and spiritual unity of all Catholics.[108] An inevitable corollary to this theme of unity is the desire to purge Catholicism of its undesirable elements. Thus, Madiran repeatedly warned the directors of *Témoignage Chrétien* about their Algerian policies. There are indications that Madiran's articles might have helped incite the right-wing agitators who stormed T.C. hawkers in many areas of France during the May 1958 crisis.[109]

Madiran is more openly hostile to the democratic framework of government than any other extreme right Catholic outside of *Pensée Catholique.* His criticism of democracy is always based on Catholic norms—never on political criteria—and is probably more effective in this way. Thus, following St. Thomas Aquinas, he advocates a government for France where the best

[106] *Verbe*, April 1957, pp. iii and iv, quoted in Henri Fesquet, *op.cit.*

[107] *Verbe*, No. 96, September-October 1958, p. v.

[108] This is a pet idea of the Catholic extreme right. No moderate or left-oriented Catholic would accept such an unrealistic proposition: most Catholics do not want to have all their activity based on their religious affiliation, and there are great conflicts, even in the spiritual realm, between Catholics of the left and those of the right, which a common religion cannot hide.

[109] Cf. *Itinéraires*, No. 21, March 1958, p. 119, and No. 24, June 1958, pp. 104-107. According to T.C., these bullies "were never Catholic militants but almost always political activists. Catholics who do not think like us, though they may dislike discussions and prefer denunciations and calumnies, never used force." See T.C., May 5, 1961, p. 2.

elements of democracy, aristocracy, and monarchy can be harmonized.[110] He rightly points out that the Catholic dogma does not necessarily lead to democracy, but he puts it in a strange context: "It is important, *especially for Spanish Catholics* to know very clearly that Christian principles cannot necessarily be confounded with the privileges and the practices of the regime incarnated by General Franco. It is important, *especially for French Catholics*, to know very clearly, in full conscience, that Christian principles cannot necessarily be confounded with the principles and practices of democracy."[111] "To pretend or insinuate that democratic 'values' have a necessary and indissoluble link with Christian values is an abuse and a prevarication. To pretend or insinuate that justice and liberty are necessarily tied to democracy is another abuse and another prevarication."[112]

Like the other Catholic extreme right publications, *Itinéraires* supports the army to the hilt. This support can affect the relations with other Catholic groups and publications. Madiran even took *La Croix* to task during the heat of the 1958 crisis for infidelity to the army in Algeria.[113]

Finally, *Itinéraires* engages in an anti-Communism of a subdued but nonetheless virulent nature: "We are agreed that today and doubtless for long to come any political activity which is not clearly designed to combat Communism risks being insignificant or for diversion only."[114]

In common with the other organizations and publications of the Catholic extreme right, there is no doubt or hesitation in the doctrine of Madiran. He has the Truth, and the security which it affords. Those who disagree with him are wrong and, to a certain degree, even sacrilegious! The men of the extreme right obviously crave an ironclad feeling of security. Catholicism gives it to them. In fairness to Madiran, he has denied

[110] *ibid.*, No. 24, June 1958, p. 53. Cf. *ibid.*, No. 42, April 1960, pp. 5-7.
[111] *ibid.*, No. 21, March 1958, p. 18. Italics in original.
[112] *ibid.*, No. 25, July-August 1958, pp. 11-12.
[113] *ibid.*, No. 21, March 1958, pp. 2-27.
[114] *ibid.*, No. 20, February 1958, p. 11.

having this obsession for certainty. Yet the obsession is perfectly clear in all his writings.

On the other hand, religion plays a totally different role with the Catholic groups of the moderate left, where it serves as a stimulus for a perpetual questioning and a perpetual doubt. There is no extreme left equivalent to *Verbe* or *Itinéraires.* Nor could there be, in all likelihood, since on the left borders of Catholicism there is an entirely different view of the place of the Church in society. The *Chrétiens Progressistes* were close to the political antithesis of the extreme right, but they were mortally wounded by the condemnation of *Quinzaine.* The final death throes ended in 1956 with the Hungarian uprising, an event which tore almost all left-wing non-Communists away from a naïve idolatry of the Communist Party.

At present the publication coming closest to the ideals of a Catholic extreme left would probably be *Esprit,* which claims not to be Catholic and which is more moderate than *Quinzaine. Esprit* calls itself a "review of Personalist inspiration, struggling against the established disorder."[115] Personalism attempts to instill a certain moral integrity in man's spirit, through stimulating both contemplation and action, including "an unending analysis of the conditions of human existence."[116] Personalists are not just semi-Christians. They want to integrate Christian truths into a more general theory of action. Personalism is not a set doctrine, but a constant questioning and self-examination.[117] The "disorder" which *Esprit* combats has been a characteristic feature in the liberal capitalist Third and Fourth Republics. *Esprit* now tends to stress more the dangers of "authoritarian paternalism."[118] From the beginning of the cold war, *Esprit* was neutralist in its foreign policy views. The Soviet

[115] Motto on frontispiece of all *Esprit* issues. The personalism of *Esprit* owes much to the thought of Maritain. See *I.C.I.*, March 15, 1960, pp. 15-23.

[116] *Esprit,* Vol. xxv (November 1957), pp. 470-471. Cf. below, Chapter Nine.

[117] *ibid.*

[118] *ibid.*, Vol. xxvi (November 1958), p. 717.

Union and the United States were criticized about equally in its columns. But for *Esprit* too, the Hungarian Revolution marked a decisive change; since the end of 1956, and more particularly since Jean-Marie Domenach has taken full control of the review, a more studious, critical attitude can be observed in foreign policy and other political spheres.[119]

On the school question *Esprit* issued a famous plan for a "National University" in 1949, which, it claimed, would solve the conflict. The plan is not significantly different from those proposed by certain enlightened Socialists. It proposes an autonomous school system free from national governmental bureaucracy, but without state support for Catholic schools.[120] When the Barangé Law was passed, *Esprit* significantly modified its proposal, advocating state payment of private school teachers outside of the clergy, and even admitting that the state could integrate certain Catholic schools as such into the new system in regions where the majority of pupils attended them.[121] This was a major concession for *Esprit*; however, like *Vie Intellectuelle, Esprit* was dissatisfied with the Barangé Law itself, primarily because of the right wing Barangé majority which dominated many years of the Fourth Republic.[122]

It is interesting to compare the positions of *Esprit* on the school question with those of now-defunct *Quinzaine*. The latter was much closer to the laic position, although it did recognize that Catholic schools perform for the moment a valuable service, in educating children for whom the state has no room. However, the solution for *Quinzaine* was a "spiritual integration

[119] Cf. *ibid.*, Vol. xxv (November 1957), p. 470 and May 1957, pp. 746-767.

[120] "Propositions de Paix Scolaire," in *Esprit*, Vol. xvii (March-April 1949), pp. 541-556. Cf. "Un statut de l'Ecole Française," *Esprit* xxvii, No. 10 (October 1959), pp. 379-391.

[121] *ibid.*, Vol. xix (November 1951), pp. 697-700.

[122] *ibid.*; *Esprit* was not dogmatically opposed to the new Debré school law of 1959, but was quite critical of those features that seemed to pave the way for rivalry between public and Catholic schools. See *Esprit*, Vol. xxviii (September 1960), pp. 1434-38. Cf. *ibid.*, Vol. xxvii (October 1959), pp. 360-378.

of Catholic school teachers into the national community," which sounds almost like gradual abolition of Catholic values.[123]

On Algeria, *Esprit* had a policy similar to *Témoignage Chrétien*, though perhaps a bit more definitely stated. Algeria is unmistakably a nation-in-being: "Algeria is becoming a nation, and all that we do to stop her makes her more nationalist."[124] The excesses of the Algerian nationalists were more comprehensible to *Esprit* than those of the French: "Violent acts of the nationalists . . . do not discredit the cause associated with them. . . . Violence resides on the French side: it is the racial contempt of the Arab, fixing of elections, the misery of slums, and the emigration of hunger."[125]

On the French political scene *Esprit* has much in common with the small groups of the non-Communist left. Most of its contributors seem to sympathize with the *Parti Socialiste Unifié*, as in the past they favored the *Union de la Gauche Socialiste* or *Union des Forces Démocratiques*. On the referendum of 1958, Domenach presented a careful analysis of why he would like to vote yes but finally chose to vote no. His main fear was that Fascist army elements in Algeria would succeed in dominating General de Gaulle and through him the entire Republic.[126]

In all these policies the relative freedom of *Esprit* should be properly understood. *Esprit* is not "Catholic" in the same sense as *Vie Catholique Illustrée*. It says things that publications with any links to the Hierarchy would not dare say. For example, the practices of the Hierarchy itself are generally outside the scope of criticism in the Catholic press. However, the following description of the activities of the Papal Nuncio appears in *Esprit*:

[123] *Quinzaine*, No. 12 (May 1, 1951), pp. 8-9. *ibid.*, No. 13 (May 15, 1951), p. 10.

[124] *Esprit*, Vol. XXVI (April 1958), p. 517.

[125] *ibid.*, Vol. XXIII (November 1955), p. 1642. A key contributor to *Esprit*, Paul Ricoeur, was recently arrested by de Gaulle's government under the emergency provisions of article XVI of the French constitution. No charges were made, but presumably Ricoeur's sympathy for Algerian nationalism was the main reason. See *New York Times*, June 10, 1961, p. 1.

[126] *ibid.*, Vol. XXVI (September 1958), pp. 294 ff.

"It is known that the Vatican Ambassador to the Republic travels throughout France and holds meetings in several cities . . . with a certain number of bishops, making them promise secrecy and obtaining their reactions. . . . By what right can a foreign ambassador convene French citizens, preside over their meeting, and pass on to them secret orders? . . . If there were a government in France, there would be immediate protests."[127]

Only the extreme right publications would dare to be as controversial as *Esprit.* Their purpose is to strengthen as much as possible their ties with the right wing members of the Hierarchy. However, they do not emphasize how far ideologically they are from the center of the Church.

IV. The Political Impact of the Catholic Press

The Catholic press represents a very wide cross section of French political thought. Its variety would make it impossible for all Catholic publications to work for any coordinated political programs. This shows once again what stumbling blocks there are for those who would favor Catholic unity of action in temporal affairs.

The political impact of the Catholic press is limited by other factors as well. Many would undoubtedly suspect that its freedom of expression is unduly limited by religious authorities. This question deserves some elaboration.

A. POLITICAL LIMITS OF THE CATHOLIC PRESS

Being Catholic is neither wholly permissive nor wholly restrictive for the Catholic press. There are varieties in the political thinking of Catholic publications, but their political freedom is not without its limits. These are of three sorts: theoretical, psychological, and practical. The theoretical limits have been well expressed by the ACA: "As soon as the sacred imperatives of faith and morals have been respected and served, there is room for everybody's personal ideas, tendencies, or

[127] *ibid.*, Vol. XXI (December 1953), pp. 786-788.

views. But this personal expression must not encroach upon the realm reserved to the Hierarchy, and all its directives must be faithfully echoed, especially in the domains of pastoral matters, Catholic Action, and social action. Also, when the Catholic publicist wants to address the clergy and Catholic Action members particularly, he must do it only with the consent of the Hierarchy and under its authority. Also, in expressing his personal ideas, the publicist must not identify them with the truth, to the detriment of the virtue of humility."[128]

The psychological restrictions are more difficult to describe. The directors and writers of Catholic publications are naturally all Catholics themselves. They have been affected by the Church social doctrine, by the national Hierarchy, and by the spirit of obedience within the Church. Without being formally restricted in their temporal activities, and while feeling perfectly "free," their Catholic background itself limits the things that they can write.[129]

It is not a simple matter to judge the practical limits to the political action of the Catholic press. At first glance there would seem to be little relation between Catholicism and specific political activities. This is confirmed by *Témoignage Chrétien*: "A Church community is not thirty friends who meet because they agree on the Algerian war. It is sixty men having a common understanding of the event which, twenty centuries ago, saved them once and for all and induced them to work together to change the world as it is, despite any differences which might oppose them."[130]

Yet in fact the Catholicism of the Catholic press does affect the range of political alternatives open to it. Catholicism does

[128] Quoted in André Deroo, *L'Episcopat Français dans la Mêlée de son Temps* (Paris: Bonne Presse, 1955), p. 147.

[129] This is a question which deserves detailed analysis, through intensive interviewing and other psychological methods which unfortunately cannot be attempted by the present study. One unusual case of a man with radical ideas who cannot express them in a Catholic publication is Georges Hourdin, who *does* feel restricted at many crises in French politics. He must often restrain himself so that his publications can preserve their apostolic character.

[130] *Témoignage Chrétien*, April 4, 1958, p. 9.

so through the specific teachings of the Church: all Catholic publications must keep their distance from the Communists, or else they risk repudiation by the Hierarchy, as in the case of *Quinzaine*. They must keep their distance from the "professional enemies" of the Church. Virtually no Catholic publication looks with favor on the policies of the SFIO in the field of Church-state relations, where it has a notoriously laic position. Noted Catholics can start philosophical schools with political significance, as did Emmanuel Mounier with his doctrine of Personalism. But none can claim that this world-view is the only valid one, for this would contradict the spirit of humility and tolerance that seems part of the Catholic heritage. These practical limits, plus the psychological and theoretical ones mentioned earlier, create some slender bonds among all Catholic publications. But they do not bring the temporal views of Catholic publications any closer together.

B. THE POLITICAL EFFECTIVENESS OF MAJOR CATHOLIC PUBLICATIONS

The political ideas of the major Catholic publications have been set forth. But do they have any effect in France? There are certain indicators which will give some idea of their influence.

The circulation figures for most major Catholic publications are significant indicators of their impact. They vary greatly among types of publications. Among daily newspapers, *La Croix*, the only Catholic representative on a national scale, is literally submerged by the other Paris dailies. In December 1958, a poorer than average month, *La Croix* printed and distributed only 92,000 copies per day, compared to over a million for *France Soir*, and almost a half-million each for *Figaro* and *Aurore*.[131] However, only about 15,000 copies of *La Croix* went to the Paris area; the rest went out to the provinces, arriving a day or more after printing, and thus unable to provide

[131] OJD *Officiel*, No. 123, February 1959, p. 4.

the "latest news." Obviously, *La Croix* is not one of the newspapers able to influence broad masses of Frenchmen.

Among weekly periodicals, Catholic publications fare better. As already noted *Vie Catholique Illustrée* prints and sells between 500,000 and 600,000 copies per week. *Pèlerin*, a similar but more pious weekly from *Bonne Presse*, has about the same circulation. The largest weekly general interest magazine in France, *Paris-Match*, has a circulation a little larger than these two combined.[132] Both *Pèlerin* and *Vie Catholique Illustrée* cover all France, though they are most popular in the West and the North.

The periodicals with immediate political aims have a much more restricted circulation than the Catholic general-interest weeklies. Both *Témoignage Chrétien* and *France Catholique* sell around 50,000 copies per week; *Homme Nouveau* sells only half that much. The largest political weekly, *L'Express*, sold 151,000 copies in mid-1958, and its nearest rival, *France Observateur*, sold 71,000.[133] In this crucial segment of the press, Catholic publications show up well against the non-Catholic publications, but not so well as in the general weekly field.

The "intellectual" and specialized reviews with political importance also have unimpressive circulation figures: around 15,000 for *Esprit* and *Etudes*, 18,000 for *Informations Catholiques Internationales*, 7,000 for *Signes du Temps*.[134]

Of course, each circulation figure has a different significance; for the three "partisan" Catholic publications the figures indicate a failure to penetrate into wide sectors of the population, and they give some indication of the militant supporters each of three tendencies represented by the publications can muster.[135] Reviews such as *Esprit* and *Etudes* are destined for an

[132] *ibid.*, No. 119, October 1958, p. 10. No. 123, February, 1959, p. 5.

[133] *ibid.*, No. 122, January 1959, p. 5. *Annuaire de la Presse Française*, 1958, p. 636. *Echo de la Presse et de la Publicité*, No. 364, May 15, 1959, p. 19.

[134] Jacques Maitre, *op.cit.*, p. 9. *Annuaire de la Presse Française*, 1958, p. 636. *I.C.I.*, April 1, 1958, p. 1.

[135] Interestingly, many militant supporters of publications are members of other Catholic groups. According to a questionnaire filled out by 7,000

elite, so the circulation figures alone have little importance. Perhaps a more balanced judgment of the influence of *Esprit* is provided by Michel François in *France Observateur*: "The influence of *Esprit* has not stopped growing abroad also. Thus, a few copies of a special issue on Spain three years ago passed secretly through thousands of hands in that country. In the same fashion, an issue of *Esprit* on Latin America seems to have contributed to a certain awakening among the intellectuals of that continent. One can even affirm that the influence of *Esprit* has been more decisive abroad than in France, where the ineffectiveness of 'committed' publications was strikingly demonstrated in May 1958."[136]

The Catholic regional press must not be ignored, although it is impossible to go into details here. For example, the *Ami des Foyers Chrétiens de Metz* distributes 43,000 copies per week, while the population of the city of Metz is less than 100,000![137] Doubtless this and most other local publications are quite nonpolitical. Nevertheless, they serve to spread throughout French society a more favorable picture of Catholicism.

Other factors limit the influence of the Catholic press. It seems to have a very small circulation outside of practicing Catholics themselves. The President of the International Union of the Catholic Press, Dubois-Dumée, said himself that "The Catholic press is, taken as a whole, a closed-circuit press, conceived only for the faithful."[138] Another limiting factor is the

---

T.C. readers, 50.5 percent were in some Catholic Action group. In addition, 9.3 percent were priests. Among the 7,000, 31.5 percent were affiliated with the CFTC, but only 9 percent were members of the MRP. However, the figures for the CFTC and MRP were far superior to any other trade union or political party. See *Chronique Sociale*, Vol. LXIII, No. 1, February 15, 1955, pp. 95-100. Cf. T.C., September 11, 1959, special supplement.

[136] "La Revue qui a Formé une Génération Chrétienne," *France Observateur*, April 2, 1959, pp. 12-13.

[137] OJD *Officiel*, No. 116, June, 1958, p. 6. A nonpolitical parish news sheet edited at Limoges is sent to 150 other parish publications with a total circulation of 140,000 or more. See OJD *Officiel*, No. 130 (October 1959), p. 21.

[138] Jacques Maitre, *op.cit.*, p. 20. But this is also a source of strength insofar as there are millions of Catholic faithful in France.

possibility that the readers of a periodical may not be agreed with all its opinions. However, it seems clear that most readers of a Catholic publication will be favorable to its general line.

Catholic ideas may lose some of their impact because most of the readers of the Catholic press also see non-Catholic dailies, listen to the radio, and are influenced by many other sources. Whenever these "outside" influences conflict with the Catholic viewpoint, the latter may be questioned or even rejected in the mind of a Catholic reader.

Circulation figures indicate the best approximations of the size of tendencies within French Catholicism. The "moderates" far outweigh either extremes, with the Catholic left selling significantly more copies of its publications than the Catholic extreme right. However, from the standpoint of dynamism of individuals and ideas, the center does not seem to show up so well. The Catholic left publications seemed better organized, with a dominant influence on many parish press committees and in the national organizations which coordinate the Catholic press. On the other hand, personal interviews and contacts bring the impression that there is as much individual dynamism on the right, and new publications with rising circulation figures would indicate that the Catholic right is finding an ever-larger public attracted to it.

Organizations of Catholic Inspiration

I. Introduction: The Nature of Catholic Inspiration

Groups of Catholic inspiration, the last major type of organization contributing to the political impact of French Catholicism, form the "outer ring" of the French Catholic structure. They are farther from the ecclesiastical nucleus than Catholic Action groups, social action groups, and most of the Catholic press. Among the many groups of Catholic inspiration, attention will be focused on the two giants, the *Mouvement Républicain Populaire* and the *Confédération Française des Travailleurs Chrétiens.* Other structures will be considered insofar as they contribute to the basic purpose of this study.

Two factors distinguish Catholic inspiration organizations from groups closer to the Hierarchy. All are distinct from the Church and from officially-mandated Catholic structures; there are no visible ties with the ecclesiastical nucleus as such, and non-Catholics are welcome in all these organizations. Furthermore, they are not at all restricted in the political role which they can play. This is obvious since one of the principal organizations to be considered is a political party. The overriding justification for including organizations of Catholic inspiration here is that all are considered by large segments of the public as being "Catholic." This general impression, though it is formally incorrect, makes it necessary to place the MRP and the CFTC somewhere within the "French Catholic family."

In practice, two main principles link these groups with the Church. First of all, the majority of individual members are in fact Catholics, resolved to apply the social doctrine of the Church wherever they can, even though the organization in which they find themselves is "neutral." Secondly, most members of the MRP and the CFTC have a strong desire to stay "in the family" even when this cannot be consecrated by an ecclesiastical mandate. It is the same for most leaders of the MRP and CFTC: some have held responsible positions in other Catholic groups; many joined the MRP to keep in the great Christian Democratic family, and their presence along with other Catholics in the rank and file is an assurance that the MRP will never stray too far from the principles of Christian Democracy.

In a sense, every activity of such a party as the MRP contributes to the "political impact" of French Catholicism, since in the minds of many Frenchmen it is *the* Catholic party. However, all the activities of the MRP are not like those of Catholic Action or social action groups. They are not explicitly or implicitly designed for a religious end, nor are they explicitly or implicitly controlled by the Hierarchy. Many have a pragmatic or political or economic, but not religious *raison d'être.* This chapter will examine whether certain activities of the MRP or CFTC are outside this general pattern—whether any activities can in fact be traced back to the core of French Catholicism. Perhaps we can begin to define such activities by seeing how historical tradition, ideology, organization, and dominant personalities bind the Catholic inspiration groups to French Catholicism.

II. The Mouvement Républicain Populaire

A. RELATIONS BETWEEN THE CHURCH AND POLITICAL PARTIES DOWN TO 1945

Until quite recent times the Church as such was often the subject of political controversy and thus directly involved in French politics. This is particularly true during the quarter-century from the beginning of the laic school laws until the separation of Church and state in 1905. It was hardly necessary for the Church to sponsor a political party of its own during this period, because most of the anti-Republican right was willing to defend the interests of Catholicism—so much so that left and right in France became identified with positive and negative views toward the power of the Church. However, during this same period a number of socially-progressive priests and laymen determined to set the Church on a more progressive course. Out of their work came some of the ideological foundations for modern Christian Democracy. But the *abbés démocrates* and the friends of Albert de Mun were closer to the structure of the modern social Catholic groups than to the MRP, for they were still closely tied to the Church.[1] De Mun's abortive attempt to form a Catholic party and the *Sillon* experiment show a certain confusion between the spiritual and temporal realms which is only natural in a period before the Hierarchy was forced to acknowledge separation of the two realms.[2]

The MRP can trace its lineal descendants back to the era of Church-state quarrels. *Action Libérale Populaire* was a political force of some importance at the turn of the century, as was noted in Chapter Two. Key men from ALP contributed to the foundation of the *Parti Démocrate Populaire* after World War I, and representatives of the latter, in turn, were among the first leaders of the MRP.[3] Marc Sangnier, older and wiser, brought many of his *Jeune République* associates into the MRP. As Honorary President of the MRP, Sangnier himself illustrated a certain continuity and an interrelation between the MRP and progressive Catholic organizations at the turn of the Century.

The most interesting thing about these historical predecessors of the MRP is their failure to attract a large clientele. The Catholic party of de Mun was misunderstood by the masses and rejected by virtually all Catholic leaders. The influence of the *abbés démocrates* was limited to the readers of their newspapers, which never had more than a few thousand subscribers.

[1] See Michael P. Fogarty, *Christian Democracy in Western Europe* (Notre Dame: University of Notre Dame Press, 1957), pp. 329-339.

[2] See Henri Rollet, *Albert de Mun et le Parti Catholique* (Paris: Boivin, 1949).

[3] Fogarty, *loc.cit.*

Though the ALP had at one time seventy or more sympathizers in Parliament, it could not survive World War I. The *Parti Démocrate Populaire* had only a handful of deputies from Brittany and Alsace. Evidently in their political action most Catholics were not joining Catholic associations in the interwar period. Instead, many Catholics could be found in the ranks of groups like *Action Française*.

What is the explanation for the failure of Christian Democratic parties to attract a Catholic clientele? Thibaudet attributes this to organizational factors: the Christian Democrats lacked their great leader—their Jaurès.[4] Perhaps this is an important factor, but the MRP attracted vast multitudes in its early years and has kept a respectable following up to now, even though it has not been a party of "personalities." The main reason seems to be the development of Catholic Action and associated groups since the 1930's. Before then, no groups were geared to train their members to think and act always as Catholics. Catholic Action, in doing this, produced large numbers of individuals who would be attracted to the parties, unions, and other groups considered "the most Catholic."

The historical traditions represented in the MRP are rich and varied; the political preoccupations and reactions of a former member of *Jeune République* will differ from those of a social Catholic industrialist looking back to the era of Albert de Mun. This creates a certain ambiguity within the MRP that contributes to its anomalous position between left and right. The best way to understand the elements in the MRP is to reduce them to three "generations": the first represents disciples of the old *Sillon*. The second and third have been described by Priouret in these terms: "If the men and women there were asked, it would be apparent that most of them are more than just practicing Catholics. Before coming to the MRP and before the MRP existed they were active members of other Catholic groups. Those under thirty came from the *Association Catho-*

[4] Albert Thibaudet, *Les Idées Politiques de la France* (Paris: Librairie Stock, 1932), p. 117.

lique de la Jeunesse Française, the JOC, the JAC, the JEC, and the JIC. Those who are between thirty and forty-five came from the *Parti Démocrate Populaire*, sometimes from *Jeune République*, and from the CFTC and the family movements. What would the MRP have been without this long preparatory work before the war? It would not have known its extraordinary development and its success would have been ephemeral if movements with the same ideas had not existed before it—especially if the Church in 1939 had not multiplied the popular groups which extended its ascendency over a part of the youth. From 1930 to the War, everything happened as if a plan had been formulated to prepare the cadres for a great French Catholic party, or at least to make such a party possible."[5]

B. IDEOLOGICAL LINKS WITH CATHOLICISM

When Thibaudet affirmed that "politics is ideas," he was reflecting a widespread viewpoint among French political observers, who usually characterize and distinguish French parties by their doctrines.[6] This is one possible way of looking at parties, provided that one does not neglect other features, such as their internal organization and their ability to participate in the power process. A doctrinal examination of the MRP is particularly useful since the MRP is tempted by a certain philosophy related to its own complex historical tradition.[7] This present section is designed to point out what Catholic elements are present in MRP ideas, and then to judge whether this doctrinalism really is significant for the activities of the MRP.

More than anything else, the MRP represents the broad tendency within French Catholicism called Christian Democracy. Catholics who are content to preserve the social inequalities of "static France," or who desire to extend the hierarchy principle from the Church to the political order, are generally at

[5] Roger Priouret, *La République des Partis* (Paris: Elan, 1947), pp. 60-61. See also *La Nef*, Vol. xi, No. 5 (January 1954), pp. 143-144.

[6] Thibaudet, *op.cit.*, p. 7.

[7] Fogarty, *op.cit.*, p. 16.

home in other political formations.[8] This Christian Democratic tendency has a rich past: "When it was born the MRP was already a century old. It was not the foundling of the Liberation, a child of chance. It is the legitimate descendant of a great family, long ignored, often scoffed at, but never sterile. It is the heir to a doctrine and even more to a tradition. . . . This is the tradition of all those who have tried for a century to reconcile Christianity and democracy; of those who undertook for four years the mission of saving Christianity, often in spite of itself. Today it is the tradition of those who try to harmonize social justice with individual liberty."[9]

Christian Democracy is hard to define, since it has been used in several different ways during its century of development. According to Willard Ross Yates, the doctrine is based on four assertions about the nature of man: ". . . that all men are responsible, free, and active persons in whom 'the spirit transcends matter' . . . that man realizes his spiritual and material well-being only as a member of society . . . that 'the aims of political action never can be finally fixed,' but 'represent a succession of stages' . . . that each man will be able to develop his faculties 'only if the entire society is organized throughout all of its structures on the basis of the primacy of man, *of every man*, respecting his liberty, permitting him to exercise his responsibilities.' "[10] According to Yates, the Christian Democrats also furnished the MRP with three "laws of history": ". . . that men, through free will, are the makers of their own happiness or misery . . . that progress occurs primarily through a change in the spiritual sphere of society . . . that the competition and cooperation of forces, spiritual families, or civilizations cause its great movements . . . progress occurs through a dialectical process in which a dominant spiritual family gen-

[8] See Priouret, *op.cit.*, pp. 70-71.

[9] Jacques Fauvet, *Les Partis Politiques dans la France Actuelle* (Paris: *Edition Le Monde*, 1947), pp. 19-20.

[10] Willard Ross Yates, "Power, Principle, and the Doctrine of the *Mouvement Républicain Populaire*," *American Political Science Review*, LII, No. 2 (June 1958), pp. 424-425.

erates its opposite."[11] Other Christian Democratic views would include according to Yates, ". . . a neo-Thomistic theory of man and society . . ." and an economic system based on ". . . the private ownership and the public management of property," as well as ". . . a decentralized social order based on recognition of individual and group rights. . . ."[12] Yates recognizes, however, that the MRP was not always faithful to its philosophical heritage, especially to the notion of political pluralism, once it had massive political strength itself.[13]

The most striking thing about these principles as stated by Yates is their vagueness. Is any democratic party opposed to the primacy and liberty of "every man"? Could not these principles be accepted just as well by a Socialist humanist like Léon Blum or a Marxian Protestant like André Philip? Or even a Mendès-France? One also has the impression that the MRP, in developing toward "dead center," has renounced those principles that seem to evoke specific programs—for example, the social control of certain private property.[14]

Still, such ideals must be included within the Christian Democratic philosophy. Among them are the notion of personalism—development of the whole man—and pluralism—the opposition to totalitarianism through competing and diverse social groupings. These notions will be described in detail in the concluding chapter.

In its practical application, the Christian Democratic doctrine of the MRP has often been used as an alternative to Communist theory, instead of simply a justification for some form

[11] *ibid.*, pp. 425-426. [12] *ibid.*, p. 421. [13] *ibid.*, p. 430.

[14] On the issue of private property, Albert Gortais is quite explicit on social controls. His statement sounds unreal today, and this underlines the inability of the MRP—or its lack of desire—to practice what it preaches: "To assure that the use of property conforms to the general interest, the state or organisms appointed by the state have the right to control the use that owners make of their property. As far as the instruments of production are concerned, the new right of property . . . will forbid capital alone to possess them, at the expense of labor in any form. Labor must, therefore, be associated in the direction of industry and in profit." *Démocratie et Libération* (Paris: *Société d'Editions Républicaines Populaires*, 1947), p. 41.

of Western democracy. The MRP leaders seem to have been stimulated by their religious background to find a positive alternative to Marx which would reconcile his progressive social thoughts with a more understanding attitude toward religion. This was especially true in the early years of the Fourth Republic, when the MRP was locked in a power struggle with the Marxist parties, which were the only other strong political forces in France. It continues, however, even today. Thus, in a recent issue of its weekly, *Forces Nouvelles*, the MRP claims to fight Communism by having ". . . a conception of man and the world: just as the Marxist conception follows from materialism, ours follows from a fully spiritualist notion of man and a fully humanist notion of society."[15]

The doctrine of Christian Democracy, an effort to reconcile the historic positions of the Church with the new style of popular government in Western Europe, is still perplexingly vague. All links between the Church and the MRP seem uncertain and fragile. In France the ideological link seems to be more historical fact and personal desire than ideological necessity. There is nothing in the essence of Christian Democratic ideals themselves that draws a man toward Rome rather than toward the Protestant Churches or toward an agnostic humanism. Nor does Catholicism necessarily lead to Christian Democracy. It just happened that those Frenchmen with both a "spiritualist" and a "democratic" orientation were usually Catholics, in the Christian Democratic tendency.

Furthermore, there seems to be remarkably little relationship between the above-mentioned ideas of the MRP and its actual behavior. As Stanley Hoffmann puts it, "As for the MRP ritual, the vague pluralistic dream which would give each social group certain rights and powers and a determinate part in production and distribution, the most important question—

[15] *Forces Nouvelles,* special issue "Face au Communisme," July 1956, p. 27. This issue has been severely criticized. *La Nef,* referring to the MRP's "practical moralism," writes, "It is this kind of reasoning which has led to the worst impasses and the most costly hypocrisy; the Indochinese war is a sad testimony of this." See *La Nef, op.cit.*, p. 147.

which direction would society take, toward what would these groups move?—has never been asked, and in practice every aspect of the MRP's ideological originality has been put under wraps for ten years."[16] The doctrinal treatises by Gortais and Gilson which were considered the essential MRP manifestos in the early years of the Fourth Republic have lost their attraction for the MRP leadership—they never were read by the mass of MRP sympathizers.[17] But all this does not mean that ideological factors have no importance to the MRP. A great deal of its strength comes from people who believe that it embodies the best traditions of Christian Democracy. In recent years these supporters have been joined by other, more conservative, Catholics, who have accepted at last the Republican form of government. So now, "liberal Catholicism," social Catholicism, and Christian Democracy—in fact, all shades of Catholic opinion short of *intégrisme*—can find a home within the ranks of the MRP.

C. ORGANIZATIONAL LINKS TO CATHOLICISM: FORMAL AND INFORMAL

The Church learned its lesson in the period around World War I. Since the early 1920's, the Church has been exceptionally prudent in expressing its political interests. No party, not even the MRP, can claim formal ties to the Church. Nevertheless, certain aspects of the MRP organization seem to draw their inspiration from the Church or Catholic Action. More important, there are several informal links between the MRP and the Church that help shed light on the true nature of this party.

On all levels of its organization the MRP includes "specialized teams" for workers, agriculture, youth, cadres and

[16] Quoted in *Esprit*, Vol. xxv (December 1957), p. 816. According to Micaud, the MRP has even rejected much of the abstraction and disembodied logic that always has characterized French Catholic politics, for a more "pragmatic" outlook. See Joseph N. Moody, *op.cit.*, pp. 202-203.

[17] Confirmed in interview with an MRP official.

liberal professions, women, overseas groups, and elected municipal officials. All but the last two have their counterpart in Catholic Action. Most of these teams are rather unimportant to the functioning and recruitment of the MRP; they are retained probably to keep unofficial ties to Catholic Action. However, the rural team is an exception; it furnishes a substantial number of MRP members and works to extend the MRP into new areas of France. Its action reflects the dynamism of the JAC and the MFR.[18] Wherever the teams function, they are a good unofficial way of keeping young Catholic Action elites "in the family," working on the social problems they know best while adding to the strength of the MRP.

The MRP has never disguised the fact that it is a Christian Democratic party. It feels particularly close to the other Christian Democratic parties of Europe, most of which have much closer and more explicit ties with the Church. At the national congresses of the MRP, delegates from the "sister parties" attend. At the congress of May 1959, these "sister parties" included the German CDU, the Belgian Social Christians, the Italian Christian Democrats, the Dutch Catholic Party, the Swiss Christian-Social Party, and several refugee parties from Eastern Europe.[19] There is, however, no organized "Christian Democratic International" as the Communists or the Socialists have. The *Nouvelles Equipes Internationales* includes many Christian Democratic leaders from various countries, but the MRP as such does not adhere to it.[20]

[18] Rural teams are dynamic, but they do not provide an unusually large proportion of MRP leaders, since many people from Catholic Action prefer to remain in the MRP rank and file. Because MRP-supporting Catholic Action groups are dispersed throughout France, it is impossible to show the Catholic Action contribution to the MRP by geographical means. For maps of MRP regional strength, see end of book. For percentage of farmers among MRP leaders (a percentage which does not exceed 12 percent, for local active members) see Daniel Pépy, "Note sur le MRP," in Duverger (ed.), *Partis Politiques et Classes Sociales en France* (Paris: Armand Colin, 1955), p. 213.

[19] *Forces Nouvelles*, May 16, 1959, pp. 15-16.

[20] Interview with J.-P. Prévost, head of the MRP group in the Senate, July 13, 1959.

Before and immediately after the passage of the Barangé Law, the informal relations between the MRP and French Catholicism seemed to multiply, as this quotation from Georges Hourdin will show: in this statement Hourdin justifies mentioning the MRP in one of the "religious" publications which he directs: "We would not waste a single minute in discussing the value of a political party, no matter how important, if the party were not directed, represented, and composed of Catholics, and if it did not commit . . . in the eyes of the man in the street, that Church which we love and that faith in God which we want to see capable of renewing the face of the earth. Whether the Popular Republican leaders want it or not, whether it pleases them or not, their activity in the technical political domain contributes in a sense to religious news. . . . The *Mouvement Républicain Populaire* could not keep the character of a nonconfessional party, in spite of the desire of its leaders to do this. . . . The chances of MRP success were linked to Catholic voters. The article published in our favor in *Osservatore Romano* during the 1951 election, the difficult vote on the Barangé Law which had such meager results, clearly attached the MRP to Christian Democracy."[21]

It appears that the informal links between the MRP and the Church declined rather quickly after the Barangé controversy. At the time of the 1956 election, Goguel remarks that practically everywhere the Hierarchy was more discreet and circumspect in its political statements, especially toward the MRP.[22]

[21] *Actualité Religieuse dans le Monde*, No. 29, June 1, 1954, pp. 3-4. The quotation is particularly significant since Hourdin himself was on the MRP National Bureau. In addition to the recommendation of *Osservatore Romano, La Croix* seemed implicitly to favor the MRP before the 1951 election. On May 18, 1951, its editor, Father Gabel, wrote, "It is natural that Catholics, in the realm proper to politics, adhere to parties claiming to follow Christian principles and giving at least some guarantees to apply them." The MRP was the only party tacitly called "Christian" at that time.

[22] François Goguel, "Note Complémentaire," in Association Française de Science Politique, *Les Elections du 2 Janvier, 1956* (Paris: Armand Colin, 1957), p. 422.

Ever since the tribulations of the early 1900's, the Hierarchy has realized the dangers of too-close affiliation to a single political party.

The ties between the MRP and Catholic Action have been particularly useful to the MRP, as has been already noted. At the end of the war, the MRP was able to set up a complete party organization very quickly because its leaders had a store of contacts throughout France, from their days in the ACJF or other Catholic Action groups.[23] If all the participants in Catholic Action and Catholic social groups were interested in political affairs within its framework, the MRP would have more young leaders than even the Communists. However, because of the character of Catholic Action, many of its members refuse political commitments. Others are attracted to the MRP not because of its Christian Democratic philosophy but because it is the "most Catholic" party, and few of these individuals desire to become active MRP leaders.

As a matter of fact, if a new authoritarian right party were to develop in the Fifth Republic, openly calling itself "Christian" and presided over by someone like Georges Bidault, a great number of the individuals just described would probably switch to it from the MRP. This is not an academic problem, for at one point Bidault seemed to be trying to establish just such a grouping.[24]

Through its Catholic Action friends and other sympathetic Catholic groups, the MRP has been able to rejuvenate itself and expand its base of operations. Now it seems to be winning back some of the strength lost earlier in its career, and even to be extending its appeal among workers and farmers. The *Rassemblement des Forces Démocratiques*, to be discussed in a moment, was essentially a movement of young workers and farmers from Catholic Action which partially succeeded in expanding the role of these classes in the life of the MRP. For example, according to a recent rules change, at least 50 percent

[23] Interview with J.-P. Prévost. Cf. Louis Biton, *La Démocratie Chrétienne dans la Politique Française* (Angers: Siraudeau, 1955), p. 61.

[24] Information from an MRP official.

of MRP national leaders must be representatives of the working class and agriculture.[25]

Is there a chance that the MRP will draw closer to the Catholic groups with which it has now only informal ties? It would seem in its best interest to keep a certain distance. The MRP is the first political party of Catholic inspiration in France not to arouse the sworn hostility of *laïques.* Future good relations between the MRP and French liberals or social democrats (under whatever party label they might appear) depend on the MRP's keeping a certain nonconfessional character. Its problem is to reconcile cooperation with laic parties (necessary for the safeguard of political freedom in France) with a continued appeal to its electorate, which, whether one likes it or not, has a certain clerical character.

D. PERSONAL LINKS OF MRP MEMBERS TO CATHOLICISM

It seems a reasonable hypothesis that most people who become MRP members or vote MRP do so because of religious factors particularly. The hypothesis can be expressed in other ways: people join the MRP to be "in the family," among fellow social Catholics and Christian Democrats working in the political sphere. This is what differentiates the MRP from the *Indépendents* or the UNR, which also count a majority of Catholics in their ranks. People become members of these parties to support a certain conception of the political order, not for religious purposes. In other words, if there were no "French Catholicism" there would still be an *Indépendent* and a Gaullist party; but the MRP would not exist. This has been true especially since the late 1940's, when the right wing elements who had entered the MRP as the "least bad" party at the end of the war found their natural homes within the *Indépendent* or Gaullist parties.[26]

[25] *Forces Nouvelles,* May 16, 1959, p. 3. However, in this issue it is stated that the "working class" includes middle-echelon civil servants and managers, as well as employees.

[26] This seems to be a widely-accepted theory in France; it was ap-

One indication that this hypothesis is accurate can be found in various public opinion polls. A French poll showed that in 1952, regular churchgoers had overwhelming political preference for the MRP, as is seen in Table 3.[27]

TABLE 3

Party Preferences in France Among Regular Churchgoers — 1952

PARTY	PERCENTAGE
Communist	1
Socialist	5
Radical	2
MRP	54
Independent	20
RPF	18

It can be assumed that the overwhelming majority of the really active Catholics trained by Catholic Action are included in the MRP figure.

Conversely, the MRP clientele includes practically no non-Catholics. Fogarty estimates that the number of practicing Catholics favoring the MRP was actually higher than the number of votes which the MRP received.[28] The 1952 French public opinion poll showed impressively how "clerical" the MRP's supporters really are. The figures are given in Table 4.[29]

---

proved by Prévost. However, Joseph Folliet of *La Chronique Sociale* disagrees—and the eminent social Catholic himself is outside the ranks of the MRP. He says that "social Catholicism . . . finds a political prolongation in the MRP, where social Catholics form the majority, but also with social Catholics in the PRL, the RPF, the UDSR, and even the Socialist Party." See *Présence de l'Eglise* (Lyon: *Chronique Sociale,* 1949), p. 52. One wonders how many Catholics in other parties really find them satisfactory prolongations of their religious principles.

[27] Poll figures from Fogarty, *op.cit.*, p. 361.

[28] *ibid.*, pp. 358-359.

[29] "Le Catholicisme en France," in Institut Français d'Opinion Publique, *Sondages,* Vol. XIV, No. 4 (1952), pp. 40-41.

TABLE 4

Breakdown of Party Supporters by Religious Practice
(figures are percentages)

Party	Devout	Observant	No Observable Practice	No Practice
Communist	0	13	10	77
Socialist	9	24	21	46
Radical	14	26	20	40
Gaullist	50	26	12	12
Independent	56	29	9	6
MRP	73	23	2	2

In Table 5 are even more revealing figures of voters who are greatly influenced by the advice of the Church when they vote.[30]

TABLE 5

Percentage of Baptized Catholic Supporters of Different French Parties Who Claimed in 1952 to be Influenced to Some Extent by the Advice of the Church in Their Decision to Vote

Party Supported	Percentage of Voters Influenced by Church's Advice		
	Much	A Little	Total
Communist	6	1	7
Socialist	2	9	11
Liberal (Radical)	0	13	13
Christian-Democratic (MRP)	43	39	82
Conservative (Moderate, Independent)	26	36	62
Nationalist (RPF)	18	38	56

[30] Fogarty, *op.cit.*, p. 361.

If the MRP must confine itself to the Catholic electorate, it finds the latter a fickle lot. In theory, France is over 85 percent Catholic, yet the MRP garners only about 10 percent of votes cast. For comparative purposes, in Holland Catholics comprise 33.5 percent of the population and the Catholic People's Party received 31 percent of the total votes in 1948, all from Catholic voters. There is some justification for Fogarty's assertion that "Practising Christians in France are less attached to their Christian Democratic party than those in any of the other countries studied here."[31]

Perhaps in recent years the situation that Fogarty described has been changing. A public opinion poll of voter loyalty patterns to political parties at local elections shows a recent increase in the loyalty of MRP voters. Percentages are given in Table 6.[32]

TABLE 6

Percentage of MRP Voters Who Intend to Vote MRP Again at the Next Election

Local Election Date	Percentage
January, 1947	78
June, 1947	64
December, 1947	40
February, 1948	34
July, 1948	46
September, 1948	32
March, 1949	41
October, 1949	39
April, 1951	41
August, 1953	65
November, 1956	66
March, 1957	80

31 *ibid.*, p. 336.
32 *Sondages*, Vol. XIX, No. 3 (1957), p. 10.

ORGANIZATIONS OF CATHOLIC INSPIRATION

Another indication of the essentially "Catholic" nature of the MRP clientele can be found in the past affiliations of MRP national leaders. The following information was given orally by the Secretary of the MRP group in the Senate, J.-P. Prévost, and covers all members of the MRP National Bureau and the National Executive Commission at the end of 1959. Of the fifty-two leaders, almost forty have had important positions in Catholic Action or similar fields!

TABLE 7

Previous Catholic Action Affiliation of MRP Leaders, 1959

NAME	CATHOLIC GROUP	
(National Bureau)		
A. Colin	ACJF. President of the MRP	
M.-R. Simonnet	ACJF. Secretary-General of the MRP	
Ch. Bosson	ACJF	
A. Pairault	USIC, Semaines Sociales. Treasurer of the MRP.	
A. Poher	FFEC	
R. L'Helguen	JOC, (CFTC)	
P. Pflimin	(*Institut Catholique*, Paris)	
R. Schuman	Third Order Franciscan	
L. Dubois	JAC	
G. Hourdin	President, *Vie Catholique Illustrée*	
P.-H. Teitgen	(*Parti Démocrate Populaire*)	
M. Schumann	(*Jeune République*)	
Francine Lefebvre	ACO, (CFTC)	
(National Executive Committee)		
R. Lecourt	FFEC	
Paul Bacon	JOC, (CFTC), MPF	(Cabinet Members)
R. Buron	Director, *Vie Catholique Illustrée*	
J. Fontanet	JEC	
R. Charpentier	JAC	
M.-M. Dienesch		
H. Dorey	(CFTC)	
N. Rombeaut	(CFTC)	(Deputies)
P. Gabelle	(CFTC)	
M. Blin	JEC	
L. Raymond-Clergue		

ORGANIZATIONS OF CATHOLIC INSPIRATION

NAME	CATHOLIC GROUP	
J. Lecanuet		
G. Boulanger	JAC	(Senators)
C. Mont	JEC	
A. Fosset	ACJF	
H. Claireaux		
M. Byé	*Semaines Sociales*	
C. Barangé		
G. le Brun-Kéris	JEC	
J. de Montgascon	ACJF	
Jean Catrice	ACJF	
G. Touquet	UFCS	
R. Pondonson	JOC	
J.-P. Prévost	JEC	(Representatives of
P. Farine	JEC, ACJF	Party Federations)
M. Lucas	ACJF	
P. Dhers	ACJF	
G. Peyroles		
J. Raymond-Laurent	(*Parti Démocrate Populaire*), *Sillon*	
E. Gabouty	*Coeurs Vaillants, Ames Vaillantes*	
J. Teitgen		
C. Ferrie	*Editions du Cerf*	
A. Edot		
R. Dorflinger		
Etienne Borne	CCIF	
J. Fonteneau	JOC	
G. Delfosse	JOC, (CFTC)	(*Militants ès Qualité*)
C. Flory	ACJF, *Semaines Sociales*	
F. Bouxom	JOC, (CFTC)	

Another way to show the "Catholicism" of the members of the MRP is to compare its areas of greatest strength with the most "Catholic" parts of France, and with regions where Catholic Action is strongest. This has been done in maps at the end of this book. The greatest strength of the MRP roughly coincides with the most Catholic areas of France, but it also extends beyond these bastions.[33] The results of the 1958 election seem to indicate that the MRP is spreading from its Western base into the south of the *Bassin Parisien* and toward the north of the *Massif Central.* From its Eastern base it is spreading into

[33] Fogarty notes the same phenomenon. *Op.cit.*, pp. 360-364.

all of *Provence*, especially the middle band of Departments stretching from the Swiss border over to Basses-Pyrénées. According to Philip Williams the MRP increased its strength by one fourth in those electoral districts where it presented candidates in 1958.[34] This seems to indicate a renewal of Catholic Action activity in its favor, and could denote a further expansion of the MRP bastions.

Finally, the appeal of the MRP throughout all social classes is another indication that its attraction is religious rather than socio-economic or ideological. "Of all major French parties, the MRP is the one which has the most balanced representation of all classes or groups," says Fogarty.[35] The MRP attracts a large proportion of old retired widows as well as young voters, workers as well as Catholic industrialists, and in this it is unique among French parties.[36]

French politics is too complex to establish a rigid identity between Catholicism and membership in the MRP. Most Catholics who are concerned about acting "within the family" will choose the MRP as their political party, but the rule does not apply everywhere. For example, in Côte d'Or, Canon Kir, the Mayor of Dijon, is the most influential political figure. One could hardly be closer to the Church than the venerable Canon, who also is *Doyen d'Age* of the French National Assembly. Yet, Canon Kir belongs to the Independent Party rather than the MRP. The MRP finds it impossible to oppose Canon Kir, and thus has not developed in Côte d'Or. The development of a right-wing "Christian Democracy" sponsored by someone like Georges Bidault might have the same results in other areas.

E. CATHOLICISM AND MRP POLITICAL ACTIVITIES

The MRP has inherited from its religious forbears a spiritualism that would put it on the right in the classic division of

[34] Information from interview with Philip Williams, in office of J.-P. Prévost, July 23, 1959. Cf. Philip Williams and Martin Harrison, *De Gaulle's Republic* (London: Longmans, 1960), p. 109.

[35] *Op.cit.*, p. 371.

[36] *ibid.*, p. 370.

political tendencies. At the same time, many of its Christian Democratic political opinions tie it to the left. There is a constant tension between the two orientations, and the MRP finds itself ill at ease in either camp. It is usually put in the center by the political analysts who insist on retaining the classic political divisions, though it would resent being termed a party of "dead center." Siegfried has described the ambiguous position of the MRP in these terms: "They are one of the pillars of the regime, the defenders of the family, but they do not constitute a cement since no majority can be constituted with them or without them."[37] This political ambiguity and the unstable political position of the MRP seem to have basically religious causes.

However, many of the specific activities of the MRP are frankly pragmatic, and can in no way be attributed to its Catholic inspiration, even though the MRP may use its spiritualist-based doctrine to justify certain actions. For example, in the May 1958 crisis, MRP leaders preferred to support General de Gaulle, the man they had been fighting for ten years, rather than their own Georges Bidault. The official reason given by *Forces Nouvelles* was ". . . Georges Bidault was condemned . . . to serve only half of a truth which it is our vocation to maintain intact and whole, against time and tide. . . ."[38] Perhaps similar considerations motivated the MRP to participate in the Debré government when less than a year before it had spoken of him in these terms: "I will surely not do M. Debré the honor of confusing his overlabored nationalist theories with arguments. I shall merely ask him to account for their perfidy and the falsehood that they conceal. . . ."[39] As early as 1946, according to Vaussard, the MRP was nothing more than ". . . a plethoric party, consumed by electoral ambitions."[40] The continu-

[37] *De la Troisième à la Quatrième République* (Paris: Grasset, 1956), pp. 192, 163, and 164.

[38] Etienne Borne in *Forces Nouvelles*, May 3, 1958, p. 12.

[39] Jean Teitgen in *Forces Nouvelles*, April 19, 1958, p. 2.

[40] Maurice Vaussard, *Histoire de la Démocratie Chrétienne* (Paris: Editions du Seuil, 1956), p. 118.

al presence of the MRP in power during the Fourth Republic ". . . effectively did nothing to stop a reversion to the worst blemishes of a politico-economic regime which must no longer be defended if it is distinctly impossible to reform."[41] Despite the Church doctrine of progress for underdeveloped nations, MRP leaders had a major part in the adventures of Indochina and Morocco. "The MRP also wanted to be social, but it upholds today the worst form of economic liberalism. It wanted to better the lot of peoples overseas, but it produced Letourneau the Indochinese, de Chévigné of Madagascar, and Bidault the Moroccan. It wanted peace in Algeria, but it makes war. It was for democracy but it has favored autocratic power. It was for the family, and Bacon infringes on the family allocations."[42] In all these activities, culminating in the abandonment of an MRP premier, Pflimlin, and the rejection of a long-time Christian Democrat, Bidault, for General de Gaulle in 1958, the MRP has shown a fairly consistent pragmatism where any "Catholic inspiration" would be difficult to find.

However, pragmatism and betrayal of principles are not qualities limited to the MRP, or to political parties only in France. Some students of the field have suggested that the MRP is rather less pragmatic than its fellow parties because of its Catholic background. "It has practised too little of *la politique politicienne*, not too much. Its history is in fact the clearest and most extreme example of the tendency . . . in all countries, for Christian Democratic politicians to treat politics as an exercise in pure principle on the one hand and day-to-day tactics on the other. The tendency is to forget, or not to think through sufficiently, the intermediate level of strategy, the 'hypothesis' or middle 'principles'. Old and experienced Christian Democratic parties like those of Holland do not suffer much from this deficiency. The MRP, true to its rather woolly antecedents, has suffered from it a great deal."[43] Other stu-

[41] *ibid.*, p. 119.

[42] Georges Morvan of *Union de la Gauche Socialiste*, formerly of *Jeune République*, in *Le Monde*, February 7, 1959, p. 6.

[43] Fogarty, *op.cit.*, pp. 338-339.

dents seem to believe that the MRP is hampered from making a few realistic political choices by the spiritualism or moralism of its philosophical background. For example, perhaps the policy of MRP leaders to continue the war in Indochina came from a desire for another "anticommunist crusade."[44] According to *Actualité Religieuse dans le Monde*, a highly-respected Catholic magazine edited by members of the Dominican Order and by Georges Hourdin, a member of the MRP National Bureau, the fall of the Mendès-France government ". . . was provoked by Catholics acting as a body, without any doubt."[45]

For the MRP the school problem was considered in a religious context as well as in a more pragmatic framework. An official MRP brochure, widely distributed before the 1951 election, proclaimed that ". . . school liberty, closely tied to religious liberty, must be effective, not only for the privileged rich, but also for the poorest families."[46]

Finally, Catholic doctrines make it practically impossible for the MRP to approve certain policies, while it is stimulated to favor others. The MRP would be very hard-pressed to favor a law liberalizing divorce or birth-control practices, while on the other hand it actively supports measures of state aid to large families, helps to continue indirect state aid to non-Communist youth organizations, and in general favors the growth of "intermediary bodies."

To conclude this analysis, we should note this effervescent quotation from François Mauriac, which paints a biased but not wholly false picture of MRP activity: "Blessed MRP! Among all the virtues in which it excels, not the least is a holy patience. It knows how to wait, and while waiting, it installs itself (Ah! dear friends of the ruined left, when are you going to grow up?) General de Gaulle will pass from the scene, but the MRP will remain. . . . For the MRP reassures. Nothing that it could do during the ten years it participated in gov-

[44] See *La Nef*, January 1954, p. 147.

[45] *Actualité Religieuse dans le Monde*, No. 46, February 15, 1955, p. 1.

[46] André Colin, *Pour la République, la Famille, Le Progrès, la Paix*, MRP *Cahiers d'Information Politique*, May 1951, p. 26.

ernments will be imputed to it. . . . When the great man who by himself occupies the vacuum created by the defeat of the left will be no more (*O soleils disparus derrière l'horizon!*) what will happen? The answer is clear: our own stolid bourgeois people, caught between a Socialism which destroys the treasury and the soldier with a machine gun, will see, rising above the vague morass of a disastrous but forgotten history, the three letters which reassure all the good and honest families of this ancient, Christian country (And certainly it is to the MRP's credit in spite of everything to have created this reflex. We recognize and admire in its militants everything that remains of generosity, disinterest, and purity)."[47]

If this were a study of the political influence of all French Catholics as individuals, doubtless hundreds of pages would be needed to describe the MRP as well as all the parties of the right. But since the study is confined particularly to French Catholicism (to groups that have definite ties to the ecclesiastical nucleus of the French Church and not to isolated individuals) we do not find the MRP always of crucial significance. The functional role of the MRP is formally distinct from the Church and Catholicism because Catholicism as such does not form political parties.

Whatever the political importance of the MRP in general, it does not seem to contribute enormously to the political impact of the ecclesiastical nucleus at the hub of French Catholicism. Perhaps the main impact is negative: the existence of the MRP as a focal point for Catholics makes it impossible for all moderate left political forces in France to unite in one strong single party. Many doctrines and some specific policies are favored by MRP leaders because the latter, as Catholics, are drawn to them. But it is too much to deduce an open participation by the Hierarchy in the political strategy of the MRP. The bishops know that many Frenchmen still have vestiges of the old "laic reflex" from the early 1900's. It seems more likely now

[47] "Le Bloc-Notes de François Mauriac," in *L'Express*, May 14, 1959, p. 40.

that the Hierarchy spreads its favors and expects returns from all the parties of the right and center—that is, all the parties that will give the Church a sympathetic hearing. Beyond this, even with the MRP, the Church will not now go. It seems desirable to leave even to the "most Catholic" political party an entire freedom. With Catholic Action, social action groups, and the Catholic press, the Hierarchy has safer and still effective ways to make a political impact if it should so desire.

III. Other Political Expressions of French Catholicism

To the left and to the right of the MRP, political groups of Catholic inspiration developed in the last days of the Fourth Republic. The 1958 crisis forced these groups to clarify their political positions, especially their relation to the MRP. The most interesting and potentially the strongest of these groups was "Christian Democracy," founded by Georges Bidault. Although the group carried the name of the progressive tendency which the MRP embodies, its goals were a world apart from the MRP. The purpose of "Christian Democracy" was to unite all conservative forces under the aegis which almost all accept: Christianity and nationalism.

Originally it seemed that Bidault would try to cajole all Catholic-inspired forces to associate with "Christian Democracy," but the MRP refused any such commitment, stating that if conservative Catholics such as Pinay, Laniel, or Duchet were in the same party with former Catholic Action members, CFTC members, and other Social Catholics, it would be impossible to get anything done. Such a vast Christian force, which would resemble Christian Democracy in the Italian or German manner, is impossible in France, said the MRP. Soon after, Bidault was effectively read out of the MRP, which he himself had founded.[48]

[48] *Forces Nouvelles*, October 18, 1958, p. 7. *Ibid.*, January 10, 1959, pp. 5-8. Bidault has been "in-again-out-again" of the MRP since the creation of "Christian Democracy." He seemed reconciled with his old party in October 1958. But certain "Christian Democracy" candidates

"Christian Democracy" did not have the opportunity in the early years of the Fifth Republic to develop into an organized party. But its real importance lies in the future. If one day the parties of the classic right find their appeal waning, "Christian Democracy" offers another set of values which they all share. If "Christian Democracy" develops in this direction, it will almost certainly provoke the splitting of the MRP into two factions, with all the more conservative elements joining Bidault, and the rest forced into a coalition with the least laic of the Socialists.[49]

On the other side of the MRP another Catholic-inspired group arose for a brief time: the *Rassemblement des Forces Démocratiques* (RFD). The RFD was made up of young leaders of Catholic Action, many of whom had positions in family, trade union, or professional organizations, or even in the MRP. Its prime movers were Roger Lavialle and Rémy Montagne, former Presidents of ACJF; Michel Debatisse, former head of the JAC; Bernard Lambert, also a former JAC officer, MRP member, and Deputy; Théo Braun, a CFTC officer; Nestor Rombeaut, a former CFTC leader and now MRP Deputy; and Guy Raclet, former President of *Jeune Patron.*[50]

---

ran against those of the MRP, and in the National Assembly Bidault is a *non-inscrit*, although in 1960 the MRP officially counted the other "Christian Democracy" deputies within its parliamentary group.

[49] In an interview, J.-P. Prévost, Secretary of the MRP Senate group, seemed to think that "Christian Democracy" was destined to widen its appeal. However, now that key prelates have made known their liberal feelings on Algeria, an alliance between the extreme right and the devout Catholic "masses" in the near future would seem out of the question.

At present it is also quite doubtful that a great "Labour Party" type of political group would result from a fusion of the MRP left with the Socialists. The formation of any party of this type, where Catholics and non-Catholics alike would be attracted, seems extremely difficult to envisage. Socialism as practiced by the SFIO seems to have little support among the masses at present, and Catholic Action members would not feel as much "at home" in a party that does not give lip service to their ideals by proclaiming its Christian inspiration.

[50] See *Le Monde*, January 20, 1959, p. 5.

The RFD was a grouping of elites rather than a mass movement. This was its fatal weakness: the lack of mass appeal finally led to its disintegration. But its members were not just uprooted intellectuals as are so many members of ephemeral groups on the French left. All its leaders had responsibilities in other Catholic organizations. The purpose of the RFD was to give these young leaders, and the social classes which they represented, more control over existing political parties. The RFD manifesto proclaimed this in more detail: "We think that the common people do not want a program made for them, no matter how good it might be. Above all they want to draw up for themselves the program that they need, according to a state of affairs in constant evolution. Thus, they should be given a determining position within political parties. . . . They want first of all to give representatives of trade union and peasant groups . . . the possibility of controlling, with a majority vote, all the directing organs of the political party of their choice."[51]

The Catholic Action experience of RFD leaders seemed to push them toward political action—effective action above all. So the RFD from the beginning decided not to start its own party, realizing that there are tremendous odds against any new political group attracting wide mass support. The Catholic Action experience also gave the RFD leaders a strong attachment to their own economic and social situations. They were led to understand that they were not just isolated individuals, but drew their fullest meaning from their occupational, social, and national identification. "It must be recognized that, on the political level, France is made up not just of 44 million citizens, but also of many economic and family organizations which represent extremely important forces."[52]

If the RFD wanted to work within a large number of political parties, it was disappointed from the start. The only major party which accepted its demands was the MRP. In

[51] Bernard Lambert, "*Les Partis Politiques, les Milieux Populaires et la Démocratie,*" in *Le Monde*, January 28, 1959, p. 5.
[52] *ibid.*

May 1959, the MRP National Congress decided to reserve half the seats in all its organs to workers and peasants, ". . . defined broadly: large-scale farmers will be considered peasants. Manual workers, monthly workers, technicians, civil servants, and middle-echelon staff will be considered workers."[53]

Some have suggested that the RFD knew all the time that only the MRP was suitable for its members. In fact, there seems to be little choice outside the MRP for a militant Catholic Action member with advanced social views, especially if effective political action is desired. The other parties of the left are either infinitesimally small, like the *Parti Socialiste Unifié*, or internally unsound, like the SFIO or the Communists. So perhaps *Témoignage Chrétien* was right in assuming that RFD leaders seriously considered only the MRP: "In the minds of several leaders, the open letter of the RFD to political parties was destined above all for the Popular Republicans. . . . The RFD leaders closest to the MRP seem to desire a democratization of the party and a change in its social composition."[54]

In the face of weak or unsuitable alternative parties, the MRP began absorbing the RFD into its structure. This caused a certain regeneration in the ranks of the MRP, though it is too early to appreciate the extent of the change, or to judge how many among the elite trained by Catholic Action were attracted to the MRP by the RFD.

Political formations of the extreme right are not treated in this section, not because they are absent from the political scene, but because all of them claim closer ties to the Church than just "Catholic inspiration." So the organizations that could be included here, such as *Cité Catholique*, or publications like *Itinéraires, Pensée Catholique,* or *Verbe,* will be found in the

[53] *Le Monde*, May 9, 1959, p. 6. The word *ouvrier* is given an exceptionally broad definition, to say the least!

[54] *Témoignage Chrétien*, February 6, 1959, p. 3. In the same article, de Montvalon warns that the RFD leaders will be sealing their political doom if they associate too closely with the MRP on the eve of another school crisis.

chapters dealing with Catholic groups more closely tied to the Hierarchy.

The Catholic extreme left is dead—at least for the moment. However, in the first years after World War II, when a residual good feeling toward the USSR plus much political naïveté on the part of certain intellectuals enlarged the ranks of the French left, the *Chrétiens Progressistes*, a group of Catholic inspiration, tried to set roots in the French political terrain. The *Chrétiens Progressistes* were never more than a few thousand Catholic intellectuals, attracted by the power and the working-class *mystique* of the Communist Party. They denied that their religion had any connection with their pro-Communist political views, justifying in this way sympathy toward a party which the Church abhorred. But while separating Catholicism and politics, the *Chrétiens Progressistes* were curiously "clerical," in that they advertised their Catholicism—something which even the MRP dares not do. Thus, their slogan was "To be of the Church, in progressivism, with the Communists." However, the *Chrétiens Progressistes* could not survive the stern condemnation of Communists and their sympathizers by the Holy Office. They finally disappeared as a Catholic inspiration group in 1951.[55] After the disappearance of the *Chrétiens Progressistes*, the viewpoint which they espoused appeared in organizations like *Jeunesse de l'Eglise*, and publications like *Quinzaine*, already described. After these disappeared in turn, the tendency itself seemed moribund. This disappearance of the Catholic extreme left is very significant; it seems to indicate that French intellectuals are at last taking a more critical view of the theories of Marxism and the French Communist Party. At the end of the war, millions thought that only Marxism could reverse decades of economic and political stagnation. Now the French economy is booming, while the homeland of Communism seems more adept at international power politics than at applying domestically the ideals of Karl Marx.

[55] See Dansette, *Destin*, p. 234. Dansette devotes all of Chapter Five to this extremist tendency in French Catholicism. See pp. 225-246.

IV. The Confédération Française des Travailleurs Chrétiens

A. INTRODUCTION: THE CFTC BRAND OF CATHOLIC INSPIRATION

The CFTC has a much different background from the MRP. The MRP began after World War II, while the CFTC dates from the end of World War I. The CFTC has evolved from close collaboration with the Church to a position that is farther from the Church than the MRP. Most MRP active members join the party because of its Catholic inspiration, while many CFTC members join that union because of economic reasons alone. In supporting the interests of the working class, the CFTC has proved its effectiveness—much better than the MRP in the political realm.

The evolution in CFTC relations to the Hierarchy can be profitably examined in detail, to show how a working class organization faced the various developments in Church-state relations in recent years. The parent union of the CFTC, the *Syndicat des Employés de Commerce et de l'Industrie*, was restricted to Catholics only—in fact, only to Catholics who had a "good reputation"—when it was founded in the Nineteenth Century![56] Even in the 1930's this union required that its members be "well known as Catholics."[57] The Confederation as a whole was open to anyone who adhered to the doctrines of *Rerum Novarum*, though no specific proof of Catholicism was required. In 1920, the CFTC repeated its firm determination to base its activity on the social doctrines of Catholicism: "These doctrines are above human economic, social, or political regimes, which are essentially imperfect and transitory. They require many things from those who follow them: respect for human liberty and dignity, guaranteed by social rights including right to individual and collective property, right of association, etc.; the maintenance of the principle of authority;

[56] Georges Levard, *Chances et Perils du Syndicalisme Chrétien* (Paris: Arthème Fayard, 1955), p. 84.

[57] *ibid.*, p. 114.

the entire accomplishing of one's duty, which is the only practical guarantee of any right; the safeguard of the family, the social group, the country, and the profession; fraternity between individuals and collectivities."[58] As late as 1936, the President of the CFTC declared that the Christian trade union movement, ". . . in order to have the right to call itself Christian, must be eternally faithful to the doctrine of the gospel and to the teachings that clarify it."[59] And in the face of the social disorders of 1936 the CFTC stuck by its Papal Encyclicals: "The CFTC claims that an effective and durable remedy cannot be found for the economic errors and social injustice which have brought the present misery and disorders, unless one seeks the remedy in the teachings to be found particularly in the Encyclicals *Rerum Novarum* and *Quadragesimo Anno.*"[60]

Clearly the prewar position of the CFTC was closer to the Catholic social groups than to those of Catholic inspiration. Its Catholicism imposed limits on its activity which were clear to all, and dictated other areas to be emphasized. The CFTC opposed the class-struggle principle down to 1945, and was against the policy of nationalization of basic industries before the war.[61] It had a special place in its social demands for the family, since "The family and not the individual is the basic cell of society and must be the key factor in determining normal social needs which production is geared to satisfy."[62]

The war profoundly shook the fabric of the CFTC; social transformations made its leaders realize that they had to open up to a wider clientele. Therefore, all explicit references to the Church were eliminated from its statutes and its ideas were aligned more closely to the other trade unions. Now its main formal tie to the Church is the statement that the CFTC is inspired by the "principles of social-Christian morality."[63] Nationalizations were accepted as they took place immediately

[58] Jules Zirnheld, *Cinquante Années de Syndicalisme Chrétien* (Paris: Editions Spes, 1937), pp. 193-194.

[59] *ibid.*, pp. 179-180. [60] Levard, *op.cit.*, pp. 167-168.

[61] *ibid.*, p. 184. Cf. Fogarty, *op.cit.*, p. 218.

[62] Levard, *op.cit.*, p. 169. [63] *ibid.*, p. 183.

after the war.[64] The CFTC Congress in June 1959 favored total nationalization of banks and envisaged the possibility of nationalizing the steel, chemical, cement, oil, and naval construction industries. The goal of the CFTC in the economic sphere has now become "democratic socialism."[65] From the behavior of the CFTC since 1945, no one could accuse it of being "yellow" or the tool of the employers, as might have been charged before the war. The CFTC has now been accepted by French workers as one of the legitimate representatives of the working class, but to be so accepted it had to sacrifice some of its Catholic ties.

There has recently been talk of dropping the label "Christian" from the CFTC's title—a move which would probably indicate the evolution of the CFTC out of the category which we are considering here. Should this happen one day, it would culminate a constant evolution away from any organic connection to the Church or any ties which seem to smack of clericalism. This development would not be an isolated instance; it has already been noted that the *Mouvement de Libération du Peuple*, a working-class Catholic Action group, evolved out of French Catholicism. And certain worker-priests before 1954 renounced the Church. So perhaps the danger is faced by any Catholic-inspired organization in the working class.

However, all members of the CFTC still realize that there is "something added" to their organization which distinguishes it from other unions. "The CFTC does something better and something that no other trade union federation can do: it defends first and foremost MAN. We are not just producers and consumers, but first of all human beings who need dignity, liberty, personal development, and true happiness."[66]

CFTC ideals force union members to take a certain distance from Marxism: "The power of Christian trade unionism lies in the members' ideal of a higher life. The members know that man depends neither on the laws of liberal economics,

[64] *ibid.*, p. 175. [65] See *Le Monde*, June 23, 1959, p. 5.
[66] *Syndicalisme Magazine*, No. 725, May 1959.

codified by the bourgeoisie . . . nor on the laws of history which are revealed only after the event."[67]

Up to now, the CFTC has wanted to remain within the amorphous category of Catholic inspiration organizations, perhaps because of these ideals. It still adheres to many of the same principles as the MRP. Other reasons why it keeps this tenuous affiliation with French Catholicism will become more apparent in a detailed study of the organic and informal ties between the CFTC and the Church.

B. RELATIONS OF THE CFTC TO THE CHURCH HIERARCHY

Before the war the CFTC had particularly close relations with the Hierarchy. A theological council existed for the CFTC National Bureau. It was made up of a bishop and prominent economic and social experts among the French clergy. On lower levels too there were Church advisors, although they do not seem to have been attached to individual unions as such. The role of the clergy in the life of the CFTC was generally limited to basic principles, as the CFTC leader Jules Zirnheld has pointed out: "The statutes of the CFTC, its principal declarations, the directives which concerned moral questions, and finally the plan of the CFTC have been the object of study and decisions by this theological council. The CFTC owes to this initial measure of security the fact that it has never wandered adventurously into error."[68] The Church was not consulted on the professional activities of the CFTC, but from Zirnheld's statement above, it appears that "professional" was narrowly interpreted.

[67] Levard, *op.cit.*, p. 188. When Khrushchev visited France in 1960, the CFTC magazine *Syndicalisme* declared that "the Soviet head of government is the master and dictator, but not the authentic representative of the Russian people in the democratic sense of the term. . . . The fact that the Russian people do not revolt cannot justify a regime which exists because of police state terror, denunciations, massive deportations, and physical liquidations. . . . This technocratic Communism has no working class spirit. . . ." See *Syndicalisme*, No. 771 (March 26, 1960), p. 1.

[68] Zirnheld, *op.cit.*, pp. 202-203.

A good picture of the functional relations between the CFTC and the Church can be seen in the struggle between Catholic employers and the CFTC in the department of Nord, just before the Depression. The employers claimed that the CFTC was "Marxist" while the CFTC claimed that workers were being exploited. The conflict was settled—but by the Church from Rome. The Holy Office itself, upon suggestions from the future Cardinal Liénart, declared that CFTC workers were "desired and encouraged by the competent ecclesiastical authority."[69] Furthermore, the Christian trade unions ". . . repudiate in principle the class struggle and collectivism in all its forms. . . . Catholics must by preference associate with other Catholics, unless necessity forces them to act differently."[70] So not only did the Church settle the quarrel, at the same time it set the limits of action for the CFTC.

At the end of World War II, all organic relations with the Church were broken. There is no longer any need for the CFTC to provide a religious presence in the working class, because this is done through such Catholic Action groups as JOC and ACO, through the *Mission de France*, religious orders and groups like *Prado*, and many other Church groups. However, the Church still encourages the faithful to join the CFTC, in preference to other trade unions. As the cardinals and archbishops said in 1945, "We earnestly remind all Catholics that their place is in the Christian trade unions which, truly professional and free, draw their inspiration from Christian morality and the Church social doctrine. Such unions must be preferred to the Socialist or Communist unions, inspired by materialist conceptions of life, of work, and of society."[71] Perhaps these encouragements tend to perpetuate a certain confessional color in the CFTC. At any rate, the French Hierarchy

[69] Levard, *op.cit.*, pp. 106-112.

[70] *ibid.*, pp. 107 and 111.

[71] Romain, *Le Syndicalisme en France* (Lille: Union des Secrétariats Sociaux du Nord, 1945), p. 137. The ACA repeated this request in 1950. Cf. Val Lorwin, *The French Labor Movement* (Cambridge, Mass.: Harvard University Press, 1954), p. 183.

has never given the MRP as specific an endorsement as this quote gives to the CFTC. Perhaps this is just the aftermath of the close Church-CFTC relations before the war, and will die in due time; or, possibly the CFTC leadership realizes that some confessional coloring could be an asset for the only major non-Marxist trade union. At any rate, it is largely this residual and hard-to-define confessional spirit that keeps the CFTC distinct from other democratic groups, notably *Force Ouvrière*. Other reasons why the CFTC would want to keep its autonomy in the labor movement will be discussed in the next section.

C. CATHOLICISM AND THE ORGANIZATION OF THE CFTC.

Before the crisis of May 1958 the CFTC was split into two camps: a "Christian" majority, which favored keeping the attributes of a Christian inspiration organization, and a laic minority, which favored a complete deconfessionalization of the CFTC and a merger with *Force Ouvrière* into one great democratic labor organization. The minority, essentially workers from heavy industry and public school teachers, whose ideas are set forth in the monthly bulletin *Reconstruction*, regularly at CFTC meetings received 40 percent of the votes. Why, if the *Reconstruction* group differed from the CFTC leadership, did it continue to participate in Christian syndicalism? It could be that members of *Reconstruction* were more motivated by their religion than they would admit. Paul Vignaux, one of their leaders, said that the CFTC ". . . constitutes the principal contribution of French Catholics to the trade union life of the country."[72] Also, *Reconstruction* is opposed to what it calls a "certain laic metaphysics."[73] More likely, though, *Reconstruction* members wanted to wait until they could persuade another

[72] *La Nef*, January 1954, p. 125.

[73] *Reconstruction*, No. 40 (July-August 1951), p. A 14. *Reconstruction* has called the CGT an "instrument of Moscow," with which limited cooperation might be possible in exceptional circumstances, but never a permanent fusion. See *Reconstruction*, II, 1960 (March-April 1960), p. 58.

ten percent of the CFTC to join their ranks, giving them a majority of the Confederation.

On occasion *Reconstruction* was practically read out of the CFTC by the majority. But all divergencies between majority and minority disappeared as a result of the crisis of May 1958. Under the pressure of the crisis, CFTC decided to modify its historic apolitical stand, to watch more carefully the development of democracy in the Fifth Republic, and to put the secondary quarrels of Church-CFTC relations into cold storage. This decision was confirmed at the Congress of June 1959, where 93 percent of the delegates approved the report of the General Secretary, and where the Confederation elected 18 *Reconstruction* members to the 44 member Federal Council.[74] As a part of the general agreement between the two factions, it appears that the "Christian" status of the CFTC will not be changed for the present.

One of the major controversies that opposed majority and minority factions in the CFTC concerned international affiliation. Most non-Communist trade unions are in the International Confederation of Free Trade Unions. In France, *Force Ouvrière* is part of this international body. But the CFTC is in another international organization: the *Confédération Internationale des Syndicats Chrétiens.* The latter includes eighteen Catholic and Protestant groups from Western European countries.[75] The position of the CFTC within this group serves to strengthen its ties with Catholicism, since many other unions in this international group feel no qualms about stressing their religious bonds.

But the CFTC does not remain in the Christian international group because it is looking for the atmosphere of a pious confraternity. There are more practical reasons for its choice: the CFTC is the dominant group in the body; its late President, Gaston Tessier, was the General Secretary of the CFTC. CFTC leaders fear that, if they were to switch international groups

[74] *Le Monde*, June 23, 1959, p. 5. See also *Témoignage Chrétien*, June 12, 1959, p. 8.

[75] Of these only two are Protestant. See Fogarty, *op.cit.*, p. 217.

now they would simply become little fish in the pool dominated by the American labor movement. The Christian international body allows the CFTC to extend its influence on the international scene because, just like the ICFTU, it influences the International Labor Organization and has other advisory activities in the United Nations. Still, despite the added prestige this gives the CFTC, *Reconstruction* has been worried that membership in the Christian international body would result eventually in a ". . . situation of confessional isolation."[76]

D. CFTC MEMBERS AND THE CHURCH: PERSONAL TIES

Does the CFTC include most unionized Catholic workers in France? There is strong presumption to believe so, although it is not something that can be proved. The religious aura around the CFTC, and the definitely laic tinge of the other two major unions would be a first indication. For a devout Catholic, especially one trained to obey the Hierarchy through participation in Catholic Action, the favor which the Church gives to the CFTC would appear virtually as a command to join it rather than the other major unions. Fogarty shows that the percentage of Catholic workers in many professions approaches closely the percentage of workers in the CFTC.[77] And a chart at the end of the book demonstrates that the Departments where the CFTC represents more than 30 percent of all unionized workers are those where the Church, the MRP, and Catholic Action are the strongest: in Brittany, the East, and the southern *Massif Central.*

One reason why the CFTC membership is difficult to analyze is the number of nonactive Catholics or even nonbelievers in the CFTC. Perhaps the number of devout Catholics in the CFTC is the same as for the MRP; however, they are drowned in a sea of other members, for among workers the CFTC is far larger than the MRP. The CFTC has upwards of 700,000

[76] *Reconstruction*, Vol. XIV, No. 2 (March-April 1959), p. 62.

[77] Fogarty, *op.cit.*, pp. 373-375. However, some of Fogarty's figures are based on the 1952 public opinion poll mentioned earlier in the chapter. These are of dubious accuracy.

members, while the worker vote for the MRP is probably around 150,000.[78]

Many young members of the CFTC who appeared to have leadership potential in the past were sent to sessions with the *Semaines Sociales*, where they became familiar with the social research undertaken by various Catholic groups, and met their "Catholic cousins." But this practice seems less frequent now than before the war. CFTC leaders are not usually the grown-up leaders of Catholic Action youth groups, as is so often the case for the MRP. Slowly, the personnel of the CFTC is breaking away from the "Catholic family" in which the MRP is still firmly enmeshed.

What are the possibilities for the CFTC to develop a stronger appeal to workers completely outside the Christian tradition? They are not too good despite evolutionary trends, if we are to believe Val Lorwin: "The CFTC is the least confessional of any of the national Catholic labor movements. It has avoided attachment to the Catholic political party, the MRP. [*sic*] Despite its independence and its showing of militancy, it is uncertain how much farther it can push the limits of recruitment in a land where the Church is still associated with the middle and upper classes and where in most regions, workers' attitudes to the Church shade off from occasional nominal conformity or indifference to hostility."[79] But in addition to reasons already given, the CFTC is too well-entrenched in certain regions and in certain occupations to sacrifice these positions for any changes in its present status. Thus, even though deconfessionalization is the only means of attracting a wider clientele, it is unlikely that the CFTC will consider this advisable.

E. CATHOLICISM AND RECENT CFTC ACTIVITIES

The CFTC and the MRP had a brief honeymoon at the end of the war, when CFTC officials were allowed to sit in Parlia-

[78] Information from Father Robinot-Marcy at *Action Populaire*. These figures also show that the CFTC does not "condition" most of its members to vote for the MRP.

[79] Lorwin, *op.cit.*, p. 189. Cf. Fogarty, *op.cit.*, p. 375.

ment and work actively for the MRP cause. But when the MRP became associated with the parties of the right the honeymoon ended, and now no CFTC national official can hold any party office.[80] In later years some CFTC members actually considered it an insult to be associated with the MRP in any way.[81] Some of the *Reconstruction* faction even came out in favor of the laic parties of the non-Communist left: "As it is now and as it can develop, the *Union des Forces Démocratiques* represents a serious hope—the only hope at present for the French left."[82]

The 1958 crisis and the advent of the Fifth Republic forced the CFTC to change its political tactics—perhaps toward more direct contact with Catholic-inspired forces. The *Rassemblement des Forces Démocratiques* was given its initial impulse by Théo Braun, a national CFTC leader, cooperating with Catholic Action elements. Braun even wanted to make the RFD a political party, to which the CFTC would be committed; this, however, was not approved. The CFTC maintained "organic connections" with the RFD, even though the elite groups constituting the RFD turned more and more toward the MRP.[83]

The indirect cooperation between the MRP and CFTC in fostering the RFD may be the harbinger of closer cooperation in the future. If the Republic itself were to be threatened by totalitarian forces from the left or the right, groups like the CFTC and the MRP would do all in their power to preserve democracy, which they view in roughly the same terms. Even without such a crisis some have predicted closer ties between the MRP and the CFTC: "In regions with strongly Christian traditions where new industrial centers are being created—Angers, Le Mans, Rennes, Troyes, Reims—teams of young militant Christians have every chance to establish a workers' movement as vigorously active in favor of workers' rights but more

[80] See Fogarty, *op.cit.*, p. 226.

[81] Etienne Borne, quoted in Fogarty, *op.cit.*, p. 227.

[82] *Reconstruction*, Vol. xiv, No. 1 (January-February 1959), p. 2.

[83] Confirmed in interview with Mme. Simone Troisgros, Vice-President of the CFTC, June 10, 1959.

liberal than the CGT. . . . In the end, there is a common language between Christian Democratic members and themselves, the same conception of the world. One is not obliged, as with the Marxists, to redefine the problem of the creation of the world."[84]

The CFTC was exceptionally active from the beginning of the May 1958 crisis. Its activities were of three kinds: appeals for preserving democratic liberties of the Republic, attempts to mobilize its mass of adherents behind the Pflimlin government, and close cooperation with other democratic trade unions, notably with *Force Ouvrière.* Illustrating the first activity there appeared under banner headlines—"The CFTC defends democratic institutions and liberty"—this comment in the CFTC magazine, *Syndicalisme,* for May 24, 1958: "The CFTC reaffirms with vigor its unshakeable attachment to the democratic institutions that France freely gave herself. These institutions are incompatible with any regime of personal power." During the May crisis the CFTC called for calm and discipline, and was especially concerned to avoid any public displays that might touch off violence. All this, said the CFTC, was ". . . the best way to help the government in this strained period."[85] The "government" in this case was the short-lived one headed by Pierre Pflimlin. Starting May 13, representatives of the CFTC and FO met every day to discuss effective measures that could be taken together. Neither the Christian nor the Socialist group was hindered in the crisis over the secondary quarrels of Marxism or *laïcité.* The army revolt of April 1961 also stimulated joint meetings between the CFTC and FO. In fact, as *Le Monde* reported on April 24, there was even a meeting with the CGT, despite its Communist leanings.

Once the de Gaulle government was firmly installed, the CFTC was not dogmatically opposed to it, though it kept a watchful eye on the continued menace of authoritarianism. With the first few weeks of the Gaullist government as a barom-

[84] Robert Barrat, in *Express,* January 15, 1959, p. 11.
[85] *Syndicalisme,* May 24, 1958, pp. 4-5.

eter, the CFTC ". . . considered that the essential general guarantees, which it demanded be safeguarded during the crisis period, were assured."[86] Considering the Gaullist Constitution, the CFTC reasoned that whether or not a democratic regime would be perpetuated depended more on the personality of the President and the health of national political forces than on the institutions. However, the CFTC noted that the Constitution seemed correct in its provisions for economic and social democracy, and called the Constitution's overseas provisions "fortunate."[87] Many CFTC members who read their union's analysis of the Constitution would probably lean in favor of its approval. Although there is nothing "Catholic" in the CFTC's sentiments toward de Gaulle or the Constitution, perhaps these sentiments would have been less tolerant if the CFTC had forsaken its Catholic inspiration.

On the school question the CFTC faced a particularly complex situation. Two teachers' unions are members of the CFTC: one for public school teachers and one for private school teachers. The first is one of the leading elements of the *Reconstruction* faction. The second is a member of the most important Catholic school pressure group, and is most anxious to improve the lot of all private schools. The two unions were so opposed to one another that the CFTC as a whole was unable to take a strong stand on the school question. However, just before the Barangé Law was passed, the CFTC came out for "effective liberty of education," which in France can only mean some sort of state aid to private schools or to their pupils.[88]

86 *La CFTC: Deux Années d'Action* (Issy-les-Moulineaux: CFTC, 1959), p. 20.

87 *ibid.*, p. 22. However, according to Georges Suffert, all CFTC national leaders except one were personally opposed to the new Constitution. See *Les Catholiques et la Gauche*, p. 97.

88 See *Le Monde*, September 7, 1951, p. 6. Both the public and the private teacher unions were rather conciliatory. Neither reflected the extreme laic or extreme Catholic views on the school question. In fact, the public school teachers' union even seemed to favor some formula to aid Catholic schools in areas where they are particularly important. See *Reconstruction*, No. 37 (March 1951), p. B-10.

In 1959, though it did not oppose the principle of state aid to Catholic schools as such, the CFTC public school teachers' union unequivocally opposed the Debré school law. The law was especially criticized for not specifying that subsidized education must be religiously neutral.[89]

F. CONCLUSION

The CFTC, almost from its inception, has been moving farther and farther from the Church. This evolution continues today, and it would be rash to assume that there will be a reversal of any trends, even though the May crisis evoked unusual behavior patterns.

At present the CFTC still remains the trade-union expression of French Catholicism, and as such it has its place in this book. Also, it seems reasonable to suppose that certain of its policies take the form they do because of the CFTC's "Catholic aura," although this cannot be proven. On the other hand, the CFTC is definitely not an apostolic group. It is not a "watered-down JOC"; if it were, it would not have any more adherents than the Catholic Action working class groups have.

If the CFTC is at the limit of the groups considered in this book, it is not the least effective. On the contrary, the French working class is so far from the Church that only the most indirect allusion to Christian principles is palatable to most workers—or can be understood by them. In this connection, the CFTC has done a yeoman's job in ridding many workers of their anti-Church prejudices. And in areas of traditional piety, the CFTC, usually the strongest trade union, has kept workers from the laic philosophies of the Socialist and Communist unions. Perhaps these considerations inspired the following judgment by Fogarty: "The main pillar of Christian Democracy in France is not the MRP, important though that party is. It is probable that far more real weight attaches to the Christian trade unions (CFTC) or to the youth movements, such as the Young Christian Farmers or Workers. . . ."[90]

[89] See *Esprit*, Vol. XXVIII (September 1960), p. 1436.
[90] Fogarty, *op.cit.*, p. 294.

The School Question and Specialized Catholic Institutions

I. *Why the School Question? Historical and Philosophical Introduction*

A. BRIEF SKETCH OF THE EVOLUTION OF THE SCHOOL QUESTION

The relationship between public and private schools in France during the past century has been a persistent political dilemma of great complexity. Whether fighting for the legal existence of Church schools or pressing for state aid, the Church has been involved in this question as in no other political matter. The place which the school question occupies for the Church Hierarchy, the Catholic press, and Catholic Action groups has already been noted: it is the one political question on which all Catholic groups can take sides.

There are also specialized Catholic groups dealing exclusively with the school question. These groups form the focal point of this chapter. They are particularly important in the perspective of this present study for two reasons. First, they illustrate the "functional efficiency" of French Catholicism in an area of particular interest to the Church. Secondly, these specialized Catholic groups assume great political significance, often beyond the bounds of the school question itself, whenever the latter comes to the forefront of French political life.

This chapter does not pretend to treat the school question in its entirety. During the sixty years that the problem of state aid to Catholic schools has existed, partisans and opponents have mobilized every conceivable theoretical argument, have sponsored innumerable pressure groups, and, during the Combes era—or from May to October 1951—succeeded in dominating the activity of the national government for months on end.

Here the concern is neither with the laic school groups nor with the political consequences of the school question as such; the school question simply serves as a framework to point out more clearly the political significance of French Catholicism.

It will be useful to sketch briefly the development of the school problem since the separation of Church and state in 1905, and even before, to clarify the reactions of present-day defenders of Catholic schools. There is no attempt at thoroughness in this sketch, simply a catalogue of the highlights of the problem.[1]

The existence of a school problem in France is related to historical factors going deep into the fabric of the French Republic. Until the Revolution of 1789, the Church had enjoyed a virtual monopoly over education in France, but since the Church was tied to the structures of government, schools were not exactly "private." Rather, education was a public service entrusted to the Church. After the revolutionary upheavals, the First Empire officially nationalized the whole school system, although private schools were allowed to exist in many instances. Since religious instruction was an integral part of the public school curriculum, the cooperation between Church and state that had existed before the Revolution was largely restored. In this atmosphere, few Church leaders had any particular desire to break the government monopoly of education and establish a private Catholic school system. Through religious instruction in the public schools, the Church could give youngsters the principles of the Catholic faith, and could thereby perpetuate a certain loyalty to the Church.

Church participation in state schools means some state control over the Church. During the first years of the Restoration

[1] The most useful bibliographic source for this sketch is "L'Histoire de la Liberté de l'Enseignement en France," in *Bulletin de Documentation des APEL et AEP*, Vol. v, No. 1 (March 1958). See also Father Villain *et al.*, *Un Problème National: l'Ecole* (Paris: Editions de l'Ecole, 1951). Note also Marguerite Bousquet, "Le Problème de l'Enseignement Primaire Privé en France depuis 1947," unpublished doctoral dissertation, Faculté de Droit, Université de Lyon, 1956.

there was little difficulty; but around the 1830's the state began to withdraw some of the privileges it had given to the Church. For example, in 1828, the Jesuits were forbidden to teach. The antagonism between Church and state gradually increased, and a strong movement to legalize private schools took hold in many Catholic circles. Thanks to this movement, three laws were passed, permitting the existence of private schools on the primary level (Guizot Law, 1833), on the secondary level (Falloux Law, 1850), and on the university level (Law of 1875). Thus at long last it was legally possible for Catholics to establish schools independent of the state.

However, as late as the first years of the Third Republic, most Catholics were satisfied with the arrangement of the 1801 Concordat. Then, a combination of events, particularly the continued loyalty of most of the Hierarchy to the *Ancien Régime*, brought a series of laws which completely modified the situation. During the two decades from 1886 to 1906 the entire structure of Church-state cooperation which had survived the Revolution fell to the blows of the anti-Church forces, through the so-called laic laws. Religious instruction was removed from the public schools, and in an excess of zeal, the Law of July 7, 1904 even forbade religious orders from teaching in private schools.

Whether the laic laws were just or unjust does not concern us here. To most Catholics, however, they brutally destroyed a vested interest which the Church had enjoyed continually for centuries: the right to perpetuate the faith through instructing the youth of France in the public schools. On the instruction of youth depends the survival of religion, so Catholics feared that the laic laws would gravely injure the position of Catholicism in France. This was the real school quarrel in France; more than the material possessions of the Church, the loyalty patterns of future generations were at stake.

It became evident soon after the laic laws were passed that they had been tactical blunders, whatever their theoretical merits or defects. They engendered a coherent and intransigent

Catholic opposition force which limited constructive political activity in the early years of this century. They perpetuated an unrealistic dichotomy between *cléricaux* and *laïques*. Also, they backfired on their supporters after World War I, when the voters selected the famous *Chambre bleue horizon.*

The period from 1906 down to the present has seen a gradual modification of the worst features of the laic laws. Slowly France seems to be moving toward a new phase in the school quarrel, where both sides are willing to compromise their extreme demands. Among the steps in this development are the Astier law of July, 1919, giving state subsidies to private technical schools; the perpetuation of the 1801 Concordat in Alsace-Lorraine; subsidies by the state to Catholic youth groups and by localities to Catholic school children; the Poinso-Chapuis decrees of June 1948, which would have given family associations the power to underwrite the education of underprivileged children in private schools, but which were never applied; the Marie and Barangé laws of September 1951, giving state aid to private school children; and finally the Debré law of December 1959, providing contractual relationships between private schools and the state and paying most private school teachers from public funds. Each of these measures marks a stage in the swing of the pendulum back toward a greater tolerance of Catholic schools and toward state financial aid to these schools. Thus, the basic legal structure of French education is no longer quite where the laic legislators left it in 1906.

During the past half-century, the evolution of the school question has been paralleled by a change in the attitude of most groups concerned with the school question. Today few responsible people question the principle that Church and state should be formally separated. At the same time, intransigent *laïques* have also lost influence, largely because their virulence has been taken over by the Communists. Few would now advocate outlawing all private education, as the extreme *laïques* once did. Catholics outside of a few extremists favor the Republic as it is now organized, so a favorite scapegoat of *laïques* has been destroyed. Also, Catholics put increasing importance on the hypothesis that a "neutral" public education can coexist with private religious education, and both can accommodate Catholic children.

B. THE NATURE OF THE SCHOOL PROBLEM TODAY

At present, if spirits are calmer on both sides, the end of the school quarrel has not been reached. More than a million Catholic families still prefer to shun the public school and give their children a Catholic school education, even if it means a certain financial sacrifice. The *laïques* of the Socialist Party or the *Ligue Française de l'Enseignement*, while accepting the principle of educational freedom, claim that children educated in Catholic schools may not be fully loyal to Republican France. The Barangé law of 1951, which provided the most obvious state subsidies for Church schools in a half century, rekindled the hostility of the *laïques*. The 1959 law also heightened tensions. As late as 1960, an official of a public school parents' association was talking like this: "On the school question no peace is possible with the Church. Either it dominates you or you dominate it. We shall not cooperate with the so-called conciliation committees, because you cannot combine fire and water."[2]

By 1959, forces favorable to the Catholic school were concentrating on a more practical argument. Since the public schools were hardly able to take care of their own pupils, the Catholic schools, the argument ran, are performing an indispensable public service. But these schools, dependent mainly on voluntary contributions, were financially unable to perform the public service adequately. The Debré government recognized the value of this argument, and through the law of December 1959, offered substantial relief. This, of course, was added to

[2] Quoted in *Le Monde*, June 7, 1960, p. 9. These sentiments were echoed in even stronger terms by Denis Forestier, President of the *Comité National d'Action Laïque*. See *Le Monde*, June 21, 1960, p. 4.

the state funds which the Barangé law allocated to private schools indirectly.[3] However, there has been such opposition to the Debré law from the laic camp that the whole principle of state aid to private schools is once more in jeopardy.

TABLE 8

Enrollment Figures and Barangé Allocations for Public and Private Elementary Schools

Year	Public Schools Pupils Aided	Public Schools Amount	Private Schools Pupils Aided	Private Schools Amount
1952	3,485,735	10,457,206[a]	772,134	2,316,403[a]
1953	3,684,320	13,263,553	864,757	3,113,128
1954	3,940,897	15,369,500	845,840	3,298,776
1955	4,796,310	18,705,611	1,010,707	3,941,757
1956	6,148,315	23,978,429	1,281,946	4,999,591
1957	6,078,461	23,706,000	1,248,660	4,869,775
1958	6,309,820	24,608,116	1,264,306	4,930,598

[a] Figures are in thousands of old French Francs.

Throughout the history of the school quarrel, theoretical and doctrinal arguments have been mobilized to justify the attitudes of all sides. Great care must be taken in evaluating them; the problem is not what principles are evoked, but whom they come from. The difference between "thesis" and "hypothesis" should be clear now. Clearly, the Pope and the French Hierarchy in their formal statements cannot openly contradict the official theses of the Church toward education, even though they may be partially inapplicable in certain circumstances. However, responsible Catholic officials are well aware that a practical situation may demand modifications of

[3] Table 8 shows the enrollment figures for public and private schools and the Barangé primary school allocations for each. It is taken from Bernard E. Brown, "Religious Schools and Politics in France," *Midwest Journal of Political Science*, No. 2 (May 1958), p. 174, and from *Liberté d'Enseignement*, 183-184 (January 1960), p. 51. By 1961, the Minister of Education announced that the Barangé law had provided over 190 billion old francs to public schools and over 39 billion old francs to private schools. The latter sum equals approximately $82,000,000. See *Documentation Catholique*, June 4, 1961, col. 739.

a Church doctrine (that is, an hypothesis). The Hierarchy and the Pope know that their theses will be interpreted as the situation warrants, so are not afraid to present a rather unrealistic thesis, so long as some verbal or doctrinal loopholes are provided.

Often the Pope will provide a rather ambiguous thesis, and then allow a lesser Vatican official to set forth the thesis in all its rigor, knowing that responsible Catholics will not feel bound by the latter.

An example of this point is a statement made by Mgr. Parente in *Osservatore Romano* a few months before the 1951 legislative elections in France: "Liberal *laïcisme,* which preaches the empty formula of a free Church in a free state, has given rise to the famous laic school, which was achieved thanks to efficient political maneuvers and under the specious pretext of freedom of conscience, even where it constituted an open insult to the moral and religious conscience of a people. . . . There is no room for the theory or for the development of a laic school, or even for an open *laïcité* of the kind favored by *Esprit.* This latter formula would mean a laic and neutral school—that is, an areligious school which is necessarily an amoral school also. This *laïcité* would be the same, even in a state which renounced the liberal *laïcisme* of the Nineteenth Century which was openly hostile to religion. . . . The Church condemns, without distinction, *laïcisme* and *laïcité,* even in the domain of the school. . . ."[4]

In *Divini Illius Magistri,* Pope Pius XI, writing in the interwar period, had been even more explicit against the religiously-neutral school: "The fact that religious instruction is assured in state schools is not enough to insure that these schools conform to the rights of the Church and of the family and are worthy for Catholic children to attend. For this to be true, all the education, all the arrangements of the school including

[4] Mgr. Piero Parente in *Osservatore Romano,* January 6, 1951, quoted in *Documentation Catholique* XLVIII, No. 1094 (May 6, 1951), Columns 519-522 and 524-525.

personnel, programs, and books must be regulated in a truly Christian spirit. Attendance at non-Catholic or neutral schools should be forbidden to Catholic children."[5] Needless to say, the "should" in the last statement could be used by Catholics who object to the seeming rigidity of this thesis. It should be compared to the declaration of French bishops in 1951: "For a Christian only the Christian school is fully satisfactory."[6] Again, exegetes with their own private notions of the school question can find justification for any opinion they might hold in the term "fully."

In line with the new tendency to be less rigid on the school question, recent declarations of Church officials seem more and more conciliatory. Cardinal Gerlier has favored *laïcité* in the sense of respect for all faiths, and the French cardinals tacitly approved the notion of Church-state separation in the new Constitution. It is only a step for Catholics to recognize the usefulness of the state schools. This was done by the Plenary Assembly of French Bishops in 1951.[7] Mgr. Chappoulie has gone even further: ". . . in a country of divided beliefs the formula of a neutral school can be the only workable formula in many cases, provided that the school takes care to respect the religious convictions of families."[8] A committee sponsored by Cardinal Gerlier extended the Church's approval of neutral schools to ". . . areas of religious indifference where practicing Catholics could not furnish enough school children to justify the existence of a Catholic school."[9] These areas actually cover great segments of France, as is shown in Map 1 at the end of the book.

[5] Quoted in *Bulletin de Documentation des APEL et AEP, op.cit.*, 19-20.

[6] *Documentation Catholique*, XLVIII, No. 1093 (April 22, 1951), Column 456.

[7] *ibid.*, Column 458.

[8] Mgr. Chappoulie, *Luttes de l'Eglise*, II (Paris: Editions Fleurus, 1958), pp. 168-169.

[9] *Note Doctrinale du Comité Théologique de Lyon à l'Usage des Prêtres du Ministère*, "Les Catholiques de France et le Problème Scolaire," in *Documentation Catholique*, April 14, 1957, Column 481.

Of course, there are still Catholic groups and bishops who are hypnotized by the "thesis," and reproach any Catholic family which sends its child to public school. In 1950 the Bishop of Vannes, Mgr. Le Bellec, refused to give the sacraments of the Church to a family guilty of this sin.[10] But the idea of monopoly either by the Church or by the state (or even by the two cooperating with one another) is out of the question in present-day France.

For the majority of Catholics the days of doctrinal discussions are over, and the time has come to seek a *rapprochement* of public and private schools, based on such pragmatic criteria as service rendered to the nation. Catholics are beginning to see that the faith of public school children can be maintained and even reinforced through effective chaplaincy systems (as now exist in many secondary schools) and through certain other Catholic public school groups to be discussed later in this chapter.

II. French Ecclesiastical Groups and the School Question

The Church Hierarchy, both in France and in Rome, is particularly concerned with all questions relating to Catholic schools. Groups have been established which enable the clergy directly to make its voice felt whenever the school question is discussed. These institutions exist both on the national and the international levels: in Rome, a number of Sacred Congregations have a particular interest in the French school question, over which the Pope personally has supreme coordinating power. This authority was demonstrated when the Debré government, in the first weeks of its existence, sent Finance Minister Pinay to Rome for a meeting with Mgr. Tardini, who is apparently the "power behind the throne" in school matters. Without at least tacit consent from Rome no government policy affecting Catholic schools would be accepted by the French Hierarchy. Unfortunately, we do not have information on the

[10] *ibid.*, February 25, 1951, Column 218.

specific groups inside the Vatican which treat the school question, so we cannot judge adequately its role in the framing of the 1951 and 1959 school laws.

In contrast to the Vatican, information is readily available on the school activities of the French Hierarchy. The Hierarchy stands at the top of a series of interlocking organizations, both laic and ecclesiastical. The two charts which follow show how these organizations are interrelated, in theory and in practice.

Theoretically, each bishop is master of the Catholic schools in his diocese. The bishop controls the curriculum of Catholic schools and approves the activities of all groups defending the interests of Catholic schools in his diocese. Among these the most important are the parish groups of General Catholic Action and the local divisions of the Catholic school parents' group, APEL. The bishop generally delegates day-to-day powers in this area to a diocese director of education. The latter is to Catholic schools what the diocese director of works is to Catholic Action.

In practice, however, many problems encountered by Catholic schools are national in scope. Individual bishops often are unable to give such problems proper attention within the diocese. To remedy the situation, certain key bishops have been delegated powers to act on behalf of the entire Hierarchy. Sometimes such activity can be informal: thus, in the early months of the Fifth Republic, before the Debré school law was passed, there were many informal contacts by Cardinals Feltin and Roques with leading political figures. The same was true during the 1951 controversy over the Barangé Law, when meetings between these prelates and leaders of the MRP and other parties were probably the key elements that finally determined the nature of the new school law.[11]

Before each national election, every French bishop publishes in the *Semaine Religieuse* for his diocese the principles which should guide the Catholic voter. Usually these principles are

[11] From interview with J.-P. Prévost, July 23, 1959.

L'ORGANISATION DE L'ENSEIGNEMENT LIBRE

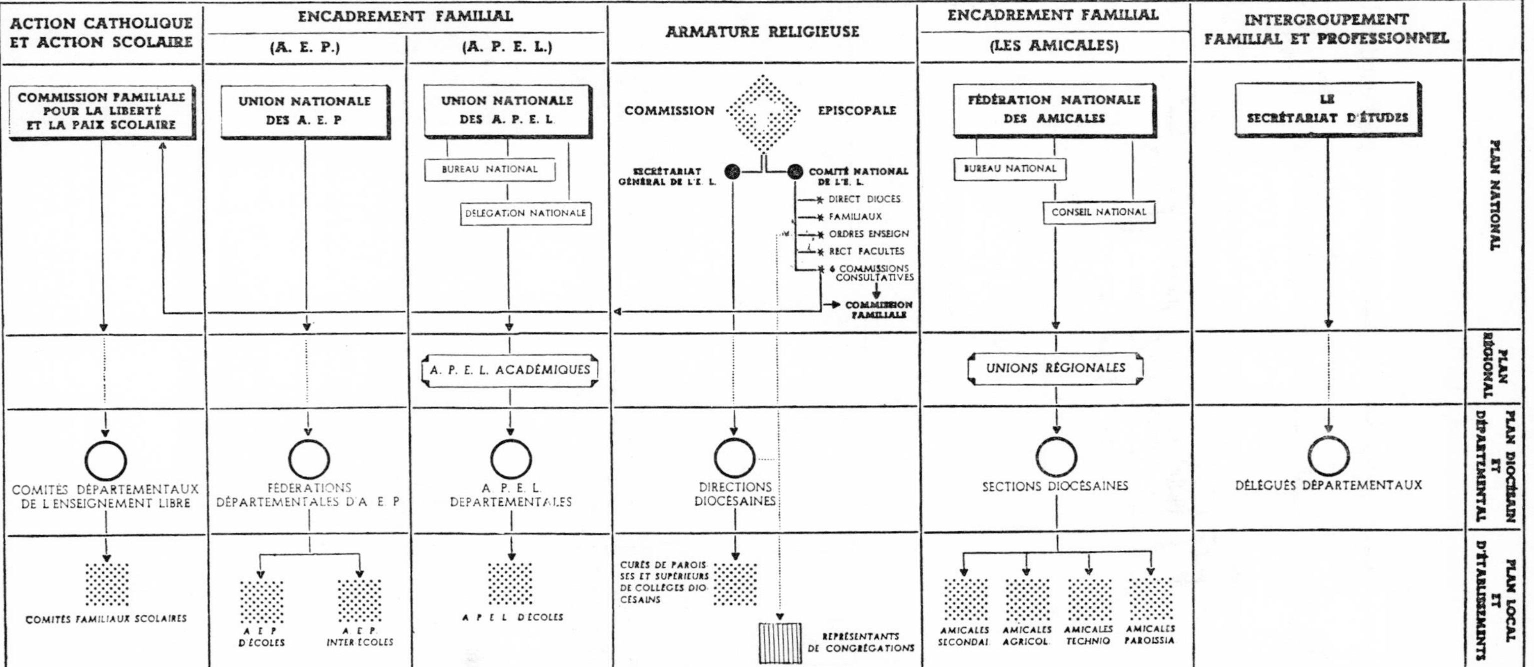

Fédération des Amicales de l'Enseignement Catholique de France: *Haut Parleur*, June 1956.

FIGURE 6. Main Catholic Education Groups: Functional Relations

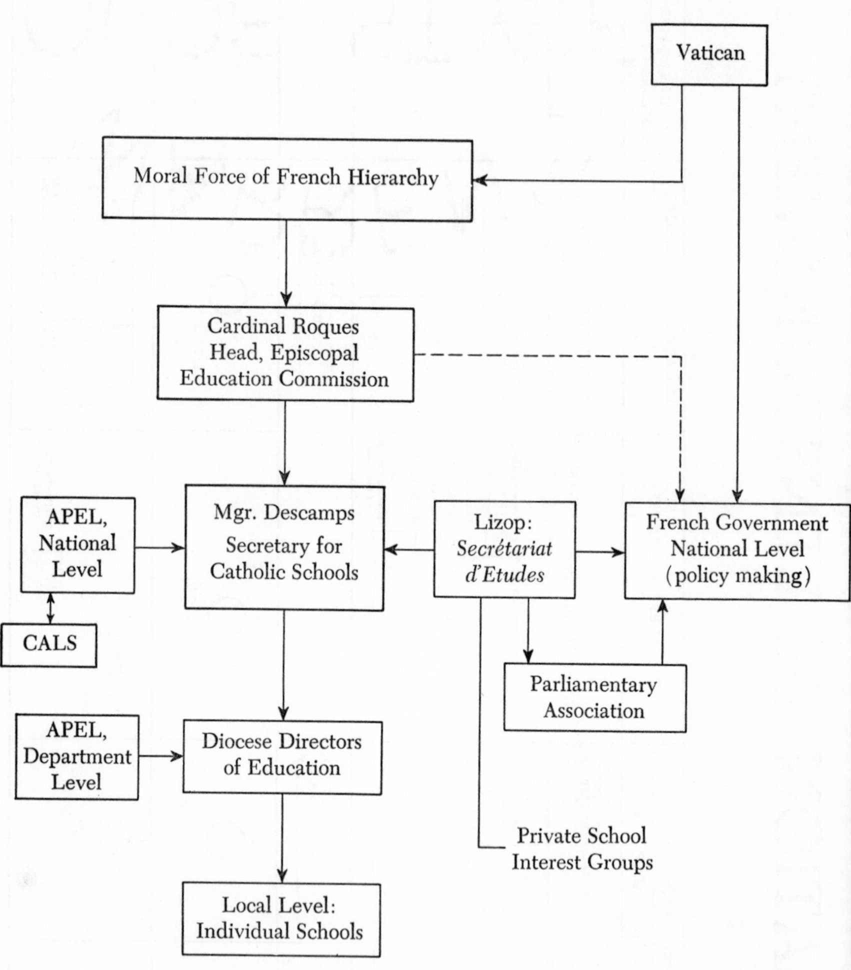

vague and general, and their impact is limited to very pious elements in the diocese. However, on the school question all bishops became much more specific, as already noted earlier. Also the statements of the French cardinals and of bishops in very clerical areas of the West often have a sizeable impact. Thus in 1951 every bishop urged his flock to vote only for candidates upholding effective educational freedom and favoring some state aid to private education.[12] In the West these instructions were generally heeded. When an official such as Cardinal Feltin makes a declaration, it automatically takes on national importance. So, widespread attention was given to the preelection statement by Cardinal Feltin that the first of all freedoms is educational freedom.[13]

The coming of the school crisis in 1951 coincided with the first Plenary Assembly of French Bishops to be held in half a century. Though this Assembly had been planned for many years, the timing was certainly due in part to the school issue. The statement on the school question issued by the Assembly, which has already been noted, had a tremendous force throughout Catholic France. By deemphasizing the "thesis" of only-Catholic-schools-for-Catholic-children, it probably helped appease some of the fears of laic groups. At any rate, the Assembly must have been effective, because it has since become an institutionalized part of the French Church.

For all specific administrative matters and many broad policy questions a national Hierarchy coordinator for all Catholic schools is needed. This function is performed by a complex of groups revolving around Cardinal Roques and Mgr. Descamps, the Secretary for Catholic Schools. Cardinal Roques is the Chairman of the Episcopal Commission on Education. He is also the President of the National Committee for Catholic Education (*Comité National de l'Enseignement Libre*). With these two positions he is able effectively to represent the

[12] Information from files at library of *Union des Oeuvres*.

[13] See Jean Charlot, "La Presse, les Catholiques, et les Elections," in Assn. Française de Science Politique, *Les Elections du 2 Janvier, 1956* (Paris: Armand Colin, 1957), p. 132.

whole French Church in dealing with the government. Thus, Cardinal Roques' basic approval was needed before any school law could be introduced in Parliament in 1951, with the hope of being passed.[14]

The Catholic Schools Secretariat of Mgr. Descamps is directly responsible to Cardinal Roques. On most specific matters of administration it is the key Catholic school group. It is the hub around which all other ecclesiastical groups dealing with schools can be placed. Direct relations exist between Mgr. Descamps and diocese officials dealing with Catholic schools, as indicated in Figure 6. Here, however, the Secretariat is always advisory, since each bishop formally controls all diocese organizations.

Acting in the name of the Hierarchy, the Secretary for Catholic Schools participates frequently in "summit conferences' with the leaders of Catholic school interest groups. These conferences generally include Edouard Lizop, who directs pressure activities within Parliament, and the President of the APEL, who is concerned with public opinion campaigns. With Mgr. Descamps representing the Church, these "Big Three" meetings can plan and coordinate strategy in the best interest of Catholic schools.[15]

Two groups under the direction of Mgr. Descamps widen the scope of his impact and assure his contact with every Catholic educational group. These are the *Comité National de l'Enseignement Libre*, and the *Commission Familiale pour la Liberté et la Paix Scolaire*. These groups are sketched out in Figure 7.[16]

Through the *Comité National de l'Enseignement Libre*, the French Hierarchy can supervise a number of Catholic groups

[14] Information from Michel Raingeard, former deputy and official of the *Association Parlementaire de la Liberté de l'Enseignement*, in interviews, January 8, 1959 and February 2, 1959.

[15] Information for this and for Figure 6 from interview with Canon Kerlévéo, Assistant to Mgr. Descamps, November 25, 1958.

[16] Information for Figure 7 is based on interviews and on *Fédération Nationale des AEP: Aide Mémoire à l'Usage des Conseils d'Administration des Associations Familiales de Gestion* (Paris: AEP, no date).

dealing with the school problem. The *Comité* is responsible for policy decisions on the various subjects taught in the Catholic schools and the types of education which the Church will offer. One of its subgroups is the *Commission Familiale pour la Liberté et la Paix Scolaire*, by far the most important group in the complex directed by Mgr. Descamps.

The *Commission Familiale pour la Liberté et la Paix Scolaire* is a coordinating group composed of one representative from each Catholic organization interested in the school question, as well as Cardinal Roques and Mgr. Descamps. It enables the Hierarchy to hear views on school subjects from all interested groups, and to pass on its instructions to them. Most Catholic Action groups send representatives to the Commission. The most important are representatives from ACGF and ACGH, for the two General Catholic Action groups, concerned with all the problems of the parish, take special interest in the school question.

III. The APEL: The Masses Organize to Defend Catholic Schools

The *Union Nationale des Associations de Parents d'Elèves de l'Enseignement Libre* (commonly known as APEL) has two aims: to organize all parents of Catholic school children into a coherent pressure group, and to use this mass base to influence public opinion at large. The APEL claims to represent almost 800,000 families, who are united in their desire to defend the interests of the Catholic schools.[17] These claims might seem well-founded, since the publication of APEL, *La Famille Educatrice*, has a circulation of 766,000.[18] However, these figures must be taken with caution. Many parents are automatically enrolled in APEL or join without understanding the policies of the group. To prove this, we offer the following quotation from *La Famille Educatrice*: "Attention, parents!

[17] See *Le Figaro*, May 12, 1959, p. 6, where these figures are quoted from information obtained at a recent APEL National Conference.

[18] OJD *Officiel*, No. 131, November 1959.

FIGURE 7

Sub-Groups Under the Episcopal Educational Commission

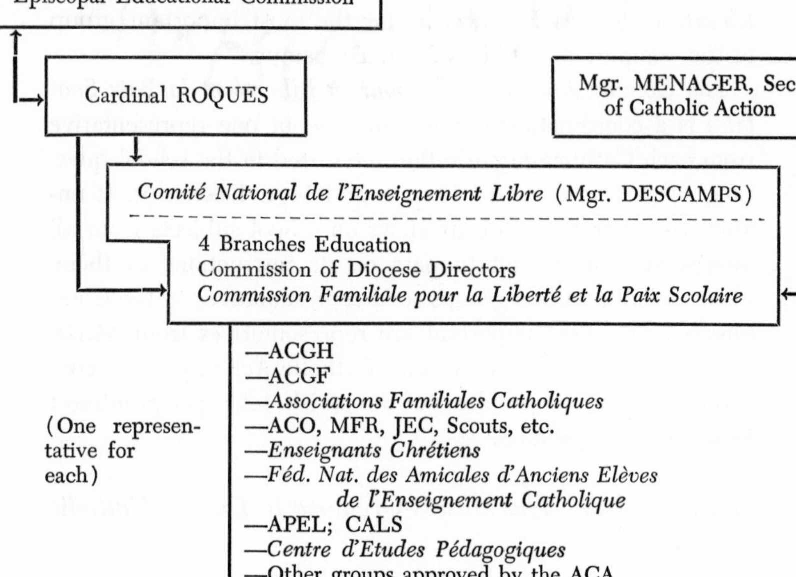

Why are you receiving this paper? Because you are a member of the APEL. . . . How did you become a member of the APEL? You were enrolled in our Association through the school which your child, or the oldest of your children, attends. Naturally, you are free to decline this membership."[19]

The APEL claims to be nonconfessional. It does include a certain number of Protestant parents, or those whose children attend laic private schools. But over nine in ten APEL members are Catholics, and there are other relations to the Church as well. One relation is the link between APEL and the *Associations d'Education Populaire*, or AEP. The AEP are the official school boards for each Catholic school. They are confessional, and the local curé has a deciding voice in their

[19] *La Famille Educatrice*, Vol. XII, No. 7 (September-October 1958), p. 12.

deliberations.[20] The AEP and APEL share the same office building and the same secretarial staff. AEP relies on APEL for any political activities since the AEP, as a confessional group, cannot directly enter into political activity. Another indication that the APEL is close to the Church is the approval that the Church gives the APEL—which the latter gratefully recognizes. The *Annuaire Catholique de France* says that ". . . an APEL section *must* be constituted around every school."[21] The APEL acknowledges its majority of Catholic members: "Our appeal is addressed particularly to all Catholics. Our APEL groups act on the level of natural law and on the family level, but their position has been many times approved by the Church."[22]

In its activities defending the Catholic schools, the APEL is particularly interested in mobilizing its masses and using them as a lever to obtain political advantages—especially at election time. Periodically APEL organizes huge conferences; the one at Caen in May 1959 included from 50,000 to 90,000 participants![23] Public opinion in France must be impressed by the massive strength of APEL during these enormous meetings. The APEL masses are also used by Monsieur Lizop for more subtle pressure tactics, as we shall see.

Until recently the demands of APEL for state aid to Catholic schools were far-reaching. APEL sought an extension of the Barangé Law to secondary schools, state funds for improving school buildings, some form of proportional sharing of state school funds based on the number of pupils in public and private schools, and state payment for all teachers' salaries.[24] These demands were always given top priority by APEL leaders, even when the regime itself seemed threatened. At the height of the crisis of May 1958, when other Catholic

[20] Cf. *Annuaire Catholique de France, 1958-59,* p. 799.

[21] *ibid.*

[22] *Bulletin de Documentation des APEL et AEP,* Vol. IV, No. 4 (December 1957), p. 18.

[23] *Le Figaro,* May 12, 1959, p. 6.

[24] See *Le Monde,* March 8-9, 1959, p. 11.

groups were girding themselves to defend the regime, the APEL proclaimed that "educational reform should be studied with a willingness on the part of all for national harmony."[25]

The arrival of a durable and effective national government has made the school activities of the APEL, like the activities of all pressure groups, less effective. The APEL has been led to modify its more intransigent demands and accept the generous settlement which the government was willing to offer Catholic schools. Thus, in recent declarations of APEL we find only vague generalities.[26]

One part of the APEL finds it hard to give up its intransigence. This is the regional organization in Western France called the *Comité d'Action pour la Liberté Scolaire*, or CALS. This regional group represents the only area of France where Catholic schools outnumber public schools. The group has often felt a compelling necessity to act in extreme fashion, and has often pulled the whole APEL along with it. An example of CALS activity is the unsuccessful "tax strike" of 1950. This was an attempt by certain people in Western Departments to withhold their tax money until the government voted to subsidize Catholic schools.[27] It is not clear whether CALS still maintains its key position within the APEL at the present time, with the Debré law offering payment of private school teachers' salaries.

On more general political questions, APEL also has an interest. Its line is closest to that of *Homme Nouveau*: conservative, even authoritarian, though without the violence of the extremists. The APEL had none of the reservations toward the de Gaulle government that were seen among moderate and left-wing Catholics, and it led an active campaign of support for the proposed Constitution. "The APEL has felt it its duty, on the occasion of the referendum, to adhere to the great

[25] *Informations Catholiques Internationales*, June 1, 1958, p. 7.

[26] See *Le Figaro*, May 12, 1959, p. 6.

[27] See Marguerite Bousquet, *op.cit.*, p. 82.

movement of renovation which must lead France to rise above its fate and better accomplish its civilizing mission in the world. . . . Christian values are a part of the French patrimony. Through the school they are perpetuated, down through the generations and the centuries. Thanks to these Christian values, our country can bring to the community of peoples, along with the lights of science, the spiritual advances which France has always bestowed on the world."[28]

In its declarations on the recent parliamentary elections, political philosophy and electoral advice were combined in the same article: "Great currents of civilization confront one another, more particularly a Christian current and a Marxist current . . . a fate without a future, limiting man's role to an ephemeral existence in the city of this world, or an infinite destiny justified by the love of the Creator and by faith in His designs. More than ever France is compelled by events to choose, and without doubt, once again her vocation is to defend and to save the Christian civilization which basically is hers. . . . No, it is not stupid to judge a candidate by his position on this school problem."[29]

Despite its mass membership, APEL's political role is relatively minor. Policies are made by elites, and APEL declarations have little influence on them. True, in each national election since 1951 the forces adhering to the Lizop Secretariat, where APEL is predominant, captured half or more of the National Assembly. But would they have done worse had the APEL not existed? More probably, the true importance of APEL is that the million-and-a-half people within its reach are open to the influence of Monsieur Lizop and Catholic extreme-right groups. At any rate, the real political importance of APEL is what Lizop made of it, so we must next consider the complex which he controls.

[28] *La Famille Educatrice*, XII, No. 8 (November 1958), p. 1.
[29] *ibid.*, p. 2.

IV. Edouard Lizop and his Legislative Pressure Group

One of the most interesting individuals in French Catholicism is Edouard Lizop, who singlehanded forged the unrelated and ineffective groups defending private schools into a coherent force able to exert great pressure on the National Assembly.

Two facets of Lizop's work must be distinguished: his power base and his pressure activities. For his power base, Lizop has created the *Secrétariat d'Etudes pour la Liberté de l'Enseignement et la Défense de la Culture.* This is a front organization, designed to bring members of various private school groups into contact with Lizop so that he can act in their name. APEL, AEP, and the *Fédération Nationale des Amicales de l'Enseignement Libre* are part of this Secretariat, just as they are members of Mgr. Descamps' coordinating group. In addition, there are groups of private school teachers, school superintendents, technical instructors, and others. The complete membership of the Secretariat follows.

Under Ambassador André de LABOULAYE, President, and M. Edouard LIZOP, Secretary General, the *Secrétariat d'Etudes* groups and represents:

—The National Union of APEL Groups
—The National Federation of Popular Education Groups (AEP)
—*Fédération Nationale des Amicales de l'Enseignement Libre*
—Group of Private Technical School Establishments
—National Union of Private Technical Education
—Society of Secondary School Principals
—Union of Directors of Private School Establishments
—Union of Heads of Primary Educational Institutions
—Union of Directors of Christian Educational Institutions
—National Federation of Nonsectarian Private Education
—National Federation of Professional Unions in Catholic Schools

—CFTC *Fédération des Syndicats de l'Enseignement Libre*
—Association of Training Centers for Nursery School Teachers
—Federation of Private Agricultural Education
—National Family Federation for Private Professional and Household Training in Agriculture.[30]

In contrast to ecclesiastical groups, the Lizop *Secrétariat d'Etudes* is officially nonsectarian and is not controlled by the Hierarchy. All participating members except the AEP are officially nonconfessional. Unlike the Descamps organization, the Lizop *Secrétariat d'Etudes* has no local branches. It is not primarily concerned with the internal administration of private schools; its work is focused outward, toward the government.

As head of the *Secrétariat d'Etudes*, Lizop represents not only all the interests of private schools, but also the 1,600,000 voters who are (more or less) connected with APEL. Lizop seems to have used this mass base to the maximum. Before the 1951 elections, he created a special group which only prospective senators and deputies could join: the *Association Parlementaire pour la Liberté de l'Enseignement.* This organization had no specific or detailed program of action, except the aim of protecting private schools. But all the deputies who joined the group pledged to follow its instructions in all matters affecting schools which would come before Parliament.[31] Before elections, each prospective deputy has an opportunity to adhere to the Parliamentary Association. Then Lizop, the APEL, and many bishops urge that only those who have joined the Association be chosen by the voters. In this way, Lizop has mobilized the power latent in millions of Catholic voters to insure that his school programs will prevail in Parliament.

After the 1951 elections, 296 deputies, just short of half,

[30] Source: private files from M. Lizop and interviews with him, November 19, 1958 and June 15, 1960.

[31] See Bernard E. Brown, "Religious Schools and Politics in France," in *Midwest Journal of Political Science*, II, No. 2 (May 1958), 169 ff.

were members of Lizop's Parliamentary Association, while other deputies were willing to cooperate with it.[32] Thus was formed the "Barangé majority"—or perhaps one can say the "Lizop majority"—which lasted through most of the 1951 legislature. Candidates pledged to Lizop's group fared less well in 1956, but in 1958 they comprised two thirds of the total National Assembly.[33] Paradoxically, the influence of Lizop seems to vary inversely with the strength of his forces in Parliament. In 1951, when he had just short of an absolute majority, he managed to keep his deputies well-disciplined, under the pressure of losing the support of APEL adherents at home. But once two thirds of the National Assembly adhered to the Association, Lizop had more difficulty in coordinating Association members. For once, they formed a coherent majority, based on other and more vital issues. This is another illustration of the difficulties pressure groups encounter in France whenever a workable party system or a strong government develop.

Actually, the final decisions on the form of the 1959 school law depended very little on the desires of the National Assembly. The Prime Minister himself, following the recommendations of a specially-constituted Commission of Inquiry, set forth the main lines of the new school law. Then the proposed law was submitted for Parliamentary approval, but the government invoked Article 44 of the French Constitution, allowing Parliament to amend the proposal only with the approval of the government. Pressure by Lizop and his followers finally forced Debré to modify the original wording of the law so that teachers in Catholic schools, even if paid by the state, would be allowed to explain in class their own conceptions of God and the world. Aside from this, however, the government firmly refused most other proposed changes.

More than any other group studied here, the Lizop *Secré-*

[32] André Siegfried (ed.), *Année Politique, 1951* (Paris: Presses Universitaries de France, 1952), p. 179.

[33] *Le Monde*, December 3, 1958, p. 16.

tariat d'Etudes and the Parliamentary Association are one-man ideas. The ingenious, aggressive personality of Lizop was necessary in constructing effective pressure groups. As noted, he succeeded admirably. But at the same time, certain personality traits have limited his effectiveness. First of all, he has not hidden his own political preferences, which are conservative. Lizop thought of running for the National Assembly on a list sponsored by Bidault, Duchet, and Morice. Finally, at the last minute, pressure from the Hierarchy forced him to withdraw his candidacy.[34] Certain parts of Lizop's parliamentary group, especially those from the MRP, were alienated by his conservative bias and tried to go over his head, to deal directly with the Hierarchy on the school question. This threatened the existence of the Parliamentary Association, but Lizop finally kept it intact. Furthermore, the personality of Lizop seems to displease a number of leaders in the Fifth Republic, for he is rather demagogic. But at the same time, Lizop has a rare amount of tact and finesse, and these qualities probably saved him from an oblivion similar to that of Pierre Poujade.[35]

V. *Teaching, Professional, and Miscellaneous Organizations*

Alongside the "triumvirate" of Mgr. Descamps, the APEL, and Lizop, there are a number of lesser Catholic groups interested in the school question. Many are associated with the three principal school organizations; others, however, are independent. It is not necessary to analyze them all; but a few do deserve attention.

The conciliatory policies of the CFTC public and private school teachers' unions have been noted in Chapter Seven. The public school teachers' union stiffened its attitude some-

[34] Information from Michel Raingeard, interview, February 2, 1959.

[35] A good deal of information for this section has been obtained from the Seminar on the Barangé Law conducted by Professor René Rémond, at the *Institut d'Etudes Politiques* in Paris, 1958-1959, as well as from interviews with M. Lizop in 1958 and 1960.

what after the passage of the Barangé Law. In 1960, its resolutions on the school problem supported the laic campaign to abrogate the Debré school law. But at the same time, this union thought that public school education still lacks something: "Public school education does not pretend to give young people a complete and exclusive upbringing. Families must be allowed to complete their children's upbringing, especially in the realm of religious practice and religious culture."[36]

There are two groups formally affiliated with Catholic Action which cater to public school teachers. One, *Equipes Enseignantes*, is designed mainly for primary-level teachers. The other, *Paroisse Universitaire*, is for secondary and university teachers. Both are designed to deepen the religious life of Catholic teachers and to convince fellow-Catholics as well as *laïques* that Catholic teachers should have a place in the public school system. The thesis that all Catholic children should be educated in Catholic schools is often used to question the right of Catholic teachers to work in the public school system; fighting this reasoning is one of the chief activities of both groups. They consider the public school a healthy place to educate one's children in the academic disciplines.

Being in Catholic Action and in the public school at the same time makes the position of *Equipes Enseignantes* and *Paroisse Universitaire* extremely difficult whenever the school question reaches the crisis stage. Both are loyal to the public school but also sympathize with the financial distress of the private schools. Thus, André Latreille, a leading member of *Paroisse Universitaire*, recently proposed ". . . financial aid to private schools through controlled subsidies and through help to private boarding schools and youth movements."[37] The national chaplain of *Paroisse Universitaire* proposed creating a state-approved confessional school system paralleling the public school

[36] *Syndicalisme Universitaire*, No. 213 (June 26, 1959), p. 1. Cf. *Syndicalisme Universitaire*, No. 222 (Jan. 27, 1960), p. 1.

[37] Quoted in *Le Monde*, July 16, 1959, p. 7. The group was divided on the 1959 school law. See *Etudes*, Vol. 305, No. 5 (May 1960).

system and receiving state subsidies. *Equipes Enseignantes* did not seem to go so far: it looked nostalgically to the day when Catholic children would enter the public school *en masse*: "For those who are most responsive to the idea of one school, where young French children of all creeds and social origins can meet and fraternize, it is painful to consider that young Catholics should be educated apart from the rest. To this 'segregation' they would object that the nation has a natural need to achieve its unity."[38]

Equipes Enseignantes was more balanced in its analysis of the 1959 school law. Though the law with its implementing decrees had some unfortunate aspects, it was deemed to be a positive step toward cooperation among the private and public school systems, as well as a definite help to the educational activities of the Church. The leaders of *Equipes Enseignantes* concluded that no final judgment can be made on the school law until it could develop in practice over the years.[39]

Teachers in Catholic schools are represented by the CFTC *Fédération de l'Enseignement Libre*, and by *Les Enseignants Chrétiens*, the counterpart of *Equipes Enseignantes*. The latter two groups both are in Catholic Action. However, the two Catholic school groups are relatively unimportant for our purposes, since their aim is generally professional in a strict sense, and pious.

A more interesting group is the *Fédération Nationale des Amicales de l'Enseignement Catholique de France*. This group is in both the Descamps and Lizop organizations. It claims to represent over 1,200,000 alumni of Catholic schools, though its national impact seems slight. Its publication, *Le Haut Parleur*, seems even more conservative than the APEL. Its motto is "Thy Kingdom Come, O Christ our King, by means of the School." However, the Federation is more interested in spreading a pious feeling among its members than in trying to influence

[38] *Equipes Enseignantes*, special issue, June 1959, p. 16.
[39] *Vie Enseignante*, No. 135 (March-April 1960), suppl. See also No. 137 (June 1960), p. 16.

others. It leaves influence to the APEL, which thus finds its mass base increased.[40]

It is interesting to note that the teachers' groups are all basically conciliatory, whether they are trade unions or spiritual organizations, from public or from Catholic schools. All of them have related conceptions of how to solve the school problem. They are closer to one another than any one of them is to the anticlerical arguments or to the theses of APEL. On the other hand, the groups of parents or alumni are much more intransigent on the school problem, and on other political problems as well. A common religion does not put them any closer to Catholic public school teachers. Here again is an indication of the wide terrain which separates Catholic left and right in France. It would be unrealistic to try to harmonize the activities of *Paroisse Universitaire* with the APEL in terms of some higher "French Catholic ideals" because the notion has entirely different connotations for the two groups, just as it did for the extremes in the Catholic press.

VI. The Debré School Law and a Permanent Settlement of the School Problem

On December 31, 1959, for the second time in half a century, the French Parliament voted to provide state resources to private schools. The Debré Law marked the culmination of years of pressure from the private school groups analyzed in this chapter. Compared to the Barangé Law, it went much further toward state subsidy of Catholic schools in several ways. First, Catholic schools were recognized as in the public interest. Prime Minister Debré stated before the National Assembly that "The state must help private schools, or rather it must help the private school teachers, whose work is useful to the whole community. Furthermore, in the present state of French society,

[40] Of course, a good many members of the Federation are also in APEL. It is only logical that parents who went to Catholic schools would send their children to Catholic schools.

much different from fifty or even thirty years ago, this aid is necessary to guarantee the practical expression of freedom of education."[41]

The Debré Law further provides various contractual relationships between private schools and the state—something which the Barangé Law had avoided by giving money to pupils rather than to specific schools. The state this time has erected a formal link between itself and a unit of the Church. Among the forms of contractual relationship open to Catholic schools, some have been declared unacceptable by the Hierarchy. Integration into the public school system has been formally ruled out. However, the Hierarchy has approved cooperating with the "contract of association," which would provide state controls over the material taught in class, as well as with the least rigid form of relationship provided by the law: the "simple contract."[42] This contract, applicable only to large and successful Catholic schools, provides for state payment of teachers' salaries and gives local government the discretion to pay for other material expenses of the school. Catholic schools are allowed to imbue every part of their curriculum with the "Christian spirit." Teaching priests and nuns are paid by the state under both the "contract of association" and the "simple contract."

Though the new school law has gone far to satisfy Catholic school interests, it cannot be considered a permanent settlement of the school question in France. For one thing, the "simple contracts" have a time limit; all must be reexamined after being in force nine years, and none can last longer than twelve years. A more serious upshot of the law is the heightened campaign by the *laïques* in France against direct aid to Catholic schools. The fact that the school issue can still en-

[41] Quoted in *Liberté d'Enseignement*, 183-184 (January 1960), p. 7.

[42] See: *France Catholique*, May 6, 1960, p. 1; Etudes, 307, No. 10, October 1960, pp. 3-18; *Documentation Catholique*, September 4, 1960, cols. 1077-78. The Hierarchy seems to prefer that primary schools adopt the "simple contract," while secondary schools can choose it or the "contract of association."

gender such widespread controversy—as much as the Algerian question itself—shows how powerful the old historical quarrels still remain in France.

Thus, despite the Debré Law, no permanent settlement of the school question is yet in sight. Whether it is practical to hope for some future settlement will depend on the moderation and willingness to compromise manifested by *cléricaux* and *laïques.*

Many members of the Hierarchy seem willing to forget the dogmatic rigors of the Catholic "thesis" toward Catholic schools, as Fauvet has noted: "The Church itself is less demanding than many of those who have appropriated its name. While reaffirming its constant doctrine in the matter, the Church puts almost as much importance on the educational and apostolic possibilities that it has kept in public secondary education, where most children study, as in the survival of private establishments where its influence is more direct."[43]

Perhaps the question is less pragmatic for the other side of the fence; books like Albert Bayet's *Laïcité Vingtième Siècle* or the pronouncements of Guy Mollet often show the beginnings of a rear-guard action to save the principle of *laïcité,* jeopardized by the hordes of UNR deputies. But even the Socialists seem to have tongue in cheek. On three occasions "neutral" commissions have been set up by the government to study the school question. In each instance they were presided over by Socialists (André Philip, Paul-Boncour, and P.-O. Lapie). In each instance they ultimately agreed that Catholic schools needed some form of state aid. The Socialists knew that the Barangé Law was coming before the 1951 elections, but this did not stop them from making alliances with MRP candidates in many Departments. Guy Mollet did the same thing in a recent municipal election at Arras.

A pragmatic attitude toward Catholic schools is no sign of a lessening of support for them. A recent public opinion poll in

[43] *Le Monde,* March 25, 1959, p. 1.

France indicated that forty-three per cent of French families would send their children to private secondary schools if they were tuition-free. Forty-seven per cent said that they would not and ten per cent had no opinion.[44] Earlier a poll showed that an overwhelming majority of those asked favored the co-existence of public and private education rather than a state monopoly.[45] In January 1949 over a third of those polled were favorable to some state subsidies to private schools.[46]

If a permanent solution to the school problem were to develop, how would it affect the position of Catholicism in French society? Certain experts consider the school problem as the only barrier to a realignment of political forces: the Catholic left would join the Socialists and the Catholic right would join moderates and authoritarians once the school problem no longer plagued France. Duverger accepts this view, and draws interesting consequences from it: "The center of gravity in the Fifth Republic, as in the Fourth, is in the alliance of Socialists, MRP, and Radicals (in their old historic forms or in new, renovated forms). . . . But this is practicable only in the present prospects of the evolution of Catholicism. . . . The first condition of this center-left alliance is the definitive solution of the school quarrel in a way which all can accept. . . . The permanent alliance of the laic center-left and the Christian center-left is the permanent nightmare of the right, for it would keep the right from power."[47] Duverger is properly foreseeing closer cooperation among Catholic and non-Catholic forces, but it must not be assumed that Catholic groups and parties as such will disappear with the end of the school problem. As indicated in Chapter Seven, individuals do not join these groups because of their position on one political question,

[44] Reported in *Le Monde,* June 16, 1959, p. 12.

[45] See *France-Monde Catholique,* No. 115 (December 1951), pp. 1-2.

[46] However, 45 percent of those polled opposed such subsidies. See *Sondages,* Summer 1950, p. 21.

[47] Maurice Duverger, "Les Objectifs Partisans," in *Le Monde,* March 26, 1959, p. 7.

but because they seek another way of expressing their Catholicism.

Any center-left agreements are bound to be extremely loose, with continued tensions between Catholics—organized as Catholics—and *laïques* who are fundamentally opposed to carrying religious considerations over into political life. Thus, we cannot wholly agree with Father d'Ouince: "The school question remains the last of our religious quarrels. It keeps Catholics permanently uneasy, feeling themselves victims of an unjustified ostracism. Once that question is solved, Catholics would feel definitively reintegrated into the nation, and delivered from an inferiority complex which has partially paralyzed their collaboration in public life."[48] One could assume from this statement that once the school problem is settled there will be no difference between Catholics and non-Catholics within the French nation. But in fact, many Catholics are anxious to maintain their own particular institutions.

If the end of the school problem will not bring the disappearance of Catholic institutions, it will probably change their attitude toward political life. In contemporary French Catholicism many groups calling themselves "nonpolitical" feel no qualms about taking sides on the school and related problems. The Hierarchy itself has tried to influence national elections so that a parliamentary majority favorable to Catholic schools could be assured. The end of the school problem would probably remove many Catholic groups from active participation in political quarrels; thus the political value of French Catholicism would be reduced somewhat. It would not be eliminated, since Catholic Action groups will always attempt a certain kind of psychological conditioning, and groups of Catholic inspiration will have political interests going far beyond the school question.

[48] Father René d'Ouince, "Aspect Politique de la Question Scolaire," in *Etudes*, Vol. 268 (March 1951), p. 295.

Concluding Remarks

I. The Philosophical Framework of Catholic Groups

A. THE "CENTRAL CORE" OF CATHOLIC SOCIAL PHILOSOPHY

Outside of a narrow range of dogma, Catholics disagree among themselves on practically everything relating to social and temporal life. Yet there are certain social principles which have very widespread acceptance among the vast majority of Catholics in France. Usually most members of the Hierarchy endorse these principles, though they are not considered as Church dogma. In fact, they have become so generally identified with Catholicism that Catholics with different views must usually explain their reasons for going against the crowd.

The purpose of this section is to set forth the main social doctrines which are widely considered as being part of the "Catholic tradition," or in other words, which form the central core principles of French Catholicism. The views of Catholic dissenters to these principles, whether they be on the left or on the extreme right of the political spectrum, will be analyzed later in this chapter. This analysis of the Catholic core philosophy, with modifications suggested by the left and the extreme right, should help explain some of the divisions which have been noted among Catholics. It should also help show why so many Catholics, even those on the extremes of the political spectrum, feel it necessary always to distinguish themselves from non-Catholics. Finally, extremist modifications of the central-core doctrines may give a clue to the future evolution of Catholic social philosophy.

Attention will first be focused on two closely connected propositions about group relations: pluralism and corporatism. Then two propositions about the individual and human nature will be examined: personalism and solidarism.

Pluralism is the justification for the existence of many autonomous entities within the social fabric. Groups must exist which are private—that is, which cannot have their existence threatened by dictatorial control or coordination by the political authority. Such groups must have the possibility of independent constructive development.[1]

Pluralism is a widespread doctrine today, even outside Catholicism. It provides one of the fundamental distinctions between our Western democracies and totalitarian forms of government, where in practice social groups are all creatures of the ruling authority. However, the Church puts a special emphasis on pluralism and cloaks it in a certain sacrosanctity. This reflects a desire to safeguard the Church, since natural law endows the family, state, and Church with a particular importance, regardless of the social context.

Catholic groups also have historical reasons for jealously maintaining group privileges. During the upheavals of the French Revolution the very existence of intermediate bodies between the individual and the state was threatened by the radical Jacobins. Their prime target, of course, was the Church.[2]

The pluralist principle is now extended by Catholics beyond the three institutions protected by natural law, so that most social groups are now covered by the principle. From their concern with pluralism it seems that Catholics, including those of the left, would be more willing to defend private groups against government controls or regulations than would most of their non-Catholic colleagues.[3]

[1] See the stimulating treatment of pluralism in the Christian Democratic tradition by Fogarty, *op.cit.*, pp. 41-100.

[2] The Le Chapelier Law of 1791 is a good example of an attempt at control of the power of intermediate bodies in France.

[3] This pluralist tradition is strong in present-day France, but it is not invariably at the base of Catholic political views. Pluralism is weak in Spain, for example, where social groupings reflect faithfully the whims of the ruling clique. Though the Vatican would theoretically prefer the ideal of a "Catholic state" over that of a "laic state," it does not seem to prefer Spanish authoritarianism over the government in France today, where independent social entities are respected. Pope John XXIII made

Christian Democrats, who are now moderates on the issue, carry the pluralist idea quite far. The emphasis on the family, a key institution for all Catholics, is particularly intense for Christian Democrats. The right of parents to choose from among many schools the educational system they want for their children is a key argument of the MRP and of conservative Catholics in favor of aid to Catholic schools. *Laïques* usually retort that the state's demands on its citizens have priority over the family's.

Pluralism applied in its fullest extent would mean also that two or more churches could coexist. While admitting this fact in practice as a hypothesis, Catholics explain that according to the "thesis" there is only one true Church.[4]

More than anything else, pluralism implies curbs on the power of the state. Believing Catholics could not accept the extreme Jacobinism of the Revolution, nor could they accept the meddling of the Combes regime in religious affairs. Today they cannot accept the totalitarian features of Communism—and this is true of the Catholic left as much as the Catholic right.

The second principle of the Catholic core philosophy, corporatism, is closely related to pluralism. In economic thinking, pluralism means a certain freedom and autonomy for all economic interest groups. Corporatism as accepted by most Catholics resembles pluralism but adds that all social groups, though autonomous, are interdependent. All must coordinate their energies for the good of society as a whole.

---

this clear in *Mater et Magistra* when he stated "We consider necessary that the intermediary bodies enjoy an effective autonomy in regard to the public authorities. . . ." See *New York Times*, July 15, 1961, p. 6.

[4] Catholics would say that other sects have no objective right to exist, since they do not possess the Truth, but the best way of eliminating them is by persuasion rather than brute force. See Fogarty, *op.cit.*, p. 43. In this way, the Church can tolerate other religions in countries like France which are spiritually divided. At the same time it can also justify the recognition of Catholicism as the only permissible form of public worship in countries as Catholic as Spain. Similar modes of thinking have occurred in other religious contexts—for example, among the Puritans of early New England.

The main principle of corporatism concerns employers and employees in the same industry: they are to be joined in one corporate body. As Elbow describes the theory in past years, this would change the character of the state: "Within such corporations, labor and management were to work together in an atmosphere of social peace for their mutual benefit, as well as that of the nation. With a minimum of state intervention, they would regulate production in quantity and quality, determine wages and hours, and provide for and administer various types of social insurance and technical education. Class strife, depressions, and insecurity would be phantoms of the past. . . . The state indeed would cease to be an oppressive leviathan, for much of its action in the economic sphere would be delegated to corporations. In turn, corporations would give counsel to the state on whatever economic-social legislation was necessary, and in this way the economic interests of the nation would secure a direct or indirect voice in the government."[5]

Also part of corporatism is the doctrine of class cooperation, rather than inevitable class struggle: "Cooperation between classes was to replace conflict between classes. Social solidarity would supplant social disharmony. Functional organizations representing industry and professions would take the place of conflicting class unions; and within each corporation, those differences which did arise between employers and employees would be settled to the benefit of the organization as a whole."[6]

Corporatists hold differing ideas on how strong the state should be in comparison to private economic groups. But all are agreed that the structure of the state should be modified. The corporate structures linking labor and management in particular industries should have direct representation in the gov-

[5] Matthew H. Elbow, *French Corporative Theory, 1789-1948: A Chapter in the History of Ideas* (New York: Columbia University Press, 1953), pp. 11-12. John XXIII in *Mater et Magistra* says it would be most desirable for workers to "be able to participate in the ownership of the enterprise itself." See *New York Times*, July 15, 1961, p. 6.

[6] *ibid.*, p. 12.

ernment. Elbow cites the ideas of an early corporatist from *Action Populaire*, Eugène Duthoit: "He believed that the Chamber of Deputies elected by universal suffrage should merely consent to taxes, while the Senate chosen by electoral colleges organized by region and type of economic activity should have jurisdiction over professional and trade interests. . . ."[7] This same formula was also desired, though not put into practice, by the MRP.[8] Biton quoted Raymond-Laurent, once an official of the *Parti Démocrate Populaire* and now an MRP leader, as follows: "Intermediary groups, some natural and others free . . . must have a juridical status which will raise them to legal institutions and give them national and regional representation, with a consultative and even a regulatory power."[9]

Corporatism seems to be especially widespread in its conservative extreme, as for example in Mussolini's Italy or Vichy France. But even in these regimes certain aspects of corporatism—for example, its criticism of classical liberal individualism—were accepted even by the Catholic left.[10] Perhaps this helps explain why many progressive Catholics, including Abbé Godin, founder of the worker-priest movement, and Emmanuel Mounier, were not opposed to the Vichy regime at its inception.[11]

In addition to its bias against classical liberalism, corporatism includes an essential feature of service to the society which attracts even the most progressive of Catholics. The Church has often condemned the abuses of capitalism and has agreed that national controls or socialization are necessary in certain economic realms. These adjuncts to corporatism in Catholic thought have probably alienated many conservative economic groups.[12]

[7] *ibid.*, p. 94. See also p. 159.

[8] See Fogarty, *op.cit.*, p. 94.

[9] Quoted in Biton, *op.cit.*, p. 99. Cf. Mario Einaudi and François Goguel, *Christian Democracy in Italy and France* (South Bend: Notre Dame University Press, 1952), p. 131.

[10] See Elbow, *op.cit.*, pp. 135 and 137.

[11] Ward, *France Pagan?*, p. 181, and *I.C.I.*, March 15, 1960, p. 21.

[12] Deroo, *op.cit.*, p. 297.

CONCLUDING REMARKS

The doctrines of personalism and solidarism focus on the individual rather than the social grouping. The term personalism is generally attributed to Emmanuel Mounier, the founder of *Esprit* and a representative of the Catholic left.[13] However, the term has been taken from its original context and used to describe a much more general concept, accepted by virtually all Catholics.[14] In this wider sense, personalism is the philosophy of individual self-development which prevents organizations, including those set up along corporatist lines, from impairing individual initiative. The primary goal of any group, according to personalist theory, should not be profit or other material advantages, but the development of the human potentials of group members and of the public at large.

Of course, personalism is not exclusively a Catholic concept, although the MRP seems to be more aware of it than other French parties. "'An individual . . . is also a person—that is, an individual being endowed with reason. . . . Capable of knowing, therefore free to choose, he can justify his acts and assume responsibility for them.' . . . What such a conception of man owes to Christianity is obvious, although its specifically religious aspect is not clearly expressed in the preceding lines, doubtless because the MRP denies that it is a sectarian party. . . ."[15]

Catholics have always preferred a term like personalism to individualism, because the latter smacks too much of human isolation and lack of relationship to other human groupings. For a personalist, the potentialities of each human being are considered, but emphasis is placed on the person in the group rather than isolated by himself.[16]

All personalists agree that the state has a duty to protect and develop the potentialities of its citizens, but there is no

[13] See Mounier's book *Le Personnalisme* (Paris: Presses Universitaires de France, 1955), especially pp. 5-17.

[14] For this wider sense of personalism, see Fogarty, *op.cit.*, pp. 27-40.

[15] Einaudi and Goguel, *op.cit.*, p. 125.

[16] Cf. Biton, *op.cit.*, pp. 75-76.

agreement on the role which the state should play in assuring this development. However, one form of state clearly conflicts with personalist principles: that based on *laissez-faire*. This is made clear even by moderate Catholics; it is an element which serves to alienate a certain conservative business group from the mainstream of Catholic thought.[17]

Solidarism is the principle that all people share duties and responsibilities to others. It insures that pluralism will not result in the atomization of individuals. Solidarism contributes the notion of class harmony to the core of Catholic thought, in contrast to class-struggle theories. This is a hard pill for the Catholic left to swallow. On the other hand, certain conservative Catholics are virtually blinded by solidarist theory; they refuse to admit that in France today class antipathies are very much in evidence.[18] More realistic solidarists, however, say that all individuals have the same basic interests and desires—even if they are not aware of this at a given moment. Thus the elimination of mutually-exclusive class sentiments is seen as good in itself and is to be actively sought. As Cardinal Suhard, the former Archbishop of Paris, said: "No more proletarians, all should be property owners! Whoever possesses, possesses for all—*must* possess for all—*can* possess for all, with the grace of our Saviour."[19] Or as Abbé Godin said: "The final aim of our work is not the conversion but the extinction of the proletariat, but that is a task that must be undertaken by human society, by the City—as a whole. We have not only to bring the masses to Christ, we have to make them into something that is no longer a shapeless mass."[20] Despite these remarks by Godin, it would seem that many members of specialized Catholic Action

[17] See John F. Cronin, *Catholic Social Principles* (Milwaukee: Bruce, 1950), p. 259. Deroo also reminds us that the Church rejects capitalism in its present form, insofar as it puts profit above the well-being of workers and perpetuates unjust divisions of wealth. See Deroo, *op.cit.*, pp. 299-300. See also Father Laurent, "Structures Industrielles," *Etudes*, Vol. 268, No. 1 (January 1951), p. 15.

[18] See *La Nef*, January 1954, p. 155.

[19] Quoted in Deroo, *op.cit.*, p. 306.

[20] Quoted in Ward, *op.cit.*, p. 188.

groups would define solidarism rather strictly: the excesses of class struggle should be eliminated, but the virtues of each social class should remain.

B. IDEOLOGICAL PECULIARITIES OF THE CATHOLIC LEFT AND RIGHT

The Catholic left is isolated from the rest of the French left by certain aspects of the Church spiritual dogma, as well as some social doctrines. For example, every Catholic must believe in the notion of original sin, even though this means automatically renouncing the idea that man is infinitely perfectible, which, in theory, is dear to the Communists.

The Catholic core principles which most affect the relations between the Catholic and non-Catholic left are the notions of class harmony and pluralism. Catholic left groups can believe that a class struggle exists at present, but they can hardly keep from wishing its modification according to the principles of solidarism. They can advocate strong state power in the economic field but can hardly favor abolition of the free groups which are necessary in a pluralist society. In this respect, the school question is particularly delicate, for no Catholic could believe in a state monopoly of education as long as Catholic schools flourish. In all these points there is great difference between the Catholic left and the Communists, of course. But even the Socialists feel uneasy about the left-Catholic stand on pluralism and solidarism.

Certain influential left Catholics were attracted to the Vichy regime just after the 1940 defeat, largely because of the corporatist principles it embodied. Abbé Godin was one of them, as was mentioned. Another was Emmanuel Mounier, the director of *Esprit*.[21] In the social theories of Mounier one finds elements of Pascal and Marx, Gabriel Marcel and Pétain. With such a background, it is no wonder that Mounier rejected the already-established social and political organizations in the declining years of the Third Republic and why he could have

[21] *Mounier et sa Génération: Lettres, Carnets, et Inédits* (Paris: Editions du Seuil, 1956), p. 265.

flirted with Vichy.[22] In the economic and social realm, Mounier evolved a concept of "socialization without state dictatorship" which brought him favor neither from the non-Catholic extreme left nor from more moderate Catholics.[23] These views are still held by *Esprit*, as shown in this recent quotation from Ricoeur: "The postulate of the immediate coincidence of the will of the socialist state with all the interests of all the workers seems to me to be a pernicious illusion and a dangerous alibi for the abuse of power by the state."[24]

There are two other points on which the Catholic and non-Catholic left definitely part company. One is the attitude toward the Church. With a few individual exceptions, the Catholic left, even when it criticizes the activity of a given Church group, maintains a spirit of filial respect. All its criticisms are constructive; none are made to please an anticlerical electorate. Secondly, Catholics are not ready to give the working masses to the Communists by default. They will not permit themselves to develop, slowly and quietly, into a bastion of the lower middle class, as the Socialists seem to be doing. A left-wing Catholic feels obliged to try unendingly to win the workers back to the Church or at least to a more objective comprehension of French Catholicism. Those who have not had such an attitude—for example, some worker-priests and a part of the Christian Progressives—soon left French Catholicism altogether.[25]

Not only must left-oriented Catholics keep their distance from Communism (for example, by neither voting Communist nor joining that Party); there obviously is a great barrier be-

[22] See introduction to Emmanuel Mounier, *Be Not Afraid*, Translated by Cynthia Rowland (New York: Harper & Bros., n.d.).

[23] Noureddine Zaza, *Etude Critique de la Notion d'Engagement chez Emmanuel Mounier* (Genève: Librarie E. Droz, 1955), p. 35. Mounier puts the state between the spiritual society, which is above it, and the people at large, who are below it. He would have certain watchdog groups insure that the state would not encroach on the legitimate interests of the other two interested parties. *Ibid.*, p. 39.

[24] *Esprit*, Vol. xxv (May 1957), p. 744.

[25] Cf. "Progressisme et Intégrisme: Essai de Psychanalyse Existentielle," in *Chronique Sociale*, LXIII, No. 3 (May 15, 1955), pp. 274-277.

tween the Catholic left and French Socialism. Though cooperation is possible on specific questions, organizational unity seems out of the question. The Catholic left is a bridge for ideas from the non-Catholic left to penetrate the rest of French Catholicism, but it is also an advanced bastion for the ideas of the Catholic central core.

Groups on the Catholic right have a much different philosophical orientation. For the Catholic left, the chief preoccupation was how to react to the majority of the French left, which often distrusts Catholic motives. But most of the French right is well-disposed toward the Church, considering it an element of social stability. There is no important anticlerical right to match the anticlerical left.[26]

Despite the absence of anti-Catholic pressures, conservatives also modify the Catholic core philosophy to suit their own needs. For example, pluralism is used as an argument for protecting vested interests, while corporatism is identified by extremists with the regimes prevailing in Spain or Portugal. In countries without a conservative corporatist or Fascist orientation, the Catholic extreme right uses the hierarchy principle to justify authoritarian political systems.

The tendency to disagree with the Communist Party, already noted on the Catholic left, is hugely overemphasized on the Catholic right, where Communism assumes satanic proportions. Generally the right dispenses with pluralist or personalist reasons against Communism and concentrates on its "innate perversity." This becomes a true obsession with the extreme right. "They consider themselves the only defenders of Christian civilization against Communism."[27]

[26] It appears, however, that many elements of the right pay only lip service to Catholicism and are violently against the progressive elements of the Church, including the more enlightened clergy. As Micaud says, "In fact, nationalism was the most vital element in the ideology of the right, their real religion rather than Catholicism, which was used as a discipline rather than believed in as a dogma." See Charles Micaud, *The French Right and Nazi Germany* (Durham: Duke University Press, 1943), p. 20.

[27] *France Observateur*, May 21, 1959.

Unlike the Catholic left, the Catholic right extends the spiritual sphere deep into temporal life. The principles of hierarchy and authority which govern the Church should also govern the state, and only a fully Catholic state is completely acceptable. Thus, the motto of *Verbe*, printed in all its issues, is "For a Christian-Social Order." For Madiran, "It is the Church which maintains and interprets the meaning of rights and duties. The Church teaches men to give unto Caesar what is Caesar's and unto God what is God's."[28] Thus the Church itself is to define the sphere of power left to the state! Even the more sensible men of the Catholic right extend the Church far into temporal life. For example, on a brochure of a large French pilgrimage group, the 1958 political crisis is explained as follows: "Not to see the finger of Our Lord in the unfolding of the events of 1958, the centenary of the apparitions of His Mother at Lourdes, is most certainly a serious lack of observation and of supernatural consciousness."[29]

Right wing Catholics stress the need for temporal unity among all Catholics—a unity based primarily on the ideals of corporatism and solidarism. Catholic unity should not be simply a spiritual principle; it should be a "unity of action," geared to winning concrete political victories.[30] This is a theme which was universally used during the separation controversy, but now it can appeal only to the Catholic right.

Perhaps the single most characteristic aspect of right-wing Catholic philosophy is the absolute assurance of possessing the Truth. Often this assurance is not openly stated, for the Hierarchy will not permit any fraction of Catholic laymen to set up their views as dogma. Nevertheless, "For the *intégriste*, nothing is doubtful; all is simple and clear."[31]

[28] Madiran, in *Itinéraires*, No. 28 (December 1958), p. 7.

[29] Quoted in *Témoignage Chrétien*, July 24, 1959, p. 9. Having presented the quotation with tongue in cheek, T.C. comments that "lacking anything better, the author of this horoscope should at least acquire a sense of humor, which is a very humble way of respecting what is sacred."

[30] See two books by Abbé André Richard: *L'Unité d'Action des Catholiques* (Paris: Plon, 1939), and *Catholiques de Partout, Réveillons-Nous, Unissons-Nous* (Paris: Propagande pour l'Unité, 1938).

[31] *Chronique Sociale*, LXIII, No. 3 (May 15, 1955), p. 278.

"The *intégriste* tends to consider his own opinions as orthodoxy and the opinions of others as heterodoxy. . . . In the famous rule of the Church, *in necessariis unitas, in dubiis libertas, in omnibus caritas*, he eliminates the last two parts. For him, all is necessary. . . . His Christianity is stripped of its immense potentials, of its tensions, of its vital paradoxes, of its tragic element, and reduced to the dimensions of small minds full of prejudice."[32]

As one moves toward the extreme right, the psychological need for security and for absolutes seems to increase. Thus, the left-wing *Témoignage Chrétien* reported recently on a meeting of the extremist organization *Verbe*: "If it is remarked to the delegates that controversial political choices are included in what they call Doctrine, although they do not seem to see it, they answer, 'How can our activity inspire partisan policies, when we want only to establish the social reign of Christ, and far beyond France alone?' It is here that one feels how difficult it is to have conversation between two almost irreconcilable mentalities. It is here that different people are tempted to mutually exclude themselves even though all remain evidently faithful to the Church."[33]

Any possibility of real understanding between the left and right tendencies of French Catholicism seems out of the question. Both extremes might feel able to live with the philosophy of the central core, but between left and right there is nothing but a *dialogue des sourds.* The Catholic right has not the monopoly of Truth that it would like, for left-oriented Catholics have equal justification to call themselves Catholics, despite their frequent *crises de conscience.* The fact that left and right still consider themselves part of the same broad spiritual family indicates how wide the appeal of French Catholicism as a religion extends, although this does nothing to increase Catholic temporal unity or political effectiveness.

[32] *ibid.*, pp. 282-283.
[33] *Témoignage Chrétien*, July 24, 1959, p. 10.

II. *The Catholic Impact on Individuals and Social Classes*

A. IMPACT ON THE INDIVIDUAL

Bringing together all the elements of this book to determine the Catholic impact in French politics is not an easy undertaking. The nature of the research accomplished makes any conclusion highly tentative. Yet, some conclusions seem fairly clear. They are of two dimensions and will be considered separately. The first dimension concerns the impact of Catholic groups on individuals, either isolated or members of a social category such as the working class. The other dimension concerns the ability of each of the broad tendencies of French Catholicism to push national political activity toward the goals and values held by that tendency.

Probably the most direct Catholic impact on individuals comes from two sources: the Hierarchy and Catholic Action. Catholic Action groups, in cooperation with the Hierarchy and through their own programs of *revision de vie*, help direct the energies of Catholics toward other Catholic-oriented social groups. The Hierarchy stimulates this desire to stay in and to extend the "Catholic family" by providing Catholic schools, by approving a Catholic press, by sponsoring Catholic professional groups, and then urging strongly that all Catholics patronize these institutions.

Catholics who care enough to go to church regularly or to take part in a Catholic Action group already have spiritual needs that are being fulfilled. Catholic school education, the process of *revision de vie*, and other pressures cultivate and extend these needs, so that only a wholehearted commitment to a whole series of Catholic groups will bring final satisfaction. Many of the Catholics who are unaffected by Catholic Action are not devout and do not desire to apply religious principles to the temporal sphere, even at the behest of the Church leadership. These are the "passives," many of whom are members of the Socialist or Radical parties or other groups with anticlerical positions disapproved by Church authorities. These passive Catholics make no practical contribution to the temporal impact of French Catholicism.

Thus, only between five and ten million Catholics have an active role in furthering French Catholic political activity.[34] This serves to explain the paradox that Catholicism, nominally the religion of the majority of Frenchmen, is only a minority social force. This difference between "active" and "passive" Catholics is recognized by most Catholic leaders themselves. One of them, the Deputy Eugène Claudius-Petit, made the following comments as the Debré Law was being considered in December, 1959: "But I am a Catholic. I am not among those who believe that their Catholicism is a private affair; I am rather one of those who think that every moment, all of our actions must be dictated by our religious faith."[35]

The nature of the spiritual need which runs over into temporal life could not be fully examined in this book. But we can speculate that this need is similar in some respects to the need of certain Communists for a *mystique* to explain the evils of this world and to stimulate attempts at curing them.[36] On the other hand, perhaps this spiritual need is just the normal human reaction to a very strong religious impulse.

Whatever the nature of the spiritual need, it leads to the creation of particularistic Catholic groupings whose members do not wish to lose their sectarian ties. This means that it is impossible to draw together all the democratic, nontotalitarian

[34] ". . . among the 40 million Frenchmen of Catholic origin, seasonal conformists, regular observants, devoted Catholics and non-Catholics are respectively 72, 16, 3, and 9 percent." Quoted from Gabriel Le Bras, *Etudes de Sociologie Religieuse*, Vol. I (Paris: Presses Universitaires de France, 1955), p. xvii. Thus, regular observants and devoted Catholics together are around one fifth of the total, or 8,000,000.

[35] *Journal Officiel de la République Française. Débats Parlementaires, Assemblée Nationale*, December 23, 1959, p. 3636.

[36] Cf. Gabriel Almond, *The Appeals of Communism* (Princeton: Princeton University Press, 1954), *passim. The Authoritarian Personality* by T. W. Adorno *et al.* (New York: Harper & Bros., 1950) has shown that a large percentage of Americans have a potential need to commit themselves to a man, a doctrine, or a cause.

groups in any professional or social category for more effective action against groups of Communists or other opponents of democracy. Without the particularism that follows from spiritual needs, the CFTC or the MRP could perhaps join their Socialist counterparts in vast democratic groupings that could more effectively compete with the Communist Party or the CGT.

As noted earlier, the universal character of the Church and the anti-class-war aspect of Catholic core philosophy seem to be leading many Catholics to modify their views toward social classes. In a country like France, where class association is still important, Catholicism might thus contribute to a breakdown of social antagonisms. However, research with the JOC, the ACO, and the CFTC indicates that being Catholic does not completely wipe out one's worker mentality. In fact, declarations of the ACO often show that worker groups may even use Christian morality to justify their social demands.

One final effect of Catholicism on individuals should be emphasized. Many Catholic groups have programs to prepare their outstanding young members for positions of social or political leadership. It is hoped that these people will go out into French society, fortified by their Catholic group experience and by their faith, to spread the interests of the Church. Interestingly, a higher priority has been given to developing a Catholic elite than to influencing the "power elite" that presently rules France. Building a Catholic elite from the ground up creates individuals who will be more loyal to French Catholicism than will an ordinary bureaucrat, and subjects the Church to less criticism by *laïques* who fear direct inroads by the Church into political life.

B. CATHOLICISM AND SOCIAL CLASSES: THE EXAMPLE OF THE WORKING CLASS

The Church and Catholic laymen's groups have been particularly concerned with the religious feelings of the French working class. It represents nearly a majority of the French population, but in large part it is quite outside the impact of French Catholicism. Bringing the bulk of the working class closer to the Church is one of the highest goals of French Catholicism. This may help to explain why the Church has engaged in many activities geared to the working class as a group, whereas for farmers, bourgeois, and other classes it generally keeps to the level of individual Catholic groups.

The chief Catholic institutions catering to the working class have already been examined. In the ecclesiastical nucleus are institutions dealing with apostolic problems in the working class and with certain temporal problems as well. There are the *Mission de France*, the Prado priests, the *Frères de Foucauld*, all of which aim at rousing a Catholic consciousness among individual workers. The *Fils de la Charité* specialize in educating working-class youngsters. All this work is coordinated by Canon Bonnet, the Secretary for the Working Class, and by Cardinal Feltin, Cardinal Liénart, who runs the seminary of the *Mission de France*, and the Episcopal Working Class Commission. Noteworthy among working-class Catholic Action groups are *Action Catholique Ouvrière* for adults and *Jeunesse Ouvrière Chrétienne* for young people. The MRP has some worker strength in its ranks through its worker teams, and the CFTC represents a large working-class force not hostile to the activities of the Church. However, neither the MRP nor the CFTC are official mandated members of French Catholicism. Finally, there are social action groups which do technical studies concerning the working class, though they themselves are not based on a working-class membership. The best examples are the *Secrétariats Sociaux* and *Economie et Humanisme*.

One index of effectiveness for the Catholic working-class groups is the number of workers who practice the Catholic religion regularly. Unfortunately, information here is unreliable and even conflicting. A poll by the French Institute of Public Opinion showed that 42 per cent of working-class men were either "devoted" or "observant" churchgoers; the figure for women of the working class was 66 per cent.[37] Fogarty, presumably using these figures, deduces that between 28 per cent and 29 per cent of the French manual laborers are regular churchgoers—though in this "laborer" category he also includes peasants.[38] However, surveys sponsored by the Church itself are much more pessimistic. For example, Abbé Daniel puts the percentage of practicing Catholic workers in the Paris region at 1.7 per cent for men and 2.8 per cent for women.[39]

Another index of Catholic impact on workers is the number who join the "most Catholic" political party, the MRP. Figures show that the worker strength in the MRP dropped by a quarter between 1950 and 1955, from 20 per cent to 14.8 per cent of the total membership. The figures include employees along with workers. A related set of figures shows, however, that workers in nationalized and private industry made up only 9.1 per cent of MRP members in 1955.[40] The small size of groups like ACO and the abrupt postwar decline of JOC would lead one to interpret these figures with a certain pessimism. However, the CFTC membership figures are still rising, so one cannot positively conclude that the Church's impact among workers is declining.

It is very difficult to make any firm generalizations about Church strength in the working class, as the conflicting figures just cited would indicate. We take more comfort in our own personal observation, based on studies of Catholic Action, that the particularism of the French working class is gradually moderating and will to a large degree disappear in the future. Workers, as they become more *embourgoisé*, will probably lose some antipathy against other social classes and against

37 *Sondages, loc.cit.*, p. 36.

38 Fogarty, *op.cit.*, p. 374.

39 Yvon Daniel, *Paroisses d'Hier, Paroisses de Demain* (Paris: Bernard Grasset, 1957), p. 171. These figures were not taken from a small poll sample, but by parish priests throughout the Paris area who noted attendance at churches on a "typical" Sunday morning, March 14, 1954.

40 See Daniel Pépy, "Le Mouvement Républicain Populaire," in Assn. Française de Science Politique, *Partis Politiques et Classes Sociales en France* (Paris: Armand Colin, 1955), pp. 214-216.

the Church. We do not prophesy American-style social conditions overnight, but it seems feasible that they can approach those in neighboring Switzerland, Germany, or Belgium. If this does happen and workers become imbued with the same social values as other French social classes, much of the working class will probably be closed to the philosophical penetration of Soviet-style Marxism. Then, probably, many workers will become receptive to the influence of the Church, just as the Church finds many worker adherents in other Western European countries or in the United States.[41]

But at the same time, one cannot ignore the social situation as it exists today. The call of the milieu today is often so strong that it seduces members of the Church itself. As was noted in Chapter Three, a number of the original worker-priests refused to obey the Vatican orders to stop factory work. And in company with their fellow workers, Catholic workers often find it difficult to resist the attraction of the extreme left in politics: "Where political behavior conflicts with religious behavior, the primacy of social factors is even more evident: Catholic fishermen can elect a Communist town government, while the a-religious small landholders and retired people in Aube and Yonne departments will vote PRL."[42]

For workers who are devout Catholics, there are usually grave conflicts between loyalty to the Church and loyalty to class. Sometimes these conflicts are partially resolved, as when the workers emphasize the "proletarian" aspects of Christ's life: "He was born in a stable—yes, a real stable. For thirty years He worked hard enough to get callouses on His hands. . . . And He was not afraid to talk to street girls so as to save them or to show the rich man who blamed Him for it where

[41] In Belgium, for example, almost all Catholic-sponsored working-class groups have a larger membership than their Socialist counterparts. See Fogarty, *op.cit.*, pp. 220-221. Fogarty cites a poll showing that as many low-income Germans attend church as those with higher incomes. *ibid.*, p. 354.

[42] Gabriel Le Bras, *Etudes de Sociologie Electorale* (Paris: Armand Colin, 1947), p. 59.

to get off. . . . Now I was beginning to understand something about His teaching and what it led to—the solidarity of men. And He was a workman Himself, a carpenter, a fellow like me. Then what about the old bigot who comes out of church between two prayers to abuse her neighbor? She's a humbug. And the so-called Catholic employer who thinks more of his machines than of his men? He's phoney. And all those people who come to church and whose life is nothing but selfishness, unkindness, injustice? They're just ersatz Christians."[43]

Often conflicts are not resolved, as when a worker joins a bourgeois-dominated parish association and thereby is cut off from his fellow workers. "In more than one region, the worker 'unclasses himself' by joining the parish milieu."[44] Groups like *Mission de France* and the Secretariat of Canon Bonnet attempt to eliminate these untenable situations.[45] Their limited success would seem to foreshadow hard times for the new secular institutes which the Vatican is attempting to establish to expand Church influence in the working class.

At present one encouraging factor for the development of Catholicism in the working class is the lack of virulent open hostility to the Church. Few workers are as antireligious as the Freemasons or the rationalists were at the turn of the century. The most prevalent attitude among workers, as the *Sondages* poll points out, is indifference and detachment rather than open hostility.[46] In the recent past, workers have been hostile to certain Catholic institutions, but this is because they seemed to be too closely tied to the bourgeoisie. The more general indifference, however, is not based primarily on class antipathies. The French working class was born outside the Church, for when the industrial proletariat first was formed at the beginning of the nineteenth century most Frenchmen were apathetic toward the Church.[47] Time will tell whether the Church can

[43] Abbé Godin, quoted in Ward, *France Pagan?*, p. 95.
[44] Dansette, *Destin*, p. 62.
[45] Cf. *Témoignage Chrétien*, May 15, 1959.
[46] *Sondages, loc.cit.*, p. 36.
[47] Cf. Dansette, *Destin*, p. 36.

attract the working class to it with as much success as it did attract the bourgeoisie, once the center of rationalistic skepticism.

Though the Church position in the proletariat has not spectacularly improved, each modest gain is significant, compared to the traditional apathy of French workers toward Catholicism. The creation of a small but dynamic elite of Catholic workers seems particularly important for the long-range position of the Church among the workers.

C. CATHOLIC IMPACT ON OTHER ELEMENTS OF FRENCH SOCIETY

In every social group the impact of the Church is limited by the number of those who are willing to abide by the Church's teachings. Only a small percentage of the working class fits into this category, and this doubtless helps explain the massive programs being carried out in the working class by many Catholic organizations. On the other hand, a different sort of Catholic effort is needed when a social group still remains imbued with respect and reverence for the Church. French farmers, for example, are more open to Church influence than workers or city-dwellers in general.[48] The French Catholic effort to extend its influence in the rural areas is mainly based on individual appeals rather than coordinated programs covering the entire peasantry. There is no mass defection of farmers from the Church, and the few mass farm organizations connected to the Church seem to be expanding, so there would seem to be little cause for concern for the future of the Church in rural France.

But even in rural areas, religious life is often more a matter of conservative traditionalism than deep religious inspiration, as Bishop Chappoulie himself admitted.[49] The Church has taken the rural world for granted and Catholic groups were allowed to develop without sufficient overall direction.

[48] See Jacques Fauvet, "Le Monde Paysan," in *Partis Politiques et Classes Sociales en France, op.cit.*, p. 174.

[49] See *Actualité Religieuse dans le Monde,* March 15, 1955, p. 5.

Public opinion polls shed some light on the general impact of the Church and other Catholic groups. The poll reported in the magazine *Sondages* in 1952 claimed that 37 per cent of the French adult population goes regularly to mass, that 26 per cent are "devoted" churchgoers, and that 14 per cent consider themselves as "fervent Catholics."[50] The last two figures should be compared to those of Le Bras, cited earlier. For Le Bras only 16 per cent of French adults can be considered "devoted" and only 3 per cent "fervent." At any rate, the 55 per cent who said they were "not at all preoccupied" with the positions of the Church when they vote must be beyond the reach of Catholic political influence.[51] Eric Stern has confirmed that most Frenchmen do not identify themselves closely with the Church. In a study of spontaneous group references in France, he found not a single identification with Catholicism.[52]

In a recent poll sponsored by *Vie Catholique Illustrée*, a sample of French young people was asked about religious habits. Eighty-five per cent of the youngsters were baptized Catholics; 82 per cent made their first Holy Communion; 78 per cent were confirmed; and 76 per cent still considered themselves Catholics. But among the young adults questioned only 34 per cent went to church regularly. The latter figure could well be an accurate indication of how many young people are open to Church social and political activity. Hourdin, however, concluding his poll report, was more optimistic about youth today: "It is, in any case, cleansed of our old religious quarrels. It is not anticlerical. It is, it seems to me, very favorably disposed to hear whoever will speak to it rigorously about religious questions, if that person will fight to make his private and public acts agree with his faith."[53]

The Church has provided Catholic Action groups for French youth open to its influence. Similar groups exist for many other

[50] *Sondages, loc.cit.*, pp. 14, 17, 19.
[51] *ibid.*, p. 25.
[52] Eric Stern, "Spontaneous Group References in France," in *Public Opinion Quarterly*, Vol. XVII, No. 2, Summer 1953, pp. 208-217.
[53] Georges Hourdin in *Express*, January 15, 1959, p. 26.

social categories. But none of these groups is designed primarily with a political end in mind. The Church realizes that it is impractical and undesirable to mobilize a social milieu for political action, just as it would be dangerous for the Church if a single giant Catholic pressure group were introduced into French political life.

III. Catholic Interrelations: The Political Significance of the Chief Catholic Tendencies

Most experts believe, and the findings of this study seem to bear it out, that the most realistic way to group Catholic organizations in the political sphere is to put them into three or four broad tendencies.[54] On one side are the representatives of the most progressive elements, whether Catholic Action groups, social action groups, publications, or even bishops. On the other side is the Catholic right, with views ranging from conservatism to extremist authoritarianism. In the center are the more moderate groups, the most faithful supporters of the "central core" of catholic social philosophy.

Any social division based on such a left-right scale leaves much to be desired. However, it can form the basis for an interesting and largely accurate view of present-day Catholic interrelations, since French Catholics themselves are preoccupied with the left-right distinction in politics. A schematic chart of the major Catholic groups follows, in which major Catholic groups are ranked from left to right. Each tendency is further subdivided into "actives" and "passives," to distinguish between Catholics who are firmly attached to their faith

[54] See, for example, the articles by René Rémond on "Droite et Gauche dans le Catholicisme Français Contemporain," in *Revue Française de Science Politique*, September and December, 1958. See also Michel Darbon, *Le Conflit entre la Droite et la Gauche dans le Catholicisme Français: 1930-1953* (Toulouse: Privat, 1953). And note the issues of *Chronique Sociale* on "Progressisme et Intégrisme" (LXIII, No. 3, May 15, 1955), and "Catholiques de Droite? Catholiques de Gauche?" (LXIV, Nos. 7-8, December 30, 1956).

Figure 8
The "Political Location" of Major Catholic Groups

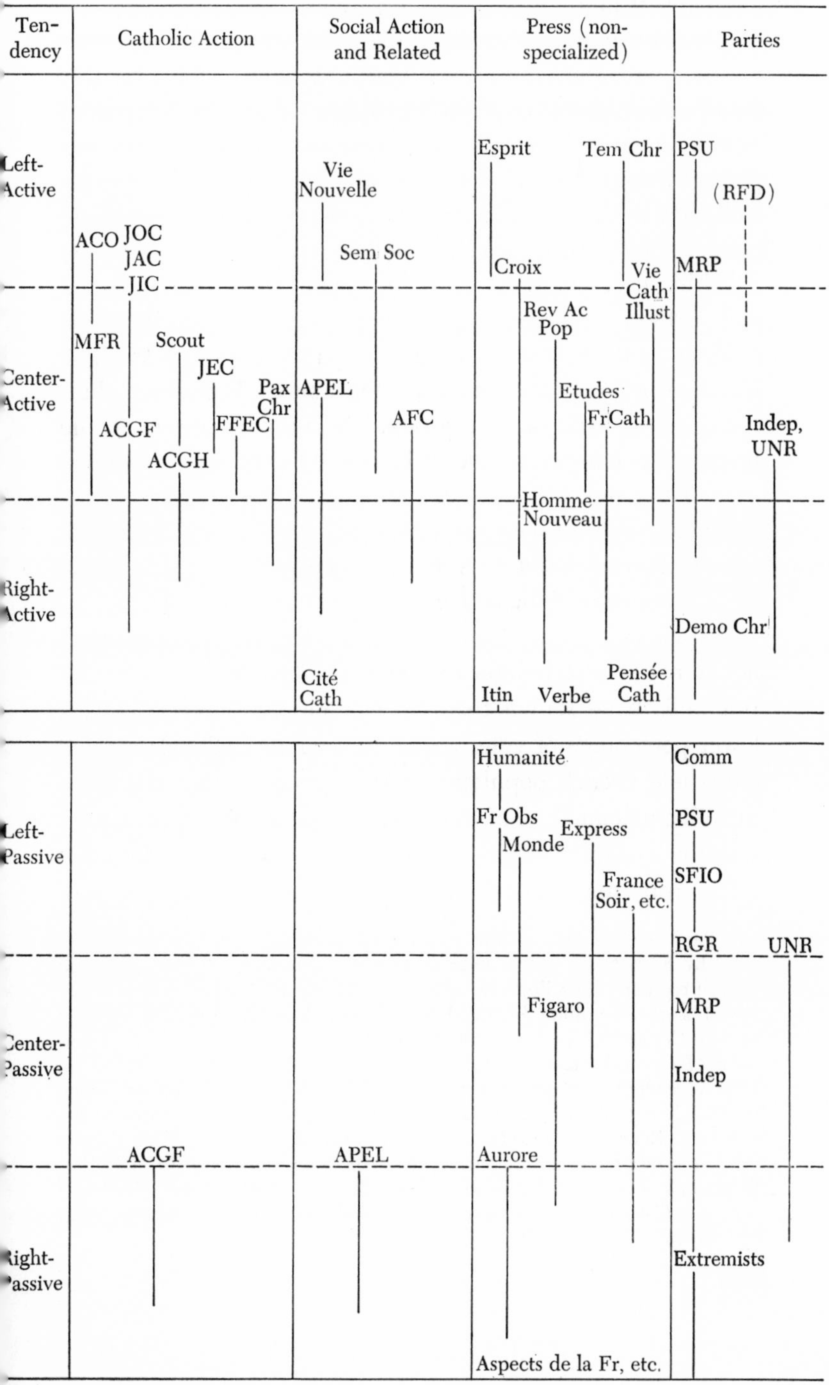

Tendency	Catholic Action	Social Action and Related	Press (non-specialized)	Parties
Left-Active	ACO, JOC, JAC, JIC	Vie Nouvelle, Sem Soc	Esprit, Tem Chr, Croix, Vie Cath Illust	PSU, (RFD), MRP
Center-Active	MFR, Scout, JEC, Pax Chr, ACGF, FFEC, ACGH	APEL, AFC	Rev Ac Pop, Etudes, Fr Cath, Homme Nouveau	Indep, UNR
Right-Active		Cité Cath	Itin, Verbe, Pensée Cath	Demo Chr
Left-Passive			Humanité, Fr Obs, Express, Monde, France Soir, etc.	Comm, PSU, SFIO, RGR, UNR
Center-Passive	ACGF	APEL	Figaro, Aurore	MRP, Indep
Right-Passive			Aspects de la Fr, etc.	Extremists

and carry it into temporal spheres by joining Catholic groups, and the broad mass of nominal Catholics who have only tenuous ties with the Church. The latter group, which probably forms the majority of Frenchmen, has been largely ignored in this book because it does not contribute to the political impact of French Catholicism in a tangible way.[55] Most passive Catholics shun groups and publications connected to Catholicism, as the preceding chart indicates.

Within each category (Catholic Action, social action, press, and parties) the organizations are ranked in Figure Eight according to their position on a continuum from left to right. The lines indicate the extent of their appeal, but do not show the numerical size of each group. This ranking system should be taken with great caution; it is meant to give only a very approximative indication of each group's position. Reading across the chart, one can have an indication of the groups which an active left-wing Catholic is likely to join, or ones which would appeal to center-right active Catholics, and so forth.

Outside of political extremes, it seems that the passive Catholics do not act much differently from the "average Frenchman." But polls have shown that the Communist Party attracts a lower percentage of votes among lukewarm Catholics than in the whole French population.[56] It is probable that the Hierarchy's condemnation of the Communists is not the reason for this; the Socialist Party is supported by many passive Catholics (though by few actives), despite the Papal condemnations of

[55] Passive Catholics are not necessarily irregular churchgoers. Figures cited by Fogarty show that over 40 percent of baptized Catholics attend church regularly. See Fogarty, *op.cit.*, p. 351. According to Le Bras, there are at least 38 million baptized Frenchmen. See "La Religion dans la Société Française," in André Siegfried, *et al., Aspects de la Société Française* (Paris: Librairie Générale de Droit et de Jurisprudence, 1954), p. 224. According to these figures, around 15 million Frenchmen would go to church regularly. This is far more than the total in all Catholic lay activities. Even if we take the more pessimistic figures of Le Bras already cited, the number of churchgoers still exceeds the membership of Catholic groups. Therefore, many churchgoers must be among the "passives."

[56] "Le Catholicisme en France," in *Sondages*, Vol. XIV, No. 4, 1952, pp. 35 and 40.

"Marxism," and the anticlerical positions of the SFIO. More than likely, one who cares to maintain even a residual affiliation with his religion is not the kind of person to be attracted by the totalitarianism and radical social positions of the Communists.

Two of the mass Catholic groups, the ACGF and the APEL, undoubtedly include a large number of passives among their members. These are probably the inactive members whose presence makes it necessary to repeat in the official publications of these groups just what the groups stand for! They join because their curé asks them, or because their children are enrolled in Church schools, but they consider their membership more in the light of its social than its religious aspects.

The preceding diagram deliberately represents the tendencies of Catholic groups on a continuum. There is no clear line between the left and the center or the right and the extreme right. Yet groups of active Catholics seem to cluster around certain positions. On the left are the social-minded progressives, with strong affinities for Catholic Action youth movements, *Vie Nouvelle*, and the PSU political party. Members of this tendency will read *Esprit* and *Témoignage Chrétien*. Moving toward the center, one finds members of adult specialized Catholic Action groups (General Catholic Action would probably seem too conservative), who read *La Croix* and *Vie Catholique Illustrée*, and who are stanch supporters of the MRP. On the right one will join a General Catholic Action group, will be an active supporter of APEL, will read *La Croix* and perhaps *Homme Nouveau*, and will vote for a classical right party or a Catholic of the Bidault tendency in the MRP. On the extreme right, one will read *Verbe* and *Itinéraires*, will be sympathetic to the anti-Communist crusade of *Cité Catholique*, and will probably be dissatisfied with all existing political parties. The Catholic extreme left, as has been mentioned, is practically nonexistent as an organized force at present.

Each of these tendencies has a particular impact upon French political life, which it would be valuable to see more clearly. Without finally solving the complex problem of what constitutes "impact" and how it is to be evaluated, some hypotheses can be made about the relative significance of each major Catholic tendency.

The progressive but nonextremist Catholic left includes a number of extremely dedicated and socially-conscious militants; they are present in the JAC, on the editorial board of *Témoignage Chrétien*, in certain circles of the clergy, notably in the Dominicans of Paris and in the *Semaines Sociales*. The energetic activity of this Catholic elite has as much temporal as spiritual significance. It is widely noted and appreciated, especially among intellectual circles in France. And its "style" is so unique that left Catholics stand out clearly from other French groups with progressive leanings. However, none of the left Catholic publications or works attains a truly mass audience. If the impact of the Catholic left is deep within individual militants, it is not widespread among the French masses.

In the center of the ideological spectrum, the active moderates have attracted a much larger segment of French society than the Catholic left. And more important, most statements of the ACA and other semiofficial organs of the French Church seem to bolster the position of the Catholic center. Most of the core philosophy of Catholicism serves to strengthen the position of the Catholic center also. Association with the Church Hierarchy brings many of the most pious—though not necessarily the most temporally active—of Catholics into this center category. Nevertheless, personal interviews have convinced the author that the leaders of Catholic center groups lack the fire and the drive of either the left or the extreme-right forces. The Catholic center seems to prefer remaining secure in its orthodoxy.

The forces of the Catholic right seem to attract both large numbers of adherents and many influential social groups, notably the Catholic-oriented business interests and certain high Vatican prelates. Thus, for example, the advertising revenue for *France Catholique*, spokesman for the Catholic right, is almost double that of *Témoignage Chrétien*.[57] However, the activity of the Catholic right entails little enthusiasm or devotion except in matters where the immediate interests of members are involved, such as the school controversy. Like the Catholic center, the Catholic right finds it hard to stand out from the French right in general, to develop autonomous positions and an impact all its own. For example, it is clear that the Catholic-oriented right and center had less influence in passing the school law of December 1959 than the more "neutral" groups, particularly the Gaullist UNR.

The Catholic extreme right has an even smaller membership than the left. Yet many of its members are influential in their own right, in the French army particularly. The activity of Catholic extreme-rightists is, therefore, more politically significant than its small number of adherents might indicate.

What will be the fate of each of these tendencies in the near future? It appears that the growth of the moderate Catholic left and center is linked to continued political stability in France. If such stability can be preserved and the Algerian conflict can be quickly ended, Catholic Action youth leaders could rise peacefully through the ranks of adult Catholic organizations without the experience of the battlefield to undermine their faith. Without political stability it may be necessary for the Hierarchy to modify its political judgments which now reinforce the prestige and impact of the center Catholic forces. René Rémond believes that the left-oriented masses have a good chance to prevail over any rightist elite, and the Church may develop a permanent orientation farther to the left; Duverger shares this view.[58] However, the Catholic right has many sources of potential strength also.

[57] See Jacques Maître, "Le Fonctionnement de la Presse Catholique en France," p. 19.

[58] See René Rémond, "Droite et Gauche dans le Catholicisme Français," in *Revue Française de Science Politique*, VIII, No. 4 (December 1958), p. 815. See also Maurice Duverger, "Les Objectifs Partisans," in *Le Monde*, March 26, 1959, pp. 1 and 7.

The right and especially the extreme right would seem to benefit from continued political insecurity in France. Uncertainty over the eventual fate of Catholic schools kept interest high in organizations such as the APEL. If the Algerian war engenders long-term political chaos, many groups where the rightist elite is strong will benefit. Eventually, some bishops might be attracted to intransigent political positions. This too would help the prestige of the Catholic right. In general, it would seem that the best hope for the extreme right to improve its political position is a continuation of crisis and insecurity. Surely men like Georges Sauge understand this; it helps explain why Sauge attempted to harass Khrushchev on his tour to France as a means of advertising to the nation his "effectiveness."[59]

Figure Nine presents in summary form some of the main constituents that seem to contribute to the political impact of each Catholic tendency. It also offers a brief analysis of the future evolution of each tendency.

This study has examined the political value of a number of Catholic groups. Patterns of interrelation have been noted among various Catholic groups which claim to be progressive or middle of the road or more conservative, but practically no politically-significant interrelations include all factions.[60] The main reason for this lack of contact lies in the widely differing viewpoints of left and right and the inability of extremist groups to accept the "central core" of Catholic social thought. But other reasons must be considered too.

If any Church agency could control and direct all Catholic groups, it would be the French Hierarchy itself. In addition to its own political role through declarations and through its

[59] The behavior of Sauge finally impelled the government to arrest him. For his aims in this matter see *Express*, December 3, 1959, p. 7.

[60] Of the Catholic officials interviewed for this book (among whom were representatives from virtually all political tendencies) none acknowledged structured contacts with leaders from an opposing political tendency.

Catholic Action auxiliaries, the Hierarchy also controls the authoritative interpretation of the Church social doctrine in France. And perhaps more important, there are local or unofficial relations between members of the clergy and virtually all Catholic groups. All except those of Catholic inspiration have chaplains or ecclesiastical advisors; many have close working relations with members of religious orders, particularly the Jesuits or Dominicans; and in many areas the local curé has a key social position.

But in spite of these activities, the Hierarchy has not given an overall political orientation to all Catholic groups. It has failed to incorporate the various Catholic groups into a unified whole. There are many reasons for this, some of which have already been explored. Perhaps the most significant is the lack of agreement among bishops in most matters outside the spiritual realm. As Rémond has said, "Especially within the Church of France, many attitudes have always coexisted, going from the most rigorous intransigence to the most tolerant liberalism."[61] And since each bishop is theoretically master in his own diocese, there is no such thing as a "majority" view prevailing among them on any important political question.[62]

Even on the school question bishops have divergent viewpoints. So any single authoritative statement from the Hierarchy on a partisan political question should not be expected in ordinary circumstances. According to Golob, the situation is similar in other countries as well: "The unity of the Catholic Church . . . should not be exaggerated. There are striking differences, from country to country and even bishopric to bishopric, in the attitudes of the Catholic hierarchy toward mat-

[61] René Rémond, *La Droite en France de 1815 à Nos Jours* (Paris: Aubier, 1954), p. 240.

[62] Even the Vatican cannot always have its way. It took five years to stop completely the worker-priest experiment. On other political questions the Vatican has no way of forcing Catholic approval of its policies without being accused of rank interference where it does not belong. See, for example, the criticism by stanch Catholic Joseph Hours of tacit Papal support for the EDC: "Les Catholiques Français et la Patrie," *Année Politique et Economique*, XXVIII, No. 123-4 (January 1955), 1-24. Cf. *ibid.*, XXXI, No. 142-3 (April 1958), pp. 81-104.

FIGURE 9. The Chief Catholic Political Tendencies: Elements of Impact

DETERMINANTS OF IMPACT	CATHOLIC LEFT	CATHOLIC CENTER
Kind of Membership	Intellectual elite; workers	"Catholic masses" plus most clergy
Degree of Activity	Very active in temporal life	Pious work stressed, without great enthusiasm
Uniqueness, Compared to Similar "Neutral" Groups	Stands out; noticed by large number of people	Hard to differentiate from other Center groups
Kind of Audience	Limited number, but many influential intellectuals and other leaders	Large in number, but not in influence
Political Impact in Foreseeable Future	Could increase if Catholic Action-trained elite succeeded in taking key places in many French organizations; probably never will attract masses	Will keep mass following, provided political stability makes it unnecessary for the French Hierarchy to change its orientations

FIGURE 9, continued.

DETERMINANTS OF IMPACT	CATHOLIC RIGHT	CATHOLIC EXTREME RIGHT
Kind of Membership	Large membership, plus economic elite; some support from Rome	Small groups, based on influential power elites
Degree of Activity	Pious work stressed, without great enthusiasm	Very active in temporal, which they insist is part of spiritual life
Uniqueness, Compared to Similar "Neutral" Groups	Hard to differentiate from other Right groups	Hard to differentiate, since most of Extreme Right considers itself "Catholic"
Kind of Audience	Large in number, with a few leaders	Small audience but certain strategic elites, especially army, Poujadist shopkeepers, and survivors of prewar extremist groups
Political Impact in Foreseeable Future	Permanent solution of school problem might decrease its temporal impact; but recent Vatican decrees bolster it	Very great if unrest and crisis make an "alternative" to the Republic feasible; now, however, this seems quite unlikely

ters of political and social policy or custom. The variation is even greater in lay acceptance, or active following, of the views expressed by the Hierarchy. Catholic uniformity is maintained strictly only in respect of the essentials of faith. The lack of unity in matters of social doctrine prevented Social Catholicism, expounded in two major papal encyclicals, from receiving greater support from Catholics, and from making far greater progress than it actually did."[63] Even if the Hierarchy found it possible to coordinate Catholic political activity in France, the chances would be against choosing such action because of the ineffectiveness of the Church during the separation crisis at the turn of the century.

Compared to the Hierarchy, the means of coordination among active lay Catholics are modest indeed. No lay Catholic has the formal authority possessed by the Hierarchy so none can pretend to impose his views in any field on the totality of Catholics. Nevertheless, some informal cooperative habits have arisen among lay Catholics. All lay members of Catholic groups have chosen to live by their faith, not just in their religious life, but also in part of their temporal life. Were this not so, they would be members of "neutral" groups. Whether or not they follow every whim of the Hierarchy, they give statements from the Vatican or bishops a "respectful consideration," whereas most lukewarm Catholics outside Catholic groups would probably ignore them.

Informal contacts among lay Catholics are often quite important, especially when contacting groups are very close in their political thinking. It has been noted that most MRP leaders have a background in Catholic Action or social Catholic groups. When Bernard Lambert, a young deputy of the MRP and one of the leaders of the RFD, was hooted down in the National Assembly as he was giving a progressive speech on Algeria, he naturally wrote an article in *Témoignage Chrétien*.[64] There are

[63] E. O. Golob, *The "Isms"; A History and Evaluation* (New York: Harper & Bros., 1954), p. 548.

[64] *Témoignage Chrétien*, June 19, 1959, p. 16. According to Georges Suffert, former editor of *Témoignage Chrétien*, as a result of contacts

doubtless many other informal contacts which cannot be known by ordinary laymen. Since virtually all leaders of Catholic groups are in Paris, a short subway ride is often easier than formalized relationship patterns.

A number of coordinating organizations for lay Catholic groups have already been noted. Some of these deal with politically significant questions; others have only a technical role. Because of the lack of cooperation among opposing political tendencies, each group concerned with political affairs invariably attracts just one tendency. Only apolitical technical groups can include representatives of all political views. Thus, the *Centre National de la Presse Catholique*, founded under moderate leftist auspices, abandoned any partisan aspirations once the conservative *Homme Nouveau* and *France Catholique* joined it. The SIPEC was founded with the hope of eventually setting forth a whole philosophy of civic education in modern France. But when members of the more conservative Catholic Action groups joined the social Catholic core of SIPEC, only technical activity could be undertaken. The RFD aspired to attracting a very wide clientele, but since it was a political action organization it was unable to attract people outside the progressive social wing of French Catholicism. Monsieur Lizop has an effective pressure group, but its subject matter limits it to right-wing Catholics.

Even inside one complex of Catholic groups—for example, inside Catholic Action—there is no social or temporal coordination relating the progressive groups representing milieux to the conservative, parish-oriented elements, despite close spiritual coordination by the Hierarchy. When an organization such as *Pax Christi* considers an international issue on which Catholics can legitimately disagree, it must either take a stand which reflects one particular political tendency, or resign itself to nonpartisan technical activity. *Pax Christi* seems now to have be-

among lay Catholic groups, an article in a Catholic review usually has a much wider impact than one in a non-Catholic publication. See *Les Catholiques et la Gauche*, pp. 28-29.

come just another Catholic Action group, with no real coordinating power over any other groups in questions relating to world peace. This is the price it had to pay for trying to appeal to all political tendencies. On the school problem itself, where most Catholics agree on basic principles, all the groups that attempt political activity are limited to one particular tendency. *Témoignage Chrétien* never endorsed the activity of Monsieur Lizop, but was favorable to the school proposals of *Esprit.*[65] A unique exception occurred during the Algerian military insurrection of April 1961, when Catholic groups from moderate left to moderate right issued a joint declaration opposing the seditious army officers. *Le Monde* of April 26, 1961 reported that the declaration was signed by the following groups: JAC and JACF, JEC and JECF, JIC and JICF, JOC and JOCF, JMC, Catholic scouts and guides, ACO, MFR, ACGH, UFCS, FFEC, *Union Nationale des Secrétariats Sociaux, Vie Nouvelle,* and *Pax Christi.* But even this declaration which, after all, only backs up the government in power, was not endorsed by ACI or by the largest Catholic Action group, ACGF.

IV. Final Remarks

Each Catholic group embodies many different individual desires: religious, moral, social and even political. The religious and moral desires, reflected in practices such as *revision de vie* and in the attitude of filial respect toward the Hierarchy, are basically the same throughout French Catholicism. It is for this reason that one can refer to "a French Catholicism" at all. But the political desires vary with the nature of the group.

[65] *Témoignage Chrétien* is quite bitter against *France Catholique*, its ideological opposite. But *France Catholique* usually seems quite gentlemanly in its criticism of T.C. In one sharp exchange, T.C. spoke of the editor of *France Catholique* in these terms: "He displays such a constant hatred of us that we are compelled to take notice of it. Without any scruples he uses the vilest methods: false comparisons, misstatements, distortions. Each month his accusations become more slanderous." See T.C., February 26, 1960.

There is no homogeneity, nor does there need to be, since the basis for all fully-Catholic groups is religious, not political, activity. These groups do not aggregate political desires efficiently because they do not consider this their prime objective. Of course, the situation is different for such groups as the MRP, and this is why such groups have been considered separately from Catholic Action and social action groups. It is also true that certain groups of the Catholic extreme right have primarily political ends, which they hide in religious terminology. The latter groups occupy a peculiar position within French Catholicism, but it is a rapidly-evolving position, which will certainly be modified in the future.

Although attachment to Catholic groups may, as was suggested in the first chapter, indirectly modify loyalty to the state, Catholic groups seldom threaten patriotism directly. The Hierarchy would like to have all one's life permeated with Catholic-approved books and movies, the Catholic press, Catholic vocational groups, Catholic schools, and so forth, but most Frenchmen probably consider their Catholicism as just one of their attributes; they also have a sex, an age, a job, hobbies, and a political opinion. Some of these attributes are often considered more important than religious affiliation, and when this is the case, the desires of the Hierarchy to raise the religious attribute above the others will simply be ignored. In this way, loyalty to the state and to the regime, even if presided over by a Socialist *laïque*, are the normal reactions of Catholics.[66] Only those of the extreme right tend to develop an uncompromising dogmatism.

[66] There are unusual cases where loyalty to the state and loyalty to the Church may conflict, and one must be chosen over the other. For example, Canon Kir wanted to receive Khrushchev during his French tour, as Mayor of Dijon. But the Bishop of Dijon, on direct order from Rome, forbade Kir, a priest, from meeting the Russian leader. The bishop noted that Kir "remained a priest, even in exercising his functions of mayor," and that he would not really have received the Russian Chief of State, but "the head of atheistic Communism." See *I.C.I.*, April 15, 1960, p. 9. After a severe *crise de conscience*, Kir finally obeyed his bishop.

On the other side of the fence, it is interesting to note that the only elements which consider that there is still a general Catholic menace to the French regime are a small group gravitating around Albert Bayet, plus the Communist Party.[67] The vast majority of neutral observers since World War II has not questioned the loyalty of most Catholic groups or of children educated in Catholic schools.

At the end of this survey of Catholic groups in present-day France, it is impossible to find any single, organized, direct political impact to which all contribute. The great crisis of 1958 showed that most Catholic groups, excepting again the extreme right, were moderate and circumspect, though some were ready to speak out if necessary to defend democratic government. But even in 1958, particular political solutions to the crisis inevitably brought disagreements among Catholics.

Unfortunately, despite de Gaulle's power, French society and French values have been sapped dangerously by the everlasting frustrations of a war in Algeria that France could neither win completely nor definitely lose. The extremists, including even certain extreme right groups connected to French Catholicism, have benefited from the frustrations of this impossible war. And no matter what the short-term results of the war itself, it seems clear that new frustrations and new social conflicts will be its legacy to French society for years to come. In the face of this destructive legacy, every friend of France must hope that she will be able to preserve free thought and expression, tolerance of political diversities, and the rule of law—the values necessary for France if she is to continue being an outstanding member of the Western democratic community. Leaders and articulate members of most Catholic groups will be counted among the devoted champions of these fundamental values in any final test of strength with the proto-Fascists.

[67] See Albert Bayet, *Laïcité Vingtième Siècle: Vers une Réconciliation Française* (Paris: Hachette, 1958), Chapter VIII.

Appendix

Maps Illustrating the Regional Strength of Catholic Groups

Throughout this book evidence has been presented showing that Catholics are politically, socially, temperamentally, and in part even spiritually divided. It is more meaningful to forsake the vague and largely meaningless concept of "French Catholicism" for divisions based on ideological affinities or on organizational types. But these are not the only possible ways to categorize Catholicism. Within different geographical regions of France there are great variations in religious fervor as well as in attachment to Catholic groups. In this appendix the regional strength of certain Catholic groups will be analyzed, to demonstrate on maps that areas of strength and weakness for different groups are closely correlated. By doing this, the following two propositions will be demonstrated.

First, church attendance is a good indication of a desire to participate in lay Catholic groups. There are virtually no areas of low average church attendance where lay Catholic forces are strong. And, with certain exceptions, the strongest areas of Catholic religious practice are the same as the bastions for Catholic groups. The West, the East, and the Center-South are the most important of these bastions. This correlation between religious practice and lay groups is as true for the MRP and the CFTC as it is for Catholic Action. This would indicate that groups of Catholic inspiration appeal to the same desires as Catholic Action does, even though Catholic inspiration groups are not officially tied to the Hierarchy.

Secondly, the absence of all Catholic activity in certain regions of differing economic and class composition indicates that Church strength might depend less on these social factors than historical and cultural differences among French regions. Events in French history have often served to reinforce the regional differences in Catholic strength. The separation of

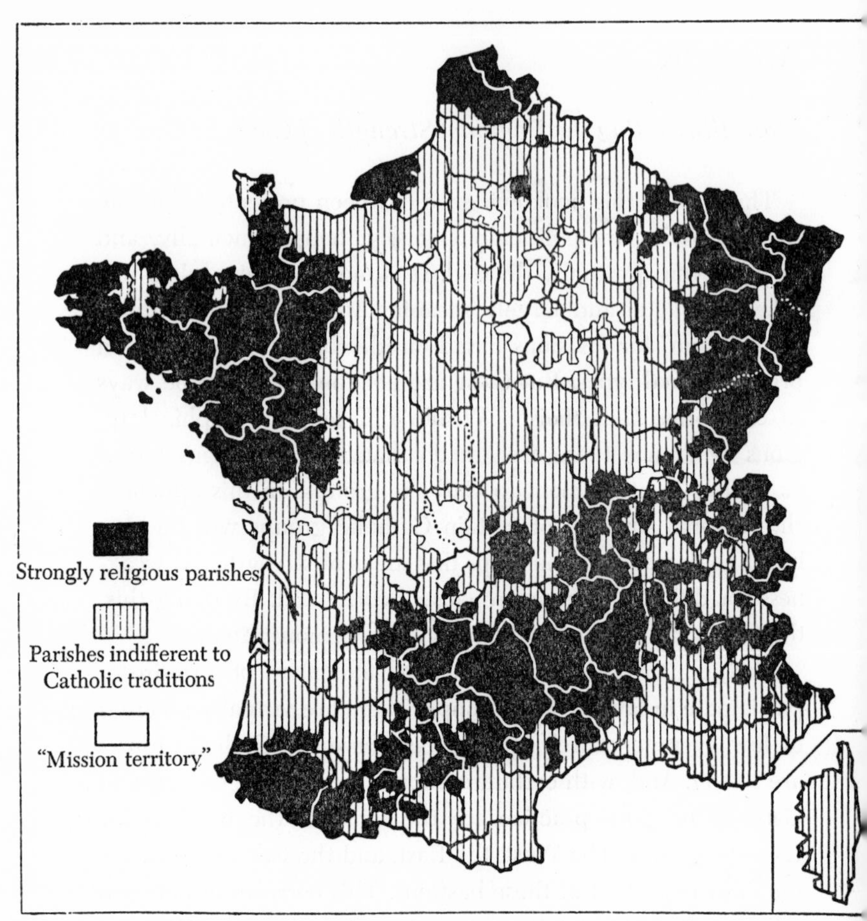

Map 1. Religious Practice in Rural France
Source: François Goguel, *Géographie des Elections Françaises, de 1870 à 1951* (Paris: Armand Colin, 1951), p. 135.

Church and state and the Barangé and Debré Laws are the most important examples in this century.

Map 1, indicating differences in church attendance in rural France, is the base map to which all the others should be referred. The map is not wholly satisfactory, since it omits religious practice in urban areas. However, it is the only one of its kind covering all of France. It is easy to find the three main bastions of religious practice from this map. Where practice is

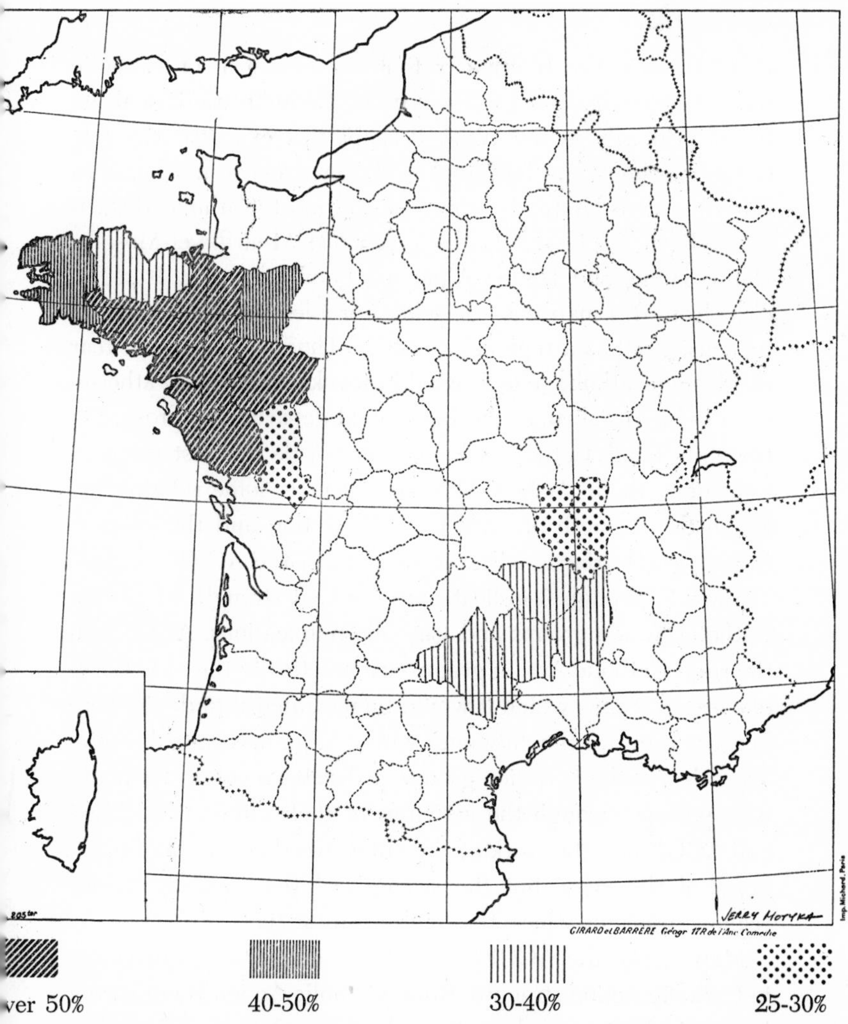

AP 2. Percentage of Children Attending Private Primary School, by Department
urce: *La Documentation Catholique*, LIV, No. 1254 (June 23, 1957), 827-28.

strong, the field is most fertile for the Catholic elite to have an impact, and for lay Catholic groups to be strong. The religious bastion in Southern France should be particularly pointed out, since it is often ignored.

In Map 2, Catholic schools in large numbers are shown to be only in areas of strong religious practice. But they are not found in all these areas. It appears that the existence of Catholic schools depends on a certain type of Catholic traditionalism, found primarily in the West. Perhaps this explains why few Catholic schools can be found in the progressive northeastern Catholic areas. Actually, some of the most Catholic departments have the fewest Catholic schools: Meurthe-et-Moselle, Haute-Saône, and Hautes-Alpes are good examples. It seems clear from this map that the school problem in France should be considered as a regional question. Those bishops who fear that losing Catholic schools would provoke widespread atheism seem to be mistaken, as the last-named departments prove. On the other hand, Catholic schools may not be the best preparation for Catholic Action. Although there is some relation between the strength of rural Catholic Action and this map, it is greatly at variance with the strength of the ACGF.

Maps 3 through 6 indicate the regional strength of certain Catholic Action groups and Catholic publications. ACGF and the rural Catholic Action groups are practically the only Catholic organizations which it would be meaningful to depict here because they are the only ones with a large mass membership. The other Catholic Action groups, as has been noted, are mainly important through the activities of their elites. With MFR and ACGF too, the work of the elites overshadows the importance of the mass, but the strength of the mass in various regions indicates where the elite has most success.

Map 4, like the ACGF map, shows interesting deficiencies in Catholic Action strength. Rural Catholic Action is not strong in certain Eastern and Northern bastions of Catholicism. The East, especially the rural areas of Alsace-Lorraine, has never been culturally or linguistically integrated into France, which could explain the difficulties of the MFR there. Perhaps the mechanized, "big-business" character of farming in the North lessens the appeal of rural Catholic Action there.

For both ACGF and MFR, local conditions often determine the success or failure of a group. If a bishop does not give

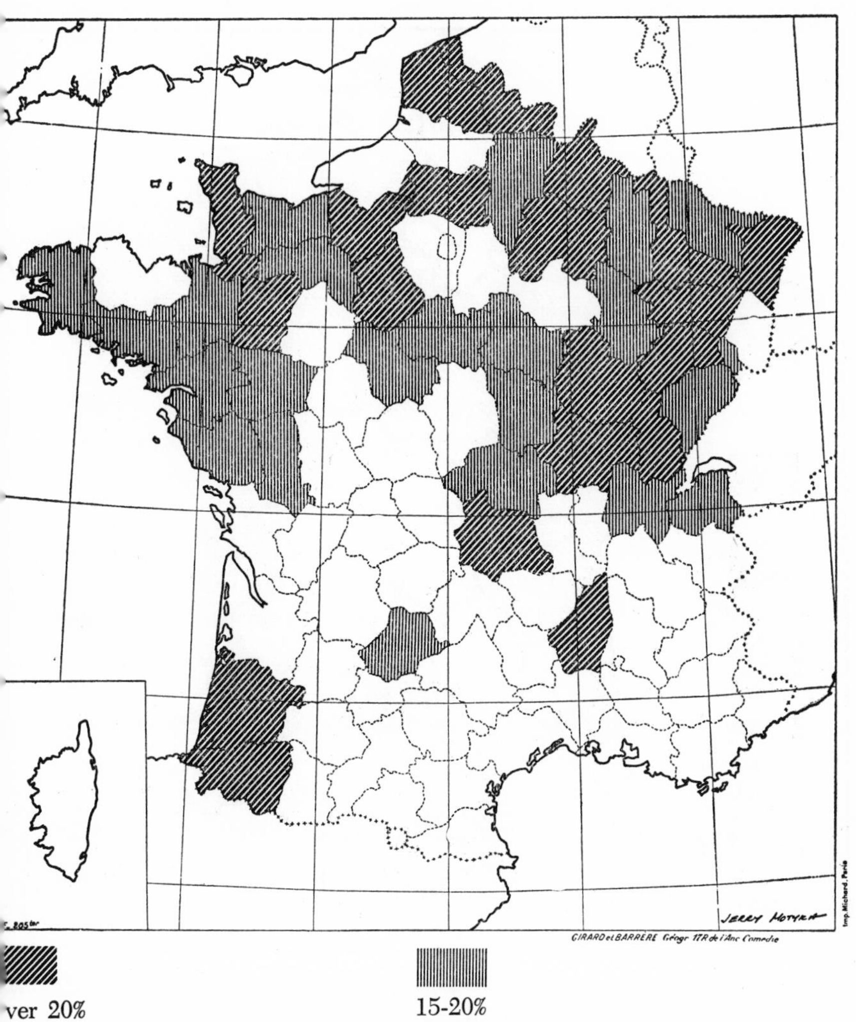

Map 3. Percentage of ACGF Members Among Frenchwomen, by Department
ource: Private files of Mlle. des Gachons, Head of Civic Education, ACGF.

wholehearted support to a particular Catholic Action group, it will not succeed. This, according to information given by one of the directors of ACGF, explains the weakness of ACGF in Côtes-du-Nord.

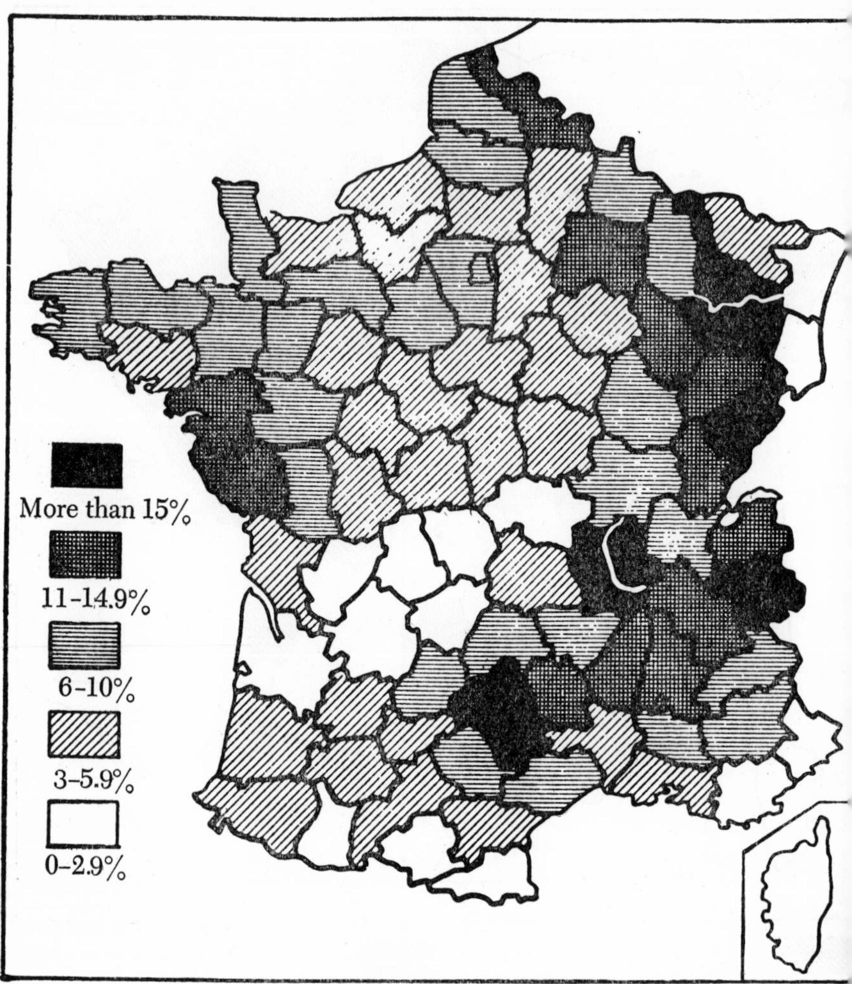

MAP 4. Percentage of Rural Catholic Action Sympathizers, by Department. Proportion of subscribers to Rural Catholic Action mass publications as compare to the active farming population of each Department.

Source: Jacques Fauvet and Henri Mendras, *Les Paysans et la Politique* (Paris: Armand Colin, 1958), p. 358.

Pèlerin is said to be particularly popular among rural Catholics, although it is designed to be a general interest Catholic magazine. The other important general magazine, *Vie Catholique Illustrée*, has a content that probably appeals more to the urban or "citified" Catholics. However, both publications have

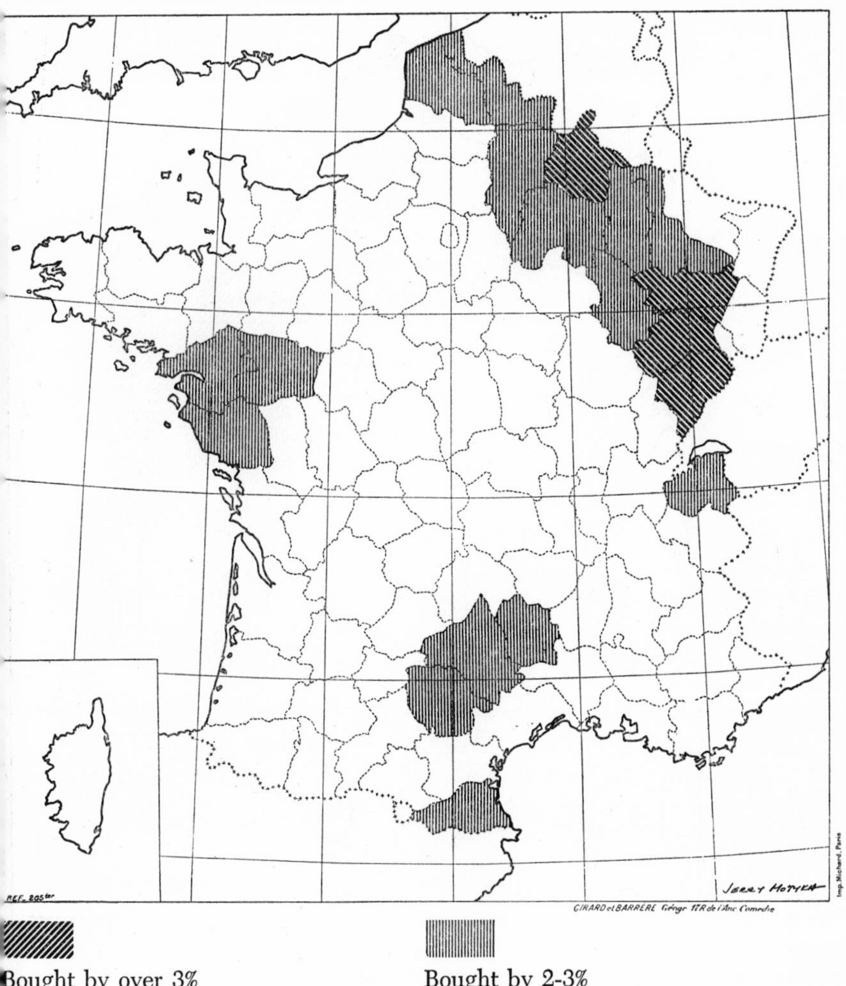

Bought by over 3% Bought by 2-3%

Map 5. Circulation of *Pèlerin* as Percentage of Department Population
Source: Private files of *Bonne Presse.* Figures for 1957.

virtually the same centers of strength; they are especially strong in the Northeast and both lack strong centers in the Center and Southwest. Most probably the strength or weakness of each publication is due to the work of local Catholic press committees. The different scales used for these two publications were necessary because of the tendency of *Pèlerin* to overestimate its strength. Both maps are simple approximations

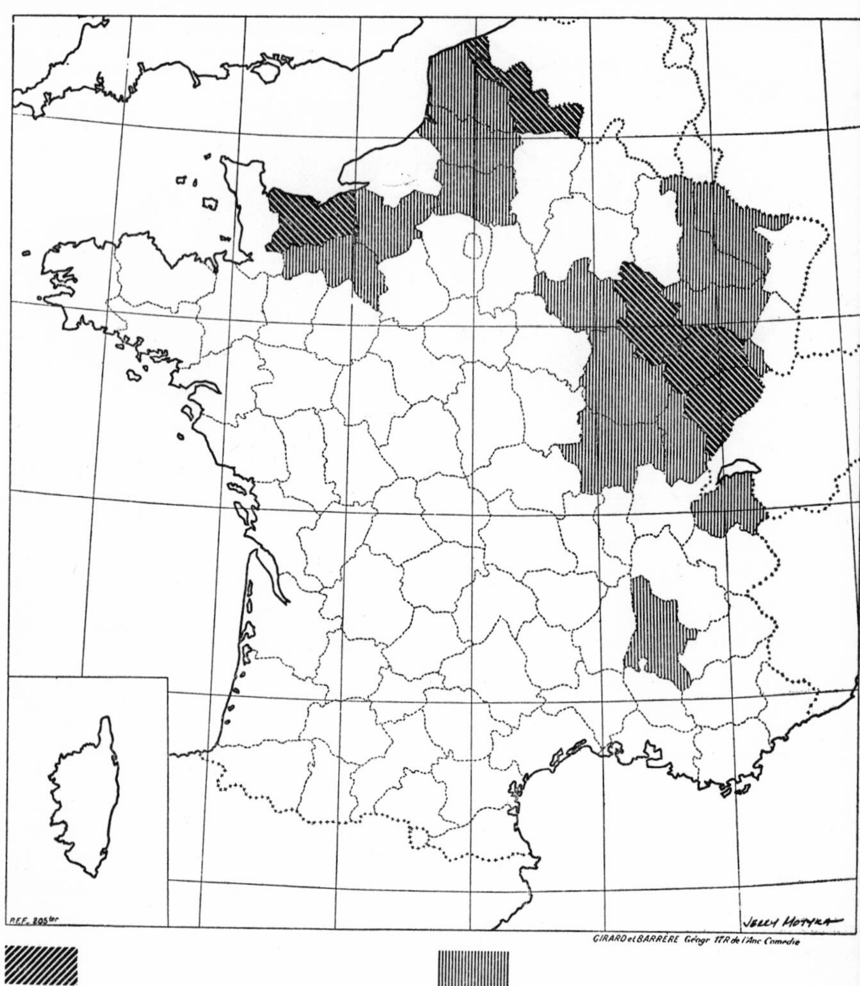

MAP 6. Circulation of *Vie Catholique Illustrée* as Percentage of Department Population.

Source: Private files of *Vie Catholique Illustrée.*

and should be taken only to show the regions where each publication sells best.

Map 7 shows very clearly how the CFTC relies on Catholics. The areas where the CFTC is the strongest trade union correspond exactly with the bastions of church attendance given in Map 1. However, there are relatively few areas where the

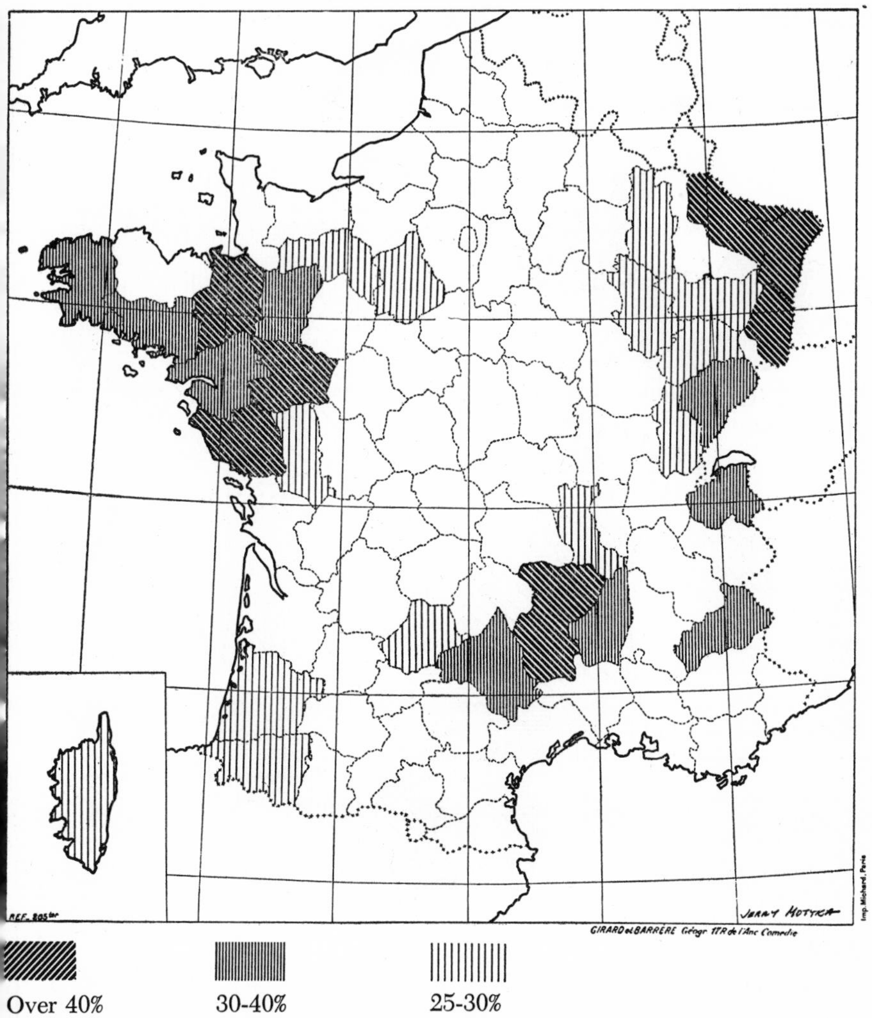

MAP 7. Percentage of CFTC Members Among All Unionized Workers, by Department.

Source. "Les élections au collège de Salariés des Caisses Primaires Départementales de Securité Sociale; Scrutin du 27 Novembre, 1955," in *Journal Officiel*, December 27, 1955, pp. 12614-12616.

CFTC does not have at least 12 per cent of the organized union strength. This is a good indication that it can attract workers who are not practicing Catholics, in addition to practically all those who are.

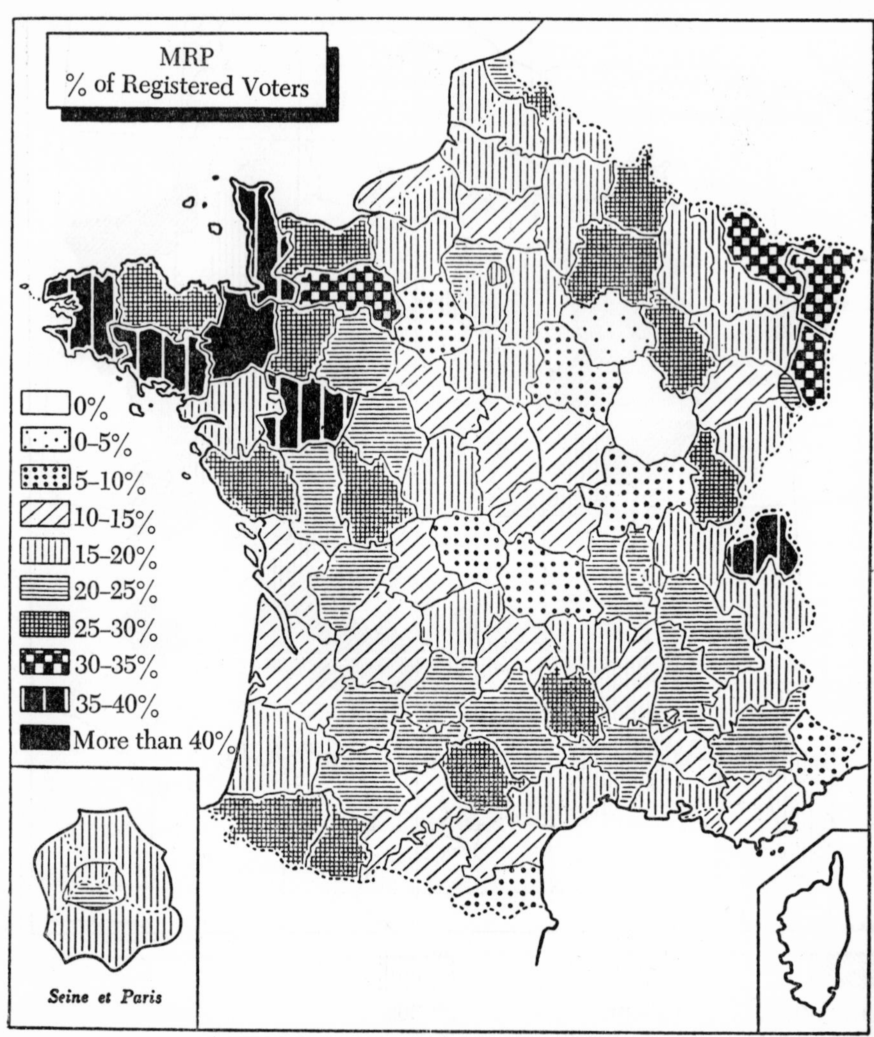

Map 8. MRP Vote in 1946, as Percentage of Registered Voters by Department
Source: François Goguel, *Géographie des Elections Françaises, de 1870 à 1951* (Paris: Armand Colin, 1951), p. 97.

Maps 8 through 11 offer interesting comparisons of the MRP regional strength from 1946 to 1958. However, the scales of the maps are not the same. Goguel considers the percentage of MRP votes as compared to the number of registered voters, while the Ministry of the Interior in 1956 considered the MRP

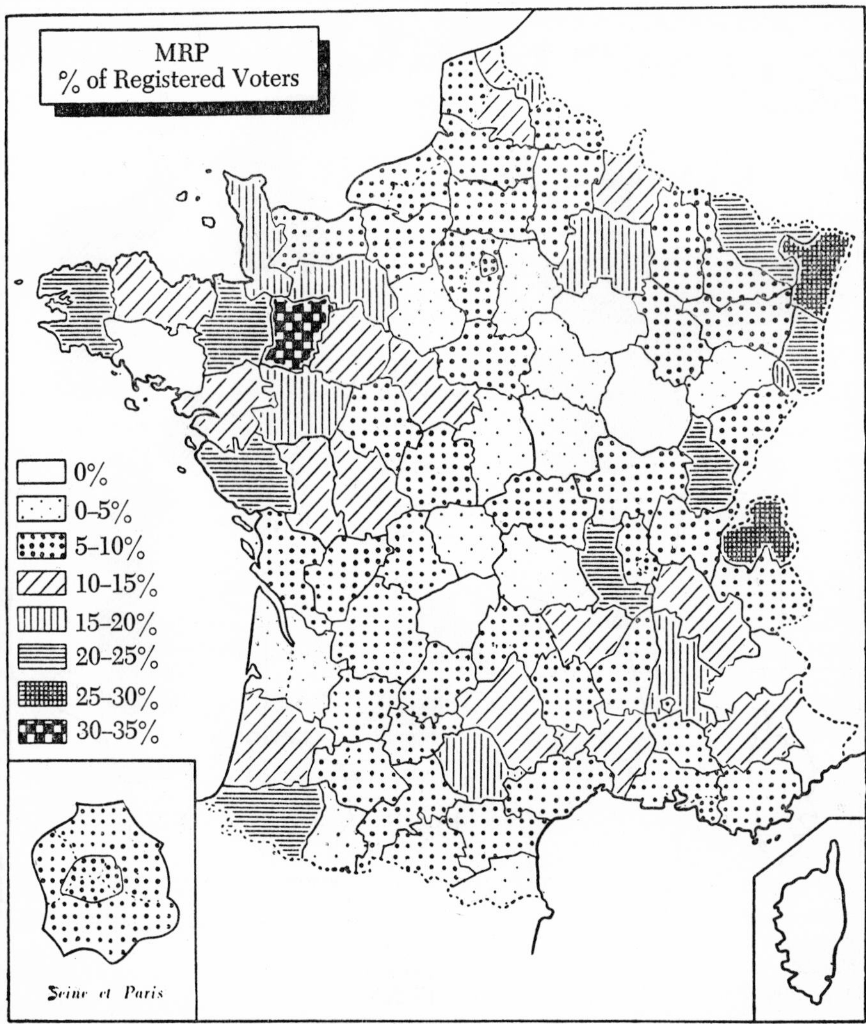

MAP 9. MRP Vote in 1951, as Percentage of Registered Voters by Department
Source: François Goguel, *Géographie des Elections Francaises, de 1870 à 1951* (Paris: Armand Colin, 1951), p. 113.

percentage of the number of votes cast. And in 1958, the election was based on single-member districts for the first time since prewar days. These differences have made it impossible to do an accurate correlation for all postwar elections based on the same criteria.

Despite the different scales, it is possible to make some

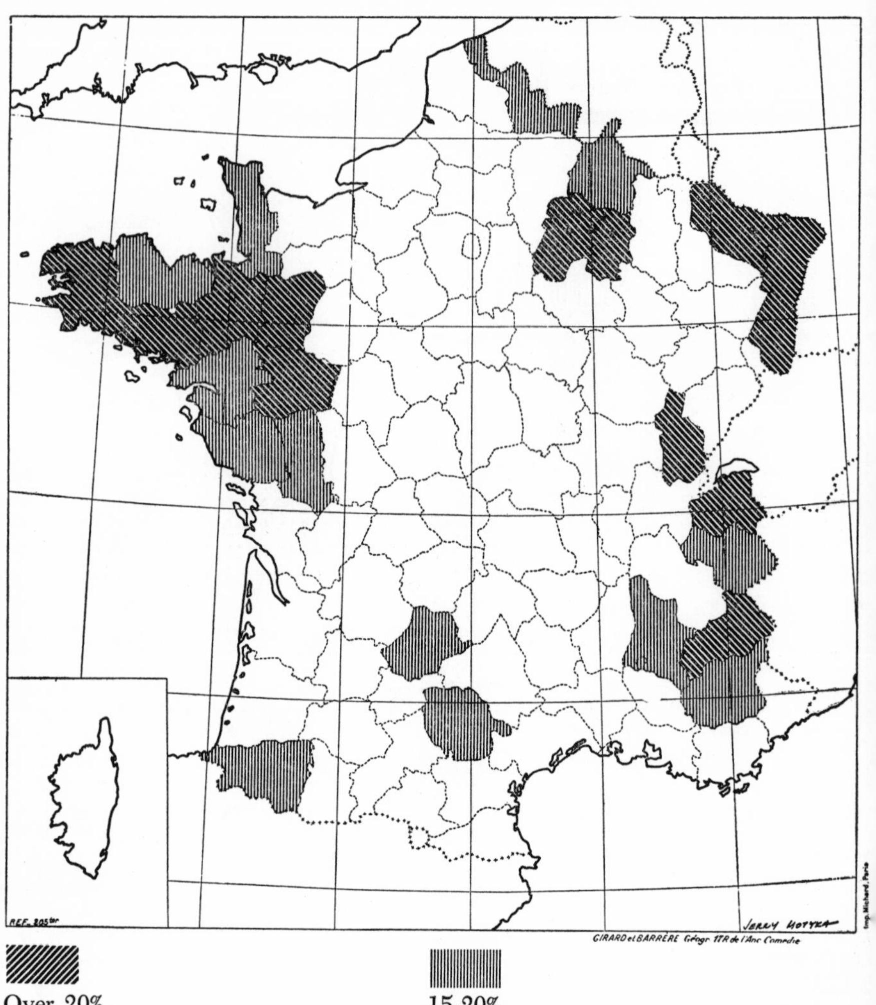

Map 10. MRP Vote in 1956 as Percentage of Votes Cast, by Department
Source: Adapted from Ministère de l'Intérieur, *Les Elections Legislatives du 2 Janvier, 1956* (Paris: La Documentation Française, 1957), p. 87.

general observations on the recent evolution of MRP strength. From 1956 to the 1958 election, the MRP definitely lost strength in Haut-Rhin, one of its bastions, Hautes-Alpes, Basses-Alpes, and Lot. At the same time, it seems to have developed new strength in areas beyond its former bastions of East and West. It is not surprising that the MRP is spreading into the South-

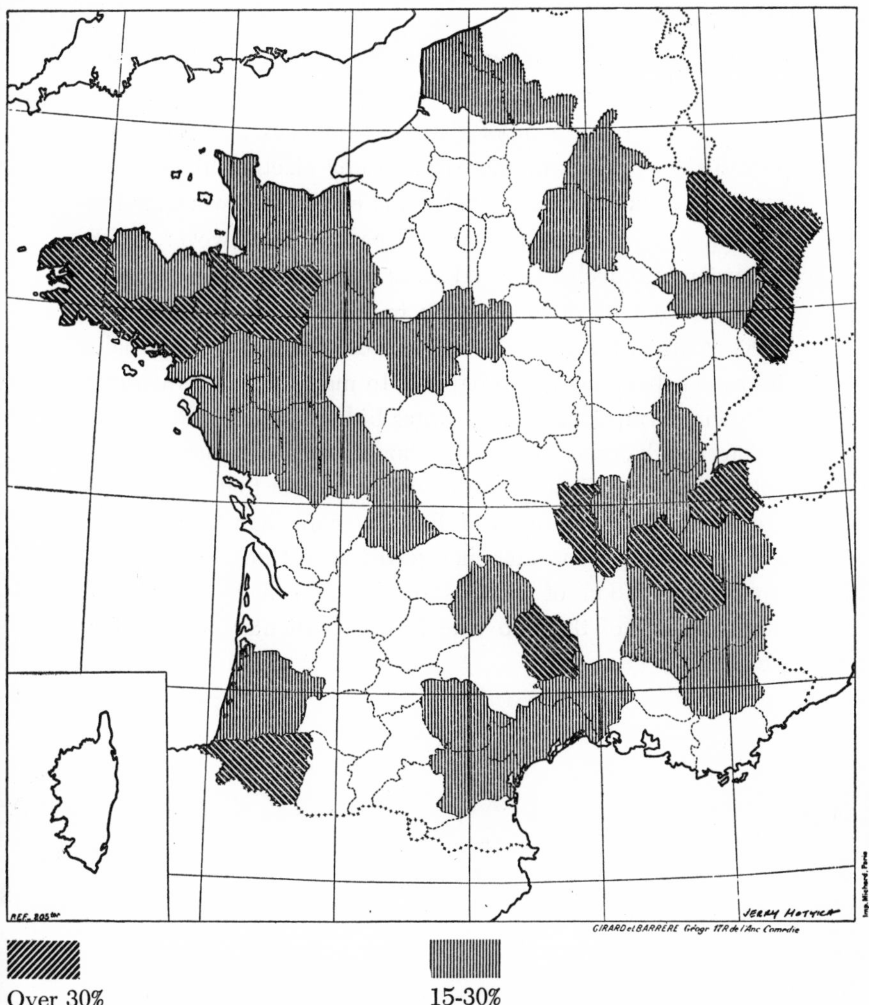

MAP 11. MRP Vote in 1958, First Round, Indicating the Departments in Which at Least One Voting District Gave the MRP More Than 15% of the Vote

Source: *Institut d'Etudes Politiques*, unpublished study of the 1958 elections.

east, since by every other criterion the departments in this region have remained fervently Catholic. It is interesting, however, that the MRP seems to be spreading eastward from its Western bastion into the relatively dechristianized Center of France.

If the MRP expansion into relatively non-Catholic areas continues, it might indicate that the patient activity of the Catholic Action-trained elite in these areas is paying dividends. There is as yet no absolute proof that this elite has materially improved the positions of the MRP in any election, though we have every reason to suspect that the elite would work for the MRP more than for other political parties. If, however, MRP expansion into dechristianized areas does not continue, we can speculate that its good showing in 1958 was due to special circumstances: the 1958 election was often based on personalities rather than on party programs. In many electoral districts, right-wing sympathizers of Georges Bidault, who could appeal to voters with conservative or authoritarian preferences, ran as MRP candidates. Finally, one should remember that even in the most dechristianized areas of France, more than 15 per cent of the population consider themselves good Catholics. An unusual combination of circumstances might have induced a large majority of them to vote in this particular election for the MRP.

Bibliographical Essay
Index

Bibliographical Essay

It would be pretentious and unrealistic to attempt to assemble all the published material from and about French Catholic groups, since there is a superabundance of such material. Even the Catholic publications of a certain political value comprise an enormous mass. However, in the midst of all this abundance, there is a scarcity of really significant material. Too many of the available Catholic publications contain little more than piety, suggestions on how to construct the best possible world, and subtle constructions to show philosophical originality. The bibliographical references to follow are intended to be as useful as possible to the researcher and scholar. Only those publications which seem most significant for the perspective of this book have been selected. For convenience, references are arranged according to chapter, and brief comments follow particularly interesting publications.

A half-dozen reference works have been particularly useful. They have been drawn on so frequently that no attempt is made to include all the articles read in them here in the bibliography. These reference works include the following: *Annuaire Catholique de France*, published in Paris by the *Presses Continentales*, with revised editions every two or three years; *Documentation Catholique*, published by the *Bonne Presse*, and *Informations Catholiques Internationales*, published by *Vie Catholique Illustrée*; the Jesuit magazine *Etudes*, and the Paris Dominican magazine *Signes du Temps*, formerly *Vie Intellectuelle; La Chronique Sociale*, the unofficial organ of the *Semaines Sociales*; and finally, the Catholic daily newspaper, *La Croix*.

In addition to the above publications, three libraries have furnished extensive information on Catholic groups: the Jesuit library at *Action Populaire*, the library of *Union des Oeuvres*, and the library of the *Institut d'Etudes Politiques*. These libraries have been of inestimable value in writing the book; of course, it is not possible to mention all the useful items in them individually.

BIBLIOGRAPHICAL ESSAY

A good part of the information in the book has come from personal interviews. Many interviews, like certain published works, are germane for more than one part of the book. When this is the case, the interviews and the books are mentioned only in the chapter where they are most relevant.

General Background for the Book

Almond, Gabriel. *The American People and Foreign Policy.* New York: Harcourt, Brace & Co., 1950.

Aron, Robert. *Précis de l'Unité Française.* Paris: Charlot, 1945.

Baboulène, Jean, *et al. La France, Crise du Régime, Crise de la Nation.* Paris: Economie et Humanisme, 1957.

Barrès, Maurice. *Les Diverses Familles Spirituelles de la France.* Paris: Emile-Paul Frères, 1917.

Berl, Emmanuel. *La France Irréelle.* Paris: Grasset, 1957.

Blanchard, Paul. *American Freedom and Catholic Power.* Boston: Beacon Press, 1949.

Catalogne, Gérard de. *Les Compagnons du Spirituel.* Montréal: Editions de l'Arbre, 1945.

Cronin, John F. *Catholic Social Principles.* Milwaukee: Bruce, 1950.

Daulnaie, J. *Si les Catholiques Voulaient.* Paris: By the author, 1956.

Davey, Elizabeth (ed.). *France in Crisis.* New York: H. W. Wilson, 1957.

Goguel, François. *France Under the Fourth Republic.* Ithaca: Cornell University Press, 1952.

Goguel, François, *Le Régime Politique Français.* Paris: Editions du Seuil, 1955.

Labasse, Jean. *Hommes de Droite, Hommes de Gauche.* Paris: Economie et Humanisme, 1947.

Lacroix, Jean. *Marxisme, Existentialisme, Personnalisme: Présence de l'Eternité dans le Temps.* Paris: Presses Universitaires de France, 1950.

Lüthy, Herbert. *France Against Herself.* Trans. Eric Mosbacher. New York: Praeger, 1955.

Marabuto, Paul. *Les Partis Politiques et les Mouvements Sociaux Sous la Quatrième République.* Paris: Recueil Sirey, 1948.

Matthews, Ronald. *Death of the Fourth Republic.* London: Eyre, 1954.

Meynaud, Jean. *Les Groupes de Pression en France.* Paris: Armand Colin, 1958.

Morazé, Charles. *Les Français et la République.* Paris: Armand Colin, 1956.

Oakeshott, Michael. *The Social and Political Doctrines of Contemporary Europe.* New York: Macmillan, 1947.

Priouret, Roger. *La République des Partis.* Paris: Elan, 1947.

Rémond, René. *La Droite en France de 1815 à Nos Jours.* Paris: Aubier, 1954.

Siegfried, André. *De la Troisième à la Quatrième République.* Paris: Grasset, 1956.

Thibaudet, Albert. *Les Idées Politiques de la France.* Paris: Librairie Stock, 1932.

Thomson, David. *Democracy in France: The Third and the Fourth Republics.* 3rd ed. London: Oxford University Press, 1958.

Williams, Philip. *Politics in Postwar France.* 2nd ed. London: Longmans Green, 1958.

Bibliography for Chapter 1

For this introductory chapter, the interviews and published works are particularly important. Most of the references mentioned here were drawn on in succeeding chapters. This is especially true for the key books, which are annotated. It should be noted that a large number of references have particular importance for the concluding chapter, just as many works cited under Chapter 9 are also relevant for Chapter 1.

CHAPTER 1: INTERVIEWS

Adrien Dansette, historian and writer, Paris, July 7, 1959. (Unless otherwise noted, interviews were held in Paris)

Professor Henry W. Ehrmann, November 25, 1958.

Jacques Fauvet, journalist for *Le Monde*, July 11, 1958.

Professor François Goguel, Secretary-General of the French Senate, July 7, 1958.

Professor Roy Macridis, November 25, 1958.

Professor Charles Micaud, Charlottesville, Va., April 8, 1958.

Father Joseph Moody, French history scholar, New York City, January 30, 1958.

Professor René Rémond, professor at *Institut d'Etudes Politiques*, Paris, many times during 1958-60. The first interview was July 1, 1958; the last was July 1, 1960.

André Siegfried, of the *Académie Française*, July 12, 1958.

Professor Philip Williams, July 21, 1958, and July 13, 1959.

CHAPTER 1: BOOKS

Brayance, Alain. *Anatomie du Parti Communiste Français*. Paris: Denoel Presses d'Aujourd'hui, 1952.

A study of the Communist Party itself and the various groups which gravitate in its orbit. The viewpoint is close to the method of this book, though sources are not given.

Chaigneau, V.-L. *L'Organisation de l'Eglise Catholique en France*. Paris: Editions Spes, 1955.

———. *Les Ouvriers dans la Moisson: Institutions et Associations Catholiques en France*. Paris: Editions Spes, 1955.

The two books of Chaigneau are especially useful for their addresses and descriptions of ecclesiastical, Catholic Action, and social action groups. However, the descriptions are of the formal-legal variety, so are insufficient by themselves.

Dansette, Adrien. *Destin du Catholicisme Français: 1926-1956*. Paris: Flammarion, 1957.

One of the key books for this study. Unlike Dansette's earlier volumes on the history of French Catholicism, this book considers only selected Catholic groups and selected problems. It has as a main theme the Catholic effort to spread into "dechristianized" social classes; consequently, most of the book considers Catholic Action and the worker-priest problem. But despite its "apostolic" preoccupations, the book discusses many political issues with perception.

Darbon, Michel. *Le Conflit entre la Droite et la Gauche dans le Catholicisme Français: 1930-1953*. Toulouse: Privat, 1953.

Not too enlightening, but the most extensive treatment of the well-known theme that French Catholicism is split into two parts.

Dogan, Mattei, and Narbonne, Jacques. *Les Françaises Face à la Politique: Comportement Politique et Condition Sociale*. Paris: Armand Colin, 1955.

Interesting statements in various parts of the book on the impact of Catholicism on French women.

Ehrmann, Henry W. (ed.). *Interest Groups on Four Continents*. Pittsburgh: University of Pittsburgh Press, 1958.

Contributions by Merle and Lavau concern French pressure groups.

———. *Organized Business in France*. Princeton: Princeton University Press, 1957.

Fogarty, Michael. *Christian Democracy in Western Europe: 1820-1953*. South Bend: Notre Dame University Press, 1957.

Another key book for this study. Although the book is wide in scope it has a good grasp of the basic evolutions within the Western European Catholic groups. There is no place to show the complex ties of each organization to the ecclesiastical nucleus, but Fogarty explains quite well the philosophical ties linking most European Catholic groups with one another.

Folliet, Joseph. *Présence de l'Eglise*. (Les Chrétiens au Carrefour, No. 2.) Lyon: Editions de la Chronique Sociale, 1949.

A series of essays on various Catholic organizations, similar to the organizations treated in this book. But spiritual and metaphysical questions predominate in Folliet's book.

Frédérix, Pierre. *L'Etat des Forces en France*, Paris: Gallimard, 1935.

Garaudy, Roger. *L'Eglise, le Communisme, et les Chrétiens*. Paris: Editions Sociales, 1949.

The institutions of the Church as seen through the warped vision of a Communist theoretician.

Golob, Eugene O. *The "Isms": A History and Evaluation.* New York: Harper & Bros., 1954.

Golob, like Thibaudet, presents "social Catholicism" as one of the main political philosophies of our time. Here the focus is on general background, without specific reference to France.

Guetzkow, Harold. *Multiple Loyalties: Theoretical Approach to a Problem in International Organization.* Publication 4 of the Center for Research on World Political Institutions. Princeton: Princeton University Press, 1955.

Hayes, Carlton J. H. *France: A Nation of Patriots.* New York: Columbia University Press, 1930.

An early and pioneering work dealing with the French educational system and other means to instill loyalty patterns in Frenchmen.

Jacquemet, G. (ed.). *Catholicisme: Encyclopédie en Sept Volumes.* Paris: Letouzey et Ané, 1950-.

There are seven projected volumes for this ambitious encyclopedia. The encyclopedia contains many authoritative articles—for example, "Action Catholique" by Mgr. Guerry, Archbishop of Cambrai. But events move so rapidly that the first part of the alphabet may be outdated when the last volume is published!

Latreille, André, and Siegfried, André. *Les Forces Religieuses et la Vie Politique: Le Catholicisme et le Protestantisme.* Paris: Armand Colin, 1951.

A general study of Church-state relations, not just confined to France.

Le Bras, Gabriel, *et al. La Société Française Contemporaine: Etudes Religieuses et Politiques.* Paris: Bibliothèque de Science Politique, 1948.

A mimeographed summary of courses given at the *Institut d'Etudes Politiques* on French Catholicism, Protestantism, and Judaism.

Lebret, L.-J. *De l'Efficacité Politique du Chrétien.* Paris: Editions de l'Economie et Humanisme, 1947.

A list of practical suggestions for operating Catholic Action and social action groups on the local and department levels.

Macaire, André. *Politique et Catholicisme dans la France Contemporaine.* Paris: Haloua, 1945.

The author is a Catholic neo-Hegelian. The book deals with general ideologies of left and right, with some treatment of how Catholics act when faced with social crises.

Maritain, Jacques. *Man and the State.* Chicago: University of Chicago Press, 1951.

Marteaux, Jacques. *L'Eglise de France Devant la Révolution Marxiste.* Vol. I: *Les Voies Insondables: 1936-1944.* Paris: Table Ronde, 1958.

A detailed but poorly organized book where fact and opinion are not clearly distinguished. The author is far to the Catholic right, and the book is a disguised polemic against Christian Democracy. A sequel, *Les Voies Exposées: 1944-1956*, has not yet been published.

Martin-Saint-Léon, Etienne. *Les Sociétés de la Nation.* Paris: Editions Spes, 1930.

A sophisticated study of the constituent elements of the French nation, with good historical material on many French social forces.

Moody, Joseph N. *Church and Society: Catholic Social and Political Thought and Movements, 1789-1950.* New York: Arts, Inc., 1953.

Part II of this vast *tour d'horizon* deals with France. The article by Vignaux on the CFTC is particularly interesting.

Rose, Arnold M. *Theory and Method in the Social Sciences.* Minneapolis: University of Minnesota Press, 1954.

Note Chapter IV, "Voluntary Associations in France."

Suffert, Georges. *Les Catholiques et la Gauche.* Paris: François Maspero, 1960.

Suffert is one of the "younger generation," who were reared

in Catholic Action youth groups and went on quite naturally into adult Catholic movements. A "man of the left," Suffert has been associated with *Témoignage Chrétien* and *Esprit*. Few Catholic intellectuals have been praised and damned more than he. His book contains an instructive study of the institutions of French Catholicism, against the background of the struggle between left and right. Also Suffert includes many personal accounts of dealings with Catholics of all ideological backgrounds. In the end Suffert is rather pleased with the integrity and the charity of most French Catholics.

CHAPTER 1: ARTICLES AND MISCELLANEOUS

Almond, Gabriel A. "Comparative Political Systems," in Eulau, Heinz, *et al. Political Behavior: A Reader in Theory and Research*. Glencoe, Ill.: The Free Press, 1956, pp. 34-42.

Almond, Gabriel; Cole, Taylor; Macridis, Roy. "A Suggested Research Strategy in Western European Government and Politics," *American Political Science Review*, XLIX, No. 4 (December 1955), 1042-49.

Brown, Bernard. "Pressure Politics in France," *Journal of Politics*, XVIII, No. 4 (November 1956), 702-719.

"Le Catholicisme en France," Institut Français d'Opinion Publique. *Sondages*, XIV, No. 4, 1952. Entire issue.

Dansette, Adrien. "Contemporary French Catholicism," in Gurian, W., and Fitzsimons, M. (eds.). *The Catholic Church in World Affairs*. South Bend: Notre Dame University Press, 1954, pp. 230-274.

Domenach, J.-M. "Religion and Politics," *Confluence*, III, No. 4 (December 1954), 390-401.

Lavau, Georges. "L'Activité de Pression Politique des Groupes Autres que les Partis Politiques (France)." *Program of the International Political Science Association*. University of Pittsburgh, September 10-13, 1957.

Maitre, Jacques. "Les Sociologies du Catholicisme Français," *Cahiers Internationaux de Sociologie*, XXIV (January-June 1958), 104-124.

Poulat, Emile. "Religion et Politique," *Critique*, No. 123-124 (August-September 1957), 757-770.

An analysis of the weak points in Dansette's *Destin.*

"Problèmes du Catholicisme Français," *La Nef*, xi, No. 5 (January 1954), entire issue.

Another key book. A number of noteworthy Catholics discuss certain problems, among which are the school question, the worker-priest controversy, and relations with German Catholics.

Stern, Eric. "Spontaneous Group References in France," *Public Opinion Quarterly*, xvii (1953), 208-217.

None of the interviewed Frenchmen mentioned spontaneously the Church or other religious institutions (p. 213).

Bibliography for Chapter 2

Two sources of information have been particularly useful in providing historical references for this book. One is the *Bibliothèque Nationale*, which has a good cross-filing system for questions antedating the Second World War. The other is the material in the French National Archives open to the public. In the Archives as a rule material is classified "secret" until it is fifty years old; therefore, the author had access to most of the official reports and documents before and immediately after the separation of church and state in 1905. The most interesting sources were found in the series F^{19} 1970 (news reports of the separation), and F^{19} 1980 (official reports on bishops' attitudes toward the separation). However, in neither of these categories were there any startling discoveries; the information merely supplemented books already published.

A number of valuable bibliographic references were furnished by Emile Poulat, of the *Centre d'Etude de Sociologie Religieuse*, and by Professor René Rémond. All these references are not included here, because the chapter is not designed to provide a complete account of the separation controversy.

CHAPTER 2: BOOKS

Barbier, Emmanuel. *Histoire du Catholicisme Libéral et du Catholicisme Social en France, 1870-1914.* 5 vols. Bordeaux: Imprimerie Cadoret, 1923.

Indispensable for its references and source material, this book is not generally available in the U.S. Abbé Barbier is on the Catholic right, but he does not let his partisanship interfere with his good scholarship. Volumes III and IV are particularly noteworthy.

Biton, Louis. *La Démocratie Chrétienne dans la Politique Française.* Angers: Siraudeau, 1955.

Bonnefous, G. *Histoire Politique de la Troisième République.* Vol. I: 1906-1914. Paris: Presses Universitaires de France, 1956.

Bonnefous, under the name of Daniel, had already edited the old *Année Politique,* which last appeared in 1906. This new history tries to fill the gap between that year and the reappearance of *Année Politique* after World War II.

Briand, Aristide. *La Séparation.* 2 vols. Paris: Bibliothèque Charpentier, 1908 and 1909.

Brogan, D. W. *France Under the Republic: The Development of Modern France, 1870-1939.* New York: Harper & Bros., 1940.

Brugerette, J. *Le Prêtre Français dans la Société Contemporaine.* Vol. II: *Vers la Séparation de l'Eglise et de l'Etat (1871-1908).* Paris: P. Lethielleux, 1935.

A more "progressive" interpretation than Barbier. The third volume, which carries the history down into the interwar period, is also helpful.

Capéran, Louis. *Histoire Contemporaine de la Laïcité Française.* Paris: Marcel Rivière, 1957.

Book by an eminent scholar; however, stops before the separation. Other volumes will follow.

Crouzil, Lucien. *Quarante Ans de Séparation (1905-1945).* Paris: Didier, 1946.

Dansette, Adrien. *Histoire Religieuse de la France Contem-*

poraine. Vol. I: *De la Révolution à la Troisième République.* Vol. II: *Sous la Troisième République.* Paris: Flammarion, 1951.

The two histories of Dansette, plus the later *Destin du Catholicisme Français* give the most comprehensive picture of French Catholicism written by a single scholar.

Debidour, A. *L'Eglise Catholique et l'Etat Sous la Troisième République, 1870-1906.* Paris: Alcan, 1909.

The *laïque* side of the question. This book complements Lecanuet and Barbier, so that we can see the separation controversy in the eyes of all main protagonists.

Duroselle, J.-B. *Les Débuts du Catholicisme Social en France, 1822-1870.* Paris: Presses Universitaires de France, 1951.

The definitive work on the subject. Superb scholarship, though perhaps too many minor details.

Ferrata, Cardinal Dominique. *Memoires: Ma Nonciature en France.* Paris: Action Populaire, 1922.

Flornoy, Eugène. *La Lutte par l'Association: L'Action Libérale Populaire.* Paris: Lecoffre, 1907.

Useful book on an often-ignored party of Catholic inspiration. But Flornoy puts perhaps too much importance in the ALP.

Goguel, François. *La Politique des Partis sous la Troisième République.* Paris: Editions du Seuil, 1946.

Goyau, Georges. *Catholicisme et Politique.* Paris: Editions de la Revue des Jeunes, 1923.

Guerry, Mgr. E. *L'Eglise Catholique en France Sous l'Occupation.* Paris: Flammarion, 1947.

Guignebert, Charles. *Le Problème Religieux dans la France d'Aujourd'hui.* Paris: Librairie Garnier Frères, 1922.

Guillemin, Henri. *Histoire des Catholiques Français au Dix-Neuvième Siècle.* Genève: Au Milieu du Monde, 1947.

Hoog, Georges. *Histoire du Catholicisme Social en France, 1871-1931.* Paris: Domat-Monchrestien, 1946.

Jacques, Léon. *Les Partis Politiques sous la Troisième République.* Paris: Sirey, 1913.

A study of the doctrines, programs, organization, and tactics of political parties which is quite advanced for its day.

Jamois, Jean. "L'Eglise Catholique et les Catholiques dans l'Etat en France depuis 1919." Unpublished Thesis, Institut d'Etudes Politiques, Paris, 1951.

Lecanuet, R. P. *Les Signes Avant-Coureurs de la Séparation (1894-1910)*. Vol. III of *L'Eglise de France sous la Troisième République*. Paris: Alcan, 1930.

Very detailed on the problem of religious teaching orders; less good on other points. The author is a priest, but also a *Dreyfusard.*

Méjan, L.-V. *La Séparation des Eglises et de l'Etat.* Paris: Presses Universitaires, 1959.

Micaud, Charles. *The French Right and Nazi Germany.* Durham: Duke University Press, 1943.

Montagnini, Mgr. *Les Fiches Pontificales.* Paris: Nourry, 1908.

Revelations of the activities of a papal nuncio, from documents taken from the former nuncio in Paris.

Morienval, Jean. *Sur L'Histoire de la Presse Catholique en France.* Paris: Alsatia, 1936.

The only substantial book on the subject before World War II. Circulation figures, unfortunately, are lacking for most prewar publications.

Narfon, J. de. *La Séparation des Eglises et de l'Etat: Origines —Etapes—Bilan.* Paris: Alcan, 1912.

The author was a journalist for *Figaro.* Though a Catholic, he favored the separation.

Paris, Edmond. *Le Vatican Contre la France.* Paris: Fischbacher, 1957.

This book is bitterly anti-Catholic, anti-Nazi, anti-Arab, and pro-colonialist. A very peculiar viewpoint!

Piou, Jacques. *Le Ralliement et son Histoire.* Paris: Spes, 1928.

By the "grand old man" of *Action Libérale Populaire.*

Poulat, Emile. *Les Semaines Religieuses: Approche Historique.* Paris: Editions Sociales, 1957.

A study of the origin, circulation figures, and metamorphoses of every *semaine religieuse* in France. Painstaking scholarship

Raphael, Paul. *La République et l'Eglise Romaine: De L'Esprit Nouveau à l'Union Sacrée.* Paris: Bibliothèque Jean Macé, 1948.

An anticlerical successor to Debidour.

Rémond, René. *Les Catholiques, le Communisme, et les Crises, 1929-1939.* Paris: Armand Colin, 1960.

Rollet, Henri. *L'Action Sociale des Catholiques en France, 1871-1914.* Vol. I: 1871-1901. Paris: Boivin, 1947. Vol. II: 1901-1914. Bruges: Desclée de Brouwer, 1958.

The worthy sequel to Duroselle, written by the head of *Action Catholique Générale des Hommes.*

———. *Albert de Mun et le Parti Catholique.* Paris: Boivin, 1949.

———. *Sur le Chantier Sociale: L'Action Sociale des Catholiques en France (1870-1940).* Lyon: Editions de la Chronique Sociale, 1955.

Seippel, Paul. *Les Deux Frances et leurs Origines Historiques.* Lausanne: Payot, 1905.

The thesis is that France is permanently divided into "clericals" and "anticlericals." Written at the height of the Dreyfus affair.

La Séparation de l'Eglise et de l'Etat en France: Exposé et Documents. Rome: Typographie Vaticane, 1905.

A white paper from the Vatican, proving that it is not responsible for the events leading up to the separation.

Thibaudet, Albert. *Les Idées Politiques de la France.* Paris: Stock, 1932.

CHAPTER 2: ARTICLES

"L'Anticléricalisme en France," *Informations Catholiques Internationales*, November 15, 1955.

"Le Cinquantenaire des Semaines Sociales," *Chronique Sociale de France*, LXII, No. 3 (May-June 1954), entire issue.

Hours, Joseph. "Les Origines d'une Tradition Politique: la

Formation en France de la Doctrine de la Démocratie Chrétienne et des Pouvoirs Intermédiaires," in Bernardin, Claude, *et al. Libéralisme, Traditionnalisme, Décentralisation: Contribution à l'Histoire des Idées Politiques.* Paris: Armand Colin, 1952.

———. "Les Catholiques Français et la Patrie," *Année Politique et Economique*, Nos. 123-124 (January-March 1955), 1-24.

Rémond, René. "L'Evolution de la Notion de Laïcité entre 1919 et 1939," *Cahiers d'Histoire*, Vol. IV, No. 1. Lyon: 1959, pp. 71-87.

Bibliography for Chapter 3

Most of the useful information for Chapter 3 came from the periodicals mentioned at the beginning of the bibliography section. Since most of these periodicals were read from cover to cover for the past few years, no attempt will be made to indicate all the articles containing helpful material. Many of the most helpful articles have already been cited in the body of the text.

Most of the interviews mentioned here were particularly important for the book as a whole. Their usefulness transcends this chapter alone.

CHAPTER 3: INTERVIEWS

Canon Berrar, Curé of St. Germain-des-Prés, and former chaplain of *Centre Catholique des Intellectuels Français*, April 17, 1959.

Canon Bonnet, Secretary General for the Working Class, and chaplain of *Action Catholique Ouvrière*, March 9 and 16, 1959.

Mgr. Foucart, Deputy Secretary of the French Episcopate, December 16, 1958.

Mgr. Ménager, Auxiliary Bishop of Versailles and Secretary of Catholic Action, January 8, 1959.

Father Odil, Assumptionnist and Editor of *La Documentation Catholique,* January 13, 1959.

Father Robinot-Marcy, Jesuit and librarian of *Action Populaire,* May 12, 1959.

Father Thomas, Dominican and staff member of *Les Editions du Cerf,* April 22, 1959.

CHAPTER 3: BOOKS

Annuaire Catholique de France, 1956-57. Paris: Presses Continentales, 1957.

Beau de Loménie, E. *L'Eglise et l'Etat.* Paris: Arthème Fayard, 1957.

Cesbron, Gilbert. *Les Saints Vont en Enfer.* Paris: Robert Laffont, 1952.

A novel, popularizing the worker-priests.

Chappoulie, Mgr. *Luttes de l'Eglise.* Paris: Editions Fleurus, 1958.

Collected speeches and articles of the late Bishop of Angers.

Congar, Father Yves. *Vraie et Fausse Réforme dans l'Eglise.* Paris: Editions du Cerf, 1950.

Daniel, Yvan, and Le Mouël, Gilbert. *Paroisses d'Hier, Paroisses d'Aujourd'hui.* Paris: Grasset, 1957.

Deroo, André (ed.). *Encycliques, Messages et Discours de Pie IX, Léon XIII, Pie X, Pie XI, et Pie XII, sur l'Education, l'Ecole et les Loisirs.* Lille: Editions de la Croix du Nord, 1957.

———. *L'Episcopat Français dans la Mêlée de son Temps.* Paris: Bonne Presse, 1955.

Descola, Jean. *Quand les Jesuites sont au Pouvoir.* Paris: Hachette, 1956.

Directoire Pastoral en Matière Sociale à l'Usage du Clergé. Paris: Editions Fleurus, 1954.

One of the more authoritative statements of the Church social doctrine in France. Approved by the Plenary Assembly of 1954 and published with the cooperation of the Secretariat of the Episcopate. Cardinal Richaud has written an annex with valuable commentary on the principles of this book.

Les Enseignements Pontificaux. Collection published by the Monks of Solesmes. Paris: Desclée et Cie., 1952.

A vast collection of papal pronouncements on various social questions. Exhaustively indexed. However, a certain emphasis is put on the documents which follow the extreme right views of the Benedictines at Solesmes. This is their answer to the too-progressive passages in the *Directoire* just mentioned.

Les Evêques Face à la Guerre d'Algérie. Paris: *Témoignage Chrétien*, 1960.

The most significant statements on the liberal side of the Algerian issue. But *Témoignage Chrétien*, with its well-known political orientation, does not include the more conservative bishops' pronouncements.

Fremantle, Anne (ed.). *The Papal Encyclicals in their Historical Context*. New York: Mentor Books, 1956.

Guerry, Mgr. E. *La Doctrine Sociale de l'Eglise*. Paris: Bonne Presse, 1957.

Guide Pratique des Catholiques de France. 4th ed. Paris: Office Nationale de Propagande Catholique, 1955.

Useful information on many Catholic organizations, though the list of them is not so long as that of the *Annuaire Catholique de France*.

Hoare, F. C. *The Papacy and the Modern State: An Essay on the Political History of the Catholic Church*. London: Burns Oates & Washbourne, 1940.

A questionable appreciation of France. Calls Premier Léon Blum a "Jewish atheist," which would seem to be a contradiction.

Houart, Pierre. *L'Attitude de l'Eglise dans la Guerre d'Algérie, 1954-1960*. Brussels: Le Livre Africain, 1960.

More wide ranging than the *Témoignage Chrétien* booklet,

though Houart also is firmly attached to the liberal position in Algeria.

Pope John XXIII. Encyclical *Mater et Magistra.* English translation in *New York Times,* July 15, 1961.

Kerlévéo, Canon Jean. *L'Eglise Catholique en Régime Français de Séparation.* Aire-sur-la-Lys: Mordecq, 1951.

A legal statement of the ties between Church and state in France.

Méjan, François. *Le Vatican est-il Contre la France d'Outre-Mer?* Paris: Librarie Fischbacher, 1957.

Monestier, Marianne. *La Mystérieuse Compagnie.* Paris: Pierre Horay, 1957.

A Catholic account of the workings of the Jesuits. Has the Imprimatur.

Neuvecelle, Jean. *Eglise Capitale Vatican.* Paris: Gallimard, 1954.

Ordo Divini Officii Ad Usum Cleri Parisiensis, Pro Anno MCMLIX. Paris: Imprimerie de l'Archevêché, 1959.

Petrie, John. *The Worker Priests.* London: Routledge & Kegan Paul, 1956.

A translation of the document written by fifty French worker-priests who refused to discontinue their activity when it was censored by the Church.

Powers, Francis J. *Papal Pronouncements on the Political Order.* Westminster, Md.: Newman Press, 1952.

Richaud, Mgr. Paul. *Annexe au Directoire Pastorale en Matière Sociale.* Paris: Bonne Presse et Editions de Fleurus, 1955.

The cardinal's version of the Church social doctrine. Can be compared with the version of Father Villain, who is probably more "progressive."

Van Lierde, Mgr. *Derrière les Portes Vaticanes.* Paris: Mame, 1958.

Villain, Father J. *L'Enseignement Social de l'Eglise.* Paris: Editions Spes, 1954.

Father Villain is a member of the Jesuit *Action Populaire*

institute. His version of the Church social doctrine follows the Christian Democratic tradition.

Ward, Maisie. *France Pagan? The Mission of Abbé Godin.* New York: Sheed and Ward, 1949.

Translation and commentary on Abbé Godin's book *France: Pays de Mission?* Godin gave the impulse that started the worker-priest movement.

CHAPTER 3: ARTICLES

Congar, Father Yves. "Jésus-Christ en France," *Vie Intellectuelle,* xxv, No. 2 (February 1954), 113-130.

Fison, J.-M. "L'Organisation Administrative de l'Eglise Catholique en France. La Nomination des Evêques," *Revue Administrative,* No. 9 (May-June 1949), 234-245.

Hourdin, Georges. "La Situation Actuelle de l'Eglise Catholique en France," articles in *Le Monde,* April 30 to May 7, 1957.

Méjan, François. L'Organisation de l'Eglise Catholique et ses Rapports avec l'Etat," *Esprit Laïque,* II (1955).

Osservatore Romano, Edition Hebdomadaire en Langue Française, passim, for 1951 and 1958.

La Revue Administrative, passim.

In addition to the articles quoted, many other articles deal with the organization of the Church. In the years 1949 to 1951 the school problem was stressed. Once the Barangé Law was on the statute books, the focus switched to structures like the Papal Nuncio or the religious orders. Sound information, though not friendly to the Church.

Les Semaines Religieuses, passim.

The library of *L'Union des Oeuvres* made available its files of clippings from all *Semaines Religieuses* arranged by subject-matter. Certain *Semaines Religieuses* from the particularly dechristianized dioceses and from the still-fervent ones were examined in more detail.

"La Situation des Prêtres-Ouvriers," *Témoignage Chrétien,* May 15, 1959.

Bibliography for Chapter 4

All the important information for this chapter came from personal interviews and the publications of the Catholic Action movements. These two sources are listed first (with no attempt made to indicate the individual articles from each Catholic Action review which were useful). Then some books of particular value in understanding French Catholic Action are listed.

It will be noted that many Catholic Action groups publish two or more reviews. One is usually destined for the "mass" of adherents and is general, easy reading. One is destined for "leaders" or "militant members," and is usually more indicative of the sentiments of the movement.

Once again the library of *Action Populaire* has been immensely helpful in furnishing practically all the publications listed below. Without its invaluable collection at his disposal, the researcher would have a hard time indeed in finding all the publications of major Catholic Action groups.

CHAPTER 4: INTERVIEWS

Mlle. Baron, Secretary of USIC and MICIAC, April 7, 1959.

Jean Bize, Secretary General of the JEC, March 18, 1959.

Canon Bonnet, Chaplain of the ACO, March 16, 1959.

Henri Catherin, Head, *Branche Aînés*, JAC, February 23, 1959.

Collette Cosnier, an editor of *Promesses* and a national officer of JACF, February 24, 1959.

M. Etcheverry, *Haute Commission à la Jeunesse et aux Sports*, June 9, 1959.

Mlle. S. des Gachons, Head of Civic Education, ACGF, March 19, 1959.

Mlle. Marguerite Guilhem, national officer, JICF, March 18, 1959.

Félix Lacambre, President of ACO (lecture), March 1, 1959.

M. Lecomte, an editor of *France-Monde Catholique* and official of ACGH, March 17, 1959.

Mlle. Michèle Lesoeur, national officer, ACI, March 17, 1959.

Jean Mazeaud, national officer, JOC, March 16, 1959.

Jean Villot, Chief of the Agricultural Workers' Section, MFR, March 3, 1959.

CHAPTER 4: CATHOLIC ACTION PUBLICATIONS EXAMINED PASSIM

ACGF: *Echo des Françaises; Militantes ACGF* (formerly *Notre Tâche*).

ACGH: *France-Monde Catholique; Animateurs.*

ACI: *Courrier des Militants.*

ACO: *Témoignage; Courrier des Responsables; Correspondance des Aumôniers.*

FFEC: *Bulletin Mensuel d'Informations.*

JAC: *Jeunes Forces Rurales; Militant à l'Action.*

JACF: *Promesses; En Equipe.*

JEC: *Action Catholique Etudiante.*

JIC: *Jeunes Equipes; Recherches—Eléments pour l'Action.*

JICF: *Jeunesse et Présence; Aux Responsables.*

JOC: *Jeunesse Ouvrière; Lettre aux Fédéraux.*

JOCF: *Perspectives Aînées.*

MFR: *Foyer Rural; Clair Foyer; Mon Village; Fiches Rurales.*

Pax Christi: *Pax Christi.*

CHAPTER 4: BOOKS

Achard, A. *Vingt Ans de JACF, 1933-1953.* Paris: Editions JACF, 1953.

ACGH. *A la Découverte de l'ACGH.* Paris: ACGH, 1959.

ACJF, Cinquante Années d'Action. Paris: Spes, 1936.

Annuaire des Services Généraux de l'Episcopat; Mouvements d'Action Catholique; Oeuvres Diverses. Paris: Action Catholique Française, 1955.

This is the "definitive" listing of Catholic Action groupings, with their goals and their publications. It is published under the direct supervision of the Secretary of Catholic Action.

Cinq Ans d'ACO: Hommes et Femmes du Peuple Devant le Message Chrétien. Paris: Editions ACO, 1955.

Commission Episcopale du Monde Ouvrier. *L'Engagement Temporel.* Paris: ACO, 1957.

This is the official statement approved by the Hierarchy on how the Catholic worker should approach the problem of joining organizations and acting within them in a "Christian manner."

Conseil Français des Mouvements de Jeunesse. *Présence de la Jeunesse.* Toulouse: Privately published, 1955.

Drujon, A. *La JEC, Quinze Ans d'Histoire.* Paris: JEC, 1946.

Fauvet, Jacques, and Mendras, H. *Les Paysans et la Politique.* Paris: Armand Colin, 1958.

Note especially the articles by Jean Labbens, "L'Eglise Catholique et l'Expression Politique du Monde Rural," pp. 327-343; and Marcel Faure, "Action Catholique en Milieu Rural," pp. 345-360.

La FNAC à l'Oeuvre dans le Domaine de l'Ecole. Paris: FNAC, 1953.

Garonne, Mgr. *L'Action Catholique.* Paris: Arthème Fayard, 1958.

d'Haene, Father Michel. *La JAC a Vingt-Cinq Ans.* Paris: Collection Semailles, 1954.

Lecordier, G. *Les Classes Moyennes en Marche.* Paris: Bloud et Gay, 1950.

———. *Le Monde Rural en Marche.* St. Etienne: Editions IGC, 1954.

De la Ligue à l'ACGF. Paris: ACGF, 1954.

Madiran, Jean. *Ils ne Savent pas ce qu'Ils Font.* Paris: Nouvelles Editions Latines, 1955.

Manuel Pratique des Sections Paroissiales, LFACF. Rennes: LFACF, 1947.

Ménager, Mgr. *Mandat de l'ACGF: Ses Exigences.* Paris: ACGF, 1958.

Ministère de l'Education Nationale. *Au Service de la Jeunesse.* Paris: Direction Générale de la Jeunesse et Des Sports, n.d.

Le Monde Ouvrier à Lourdes. Paris: ACO, 1958.

Perspectives Apostoliques. Paris: ACO, 1954.

Pour Comprendre la JAC, par un Groupe de Dirigeants. Paris: JAC, 1945.

René Rémond. "L'ACJF et la Jeunesse Ouvrière," *Vie Intellectuelle* xxvii, No. 3 (March 1956), 26-41.

Sales, Claude. *Où Va la JEC?* Paris: Editions de l'Epi, 1954.

Trente-Troisième Conseil National de la JOC Française: Rapport. Paris: Equipe Ouvrière, 1958.

Vauthier, Emile. *Initiation à l'Action Catholique: Essai de Théologie Pastorale.* Langres: Bureau de l'Ami du Clergé, 1955.

Bibliography for Chapter 5

The books and articles used in writing this chapter have already been mentioned in previous chapters (see books by Folliet, Lebret, and *Nef* issue in bibliography for Chapter 1; by Rollet and Duroselle in bibliography for Chapter 2; by Richaud in bibliography for Chapter 3). These references will not be given again in detail. Here are listed only the essential interviews for Chapter 5 and the publications of social action organizations which were inspected *passim.*

CHAPTER 5: INTERVIEWS

J.-P. Amalric, national officer of *Vie Nouvelle*, April 10, 1959.

Canon Berrar, former chaplain of CCIF, April 17, 1959.

Mlle. Thérèse Doneaud, national officer of UFCS, April 7, 1959.

M. Garin, national officer of the CFPC, April 13, 1959.

Michel Rigal, Commissioner-General of *Scouts de France*, March 23, 1959.

Henri Théry, liaison officer between *Secrétariats Sociaux* and *Semaines Sociales*, March 20, 1959.

CHAPTER 5: REVIEWS OF SOCIAL ACTION GROUPS

Action Populaire:
Revue d'Action Populaire; Cahiers d'Action Religieuse et Sociale.

Associations Familiales Catholiques:
Tâches Familiales.

Chronique Sociale:

La Chronique Sociale de France. See especially Vol. LX, No. 3 (June 1952), "La Chronique a Soixante Ans," and Vol. LXII, No. 3 (May-June 1954), "Cinquantenaire des Semaines Sociales."

Cité Catholique:

Verbe. See also Planchais, Jean. "Le Catholicisme Dur," *Le Monde*, June 26, 1958; and Fesquet, Henri. "Verbe, Revue de la Cité Catholique, Renie les Principes de la Révolution," *Le Monde*, July 9, 1958.

CFPC:

Documents et Commentaires.

Economie et Humanisme:

Economie et Humanisme.

Scouts de France:

La Route; Le Chef.

Secrétariats Sociaux:

Service d'Information et de Propagande pour l'Education Civique: "Notes d'Actualité," "La Démocratie Organique," mimeographed pamphlet, February 8, 1959. Also reports of yearly *Semaines Sociales.*

UFCS:

La Femme dans la Vie Sociale.

Vie Nouvelle:

Vie Nouvelle.

Miscellaneous:

Itinéraires; Paternité-Maternité; Pensée Catholique; Mouvement de Libération Ouvrière: *Vie Populaire.*

Bibliography for Chapter 6

CHAPTER 6: INTERVIEWS

M. Boilet, President of the *Association Nationale des Périodiques Catholiques de Province*, April 22, 1959.

M. Brichard, Secretary of the *Centrale Technique d'Information Catholique*, December 3, 1958.

Mlle. Duclos, Secretary of the *Centre Nationale de la Presse Catholique*, April 16, 1959.

Jean de Fabrègues, Editor of *La France Catholique*, April 23, 1959.

Georges Hourdin, President of *Vie Catholique Illustrée*, May 5, 1959.

Mlle. de Lesseps, *Librairie Alsatia*, May 22, 1959.

M. E. Lethielleux, owner of *Librairie Lethielleux*, July 21, 1959.

Jean Madiran, director of extreme-right publication *Itinéraires*, July 4, 1960.

Jacques Maître, researcher for the *Centre de Sociologie des Religions* and expert on the Catholic press, September 11, 1958.

Serge Montini, *Editions du Seuil*, June 2, 1959.

Robert de Montvalon, Editor-in-Chief, *Témoignage Chrétien*, April 16 and May 5, 1959.

Father Odil, Editor of *Documentation Catholique*, January 13, 1959.

Father de Parvillez, Secretary-General of the *Comité Catholique du Livre* (correspondence).

Jean Pelissier, Head of *Les Informateurs Religieux*, July 11, 1959.

M. de la Potterie, Head of Documentary Service, *Union des Oeuvres*, March 24, 1959.

Jean-Claude Renard, *Editions du Cerf*, April 22, 1959.

Father Richard, Editor of *Homme Nouveau*, May 23, 1959.

M. Villette, Publisher of *Les Editions Ouvrières*, June 25, 1959.

CHAPTER 6: REVIEWS AND OTHER PUBLICATIONS READ PASSIM

La Croix
Homme Nouveau
Panorama Chrétien
Pensée Catholique
Vie Catholique Illustrée
Esprit
Itinéraires
Courrier Français de Bordeaux
Paternité-Maternité
Témoignage Chrétien
France Catholique
Notre Courrier, CTIC
Pèlerin
Verbe

CHAPTER 6: BOOKS AND ARTICLES

Annuaire de la Presse Catholique et de l'Edition. Paris: Centre d'Informations Catholiques, 1950.

Annuaire de la Presse Française et Etrangère et du Monde Politique. Paris: Chambre Syndicale des Editeurs d'Annuaires, 1958.

Although very general, this yearbook has an entire section on the Catholic press, which gives circulation figures for many publications.

Bodin, Louis. "La Presse Catholique de France: Ses 'Patrons' et ses 'Inspirateurs.'" *France Observateur,* May 5, 1955, pp. 16-17.

Charlot, Jean. "La Presse, les Catholiques, et les Elections," in Duverger, Maurice *et al. Les Elections du 2 Janvier, 1956.* Paris: Armand Colin, 1956, pp. 131-141.

Devisse, Jean. "Les Forces Spirituelles et la Politique Extérieure de la France," in Association Française de Science Politique. *La Politique Etrangère et Ses Fondements.* Paris: Armand Colin, 1954, pp. 35-61.

Catholic ideas are shown through examining a dozen or so key Catholic publications and noting their reactions to selected themes.

Echo de la Presse et de la Publicité, No. 364 (May 15, 1959).

Here most of the declared circulation figures for Catholic publications are given, for late 1958. The *real* circulation, which is the declared figure minus unsold copies, is impossible to ascertain from these figures, however.

François, Michel. "La Revue qui a Formé une Génération Chrétienne," *France Observateur,* April 2, 1959, pp. 12-13.

An analysis of the ties linking *Esprit* to French Catholicism.

Gabel, Father E. *La Presse Catholique: Pour Quoi Faire?* Paris: Alsatia, 1957.

Hourdin, Georges. *La Presse Catholique.* Paris: Arthème Fayard, 1957.

"Le Livre Religieux en France," *Informations Catholiques Internationales*, xxv (June 1, 1956), 17-25.

Madiran, Jean. *Ils ne Savent pas ce qu'Ils Font.* Paris: Nouvelles Editions Latines, 1955.

Although already cited in a previous chapter, this book, written by an extreme-right author, has interesting information on the sources of wealth of the Catholic press.

Maître, Jacques. "Le Fonctionnement de la Presse Catholique en France." Mimeographed study for the June 1957 round-table discussions of the French Political Science Association: *Les Intellectuels dans la Société Française Contemporaine.*

This is the most valuable study of the Catholic press in France. Especially good in its analysis of the chief Catholic publishing houses. Interesting hypotheses on the "real" influence of the Catholic press.

Mondange, Jean. *L'Information Catholique.* Vol. I: *Une Industrie Nouvelle: la "Fabrication" de l'Opinion Publique.* Vol. II: *Comment Diffuser la Pensée Chrétienne.* Vol. III: *La Presse d'Aujourd'Hui.* Paris: Editions de l'Hirondelle, 1950-1951.

———. *Le Chrétien Devant l'Information.* Paris: CTIC, 1957.

Office de la Justification de la Diffusion. *OJD Officiel. Passim.*

The OJD has a way of checking the "real" circulation figures for member publications. Most of the major Catholic publications are members of the OJD, so there is a sure way of knowing how much of their material comes before the public's eye. However, the OJD does not service non-members.

Syndicat des Editeurs de Paris. *Livres Catholiques, 1951-1955.* Paris: Syndicat des Editeurs, 1955.

Lists all Catholic books published by recognized publishing houses during the period.

"Témoignage Chrétien," *Informations Catholiques Internationales*, June 15, 1957, pp. 13-24.

Veuillot, François. *Sous le Signe de l'Union.* Paris: L'Union des Oeuvres, 1948.

Bibliography for Chapter 7

The following references do not represent all the information available on the MRP or the CFTC. As in the main text, the emphasis here is on the "Catholicism" of the two groups.

MRP: INTERVIEW

J.-P. Prévost, Secretary of the MRP Group in the Senate, July 13 and 23, 1959, and June 15, 1960.

MRP PUBLICATIONS, STUDIED PASSIM

Aube, daily newspaper published until July 1951.
Forces Nouvelles, weekly magazine.

MRP: BOOKS

Biton, Louis. *La Démocratie Chrétienne dans la Politique Française*. Angers: Siraudeau, 1954.

Interesting pages on how Christian Democracy fits into the present political and religious climate of France. Otherwise, the book is similar to Einaudi and Goguel.

Einaudi, Mario, and Goguel, François. *Christian Democracy in Italy and France*. South Bend: Notre Dame University Press, 1952.

Fauvet, Jacques. *Les Forces Politiques en France*. Paris: Le Monde, 1951.

———. *La France Déchirée*. Paris: Arthème Fayard, 1957.

———. *Les Partis Politiques dans la France Actuelle*. Paris: Le Monde, 1947.

Gay, Francisque. *Les Démocrats d'Inspiration Chrétienne à L'Epreuve du Pouvoir*. Paris: Bloud et Gay, 1950.

Goguel, François. *France under the Fourth Republic*. Ithaca: Cornell University Press, 1952.

Gortais, Albert. *Démocratie et Libération*. Paris: Société d'Editions Républicaines Populaires, 1947.

Havard de la Montagne, Robert. *Histoire de la Démocratie Chrétienne, de Lamennais à Georges Bidault. Les Origines et les Egarements du MRP*. Paris: Amiot-Dumont, n.d.

The book was probably published in 1948. According to the author, there is something anti-Christian in accepting the Revolution of 1789 and the Republics based on it.

Lenoir, Jean. *Essai sur la Démocratie Chrétienne.* Monte-Carlo: Regain, 1954.

Priouret, Roger. *La République des Partis.* Paris: Elan, 1947.

The author predicted a decline of political parties in any future stable French government. The events of the past year have partially borne him out.

Raymond-Laurent. *Les Origines du MRP.* Paris: Editions du Mail, 1947.

Siegfried, André (ed.). *L'Année Politique,* years 1951 and 1958. Paris: Presses Universitaires de France, 1951 and 1958.

The day-by-day account of political activities of importance to France. The volumes covering the Barangé crisis and the change of Republics were particularly helpful.

Vaussard, Maurice. *Histoire de la Démocratie Chrétienne: France, Belgique, Italie.* Paris: Editions du Seuil, 1956.

MRP: ARTICLES AND PAMPHLETS

Duverger, Maurice. "Les Otages," *Le Monde,* July 22-23, 1951, p. 4.

The Barangé Law, says the author, was forced on the MRP by the RPF and other parties of the right, to insure that the MRP could not be associated in the future with a center-left coalition.

Ehrmann, Henry W. "Political Forces in Present-Day France," *Social Research* xv, No. 2 (June 1948), 146-169.

Micaud, Charles. "The Politics of French Catholics in the Fourth Republic," in Moody, Joseph (ed.), *Church and Society.* New York: Arts, Inc., 1953.

"Le MRP, Parti de la Quatrième République." (Brochure). Paris: MRP, n.d. but before 1946.

Noether, Emiliana P. "Political Catholicism in France and Italy," *Yale Review,* XLIV, No. 4 (Summer 1955), 569-583.

"Origines et Mission du MRP." (Brochure). Paris: Les Cahiers de Formation Politique du MRP, 1951.

Pépy, Daniel. "Note sur le Mouvement Républicain Populaire," in Duverger, Maurice (ed.). *Partis Politiques et Classes Sociales en France.* Paris: Armand Colin, 1955, pp. 209-218.

Yates, Willard Ross. "Power Principle and Doctrine of the Mouvement Républicain Populaire," *American Political Science Review,* LII, No. 2 (June 1958), pp. 419-436.

CFTC: INTERVIEW

Mme. Simone Troisgros, Vice President of the CFTC, June 10, 1959.

CFTC: PUBLICATIONS CONSULTED PASSIM

Syndicalisme CFTC. Official CFTC weekly. 125,000 circulation.
Reconstruction. CFTC "left wing."

CFTC: BOOKS AND ARTICLES

Bigo, Father. "Le Syndicalisme Chrétien," unpublished lecture notes from course at *Institut Catholique,* 1955-56.

"La CFTC: Deux Années d'Action." Brochure for Thirtieth National Congress, CFTC. Issy-les-Moulineaux: CFTC, 1959.

"La CFTC," *Vie Intellectuelle,* XXVI, No. 7 (July 1955), 137-152.

Levard, Georges. *Chances et Périls du Syndicalisme Chrétien.* Paris: Arthème Fayard, 1955.

The most complete contemporary discussion of the CFTC, by its secretary-general.

Lorwin, Val R. *The French Labor Movement.* Cambridge, Mass.: Harvard University Press, 1954.

Romain (pseudonym). *Le Syndicalisme en France.* Lille: Union des Secrétariats Sociaux du Nord, 1945.

A very pious interpretation of the labor movement.

Zirnheld, Jules. *Cinquante Années de Syndicalisme Chrétien.* Paris: Spes, 1937.

The historical development of the CFTC by its first secretary general.

Bibliography for Chapter 8

Appreciation is hereby expressed to Professor René Rémond for permission to participate in his seminar on the events leading up to the Barangé Law, given at the *Institut d'Etudes Politiques* in Paris. The seminar and the sources assembled by the students furnished invaluable material for this chapter. In addition, the libraries of *Action Populaire* and *Union des Oeuvres* were also well-supplied with information on the school question. Finally, many useful documents were examined at the library of the *Ligue Française de l'Enseignement*, access to which was kindly given by President Albert Bayet.

CHAPTER 8: INTERVIEWS

Albert Bayet, President of the *Ligue Française de l'Enseignement*, October 1, 1958.

Canon Kerlévéo, Associate Secretary General of the Secretariat for Catholic Schools, November 25, 1958.

Edouard Lizop, Secretary General of the *Secrétariat d'Etudes pour la Liberté de l'Enseignement et la Défense de la Culture*, November 19, 1958, and June 15, 1960.

M. Le Pichon, staff writer for the *Associations de Parents d'Elèves de l'Enseignement Libre* (APEL), November 27, 1958.

M. Raingeard, former Deputy from Loire-Atlantique and Parliamentary Secretary of the *Association Parlementaire pour la Liberté de l'Enseignement*, January 8 and February 2, 1959.

CHAPTER 8: PUBLICATIONS EXAMINED PASSIM

Action Laïque. Review of the *Ligue Française de l'Enseignement*. Strongly against any aid to Catholic schools. Has a tinge of even more forceful anticlericalism.

Bulletin National des Instituteurs et des Institutrices Catholiques de l'Enseignement Public.

Documents Pédagogiques. Review of Lizop's *Secrétariat*.

Enseignement Libre. Review of the *CFTC Syndicat de l'Enseignement Libre.*

La Famille Educatrice. Review of the APEL.

Liberté d'Enseignement. Lizop's publication. Successor to *Documents Pédagogiques.*

Syndicalisme Universitaire. Review of the CFTC public school teachers' union.

Various *Semaines Religieuses,* particularly those of the Dioceses of Angers, Limoges, Nantes, Paris, Périgueux, Quimper, Reims, Rennes, and Vannes.

CHAPTER 8: BOOKS

Bayet, Albert. *Laïcité Vingtième Siècle: Pour une Réconciliation Française.* Paris: Hachette, 1958.

Benabarre, Father Benigno. *Public Funds for Private Schools in a Democracy: Theory and Practice.* Manila, P.I.: Our Lady of Montserrat Abbey, 1956.

An exhaustive comparative study of the legal position of Church schools in most of the Western Democracies.

Bousquet, Marguerite. "Le Problème de l'Enseignement Primaire Privé en France depuis 1947." Unpublished doctoral dissertation, Faculté de Droit, Université de Lyon, 1956.

The most complete work available on the events which culminated in the Barangé Law.

Chabernaud, Germaine. *Cartes Sur Table.* Poitiers: Editions des Cordeliers, 1951.

A public school teacher tells why all Catholic youngsters should attend private Catholic schools!

Garail, M. *Pour une Ecole Nouvelle, Démocratique et Nationale.* Paris: Editions du Témoignage Chrétien, 1947.

Represents the views of *Témoignage Chrétien.*

Kerlévéo, Abbé. *L'Enseignement Libre, Service Privé d'Intérêt Général en Droit Public Français.* Paris: Secrétariat Général de l'Enseignement Libre, 1956.

Méjan, François. *Les Lois Marie et Barangé. Répercussions sur les Rapports de l'Eglise Catholique et de l'Etat.* Paris: Société Universitaire d'Editions et de Librarie, 1954.

Pelissier, Jean. *Grandeurs et Servitudes de l'Enseignement Libre.* Paris: Bonne Presse, 1951.

Secrétariat Général de l'Enseignement Libre. *L'Enseignement Catholique Français.* Paris: SGEL, 1957.

Villain, Father *et al. Un Problème National: L'Ecole.* Paris: Editions de l'Ecole, 1951.

CHAPTER 8: ARTICLES

Brown, Bernard E. "Religious Schools and Politics in France," *Midwest Journal of Political Science,* II, No. 2 (May 1958), 160-178.

Comité Théologique de Lyon. "Les Catholiques de France et le Problème Scolaire: Note Doctrinal à l'Usage des Prêtres du Ministère," *Documentation Catholique,* 1957, pp. 467-484.

"Laïcité et Paix Scolaire," *Esprit* XXVII, No. 10, October 1959, whole issue.

"Les Données Actuelles de la Question Scolaire," *Informations Catholiques Internationales,* No. 93 (April 1, 1959), pp. 13-23.

Lizop, Edouard. "Les Lois Scolaires," *Revue des Deux Mondes,* April 15, 1956, pp. 662-672.

Méjan, François. "Evolution de la Législation Scolaire," *Revue Administrative* XXV (January-February 1952).

———. "L'Organisation de l'Eglise Catholique dans ses Rapports avec l'Etat: L'Aide Publique à l'Enseignement Privé," *L'Esprit Laïque,* No. 2, 1954.

d'Ouince, Father René. "Aspect Politique de la Question Scolaire," *Etudes,* 84, Vol. 268 (March 1951), pp. 289-307.

"Pour la Justice Scolaire," *Documentation Catholique,* 48, No. 1094 (May 6, 1951), 513-571.

"Propositions de Paix Scolaire," *Esprit,* XVII, No. 154 (March-April 1949), whole issue.

Simon, Pierre-Henri. "La Guerre des Principes: Laïcité, Justice, Liberté," *Etudes,* 89, Vol. 289 (May 1956), 176-190.

Sorre, Maurice. "Etudes Critiques, Eglise, Ecole, Politique," *Cahiers Internationaux de Sociologie,* VIII (1950), pp. 134 ff.

Bibliography for Chapter 9

In addition to the references below, many books listed for Chapter 1 were also helpful here.

CHAPTER 9: BOOKS

Boulard, Canon. *Paroisses Urbaines, Paroisses Rurales.* Paris: Casterman, 1958.

———. *Premiers Itinéraires en Sociologie Religieuse.* Paris: Editions du Cerf, 1945.

Elbow, Matthew. *French Corporative Theory from 1789 to 1948.* New York: Columbia University Press, 1953.

The study does not deal with the Fourth Republic. Much valuable information on the background of solidarism and pluralism as well as corporatism.

Evans, J. W., and Ward, Leo R. *The Social and Political Philosophy of Jacques Maritain.* New York: Scribner, 1955.

Le Bras, Gabriel, *et al. Etudes de Sociologie Electorale.* Paris: Armand Colin, 1947.

Note especially the article by Le Bras, "Géographie Electorale et Géographie Religieuse," pp. 44-66.

———. *Etudes de Sociologie Religieuse.* 2 vols. Paris: Presses Universitaires de France, 1955 and 1956.

Loew, Jacques. *Journal d'Une Mission Ouvrière, 1941-1959.* Paris: Editions du Cerf, 1959.

Mounier et sa Génération: Lettres, Carnets, et Inédits. Paris: Editions du Seuil, 1956.

Mounier, Emmanuel. *Be Not Afraid: Studies in Personalist Sociology.* Trans. Cynthia Rowland. New York: Harper & Bros., n.d.

———. *Le Personnalisme.* Paris: Presses Universitaires de France, 1955.

Pin, Father Emile. *Pratique Religieuse et Classes Sociales dans une Paroisse Urbaine, Saint-Pothin à Lyon.* Paris: Spes, 1956.

République Française, Ministère de l'Intérieur. *Les Elections*

Législatives du 17 Juin, 1951. Paris: La Documentation Française, 1951.

———. *Les Elections Législatives du 2 Janvier, 1956.* Paris: La Documentation Française, 1957.

Ryan, John A. and Boland, Francis J. *Catholic Principles of Politics.* New York: Macmillan, 1940.

Richard, Abbé André. *Catholiques de Partout, Réveillons-Nous, Unissons-Nous.* Paris: Propagande pour l'Unité, 1938.

———. *L'Unité d'Action des Catholiques.* Paris: Librarie Plon, 1939.

Siegfried, André. *Tableau Politique de la France de l'Ouest sous la Troisième République.* Paris: Armand Colin, 1913.

———. *Géographie Electorale de l'Ardèche sous la Troisième République.* Paris: Armand Colin, 1949.

Zaza, Noureddine. *Etude Critique de la Notion d'Engagement chez Emmanuel Mounier.* Genève: Librarie E. Droz, 1955.

CHAPTER 9: ARTICLES AND MISCELLANEOUS

"Catholiques de Droite? Catholiques de Gauche?" *Chronique Sociale* LXIV, No. 7-8 (December 30, 1956). Entire issue.

Leading Catholic officials and students of Catholicism answer questions asked them by the magazine, which attempts to see whether the notion of a duality in French Catholicism between left and right is generally acceptable. Most answers recognize that Catholics are profoundly divided, though many reject a simple dichotomy.

"Chrétien dans ma Commune," brochure edited by the *Mouvement Familial Rural.* Paris: MFR, n.d.

Henry, Jean-François. "Eléments pour une Etude des Survivances de l'Intégrisme dans le Catholicisme Français Contemporain." Unpublished thesis for the *Institut d'Etudes Politiques*, 1957.

"Intégrisme et National Catholicisme," in *Esprit* XXVII, No. 11 (November 1959), pp. 515-543.

MacRae, Duncan, Jr. "Religious and Sociometric Factors in

the French Vote, 1946-1956," *American Journal of Sociology*, Vol. LXIV, No. 3 (November 1958), 290-298.

Maître, Jacques. "Les Dénombrements de Catholiques Pratiquants: Tableau des Enquêtes, Diocèses de la France Métropolitaine," *Archives de Sociologie des Religions*, III (January-June 1957), 72ff.

According to this exhaustive study, there is no complete, standardized study of religious practice which extends to all dioceses in France.

"Progressisme et Intégrisme," *Chronique Sociale*, LXIII, No. 3 (May 15, 1955), entire issue.

Rémond, René. "Droite et Gauche dans le Catholicisme Français," *Revue Française de Science Politique*, VIII, Nos. 3 and 4 (September and December 1958).

Index

INDEX

INDEX